BROADMOOR INTERACTS:

CRIMINAL INSANITY REVISITED

BROADMOOR INTERACTS:

Criminal Insanity Revisited

A Sequel to Partridge's
'BROADMOOR: A History of Criminal Lunacy
and its Problems'

for the period between the
MENTAL HEALTH ACTS OF 1959 and 1983

and

A Psychological Perspective on its
Clinical Development

by

D.A. Black, MA (Cantab), FBPsS,
Chartered Clinical & Forensic Psychologist, retd. 1996
Director of Psychological Services, Broadmoor Hospital,
1959-1986
Visiting Lecturer in Clinical Psychology, University of
Southampton, 1970-71
Cropwood Fellow, Institute of Criminology, Cambridge
University, 1975
Mental Health Act Commissioner, 1986-1990

BARRY ROSE LAW PUBLISHERS LIMITED
CHICHESTER

DEDICATION

This book is dedicated to

the staff and patients of

Broadmoor Hospital,

neither of whom are publicly understood

CONTENTS

Contents

PART II - THE WAY IT WENT

Contents

PART III - WHAT IT MEANS

Contents

ACKNOWLEDGEMENTS

The views expressed in this book are the author's and should not be taken as necessarily representing those of his former employer, the former Department of Health and Social Security, or its present successors, or the local managers of Broadmoor Hospital at that time or since.

The recollection of facts and events are also the author's and it would be surprising if errors had not arisen after all this time. Nevertheless, it has seemed important to try to set down as much as can be recollected of this unique period of Broadmoor's history, which could otherwise become forgotten. Those still able to recall the early years of the 1959 Act are now sadly dwindling and the growing number of accounts of subsequent developments are already tending to obscure memories of what went before. Apologies are therefore tendered to all those who find errors or omissions in what must inevitably be a personal and selective account. Personal recollections, however, often add interest and I can only hope that there may be an element of this which will compensate for the mistakes.

The history was compiled over an 18 months period during 1998-2000, after which drafts were placed in the Psychology Department and the Staff Library (now the Patrick McGrath Library) for scrutiny and so that corrections and amendments could be suggested. A third draft went to a long standing friend and colleague, John Graham White, whose distinguished career in clinical psychology, extending from before the Second World War, concluded with spells with the Management Board for the special hospital for Scotland (the State Hospital at Carstairs) and with the Mental Health Act Commission for England & Wales. His suggested additions and amendments have been invaluable, as have also the comments he has supplied for the Preface. A fourth copy went to Nigel Walker, emeritus Wolfson Professor of Criminology at Cambridge University and a member of the former Butler Committee, who has supplied the Foreword. He, too, has drawn attention to places where amendments and clarifications were needed. I am deeply grateful to both these eminent colleagues for their contributions and all their help.

The original draft in a now obsolete MS-DOS text has been transformed into a WINDOWS format by Haeley Reeves, to whom further gratitude is expressed.

Graphics and tabulations throughout are either the author's own or adaptations by the author of originals deriving from either his own department records or those of SHRU (the Special Hospitals Research Unit). A number of these have appeared in several publications subsequently:

Several of those in Chapter 4 have previously appeared in Black, 1973 (published by the Special Hospitals Research Unit, London); in Lloyd-Bostock, 1981 (published by the Centre for Socio-Legal Studies, Oxford); and in Gunn & Farrington, 1982 (published by Wiley, Chichester).

Likewise those in Chapter 16 are adaptations of some also supplied for Gunn & Farrington, 1982, and of one for Farrington & Tarling, 1985 (published by The State University of New York Press, Albany, NY).

The tabulations in Appendix A are adaptations of those used in a report of the British Psychological Society, 1993, and the Society's 'Professional Psychology Handbook', 1995 (published by the BPS, Leicester).

To all these sources grateful acknowledgement is made, as it is also to the Cropwood Fund which enabled the work from which Chapter 16's material derives.

The photographs of Broadmoor a century later were taken by the author, with official permission, for a conference and lectures in Canada in 1969. Further pictures were taken in the mid-1980s, during the course of the Broadmoor Hospital rebuilding, to show features of the reconstruction or to record what was about to be changed or demolished. A condition of taking such pictures is that patients, if shown, must not be recognizable.

I have been encouraged in this present endeavour by my family and by many friends and former colleagues who have urged that it should be done, in particular the librarians at Broadmoor, Alison Farrar and Judy Phillips, who say the lack of a follow-on from Partridge is an embarrassment. Appreciation is also due to a great many others - more than could possibly now be comprehensively recalled. Nevertheless the unique position and personality of the late Dr Patrick McGrath must be acknowledged, head of the hospital for most of the period of the 1959 Mental Health Act, who steadfastly supported developments in clinical practice, research innovations and the reporting and publishing of the results. But also acknowledged must be the loyalty and support of my own department over the years who made the job not only feasible but exciting. Finally, of course, there are the patients, without whose tragic lives there would have been no history. I hope we helped them.

A PSYCHOLOGIST'S PREFACE

By John Graham White

A history of Broadmoor might seem of little interest to anyone other than those who work there. Even its residents, the patients, might be expected to be sceptical of the place while there and to want nothing to do with it once they had left. The public, of course, is intrigued by its more sensational aspects, such as details of its inmates' crimes, their escapes, and any scandals about the way the hospital is run that might from time to time make the headlines. Beyond that they are probably happy to know nothing, trusting that the violent perpetrators of their worst fantasies are safely locked up for the rest of their lives where they can do no further harm. Except, of course, that the majority are *not* locked up for life. A few are but the majority recover from the mental disorder that put them there and they return, probably first of all to some local form of supervised care and then to the open community to resume their lives.

Broadmoor, however, as this history sets out to tell, is not the place of popular myth and misconception. A 'special' hospital for the special few who have offended dangerously whilst insane (now mentally disordered), both its history and contemporary role serve to highlight our understanding of mental disorder in general. Through the magnifying glass which is Broadmoor we can see 'writ large' the problems of mental disorder in general and, for good measure, a great deal about criminality too. Critically, we are able to perceive, not only what each comprises, but how we might better deal with them, both in a remedial sense and through the due process of the law.

When setting out to relate the more recent history of this national institution, largely because so much of significance had happened since the now much out-of-date history told by Partridge and no one else looked as though they were going to do it, such claims seemed somewhat grandiose to the mind of a scientist. The reader should reach this conclusion for him or herself, from following the history. However, subjecting the draft to the critical appraisal of a much respected senior colleague, John Graham White, he maintained that this was more than a history of eight hundred patients and that its wider message should be made explicit at the outset. Natural reticence led to the suggestion that he might like to be the one to say this, which he has done - let him, therefore, take up the theme from here himself.

"Nothing stands still. Like the brittle surface of Planet Earth itself we, its inhabitants, are constantly on the move; and even institutions like Broadmoor, whose patients spend years and not just weeks or months there before they are discharged, are certainly not standing still. That is the most striking message of the present history.

"'Broadmoor Interacts' is a story of institutional change. Progressively over the past century, as Partridge in his history of the preceding period and now the present author clearly demonstrate, Broadmoor has become much less a holding pen for people whom our society has not known what to do with but, rather, a therapeutic institution and testing ground for searching scientific inquiries on the part of related disciplines: medicine, psychology and sociology and their related sub-systems. What this history describes is not only the development, over the years between the two Mental Health Acts

(1959 and 1983), of a serious therapeutic environment for some of the most severely psychologically disabled and socially disadvantaged people on this island; but it also illustrates in detail a considerable intellectual effort to understand the individual patient's needs.

"By the beginning of the 19th century it had become quite clear to government that the law alone should not be expected to deal with the problem of the 'criminal lunatic' (nowadays the 'mentally disordered offender'); and so medicine was called in to share the burden and, along with medicine, of course nursing. (To begin with, nurses may have been hard to distinguish from prison officers, since probably their most important duty was seen as ensuring high security for both their patients and the rest of society.) After the doctor and nurses came the social worker, initially to prepare the social context in which the mentally disordered offender was to start living again when discharged, and later to help prepare the patient *before* discharge for the realities of life outside. Since it soon became clear that many of Broadmoor's patients had missed out on basic education as well as occupational training, teaching staff and occupational instructors came to be appointed. As follow-up studies of ex-patients' lives during the 'interacts' period have shown, post-discharge employment was significantly related to their self-esteem and both finding and keeping a rewarding job as well as building and maintaining self-esteem were vitally important for integration in the community. Hence the need for post-discharge supervision.

"Psychology was a late comer to the Broadmoor scene, not surprisingly since it had taken its parent science the first half of the 20th century to establish itself as an independent academic discipline. Although psychologists had been working at the Home Office before the second world war, the author of the present history was the first to have held a full-time NHS clinical appointment at Broadmoor. The post-war years saw giant strides in research into the applicability of psychological knowledge and techniques to understanding abnormal behaviour and to ways of changing it, that is, in the present context to diagnosis and treatment. Relating observable and measurable behaviour to physiological processes such as nervous system arousal and linking emotional states such as anxiety or sexual excitement to corresponding physiological changes led to the design and construction of many new methods of measurement.

"At Broadmoor, clinical psychology progressed during this period from the initial psychometric testing of a patient's intellectual functions and personality traits to the extremely intricate work well illustrated in the research into the physiological changes accompanying sexual arousal in response to images of different kinds of sexual activity. (This research was undertaken with particular reference to those patients described as suffering from psychopathic disorder.) On the treatment side, psychology's most substantial contribution to helping people change their ways of behaving has depended to a large extent on studies during the past century of the learning process in animals and humans; and it is to those sources that it has had recourse at Broadmoor in its strategies to help patients acquire social skills, to control anger, to assert their point of view in company, and generally to relate effectively to others.

"What becomes increasingly clear from the present history is that the care and treatment of the mentally disordered offender relies heavily on a closely collaborative enterprise on the part of all the different disciplines now involved. The many difficulties in the way of achieving such collaboration range from lack of numbers to serve each clinical team in the hospital to the problems of professional jealousy between disciplines. The present author dodges none of these problems. While on balance most of the changes during the period he worked at Broadmoor appear to have been positive from the point of view of understanding and rehabilitating the patient, some changes appear to have had negative results. For example, with the growth of clinical teams, each led by its responsible medical officer, came the demise of the unitary hospital and its transformation into a small number of 'mini-hospitals'. That development allowed closer attention to be given to the needs of the individual patient; but it also led to a greater predominance of 'medically oriented thinking' and the loss of many of the therapeutically useful 'whole hospital' activities of the earlier period. In those activities patients became members of small working groups and sports teams, acquiring skills for themselves as well as contributing to the hospital's economy.

"One very certain message to emerge from this history is the pressing need for a joined-up service between the special hospital and the various local units into whose care the ex-patient is returned, whether regional secure unit, psychiatric hospital or community health service. The result otherwise is that much, if not all, of the diagnostic and therapeutic work, plus education and occupational training, undertaken in hospital is liable to be dissipated on discharge. Pharmacology can restore to normality and sustain physiological functioning in those of us who enjoy the advantages of an adequate economic, social and educational background. Those advantages, however, are conspicuously lacking in a majority of Broadmoor's patients. Hence the importance of all the therapeutic, educational and occupational inputs to their treatment package during their stay in hospital as well as the need to sustain them thereafter.

"The intricacies in terms of time, personnel and management of providing a service appropriate to the needs of the mentally disordered offender illustrate very clearly why such a service cannot painlessly accommodate the changes required by new acts of parliament and especially not those of two acts within a 25 year period. Nor, incidentally, can such a service as here described be cheap. Fortunately for the taxpayer in England and Wales, the population of the present three special hospitals has been reduced and has not risen above 1,700 annually in the past decade. If Kaye's and Franey's estimate of the number of staff required to cater for the needs of a 200-bedded secure psychiatric unit is 500 then clearly this form of care is expensive; but so is all hospital care.

"In Part III the author provides us with a remarkably dispassionate appraisal of Broadmoor's work over the period of his history. These final chapters are particularly rewarding, serving as they do as a summary of the impact of the 1959 legislation on the diagnosis and treatment of Broadmoor's patients as observed from inside the hospital, and including a close scrutiny of the law and its adequacy for its task in relation to the special hospital patient.

"To conclude: although I have been a friend and colleague of Tony Black since we both worked in Liverpool in the 1950s this history of his has been an eye opener to me. His tracing of the evolution of the concept of mentally disordered offenders and of the appropriate conditions for their accommodation, as well as of the insights into the nature of their disorders and relevant treatment strategies, should be compulsory reading for anyone contemplating working in a special hospital, secure psychiatric hospital or in any of the rehabilitation services outside hospital."

So there it is: the plot divulged. The reader does not have to persist to the end to discover it. Alternatively, however, it might encourage the more inquiring reader to take a look at the book in the first place if they know it is not just the story of Broadmoor. Enigmatic it might be but isolated it is no longer. It is indeed the magnifying glass through which we may see more clearly the concepts and reappraisals we need to make about sadness, madness and badness generally.

FOREWORD

by Nigel Walker

When I first read Ralph Partridge's short history, many years ago, I wondered what made one of the Bloomsbury group choose Broadmoor as a subject. I managed an introduction to his widow, Frances Partridge, but she could not help. It is possible that a friend, such as John Strachey the psychoanalyst, made the suggestion. Even so, Patridge's qualifications for undertaking the task were not obvious. He was not medically or psychologically trained, nor was he an 'insider'.

This not to belittle his contribution; nor does Tony Black do so. But he has the advantage of being both an insider and a professional. For the latter half of his history Partridge could visit and talk to staff, but he was not a resident or a confidant and if any of the staff were critical he does not record it. By contrast Black, for nearly the whole of the period which he chronicles, was the senior clinical psychologist of the hospital, in the confidence of the Medical Superintendent and the other psychiatrists, and on friendly, if not exactly confidential, terms with the formidably uniformed members of the Prison Officers' Association who formed the nursing and custodial staff. His understanding of the problems of both psychiatry and management gave him an insight into what was going wrong - but also into what was going right. For he defends Broadmoor against many of its critics, both journalists and professionals. He even doubts Partridge, who gives the impression that staff treated patients' crimes as a taboo subject for discussion with them: how could an outsider be sure of this?

Black has his own criticisms, of course. Both the state of the law and the mind-set of many staff - especially the POA - delayed obvious improvements. The expansion of the inmate population and staff meant that what began as a compact little team of professionals divided into several 'clinical teams', with less intercommunication of information and ideas. He also describes the scepticism with which clinical psychology, with its own tests and theories, had to contend at first. He has his own axe to grind; but some axes need a bit of sharpening. This book fills a gap that has existed for too long.

Nigel Walker
Cambridge

INTRODUCTION

THE EXISTING HISTORY

Inevitably many books have been written about Broadmoor. It's that sort of place. Most of them have been written by - or about - people who have been there as patients. By contrast, those who have worked there have mainly published papers in medical, legal and scientific journals, and chapters in books. Only one book exists, however, which gives a comprehensive account of the reason for Broadmoor's existence and its internal organization and functioning. This is entitled simply 'Broadmoor', was written by Ralph Partridge and published by Chatto & Windus in 1953.

Partridge's book is a fascinating and authoritative account of the history of criminal lunacy legislation and the thinking behind it, together with a description of the way mentally disordered offenders, as they are now called, have been dealt with over the years, culminating in what was, by 1953, modern psychiatric treatment.

THE LEGISLATIVE CHANGES POST-PARTRIDGE

In 1948 the National Health Service had been born and asylums became mental hospitals. 1953 was sufficiently soon after the war that Broadmoor, and indeed the entire psychiatric service of the time, was still functioning under pre-war legislation. Between 1954 and 1957, however, there was a Royal Commission (the 'Percy' Commission) which led to the Mental Health Act of 1959. This embodied radical changes which, in effect, 'medicalized' what had previously been mainly a social expedient. Admission to a mental hospital, if not accepted voluntarily, was made a medical matter and no longer dependent upon a magistrate's ruling.

The term 'Mental Disorder' was introduced, with its four sub-categories of 'Mental Illness', 'Mental Subnormality', 'Severe Mental Subnormality' and 'Psychopathic Disorder', the last-named being an innovation to cater for persistent antisocial behaviour not definable as mental illness but nevertheless attributed to 'abnormality of mind' (it was not, however, incorporated into the Scottish Mental Health Act either in 1959 or 1983). The 1983 revision retains the same classification except that it substitutes 'impairment' for 'subnormality'. The 1959 Act also explicitly enabled transfer of patients to take place between the special hospitals and local psychiatric hospitals.

A couple of years earlier, in 1957, a new Homicide Act had sidelined the old McNaughtan[1] Rules and included the much debated 'diminished responsibility' concept whilst later, in 1965, came the act to abolish capital punishment. These legislative changes, as we shall see, also brought great changes to the make-up of the patient population and hence the running of Broadmoor.

CLINICAL CHANGES

As if these legislative changes were not imposing enough adaptational challenge upon Broadmoor and the other special

---

1. McNaughtan enjoys a variety of different spellings, not resolved even by reference to his hospital case notes. This history follows Richard Moran's biography *(Knowing Right from Wrong*, 1981, Free Press) which confirms the spelling used by McNaughtan and his family.

ntroduction*

hospitals, other radical changes were taking place in psychiatric medicine. An explosion in drug development characterized the 1950s and 1960s which enabled more rapid and effective treatment for many mental illnesses and resulted in the 'opening of doors' in what had previously been largely locked and enclosed institutions. This, with the facility for transfer of patients between local and special hospitals, put a considerable load upon the special hospitals of those chronic psychiatric cases who failed to respond to the new drugs and whose sometimes hazardous behaviour required more security than the now 'open' mental hospitals could provide.

New medical specialisms and entire new professions were emerging which were contributing their ideas and practices to the mental health field, whilst long established professions, like nursing, were developing new ideas and practices. The 'clinical team' was soon to be born. All these changes brought opportunities to the special hospitals but also put them under great strain. They had to respond and adapt to the pressures of both a rising admission rate and the public spotlight always directed at a place which holds people who are little understood and therefore arouse fear and suspicion.

THE RESULTING CONFLICTS

Small wonder then that the 'post-Partridge' phase in Broadmoor's history is punctuated with criticism and uncertainty. A fresh look at how Broadmoor fared after Partridge's account ends is overdue. Another Mental Health Act, in 1983, has replaced the innovative 1959 Act, reflecting further advances in diagnosis and treatment, together with re-thinking on the 1959 Act's effects where civil liberties and public safety are concerned.

Although this Act is not as radical as the 1959 one, it has

brought changes of its own which have continued both the stresses to which the special hospitals must adapt and the criticisms which have always been directed at them. The 1983 Act embodies much of the philosophy of the late 20th Century in which civil rights and personal freedoms for a long time seemed to outweigh personal obligations and responsibility. People have come to expect that they should be able to enjoy both total freedom and total safety, regardless of the impossibility of this in a fallible world and that, at places like special hospitals, they are mutually incompatible. Freedom for mentally disordered people means reduced public safety whilst total public safety means restricting the freedom of mentally disordered people. A balance has always had to be struck. In the cold war era Dr Patrick McGrath, medical superintendent at Broadmoor for most of this period between the 1959 and 1983 Acts, and who occupies a comparable position to that of Dr Stanley Hopwood in Partridge's history, used to say that he must be doing things about right when the letters in his postbag accusing him of being a 'red-under-the-bed' balanced out those which accused him of being a 'fascist pig'.

CALLS FOR CLOSURE

With the 1983 Act have come fresh calls for the closure of the special hospitals. These are not new; they were always being voiced. Setting aside some obvious inconvenience in relocation, the special hospitals staffs probably would not greatly object. Their skills would still be needed elsewhere in the system, especially as the skills of nursing 'refractory' patients were being lost. This however, would also mean relocating the patients. Dispersal of responsibility to local authorities requires instead many small secure units scattered around the country, a strategy proposed by the 1975

('Butler') Report on Mentally Abnormal Offenders and gradually implemented since. Broadmoor, if it were closed in its present capacity, would probably reopen in modified form as one of these for its local area. No government would want to waste the considerable costs of the rebuilding and modernization that has been taking place in recent years.

THE CONTINUING NEED

But this only removes the problem one step further on. Full rehabilitation of 'mentally abnormal offenders', or mentally disordered patients generally, means gradual 're-entry' into the normal world as they respond to treatment and learn to cope safely with normal life. It is at this point that public safety becomes less than total and conflicts with much *fin-de-siècle* thinking. Yet to detain permanently all formerly dangerous mentally disordered patients deprives them all of their civil liberties for the sake of perhaps 5% to 10% who might be dangerous in the future (and who should be spotted becoming so under adequate aftercare provisions). It also insults the professional knowledge, skills and efforts of those staff who have assessed and treated them and would require the building of a further Broadmoor every decade - an expense which no government would contemplate (and there are not many votes in mental disorder!)

Small wonder then that local authorities are reluctant to take on the problem of finding and funding accommodation for people in their midst who might constitute a hazard to the local populace, and their own re-election, whilst also escalating their costs: the budgets for community care, residential units, psychiatric services, social services, the probation service and the police force would all rise. Local authorities instead prefer to pay for them to reside in units around the country which specialize in this sort of problem. As special hospitals shrink, independent units multiply.

So the special hospitals, funded and managed during this 'inter-acts' period by central government, continue to exist and, under present conditions, look likely to go on doing so.

THE HISTORICAL PERIOD COVERED

This book examines how Broadmoor has evolved since Partridge's account and during the 'inter-acts' period of 1959 to 1983; how it has 'interacted' with the rest of the NHS's psychiatric hospitals and regional secure units, the prisons and the community; how it has, in effect, created its own community on its 400 acre site; and how its staff has provided the same range of psychiatric services in the context of close supervision and a secure perimeter that would be found in the rest of the NHS.

It does not go beyond 1983 for a number of reasons. The period of the 1959 Mental Health Act, firstly, provides more than enough change and evolution for one book. Secondly, the author retired soon after the 1983 Act took effect and was not in a position to recount what happened next. Thirdly, a further book has appeared that tells of life at the special hospitals under the changed management system following the 1983 Act (Kaye & Franey, 1998). Although this does not follow the Partridge formula, it takes the story forward through the initial years of the next Act. This makes it all the more important to give an account of the intervening years between Partridge and Kaye & Franey (the 'Inter-Acts' era) but removes the need to go further. It does, however, mean that ideas, theories, principles and practices will have changed since those described in this history. Things quickly become out of date and superseded. A history must trace ideas and developments and it is noticeable that what is recounted here is already seen to be inadequate in comparison with current practice. But it also shows how present day thinking and procedure came about.

AUTHORSHIP PROBLEMS

Partridge was a professional writer, invited to write a first ever account of Broadmoor. To do so he spent some time in and around the hospital, getting familiar with its history, its patients, its staff, its work and its traditions, as well as its legal context: the lunacy laws.

The present continuation, in contrast, has been compiled by a former member of the staff who spent most of a lifetime's career there. Whilst this means that I might be expected to have observed and penetrated further into Broadmoor's 'soul and psyche' than Partridge could have done, it also means that I could have put too much personal and professional 'spin' on it, as current jargon has it. Of course, I cannot be sure that I haven't, even though I have tried to be even-handed: only others can judge that. I hope that at least I have faithfully recounted the historical events. If there are errors, these will be the result of inadequate knowledge, memory or understanding, not of any intent. I have tried throughout to make clear where I am recounting history and where I am trying to promote a viewpoint or arguing for change, which I have done intentionally, not inadvertently. The fundamental issues involved, the new fields of advancing knowledge and a general level of public ignorance and misinformation, all call for this.

PUBLIC MISCONCEPTIONS

Where service developments are concerned, too, I have a 'case to make' and, again, have intentionally departed from impartial history. Broadmoor - the place, the work, the patients, the purposes and the law governing it - are largely unknown to the public and, worse still, as I have indicated, frequently misunderstood and misrepresented. This unfortunately extends beyond the general public to people in public office, one's professional colleagues around the country and, probably more significantly because of the publicity they generate, members of the media. Staff members' repeated explanations of the basic facts of Broadmoor's existence and purpose become like the proverbial gramophone needle stuck in its groove. They invariably have to preface any public lecture or conference paper with substantial basic information, otherwise what they have to say will not be understood. I have, therefore, deliberately addressed this ignorance and, worse, misinformation, with attempts to set records straight.

PROFESSIONAL BIAS

I will also obviously know my own field best and any disproportion of this history's content will no doubt reflect this, too. However, I feel I also have a 'case to make' here, on behalf of my own profession, which it will again be as well to declare at the outset. Psychology has given rise to professional applications relatively recently, these having developed largely since the war which had not long ended when Partridge wrote.

The war was responsible for many rapid advances in, for instance, the location of brain function (from wartime head injuries), the assessment of skills and abilities essential for wartime personnel placement, and the assessment of personality and neurotic disorders brought into prominence through battle experiences. These gave a boost to the post-war development of applied psychology, including clinical, and although in the mental health field the latter is still a small profession it has grown exponentially in numbers and in its contribution to the understanding and relief of human distress. Its applications, as well as research, have a large and ever-growing literature. Nevertheless, it is still often overlooked in accounts like this.

Astonishingly, neither psychology nor psychologists appear in the index to Kaye's & Franey's book, nor are any psychologists associated with the special hospitals cited in the bibliography, despite the influence of psychology on Broadmoor's work by that time. Of course, psychology does not have either the statutory legal responsibilities borne by the medical (psychiatric) and social work professions or the day-to-day continuous care responsibilities on the wards borne by the nursing staff . Yet it is psychology which supplies much of the core knowledge used by all of these professions in the field of mental disorder. This history, therefore, provides an opportunity to include, in a period that featured a wealth of development and expansion deriving from psychology, the results of the work of psychologists themselves. Whilst the space given to this may be thought to be an over-correction or a personal indulgence, I believe any dispassionate assessment of what I have described would confirm, not merely psychology's growing presence on the 'inter-acts' scene, but the scale and significance which this history has given to it.

JARGON

A further risk of an account by a specialist is that there will be too much jargon. I am well aware of this. A certain amount is inevitable if the advances in our understanding and treatment of complex clinical conditions in the context of equally complex legislation are to be adequately told. I have tried, however, to convey these complexities in as straightforward and uncomplicated a manner as possible. That risks the error of approximation. But this is a history and not a technical explanation. I have referred the reader elsewhere for scientific and professional details although, again, I have tried to keep references to a minimum. The ones quoted will lead the reader to where others may be found.

CONFIDENTIALITY

Confidentiality requirements derive from codes of professional conduct and from the Official Secrets Act applying to government employees. Individual patients may not be identified or their treatment discussed and confidential matters concerning what was then the Department of Health & Social Security, and earlier the Ministry of Health, may not be divulged or criticized. Patients have been described anonymously, without reference to their individual clinical conditions. Some have been referred to by name but have published books on their experiences in Broadmoor, so have put themselves into the public domain. Again, there is no discussion of their clinical conditions.

Descriptions of the hospital's security and clinical procedures are within confidentiality requirements. They would feature in the routine discussion sessions with the weekly parties of professional visitors to the hospital as well as in lectures and conference papers. It was always the policy and practice of the DHSS and of Dr McGrath and the local Broadmoor management that this kind of information should be more widely known and better understood.

As said already, there has been too much mystery and misinformation about Broadmoor. Dr McGrath resisted trivial, flippant and sensational reporting but, conversely, welcomed and encouraged factual portrayals of the hospital's patients and work.

References to the DHSS and the MoH, its predecessor, have also remained descriptive of their functions in relation to the hospital. Any criticisms would have been put directly to the hospital managers, locally or at HQ in London. In fact, it would be the duty of a DHSS employee, especially one responsible for the delivery of specialist services, to make known observations on deficiencies or improvements. If a PQ (parliamentary question) arose in a field to do with Broadmoor then the head of the appropriate service would be expected to provide the 'briefing' necessary for the minister's reply.

LITERARY STYLE

Finally, and on a quite different note, grammatical errors will inevitably have occurred. Some of these, however, have been intentional. Colloquial speech conventions have been used at times in the interests of making complex material read more easily, such as using the plural of a verb where a collective noun should strictly take the singular: 'a number of reasons *were* given' seems to read less jarringly. I hope I will not have offended too many readers.

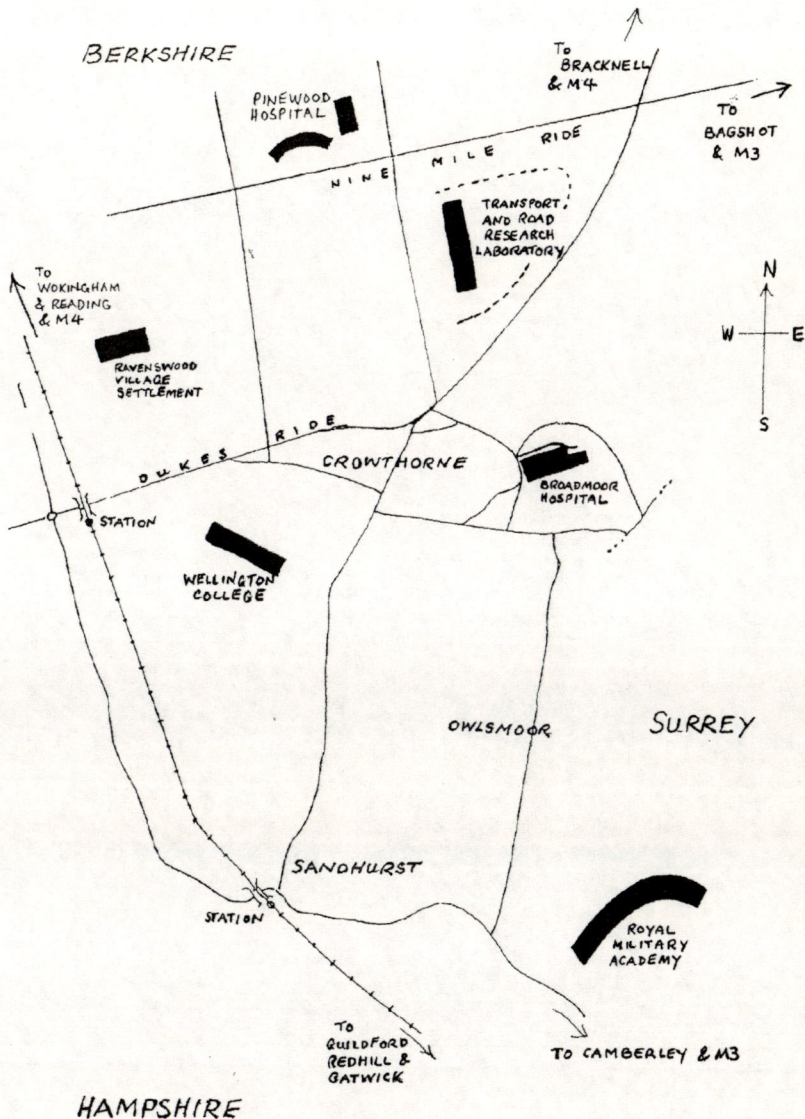

BERKSHIRE

PINEWOOD HOSPITAL

NINE MILE RIDE

TO BRACKNELL & M4

TO BAGSHOT & M3

TRANSPORT AND ROAD RESEARCH LABORATORY

TO WOKINGHAM & READING & M4

RAVENSWOOD VILLAGE SETTLEMENT

N
W E
S

DUKES RIDE

CROWTHORNE

BROADMOOR HOSPITAL

STATION

WELLINGTON COLLEGE

OWLSMOOR

SURREY

SANDHURST

STATION

ROYAL MILITARY ACADEMY

TO GUILDFORD REDHILL & GATWICK

TO CAMBERLEY & M3

HAMPSHIRE

BROADMOOR'S LOCATION

PART I

THE WAY IT WAS

CHAPTER 1

THE LEGAL POSITION BEFORE 1959

Broadmoor is not and never was a prison, although it is often erroneously referred to as one and its patients, equally wrongly, are often referred to as prisoners. Maybe this is because of its similarity of name with Dartmoor.

'IT'S NOT WHERE YOU THINK IT IS'

'Moor' has the misty mystique of a location somewhere on the country's margins, whereas many people are surprised to learn the 'moor' is in fact a piece of heathy highground on the Surrey-Berkshire border, a dozen miles from Reading and some twenty from both Windsor and Guildford. Its nearest towns are Wokingham, Bracknell and Ascot in Berkshire and Camberley in Surrey. Its nearest neighbours are the Royal Military Academy at Sandhurst, the Staff College in Camberley, and Wellington College and the Transport Research Laboratory in Crowthorne itself. In fact, Crowthorne did not exist at the time Broadmoor was opened in 1863 and early references are to its location in the parish of Sandhurst. Crowthorne grew up as a village community serving the population that arose between Broadmoor 'up the hill' and Wellington College 'down the hill'. Both establishments were built on Crown land, the one out of legal necessity and the other to mark a grateful nation's memory of the conqueror of Napoleon.

Partridge describes all this but it is worth repeating because so many people, even nowadays, are vague on Broadmoor's whereabouts. Staff who attend meetings in London, say, are familiar with expressions of appreciation for their having travelled a long way to attend and are torn between putting the, often distinguished, person right or, to avoid embarrassment, letting the misconception continue.

What has all this to do with Broadmoor's legal context? It underlines the ambivalence with which Broadmoor is viewed, for it is more than the name that establishes Broadmoor as a distant prison in so many people's minds: after all, it is specifically intended for dangerous people; it is surrounded by high walls; its doors are locked; and its windows barred.

REFUGE, NOT PUNISHMENT

Yet Broadmoor was always a place of refuge, not punishment, for those who had committed violent and often abhorrent acts in what was clearly a deranged state of mind and who could not be held responsible for their actions in the way a sane and reasonable person has always been.

This apparently quite reasonable distinction in the context of a number of dramatically public crimes underlies the decision to build an asylum - a place of refuge - for people who were demonstrably mad at the time of their crime. Partridge describes the historical background in full, highlighted by a number of sensational public cases of people who shot at monarchs and prime ministers. King George III was shot at by James Hadfield in 1800; Queen Victoria was shot at by Edward Oxford in 1840 and Roderick Maclean in 1882. Spencer Perceval, the prime minister of the time, was shot and killed in 1812 by John Bellingham, whilst the private secretary

2

to prime minister Sir Robert Peel was shot and killed in 1843 by Daniel McNaughtan, whose name is attached to the 'rules' which emerged to define criminal insanity.

Although the legal framework is different today it is instructive to summarize the situation described by Partridge and which still determined the position of patients in Broadmoor up to the time of the 1959 Mental Health Act (implemented in November 1960). If we are to see how the 1959 Act affected Broadmoor, its patients and its life, we need to recall the legal state of affairs that existed until that time.

NOT ANSWERABLE FOR THEIR ACTIONS

As Partridge says, history is replete with the puzzles posed by the mad, initially considered the province of the church. Medicine then emerged to offer alternative explanations, although from being burned as a witch to being shackled and flogged - often the recommended treatment for lunacy - might not seem much of an advance. The high profile cases of monarchs and prime ministers shot at by madmen, however, gave impetus to the legal enactment of medical advances. Clearly the assertion on trial for high treason that Hadfield's attempted murder of the King was on the instructions of God, who had commanded him to save the world through the sacrifice of his own life (treason was punishable by death and so would ensure his swift and sure end), was not the act of a normal criminal. Instead of being punished or put to death, they should be detained in an asylum for the appropriate treatment of their disorder.

Although the insane were already detained in asylums, these could not be relied upon as sufficiently safe to prevent the likes of Hadfield absconding to repeat their crimes. The Criminal Lunatics

Act was rapidly passed later in 1800 and gave rise to the identification of buildings in Bethlem Hospital, London and Fisherton House, Salisbury, for such cases until these became inadequate and Broadmoor was built, opening in 1863, seven years after the decision taken in 1856. (The current extensions and rebuilding were announced by the then Minister of Health, Enoch Powell, at the centenary celebrations in 1963 and the rebuilding was only partially complete at the time of the 1983 Mental Health Act - 20 years on!)

Yet the vagaries of public events - the eminence of the victim, whether he was killed (Spencer Perceval) or survived (King George III) and the heroic history or otherwise of the perpetrator (Hadfield had been wounded serving his king and country) - did much to vary the view taken of madness: was he sane enough to deserve punishment or mad enough to escape it? Partridge quotes the direction of the Lord Chief Justice to the jury in Hadfield's case: "It is necessary for me to submit to you whether you will not find that the prisoner, at the time he committed the act, was not so under the guidance of reason as to be answerable for this act, enormous and atrocious as it appeared to be". Had this view prevailed, says Partridge, the law could have saved itself a century of argument and opposition over medical evidence. So 'sane enough to receive punishment' gave way to 'mad enough to escape it' in the McNaughtan Rules.

Daniel McNaughtan had shot and killed the Prime Minister's, Sir Robert Peel's, private secretary, apparently in mistake for the prime minister himself, and did not have the illustrious military career behind him that Hadfield had had. In 1843, therefore, in response to the House of Lords by a bench of judges, the rules were framed, the crux of which to persist in this context being: "Was the prisoner at the time of the crime suffering from such a defect of reason from disease of the mind as not to know the nature and quality of the act he was doing or not to know that it was wrong?" This was to give rise to time consuming arguments in court between medical and legal experts right up to the time of the 1957 Homicide Act with its use of the concept of 'diminished responsibility' and the 1959 Mental Health Act with its categories of mental disorder, any of which, if established and accepted in court, could be sufficient for the defendant to be detained for treatment instead of sentenced to imprisonment.

It should be pointed out, of course, that a range of provisions and procedures operated for the protection and treatment of what were formerly known as 'pauper lunatics' as well as the various categories of 'defectives'. The latter were not Broadmoor's concern, but the Lunacy Act of 1890, for instance, provided for a 'reception order' for care of the former which might have been its concern if the offence was serious enough. Later, during the middle of the 20th century, probation was another avenue for provision of psychiatric treatment but, again, would not have been considered appropriate for the seriousness of the offences of Broadmoor patients. Walker & McCabe (1973) give a full account of these provisions and the often droll vacillations that marked the fitful progress in parliament of the proposals for reform. It was really only after the interruptions of the two wars that the situation was clarified and resolved by the 1959 Mental Health Act.

GUILTY BUT INSANE OR INSANE ON ARRAIGNMENT: 'PLEASURE PATIENTS'

The position then, up to the time of the 1959 Act, was that a defendant who successfully pleaded insanity could be found 'guilty but insane' and detained at Her Majesty's Pleasure, which meant at Broadmoor 'Institution' for people of normal intelligence or one of its sister institutions, Rampton or Moss Side, for those of subnormal intelligence (as the term then was). Note the name change from 'Asylum' to 'Institution' following the 1948 National Health Acts.

Alternatively, someone who was still insane at the time of trial (as distinct from the time of committing the crime) so that they were unable to 'instruct counsel, challenge jurors, make a plea or understand evidence' would be found 'insane on arraignment' and also detained at Her Majesty's Pleasure. Here, of course, the trial not having been concluded, the matter technically remained outstanding and a resumed or new trial could take place at a later date when the, by then, 'patient' had sufficiently recovered as to be able to 'instruct counsel ... etc.' In practice this never happened as the illness and its subsequent treatment were regarded in the same light as someone having been committed to Broadmoor as 'Guilty but Insane' who would be discharged when fit and recovered from insanity, such discharge being supervised and conditional until made absolute at some indefinite later date. Technically, this was wrong as the lack of conclusion of a trial left undetermined whether the person indicted might not have been found 'not guilty'. However, 'guilty but insane' was also technically a 'not guilty' finding. Originally it had been 'not guilty by reason of insanity' (as it is again now) until one of the cases of an attempt on the life of Queen Victoria who, having been the victim of the attempt and observed clearly what was intended towards her, insisted on the change of terminology and is reported to have said: "insane he may have been but not guilty he most certainly was not as I saw him fire the pistol myself!"

As indicated by Partridge, both these above types of patient were known as 'pleasure' patients in the hospital, because both were detained 'until Her Majesty's Pleasure be known'. The subdivisions were known as GBI for the 'guilty but insane' and

6

IOA for the 'insane on arraignment'.

TIME-SERVING PRISONERS TRANSFERRED WHEN INSANE

The other group of patients were the 'time men' (and women too, of course, but they were fewer). These would be prisoners sentenced in the normal manner who were found later to be insane, in the view of a panel of examining doctors, and transferred to Broadmoor. Such an examination would always take place in the case of a capital crime (i.e.: carrying a death sentence) but transfer to hospital could also occur with lesser offences. In the days before the abolition of the death penalty this gave rise to some odd phraseology in offender classification, both 'life' and 'death' occurring (life in the case of a life sentence for, say, manslaughter, and death in the case of a death sentenced murderer subsequently found to be insane by a panel of doctors).

DISCHARGE

Discharge from one of the state institutions was a matter for agreement at the Home Office. Despite the special hospitals (state institutions then) being Ministry of Health establishments, their patients were detained as a result of a court process (either directly for the 'pleasure patients' or indirectly for the 'time patients' transferred from prison). This was, therefore, a Home Office matter. In other words, whilst their staffs were and still are employed under NHS conditions and provide standard NHS psychiatric care and treatment, making them the administrative concern of the Ministry (now Department) of Health, the patients were a Ministry of Health responsibility only where their care and treatment were concerned; they were a Home Office responsibility where their admission and discharge were concerned. After the 1959 Act, as we shall see, the position becomes more variable.

Prior to the 1959 Act therefore, and as described somewhat discursively and anecdotally by Partridge in Chapter 9 of his book, HMP patients were discharged when recovered and when recommended as both stabilized and unlikely to relapse. Discharge was conditional, dependent upon the social worker finding a suitable place to live, a job and someone to be responsible for the patient, most commonly a spouse or other close relative. Discharge would usually be made absolute after five satisfactory years outside but could be shorter or longer. Recall could occur in the case of danger signals as the essence of 'HMP' was, of course, that the ex-patient's future life remained dependent upon 'Her Majesty's Pleasure'.

'Time' patients were different. In the case of someone transferred on a fixed sentence, an absolute, not conditional, discharge took place on expiry of sentence. This however, would be on expiry of the whole sentence, remission for 'good behaviour' being an irrelevant factor where mental disorder was concerned. This would often give rise to resentment on the part of some patients who saw it as unfair and that they would have been better off in prison. In fact, where recovery had clearly occurred and been maintained before expiry of sentence it would sometimes happen that transfer to prison could be arranged, there to derive benefit of remission. Such an incentive could be beneficial where the patient's resolve to comply with treatment was concerned. Conversely, if still suffering from mental disorder at the time their sentence expired, arrangements would be made for an appropriately qualified person from their usual home area to be available to 'certify' them on discharge, so that they could immediately be admitted to a local mental hospital for continuation of treatment.

'Time' patients who had been transferred to Broadmoor under life sentence or a respited death sentence originally would not have an expiry date, of course. They could, however, be returned to prison to continue sentence if and when they recovered from their mental disorder, where they could become eligible for parole review.

As with Partridge's book, the discharge process (and 'transfer', too, after the inception of the 1959 Act) will be discussed from the clinical point of view in a later chapter. The present chapter is concerned with the way the law determines a patient's arrival and departure from the hospital and, thus far, has summarized the position before the 1959 Act which is well discussed by Partridge. It is the situation in Dr Hopwood's time, which continued through Dr James's into Dr McGrath's superintendentship, which needs to be understood if we are to trace the changes introduced by the 1959 Act and the way the hospital coped with these in Dr McGrath's time.

SUMMARY

Before the 1959 Mental Health Act, committal of an offender to a mental hospital required a court to accept that s/he was 'insane'. The criteria for offences of such severity that Broadmoor was necessary were the 'McNaughtan Rules' (other avenues were available for lesser cases). The law had recognized for more than a century that insane offenders should not be held responsible for their actions and should be committed instead to an asylum (later called a mental hospital). The McNaughtan Rules were met if the defendant could be held not to understand the nature of his/her offence or that it was wrong. Not even all forms of psychosis (the technical term for insanity), however, necessarily met these rules, let alone the neurotic disorders, and some epic court tussles marked their use.

Those where a court did accept the McNaughtan criteria were, however, acquitted by the 'Guilty but Insane' verdict. If the court found them unfit even to stand trial then it did not proceed and a finding of 'Insane on Arraignment' was recorded. Both 'GbI' and 'IoA', as they were known, were then detained at 'Her Majesty's Pleasure' (known as 'HMP') which invariably meant in a secure mental hospital.

Convicted prisoners who became insane in prison could also be sent to such a hospital for the duration of their sentence and this included, in those pre-abolition of capital punishment days, those on life sentence or whose death sentence for murder had been 'respited'.

Recovered patients in Broadmoor could be conditionally discharged if the Home Secretary sanctioned this and transferred time serving prisoners could be released on expiry of sentence, or returned to prison on recovery to be considered under the parole system.

In 1957 the Homicide Act introduced 'diminished responsibility' which allowed consideration of insanity criteria broader than McNaughtan and, more importantly if accepted, for the conviction to be reduced to manslaughter. Whilst this did not oblige the court to impose a particular sentence it allowed a life sentence and this was significant in the days before the abolition of capital punishment in bringing a committal to a secure mental hospital (as it still does on the rare occasions that it continues to be used). This in turn made the old McNaughtan Rules largely redundant. The scene was therefore set for a reform of mental health legislation itself and this is the subject of the next chapter.

CHAPTER 2

THE LEGAL POSITION AFTER 1959

The 1959 Mental Health Act was a major piece of reforming legislation. It was a medico-legal advance on behalf of 'mental patients' (later 'psychiatric patients' but no longer, note, 'lunatics') on what had previously been legislation designed principally for public protection. Its very first words state that it repeals, in one sweep, the Lunacy and Mental Treatment Acts of 1890 to 1930 and the Mental Deficiency Acts of 1913 to 1938.

MENTAL DISORDER AND ITS FOUR CATEGORIES

Of first concern in Broadmoor's context is the specification of the term 'mental disorder'. The Act's definition of mental disorder in Section 4(1) may be criticized as insufficient but, for its time and for an Act of Parliament (in contrast with a scientific or medical definition), it was a huge step forward, viz: *"In this Act 'mental disorder' means mental illness, arrested or incomplete development of mind, psychopathic disorder, and any other disorder or disability of mind; and 'mentally disordered' shall be construed accordingly."*

The first category of mental disorder - 'mental illness' - is not further defined but Section 4 Subsections (2) and (3) define 'subnormality' and 'severe subnormality' as states of: *"arrested or incomplete development of mind which include subnormality of intelligence and are of a nature or degree which: (Subsection 3) requires or is susceptible to medical treatment or other special care or training*" in the case of subnormality; and (Subsection 2) "*that the patient is incapable of living an independent life or of guarding himself against serious exploitation, or will be so incapable when of an age to do so*" in the case of severe subnormality. Whilst these categories did not concern Broadmoor at that time, they concerned the other special hospitals. Section 4(4), however, in the Act for England & Wales but not Scotland, did concern Broadmoor and said: "*psychopathic disorder means a persistent disorder or disability of mind (whether or not including subnormality of intelligence), which results in abnormally aggressive or seriously irresponsible conduct on the part of the patient, and requires or is susceptible to medical treatment*". The usual catch-all provision of '*any other disorder or disability of mind*' was added, envisaging, say, the effects of head injury, but was never used in Broadmoor, a specific category always being insisted upon. Where head injury cases did occur they were always categorized in terms of their effect, i.e.: of a mental illness.

Of course, as Chapter 1 has mentioned, there had been other provisions than the McNaughtan Rules for the care and treatment of the insane and lesser mental disorders but, in the context of Broadmoor's function as a secure institution for the most dangerous, it is these rules that had effectively governed the admission of its patients. In the space of only two or three years, therefore, first: the 1957 Homicide Act freed the law from the McNaughtan Rules and could consider 'diminished responsibility' instead; and then: the 1959 Mental Health Act set out four categories of 'mental disorder' by which to consider diminished responsibility. To consider the full implications for Broadmoor it is necessary to look further into the new legislation.

THE HOSPITAL ORDER

Part IV of the 1959 Mental Health Act (Sections 25 to 59) set out a whole new structure and conditions for compulsory admission of people who needed observation and/or treatment for their own or others' protection (people could continue to be admitted voluntarily, of course. Section 5 of the Act dealt with 'informal admission' of patients to hospital for treatment). Part V of the Act (Sections 60 to 80) set out the equivalent conditions for the admission to hospital of patients concerned in criminal proceedings and the transfer to hospital of prisoners under sentence and people on remand awaiting trial. Such admission to hospital could be effected by either the magistrates' court or a higher court, when it would be an alternative trial outcome to a sentence, as a result of medical evidence of mental disorder being accepted. This evidence, therefore, no longer had to address the complex questions of insanity under the McNaughtan Rules but instead had to attest the existence of a 'mental disorder' as defined under the new Act: one of the four sub-categories (or, sometimes, a combination of some of these) had to be said to exist. If so, and if accepted by the court, it would no longer be a case of 'guilty but insane' (GBI) and detention 'until Her Majesty's Pleasure be known' (HMP) but a guilty finding and then the making of a 'hospital order' under Section 60 of the Act because of 'mental disorder' (which had no time limit). A change of major significance to be noted in this was that the verdict was no longer an acquittal, as GBI had been. GBI was an actual verdict of the court and amounted to an acquittal, even if placement in a secure hospital was the result. A classification of mental disorder, by contrast, was not a verdict of the court but was the classification reached after the verdict in the light of the acceptance of evidence of such disorder. Although it resulted in a hospital disposal and not a prison sentence, it was still the result of a conviction.

WHICH HOSPITAL: THE 'RESTRICTION ORDER'

Committal under a hospital order did not need to be to a special hospital unless the person concerned was considered likely to be a continuing danger to the public. For instance, a mentally ill person before the court for petty theft could be sent under a Section 60 order to his or her local psychiatric hospital. Only if the person was thought to be a potential further danger would the hospital order be implemented at a special hospital. In this case, a further provision in the new legislation would usually also be used. This was for a 'restriction' to be placed on subsequent discharge, under Section 65, which meant that authority for the eventual discharge was 'restricted' to the Secretary of State, Home Office. (NB: this did not mean that 'restrictions' were put upon the discharged patient's freedom of movement, a frequently made misinterpretation of the term). In other words: someone under such an order could not be discharged from a special hospital on the authority only of the hospital; there had to be an endorsement by the Home Secretary.

Early use of this order was often made with a time limit, say of 10, 15 or 20 years, which also gave rise to misunderstandings, although more usually on the part of the press who interpreted it as a 'sentence'. Too short a time limit, in the opinion of the press, would often be criticised on the assumption that that was when the patient would be discharged when, of course, it meant that that was the period during which any discharge proposal (due to recovery from mental disorder) needed the Home Secretary's agreement. The Section 60 Hospital Order remained operative and a decision to discharge might well not be made until much later. It could then, of course, be effected by the hospital without the need for the Home Secretary's approval. Later on courts reacted to this situation by tending to make 'restriction orders' without limit of time so that discharge, *whenever* it was recommended, invariably became a matter for the Home Secretary's endorsement.

Committal to hospital under a court order *without* the addition of restrictions could be made either by a magistrates' or a higher court. If a magistrates' court considered that a restriction order needed to be added then, of course, there would be a further remand for a higher court hearing and this remand period could be spent either in prison or in hospital, as appropriate.

TRANSFER OF PRISONERS

Convicted prisoners could be transferred to hospital just as were the 'Time' patients under the old legislation but they were now subject to the same sort of provisions in the new Act as people sent under a hospital order direct from the court. Section 72 covered these; and Section 74 covered 'restrictions' on discharge (viz: Home Secretary's agreement required) just as did Section 65 for cases direct from court on a hospital order.

People on remand awaiting trial could also be transferred to Broadmoor pending trial although it was more usual in those days for any psychiatric investigations to be carried out during remand in prison rather than transferring someone to Broadmoor for this. It was not until the 1983 Act, with sections specifically for this purpose, that transfer to Broadmoor on remand became a significant feature, allowing more extensive assessments over a longer period and, equally importantly, a trial run for the feasibility of treatment.

TRANSFER OF 'CIVIL' PATIENTS

The last route for arriving in Broadmoor was by transfer from a 'county mental hospital' (later known as a 'district psychiatric hospital'). The equivalent for the other two English special hospitals - Park Lane was not yet built - was transfer from a local mental subnormality hospital (later called a 'mental handicap hospital' and later still a unit for 'people with learning difficulties'). Part IV of the Act (i.e.: the 'civil', not 'criminal' part) contained provision for this in Section 41. As this section covered 'transfers between' hospitals it also made explicit a procedure only effected with difficulty previously - the transfer of special hospital patients to another psychiatric hospital.

This was a major advance for it set up an avenue of exchange that both greatly facilitated the transfer out of patients no longer considered to need the security of a special hospital but also, in facilitating the same avenue in, it opened Broadmoor and its sister hospitals for the first time to non-offender patients. It may very well be argued that the distinction is a fine one, for those transferred in would have been moved because of some significant violence on their part - for example: attacking staff or other patients, or setting fire to something in the hospital - but nevertheless they would not have been through the courts and remained 'civil' patients. This was to create a significant change in the perception, status and legal position of this group of the hospital's residents.

DURATION AND DISCHARGE OF COMPULSORY ADMISSIONS

Before considering the last few aspects of admission conditions and categories under the 1959 Act it will be helpful to jump ahead a little and consider how long these compulsory admission orders were intended to last, whether under the civil or the criminal Parts of the Act. The civil Part IV had three avenues of admission, the shortest being for 72 hours (3 days). This was for emergencies when a second doctor was not available to authorize an admission requested by a mental welfare officer (social worker nowadays) or the nearest relative. Otherwise two doctors were required for longer admissions and one of these had to be 'recognized' for the purpose as having special qualifications (i.e.: a psychiatrist). Section 25 was for observation and expired after 28 days. By that time it was considered that it should be possible to establish whether a longer Section 26 order for treatment was needed or not. Section 26 expired after one year. It could be renewed for a further year and then, if necessary, for further periods of two years at a time.

Now here is the reason we need to consider these 'civil' categories of admission, for the 'criminal' categories did not need renewal; by and large they continued until either: the 'responsible medical officer' discharged the patient (Section 60); or his discharge recommendation was endorsed by the Home Secretary (Section 65 and prison transfer equivalents); or the patient made a successful application for discharge to a Mental Health Review Tribunal. However, if the patient was already someone transferred from a local psychiatric hospital under Section 26 and needed renewal after the lapse of two years, or if the patient was a transferred prisoner whose sentence had expired and a Section 26 order was needed, and if the category of mental disorder under which they were held was either subnormality or psychopathic disorder, the civil part of the Act allowed this to happen only until the age of 25. Then they could no longer be detained, unless their classification could be changed so that they could now be said to suffer instead from 'severe' mental subnormality or mental illness, neither of which had an age limitation. The 'criminal' Part of the Act did not have this limitation for Sections 60 (Hospital Order) or 72 (transfer from prison).

GUARDIANSHIP

One more new committal category needing mention is the creation under Part IV (i.e.: the non-criminal part of the 1959 Act) of 'guardianship' conditions which enabled the committal of people, in need of care and protection for their own safety and benefit, to the supervision of a specified person or authority. The conditions were similar to those of a parent and generally intended for those designated in those days as 'mentally subnormal' with the guardian usually being a social services department. Guardianship was more relevant to the other special hospitals where the subnormal and severely subnormal were sent and no case of guardianship occurred at Broadmoor during the time of the 1959 Act. With the increasing emphasis on community care over the years and the introduction in the later 1983 Mental Health Act of statutory aftercare for people discharged from several of the compulsory sections of the Act, the Guardianship provision perhaps deserves more attention and use than it has had. Taking on responsibilities of the parental kind for problematic people, however, is clearly not popular and is fraught with difficulties so its relatively little use is perhaps not surprising.

INSANITY AND 'HER MAJESTY'S PLEASURE'

We should not leave discussion of the new variations in ways of arriving at Broadmoor without brief mention of the old 'Her Majesty's Pleasure' provision which still continued to exist for treason and some armed services' offences. There also remained, of course, numerous patients in Broadmoor at the time the 1959 Act came into force who had been admitted originally as 'HMP' through being insane on arraignment or found guilty but insane. Section 71 in the 'criminal' Part V of the Act made provision for these who were to be treated in the same way as someone committed under a hospital order (Section 60) together with an order restricting discharge (Section 65).

Later, in 1964, the Criminal Procedure (Insanity) Act was introduced which dealt further with the position of those who might still plead insanity or be found insane on arraignment, although the circumstances where this would be needed were greatly reduced by virtue of the 1959 Mental Health Act and the 1957 Homicide Act. The Criminal Procedure (Insanity and Unfitness to Plead) Act 1991 has more recently further updated the situation in the light of another (1983) Mental Health Act and periodic Criminal Justice Act revisions. Meanwhile it is worth noting that the 'not guilty by reason of insanity' wording has been restored, making clear the original meaning and that the verdict is an acquittal (although with significant restrictive consequences). Queen Victoria is no longer around to take umbrage!

SUMMARY OF PROCEDURES

To summarize all this tedious but unavoidable legislative detail:

1) The new legislation still brought patients into Broadmoor either directly from the courts or by transfer from prison. However, it now also brought them from other psychiatric hospitals as well.
2) The reason it brought them was broadened and updated from the old 'insanity' concept and no longer needed the constricting definitions of the McNaughtan Rules. Instead, it was based on the new categorization of 'mental disorder' which was defined in terms of four sub-categories, two of which were relevant to Broadmoor: 'mental illness' and 'psychopathic disorder'. This was to make the process greatly more flexible and, therefore, widen the range of psychiatric conditions eligible for

Broadmoor.

3) The kind of criminal act committed by a mentally ill or psychopathic person was also revised, and this continued through the lifetime of the 1959 Act, so that Broadmoor and its sister special hospitals were increasingly reserved only for those who were dangerous. People before the courts who met the Mental Health Act's criteria and who were not dangerous could equally be committed under Section 60 to a local psychiatric hospital.

4) The period of detention under the new legislation was still indefinite and discharge was dependent upon the recommendation of the RMO or a successful appeal to a MHRT. In the case of the majority of patients who were 'restricted' or transferred from prison, the endorsing approval of the Home Secretary was also required. Only those transferred from another hospital under the civil Part of the Act or from prison under a fixed sentence would leave at the expiry of their order or sentence unless detained further under a fresh section.

MENTAL HEALTH REVIEW TRIBUNALS

Let us now move on to consider what changes the new legislation brought to the legal position of the patients once arrived within Broadmoor. We shall consider later how the legislative changes affected the clinical mix of patients and, therefore, their treatment and life generally within the hospital but, for the present chapter's purposes, probably the most significant and noticeable legal change resulted from the creation in the 1959 Act of a new body: the Mental Health Review Tribunal (MHRT).

Although this was not synonymous with the old Board of Control, which had been quietly pensioned off by the new Act, it took over some of its functions. Other functions - and greatly expanded too - were not to be revived until the 1983 Mental Health Act when a Mental Health Act Commission (MHAC) was created to oversee the administration of the Act and the concerns and complaints of patients. Meanwhile, the MHRT system provided a means of appealing against continued detention by 'sectioned' patients, whether under Part IV (civil) or Part V (criminal) of the Act.

MHRTs are organized on a regional basis - there is not just one Tribunal for the whole country - so the tribunals for the areas in which the three special hospitals are situated are in need of a larger panel of tribunal members to draw upon: all the special hospitals' patients are 'detained' whereas only a small number in any one regional psychiatric hospital will be.

Patients detained under different sections of the Act were and are able to appeal to a MHRT for a hearing after a specific interval (different for different detaining sections) and thereafter again at two-yearly intervals (this became yearly with the 1983 Act).

The Tribunal is chaired by a lawyer and comprises also a psychiatrist and a lay member. The psychiatrist visited (and still does - the 1983 Act maintained Tribunals, with some revised composition and functions) a few days in advance of a hearing to make a preliminary assessment. He or she would consult with the patient's 'responsible medical officer', or RMO, a consultant psychiatrist, and any other staff he or she thought relevant, and would have access to the case notes and medical records, so that other reports would also be available, legal or clinical.

At the subsequent Tribunal hearing the RMO would invariably be called, although other staff 'witnesses' less often so. Patients could have legal assistance and be legally represented, although legal aid was not made routinely available for this until the 1983 Act. Occasionally 'open' Tribunal hearings would take place when members of the public could attend (including, of course, staff if they wished and were off duty).

The Tribunal's recommendations were mandatory for someone detained without a restriction order but needed Home Office agreement where a restriction order existed. (This has changed with the 1983 Act and a tribunal's recommendations, if the presiding lawyer is a QC, cannot be overruled by the Home Office.) The conditions and regulations for MHRTs are numerous and governed by similarly numerous 'Rules'. These are detailed in Section 124 and were also periodically augmented or amended by the Lord Chancellor under whose jurisdiction the MHRTs fall. Changes occurred in the lifetime of the 1959 Act and, again, with the 1983 Act. It would not be appropriate in the present context to detail all these. Anyone wishing to pursue legal issues in more detail should consult the Acts themselves and the various commentaries and manuals available on them.

Tribunals have been viewed with mixed feelings by both patients and staff but there is no doubt that an independent outside authority of some sort must exist for monitoring the situations of people compulsorily detained in closed institutions. Whilst the necessity to produce reports for Tribunals is no doubt irksome for psychiatrists and other staff it is one of the ways that ensures a patient's condition and circumstances are constantly under review.

The mixed feelings on the part of the 'RMO' (the consultant psychiatrist) and other staff arise quite understandably from their view that, since they are with the patient all the time, they must surely know him or her better than any outsider could, especially on only a brief visit. The mixed feelings on the part of the patient will depend upon whether they are well recovered from their mental disorder or not. If not, they might well have any prejudices or delusions accentuated by their RMO's opposition to their appeal. If they are largely recovered, then they might argue that a Home Secretary and his advisers are unlikely to decide to discharge a formerly dangerous person on the recommendation of a Tribunal alone when their own RMO is not prepared to make a recommendation.

On the other hand (and this has tended to happen more frequently in recent years with the difficulty in persuading local psychiatric services to accept a Broadmoor patient on transfer) an RMO might encourage a patient to appeal to a Tribunal in the expectation that favourable corroboration will encourage the local health authority to accept the patient on transfer.

In between these extremes there was the strategy of an RMO, who perhaps did not feel able positively to recommend a discharge but did not oppose it either. The patient was, therefore, encouraged to test the matter through a MHRT appeal.

This touches on a subtle difference of emphasis in the 1959 Act generally, by comparison with its successor. The ethos of the 1983 Act is one of not detaining someone compulsorily unless there are very good reasons to do so. The 1959 Act provided for detention until there were very good reasons not to.

SUMMARY

The 1959 Act made two fundamental changes to the pre-war legislation. Compulsory committal to a mental hospital became a medical instead of a legal matter (albeit with legal provisions and safeguards) and the 'mental disorder' on which this was to be based was defined much more widely than the 'insanity' rules which it replaced. These changes applied to both the civil and the court routes into hospital.

Many more mentally disordered offenders than previously were able to obtain the care and treatment they needed by means of a hospital order of the court. They did so, however, as convicted persons (there remained an updated version of the former legislation for the 'insane' but its use was confined to a minority).

The previous legislation had provided only for the insane, treated them as not responsible for their actions and acquitted them (albeit in somewhat equivocal terms: the original verdict of 'not guilty by reason of insanity' was changed, at Queen Victoria's insistence, to 'guilty but insane' but the result was still indefinite incarceration, although in an asylum rather than a prison). Those found to be mentally disordered while in prison could once again be transferred to hospital for treatment but, in addition, psychiatric patients in district hospitals who became too dangerous in such settings (bearing in mind that doors were increasingly being unlocked) could also now be transferred to the security of a special hospital.

Apart from the legal status of being convicted instead of acquitted and, although allowing a much wider range of mentally disordered people to obtain care and treatment instead of being imprisoned, a fundamental consequence of this change was the sidestepping of the controversial issue of legal responsibility. Lawyers, legislators, the medical profession, and philosophers even, had pondered and argued over this for centuries, to little avail. So it was probably as well that the issue was now sidelined. As long as a court was prepared to accept medical evidence of mental disorder, offenders could now be sent for treatment after conviction and questions of their responsibility didn't arise.

Where eventual discharge was concerned, the same safeguards existed as previously and these knotty philosophical issues again hardly mattered. More mentally disordered offenders than previously were now receiving care and treatment under secure conditions and would only be released upon society, in the case of the dangerous ones, when the Home Secretary of the day agreed the doctor's discharge recommendation. There was now, however, the important new safeguard for the patient in the creation of the Mental Health Review Tribunal. This was to consider appeals from patients whose discharge was being denied.

CHAPTER 3

THE PATIENTS AFTER 1959:
MENTAL DISORDERS

CATEGORIES OF MENTAL DISORDER

Partridge describes the types of patient to be found in Broadmoor during its lifetime, up to the immediate post-war period. He also contrasts the types in the 'HMP' category (direct from court) with those transferred from prison, frequently using the term 'convict class' to describe the latter (a term that would be shunned today).

It is interesting how the terminology had changed by the 1960s (the 1959 Act took effect from November 1960), reflecting partly the changing times and partly the change in the mix of patients as a result of the new legislation. The 1959 Act allowed a greater range of psychiatric conditions to be considered under 'mental disorder' than it had done under the McNaughtan Rules for insanity. The same patient groups are there but they are described differently and they are augmented by other categories not there previously. The breakdown does, nevertheless, roughly follow those described by Partridge. However, the categories of 'mental disorder' are medico-legal ones and we must look within them for the diagnostic groupings.

Hospital statistics in the 1960s show the main breakdown between 'Mental Illness' and 'Psychopathic Disorder' among new admissions fluctuating between 3:1 and 4:1, that is to say there were some 75-80% Mentally Ill to 20-25% Psychopathic Disorder.

Within these groupings were to be found the psychiatric diagnostic categories roughly equivalent to those described by Partridge. A tabulation is the easiest way to show how his groupings and those of the 1960s compare, together with the proportions of each in the resident population at the end of the 1960s (by then the 1959 Act had had time to settle in and show trends):

TABLE 3.1

Partridge	Post 1959 M H Act	Ratio	%age
Organic Reaction Type	Organic Disorder	1	6%
Schizophrenic Reaction Type	(Schizophrenia ((Paranoia	9 \ 10 1 /	56% \ 62% 6% /
Affective Reaction Type	Affective Disorder	1	6%
Hysterical Type	Does not appear so described		
Does not appear so described	Psychopathic Disorder	4	25%

SCHIZOPHRENIA

By far the largest category in all the eras of the hospital's life is that of schizophrenia. This is not surprising in view of its nature as a psychosis, that is to say a mental disorder characterized by loss of contact with, or distortion of, reality: reasoning ability is impaired and inefficient or inappropriate responses are made, sometimes with incongruous emotional responses in addition. Psychotic states are typified by delusional thinking and often hallucinatory experiences as well. This is where people may believe ideas that are fanciful,

26

bizarre or untrue or see or hear things that are not there.

It is repeatedly and rightly said that this condition does not necessarily or always give rise to hazardous behaviour. This is so. Only very few develop irrational ideas that lead to violence. Even those who foment hostile thoughts rarely act these out in more than angry mutterings, swearing or verbal abuse. The great majority retreat into a world of delusional harmlessness, distressing to themselves and others but not otherwise dangerous.

The problem, of course, is predicting beforehand which are the few who will be harmful at some later date, which will become a matter for discussion later on in this history. At this point it is relevant to note that, in a small minority of cases, delusions can build up into overwhelmingly strong forces for violence when they turn upon some persecutory belief. Likewise hallucinations, more frequently auditory than visual, can be taunting, goading or abusive voices which over time push some sufferers into a violent reaction.

A typical case illustration of the harmful variety of the hallucinatory condition is the man who repeatedly heard abusive voices. On one occasion when travelling on a bus he imagined these to come from the passenger behind him, causing him to turn around and stab the person. He had taken to carrying a knife because of the incessant insults and commands of the voices and the crime had occurred when he could tolerate the taunting voices no longer.

An example of an exactly similar hallucinatory condition but which had no such dangerous consequences would be the man whose voices insulted him with denigrating remarks about his appearance and who, therefore, shut himself away in his house to avoid other people. Yet a third example, of similar hallucinations which caused a violation of the law but a less harmful and certainly non-violent one, would be the woman whose hallucinatory voices insulted her looks until she shoplifted cosmetics to remedy the matter.

These illustrations of three quite different outcomes to similar psychotic processes demonstrate the inappropriateness of the often asked question when attempting explanations: "aren't they simply evil?" Of course a harmful outcome may be described as 'evil' but, when the precipitating process is similar to that of unharmful outcomes it is hardly appropriate to describe the one person as 'evil' and not the others. Perhaps, then, the different motivation to the same hallucinatory process may be described as 'evil'? This seems equally inappropriate, however, when one considers that the hallucinatory voices in all the cases were insulting to an unbearable degree. Finally, then, perhaps the chosen solution was 'evil': to turn round and stab the supposed source of the insult was evil; to steal the means of improving one's appearance was still 'evil', although less so, whilst retreating from the world was pathetic but not 'evil'? This seems a tortuous set of distinctions and illustrates the inappropriateness of ascribing evil outcomes to evil motivation. The differences resulted not from some evil personal source but from different personal habits and tendencies in dealing with life pressures and stresses.

Turning to delusions without necessarily any hallucinatory accompaniment brings to mind the woman who believed she was the reincarnation of the Virgin Mary (and there are invariably several men in Broadmoor at any one time who believe they are the reincarnated Jesus Christ). Such delusions might be thought to result in benign works, not violent ones and, indeed, this is the more common picture to be met in most psychiatric cases with such preoccupations. Our patient, however, imagined that she had given birth to an infant Jesus who had been kidnapped by the Pharisees whereupon she had broken into the residence of the supposed Pharisees and retrieved the baby. Needless to say, the residence was of a pair of innocent and distraught parents and the ensuing hue and cry resulted in the apprehension and conviction of our patient, with the making of a hospital order.

AFFECTIVE DISORDER

When the delusions are ones of either lack of self worth or, the opposite, self-aggrandisement, with extremes of mood in keeping with the delusions, then 'affective disorder', or 'affective psychosis' if there is loss of reality, is the appropriate description. Depression is the more common, without periods of elation, and is accompanied by slowness of actions as well as of thinking and depressed mood. Mania is the opposite condition, comprising overactivity and delusions of grandeur and omnipotence. Because both of these extremes of mood and delusions can often occur alternately in cycles within the same person, the clinical condition of 'manic depressive psychosis' is also a common diagnosis in this group of disorders.

This group featured in Partridge's account as the 'affective reaction type'. From the 60s onwards, psychiatric thinking often tended to include patients featuring grandiose delusions of the manic type with the schizophrenics, largely because other delusions and psychotic symptoms also tended to coexist with them and the affective element was less prominent. This left those with depressive inactivity and delusions of worthlessness to comprise the bulk of the 'affective disorder' category, with a smaller group of those who fluctuated between the manic and depressive extremes.

Typically in the affective disorders it is the emotional element that is irrational rather than the reasoning (the 'affect' rather than the 'cognition', in technical terms), which is what has given rise to the name. However, neat and clear distinctions are the exception and the occurrence also of disordered thinking is what will often put the sufferer into the schizophrenic rather than the affective category, together with the similarity of treatment.

What leads to violence in these extremes of elation or depression? The depressives are the more easily explained. Typical is the man who becomes overwhelmed with feelings of worthlessness, believing (to a delusionally, that is to say irrationally, excessive degree) that he has brought disaster upon all around him, particularly his family, to the point of having perhaps contaminated them with some disgraceful disease (VD was the typical one when it was seen as more disgraceful than it is today). Maybe work and money worries, or personal or family problems, will have accentuated the situation, whilst often strong religious beliefs will have been an influence too, ultimately persuading him that salvation for him and his family is only to be found through dying and passing on to the life hereafter. Many who fit this category achieve their aim. Those who botch the suicide that was intended to follow the killing of their family, or whose resolve fails them, are the survivors who used to come to Broadmoor and, increasingly as their condition is better understood, now go to ordinary psychiatric hospitals instead. They are a danger only to themselves and possibly any remaining members of their families, not to the public at large.

At the other extreme of mania the irrationally inflated feelings of grandiosity, power and invulnerability less often lead to harmful violence, except by accident. In such states the feeling may be out of control and irrational but is more often benignly intended. For instance, one Broadmoor patient, having believed the Queen to be in great danger from some plot, deemed it his duty to save her and drove his car in manic over-excitement to Buckingham Palace to warn her, tragically killing a pedestrian on the way. Other variants of the manic form of psychosis may result in their sufferers believing that they have supernatural powers. This can lead them more often to self-destruction than the destruction of others, as when they believe they can fly and therefore throw themselves off a building. As shown in the proportions in Table 3.1, this group was small by comparison with the schizophrenic group although, as has been said, there will be manics (who have not shown cyclical swings to depression in between their manic phases) who may have been included with the schizophrenics.

PARANOIA

When the delusions are persecutory to the exclusion of other schizophrenic symptoms, i.e.: the personality is 'intact' (well preserved, without intellectual impairment or emotional disturbance) and particularly when the delusions concern only one subject or person ('mono-delusional'), then a diagnosis of 'paranoia' will be used.

This is the type beloved of novelists and TV scriptwriters where the 'paranoiac' (not a clinical term any more than 'maniac'; the correct terms are paranoid and manic) typically develops the idea that someone is plotting their downfall and intends them harm. What also makes this type popular with fiction writers is the difficulty and length of time it often takes to establish that the beliefs are really delusional, which therefore makes a good story. They often sound plausible and convincing - one feels that, just possibly, such things *could* happen - and take some time to disentangle. Dr Edgar Udwin, a consultant psychiatrist at Broadmoor during this 'inter-acts' period, told of a patient at his previous hospital who repeatedly referred to what was thought to be the delusion of a Chinese man who would bring him a great deal of money, until one day the said Chinese man turned up at the hospital with a large cheque for the patient! (It was some kind of investment return, of course.)

A more typical example of paranoia resulting in a need to be placed in a special hospital is that of the man who increasingly interpreted over time the confidential conversations of his factory colleagues as plottings against him. Gradually, also, he saw any minor breakdown of his machinery, mislaying of tools and even, ultimately, leg-pulling and jocular remarks, as having sinister and malign significance. Whilst this scenario is, unfortunately, not uncommon, it usually results in the aggrieved and now paranoid person simply leaving the job, giving his colleagues a lot of 'aggro' or else making an official complaint. He would be regarded as a nuisance but probably not a 'psychiatric case'. The patient in question, however, decided upon sabotage of the machine operated by the man he saw as the ringleader of the plot. The intention was perhaps simply a machine breakdown but, unfortunately, the resulting malfunction resulted in the injury of the work colleague. Tracing the incident to the aggrieved 'paranoid' individual brought about his committal under the Mental Health Act.

Another and quite different manifestation of a paranoid delusion involved a woman on the staff of a large residential establishment who developed the delusion that one of her colleagues was possessed of the devil (a not uncommon delusion). An evil influence was believed to emanate from this person's eyes (another not uncommon delusion) and, after some length of time privately nursing this delusion, our patient decided action had to be taken to eliminate the evil. She did this, tragically, by killing the object of her delusions and gouging out her eyes.

Without a violent or other tangible outcome such cases will often not come to light because the paranoid often keeps things to him or herself and the delusions may not be apparent. Even at home, at work, or if seen by a GP or at a local psychiatric centre, a delusion may often be missed. The paranoid basis may only be revealed when, tragically and too late, some violent act occurs which brings the perpetrator to notice and into a special hospital.

The diagnosis is puzzling no longer but has been resolved by the criminal consequences.

It is difficult to know if the 'schizophrenic reaction type', as described by Partridge, has grown or not, as Partridge does not give figures that allow comparisons. From the way he discusses the various diagnostic groups they would seem to be more evenly divided than they were in the 1970 table above. If so it is probably not so much that the schizophrenic group grew post-1959 as that it attracted other subgroups within it in the ways described above.

ORGANIC DISORDERS

Where the 'organic reaction type' was concerned, the prominence given to epilepsy has noticeably declined post-1959. Advances in charting organic damage, in treating epilepsy and in understanding psychosis tend to have reduced the numbers and transferred some other types of so-called 'epileptic' confusional states more appropriately into the schizophrenic category, again inflating that group. Again, under both the former McNaughtan criteria as well as the new 'mental disorder' criteria it became increasingly more unlikely that a disorder typified by occasional fits could be held in court to be something impairing judgement and actions. There had always been doubts and arguments about the possibility of committing dangerous acts (or any other type of act), associated with a fit and of which one had little or no memory, although there is no doubt automaton-like behaviour occurs sometimes prior to or following a fit. However, there was by now increasing control of epilepsy with advances in medication and the shrinkage in this category post-1959 no doubt reflects this.

Case illustrations of epilepsy are difficult to give. As the organizations dealing with the conditions are always concerned to point out, most epileptics are indistinguishable from other people except when they are suffering a fit. They are sometimes said to be more irritable than others, and sometimes vague, especially when building up to a fit, but this is a notoriously unreliable discriminator. There is certainly a tendency for confusion and disorientation following a fit, which is hardly surprising, and it is to this 'post-ictal' period that violent acts have usually been ascribed when epilepsy has been successfully pleaded as a defence.

Amongst infectious organic conditions, GPI (General Paralysis of the Insane, a syphilitic condition nowadays invariably treated before it reaches that state) is surprisingly reported by Partridge as an uncommon condition in Broadmoor; surprising because it was common in county mental hospitals of that era, although dwindling not only because of the better modern knowledge and treatment of the condition but because the original sufferers were by then growing older and dying out. Presumably in its later stages, and although accompanied by great confusion, its sufferers were too helpless to be of much danger to others in their behaviour.

Poisons, another of Partridge's organic categories, including alcohol and drugs, probably remained a constant small trickle, although later on one might expect the growth of the 'drug culture' to increase the numbers in this subgroup. The main feature would be the proportion of alcohol abusers who reach the stage of 'Korsakow's syndrome' where not only liver but brain damage occurs.

Deterioration from old age or arteriosclerosis continued in the small 'organic' group and would be expected to rise with the increasing numbers of people living to an older age. Thus 'Alzheimers' is now in everyday parlance but was then an abstruse term known only to the clinical professions. Together with 'Pick's Disease' it figures amongst the senile and pre-senile dementias which contribute to this category.

Specific head injuries and brain tumours continue to appear in the 'organic' group, probably tending to dwindle somewhat as the people who suffered head injuries during the two world wars would gradually die out.

Case illustrations for these other organic conditions are again difficult to distinguish from functional psychosis. The confusion and disorientation arising from the damage, from whatever cause but differing according to the site in the brain that is damaged, may give rise to a clinical picture in some ways similar to schizophrenia. Differences are largely in a lesser incidence of hallucinations (except in alcohol toxicity) and a greater incidence of memory and learning loss, assessment of which is often crucial to differential diagnosis. This comprised the essence of a research project in my early days in clinical psychology where the distinction in the 60s and 70s age groups was often crucial (to give ECT could be helpful to an elderly depressive but harmful to an early dementia). Whilst the typical organic dementia case would merely become sadly confused, incapable and self-neglecting, perhaps wandering off and coming to harm from traffic or going out into the rain and snow in their night clothes, a case involving violence and needing to come to Broadmoor would more likely be of someone harbouring delusions of the infidelity or malign intent of their partner and then sadly injuring or killing them with, say, a kitchen knife or garden implement.

These are the categories Partridge describes in the 'Organic Reaction Group'. In 1970 we see that they constituted 6% of the resident male population of Broadmoor.

NEUROTIC DISORDERS

This brings us to the Hysterical Type described by Partridge, which does not figure in the categorization post-1959, and the Psychopathic Disorder group which certainly does, specifically included and defined in the 1959 Act.

Despite the broadening of the range of mental disorders that would be eligible for committal to Broadmoor under the 1959 Act compared with the McNaughtan Rules, hysteria did not assume significant proportions to the extent of amounting to a category for statistical purposes. This might seem surprising: if it managed to get by the stringent McNaughtan criteria, why not the more broadly defined 'mental disorder' criteria? The answer is likely to lie partly in each of three directions.

Firstly, hysteria is, as Partridge points out, a sub-category of the larger category of 'Neurosis'. However, this category does not appear in the statistics either. The reason is probably, and despite the apparently more liberal concepts of the new legislation, that both courts and medical witnesses were still disinclined to use mental disorder as a 'responsibility-disabling' condition when the sub-category was 'neurotic' because medical experts knew, and the court would therefore be told, that this was not a condition which rendered the sufferer unable to appreciate the significance of what they were doing (the essential core of the McNaughtan Rules).

Secondly, the irrationality of some hysterical behaviour might well tend to be regarded as psychotic rather than neurotic in the post-1959 era, particularly if other accompanying irrationalities could be demonstrated which might help to support a mental disorder defence.

Thirdly, the introduction of the category of 'Psychopathic Disorder' in the new legislation provided a convenient alternative for assimilating some of the hysterical conditions that might arise in association with violent behaviour. To the extent that hysterical behaviour tends to occur in extravert personalities similar to the psychopathic (i.e.: acting out rather than internalizing their problems and conflicts) the new category would be seen as a convenient way of assimilating an otherwise awkward group where the new Act was concerned.

Thus: hysterical behaviour, in contrast with the lay idea of 'histrionic' tantrums and excesses, more broadly consists of dealing with one's problems and stresses by means of 'blaming someone or something else'. In everyday 'normal' circumstances this is commonly the blaming of an object like one's car or one's telephone; or of another person such as a family member, for failing to function or to do something properly. It reaches a 'neurotic' or disabling level when the tendency is so frequent or gross that one's ability to carry out life's normal functions are impaired or the lives of others are disrupted. Even then, this may amount only to a gross nuisance and not necessarily be recognised as indicating a need for help or treatment unless the hysterical reaction is violent or someone suffers as a consequence. The perpetrator's explanation of his/her behaviour (it is by no means confined to women, as Partridge implies) may then seem so bizarre as to suggest psychosis or, in the days before the abolition of capital punishment, to be regarded more compassionately as psychotic by medical witnesses, or juries, or both, so that a hospital committal was effected instead of the death penalty. Partridge hints at this in connection with a number of cases and categories.

Hypochondriasis may be thought of as a variant of 'hysterical avoidance' inasmuch as, here, it is one's own ill health that is held responsible for not fulfilling some irksome responsibility. 'Conversion hysteria' is an extreme form of the condition where the patient is said to have 'converted' the stress into something physically incapacitating which avoids facing the psychological consequences of the challenge or stress. This might involve the apparent paralysis of a limb or, in the case which figured in an early behavioural treatment published by Don Walton and myself, loss of a function such a speech. This had apparently enabled the patient to avoid consenting to a marriage she did not want whilst also to avoid refusing the marriage which would have brought intolerable family disapproval and pressure.

With the abolition of capital punishment in 1965, therefore, and the inclusion of 'Psychopathic Disorder' in the 1959 Act, an alternative avenue was created for some of the violent manifestations of hysteria and other neurotic disorders to be committed for the secure treatment they were seen as needing.

PSYCHOPATHIC DISORDER

This then, brings us to consideration of the 'Psychopathic Disorder' category itself. Partridge mentions the disorder and that there were psychopaths in Broadmoor prior to 1959 although, like the hysteria cases discussed above, admitted usually because of some other aspect of their condition or behaviour that led a jury to decide they sufficiently met the McNaughtan criteria to be sympathetically dealt with in that way.

Psychopathy is a complex and much argued disorder which has spawned numerous scientific papers and books in its own right to which readers must turn for a fuller picture. Nevertheless, it demands attention here and the enigma is not difficult to appreciate.

Basically, psychopathic behaviour is characterized by a cluster of antisocial qualities such as aggressiveness; impulsiveness; callousness; failure to conform to social and legal constraints, to maintain relationships, to persist in a job, or generally to keep within what would be regarded as the normal bounds of behaviour. Such a description, however, as will be immediately apparent, simply describes an antisocial behaviour pattern which could be said to apply to many so-called 'normal' people and certainly to many people in prison not called 'psychopaths'. How then is this antisocial group to be defined differently so as to identify those who seem to be regarded as in need of care and treatment rather than punishment? That they are different is repeatedly recognized, even among 'normal' criminal groups in prison where they are shunned or feared as 'weird' or 'psycho' but not 'nutters' or 'schizo' as the mentally ill are recognized. The degree and intractability of the psychopath's antisocial attributes are somehow more extreme and gross so as to mark them out from other people who have broken the law. In fact they are not simply equatable with criminals as most criminals do not display the degree or uniformity of callousness, heedlessness or lack of feeling of psychopaths. Most criminals are selectively antisocial and can be passionately loyal to their families and friends in a way that psychopaths tend not to be. Many criminals are also well able to plan ahead carefully as psychopaths usually do not.

We have, therefore, a string of antisocial features of a comprehensiveness and degree which largely distinguishes psychopaths from the great majority of 'ordinary' criminals. Largely. But not exclusively. Small wonder that a classification listing such characteristics is greeted by public and press in notorious cases as a 'con' or 'let-off' by 'woolly minded do-gooders'. And yet, with monotonous regularity, these psychopathic cases are widely agreed by all concerned inside prison or special hospital to be different and in need of some kind of help rather than punishment.

Having recognized the widespread agreement that a type and degree of antisocial personality pattern exists which is different from 'mere criminality' (another contentious term) there then arose the problem of how to define it within legislation to provide the care and help so widely agreed to be appropriate and necessary. The Mental Health Act is couched in medico-legal terms, being intended to provide care within a medical rubric for conditions that conform to a medical description or diagnosis. Section 4(4) of the Act says: *"In this Act 'psychopathic disorder' means a persistent disorder or disability of mind (whether or not including subnormality of intelligence) which results in abnormally aggressive or seriously irresponsible conduct on the part of the patient, and requires or is susceptible to medical treatment."* This actually allows a wider range of people to be categorized as psychopathic than the characteristics described so far in this chapter would indicate, but then Acts of Parliament are framed in briefer and more general terms than a textbook. In any case, the phrase 'disorder or disability of mind' leaves room for specialist evidence to direct attention to whichever aspects of a defendant's behaviour can be established to the court's satisfaction as relevant to the disorder in question.

Although this provision of the 1959 Act has by and large worked, that is to say that numerous people have found their way to Broadmoor and the other special hospitals who properly should have and who have derived benefit from so doing, the categorization has still been argued and disputed and further changes were introduced in the subsequent 1983 Act. However, these changes were not to the definition but to the ensuing provisions. The final phrase in Section 4(4) above: *"and requires or is susceptible to treatment"* was removed and the provision inserted elsewhere that committal to hospital was dependent upon the condition, once established and accepted, being treatable. This has opened up a whole new field of fresh problems which fortunately do not concern us here in the context of the purpose and running of Broadmoor during the period after Partridge and as a result of the 1959 Act. It does, however, serve to remind us of the continuing debate over the problem of psychopathy.

Basically, the problem of psychopathic disorder has been that the evidence required in medical terms has been both tautological and non-medical. It is tautological to the extent that the characteristics attested to support a contention that the condition exists in a case before the court are not independent and distinguishable from the very offending behaviour for which the defendant stands trial and which it is the duty of the court to assess. Medical evidence in the case, say, of schizophrenia, will refer to signs and symptoms of disrupted, impaired and irrational thinking, including hallucinations or delusions, all of which should be independent of the particular thinking and offending behaviour which is the subject of the trial. Even with schizophrenia this is sometimes difficult and is disputed as truly independent in comparison with the more tangible symptoms of physical diseases. But it is both easier and clearer than the process of independently establishing the existence of psychopathic disorder. Medical evidence here will not usually be able to point to 'causes' of psychopathy other than manifestations of the same aggressiveness, impulsiveness, callousness and failure to plan, persist or to maintain social and personal relationships which are at issue in the court's evaluation of the case being tried. What usually swings the balance in the end towards acceptance of the classification is the wide ranging, comprehensive and extreme nature of such a menu of disastrous behaviours and failures.

Such evidence is also non-medical in that it is social and personal behaviour that comprise it, not underlying pathological processes. In other words, the evidence for some inferred underlying pathology is the array of excessive behaviours of the kind that are on trial. At the time of the 1959 Act's inception, there was no satisfactory independent evidence of an underlying physical, physiological or neurological pathology to psychopathic disorder and, although such independent evidence is now emerging, it is still disputed. Some say it is merely a correlate, others that it is a result and not a cause. The early evidence tended to be psychological and, now with neurophysiological advances, this has been where the main thrust of developments on psychopathic disorder have occurred.

Since the arrival of psychology at Broadmoor is one of the developments that mark this 'inter-acts' period the subject will arise later in more detail. Nevertheless, at this point it will be helpful to distinguish the role of psychology, as that of a scientific discipline which deals with the 'mental processes' underlying all behaviours, and contrast it with the role of psychiatric medicine which is concerned with the pathological processes that account for the abnormal ones. Using the analogy of the computer, the camera, or the hi-fi, psychology may be said to be concerned with the programme in the computer, the picture on the film or the music on the disc, whereas medicine may be said to be concerned with the actual components, circuitry, capacities and voltages of the equipment and faults, malfunctions or fluctuations of these.

It is in the psychological domain, then, that explanations and definitions have been forthcoming for psychopathic behaviour, superimposed on a different neurophysiological 'specification' for psychopaths, rather than a malfunctioning system. Given all this, it is rather surprising that the legal definition in the 1959 Mental Health Act, operating on medical evidence, has turned out to have done the job it was intended to do as well as it has. To the extent that the explicit admission to Broadmoor, rather than to prison, of people in this category has resulted in the successful treatment and discharge of so many is a pointer towards getting the definition and concept sorted out and improved. The topic will arise again during this history, when research into the conditions, offences and treatments developed in this inter-acts period is discussed again, seeing that between a fifth and a quarter of the admissions to Broadmoor following the implementation of the 1959 Act were categorized as Psychopathic Disorder.

We cannot leave the subject, however, without noting that the medico-legal definition has allowed individuals to be admitted in this category that do not strictly accord with the psychological and neurophysiological characteristics to have emerged from research up to and especially following the implementation of the Act. 'Psychopathic Disorder' has tended to become expanded to 'Personality Disorder' generally and to include instances where 'Neurosis' would have been the preferred classification (which brings us back to the 'hysteria' category to which Partridge refers). Instances have arisen where highly emotionally disturbed people have caused damage and harm to the properties and possessions of others, often family or friends, possibly including harm to the people themselves and often including harm to themselves. Being so clearly disturbed as well as having caused harm they presented no great problem in being included in the Act's loose definition of 'psychopathic disorder', or even of 'mental illness', and both medical witnesses and the court as a whole had no difficulty in seeing the Act as the appropriate vehicle for placing them in hospital rather than sentencing them to imprisonment or some other penal outcome. Clearly many of these could not be said to be callous and unfeeling - if anything they suffered from an excess of emotional feeling - whilst they often were far from lacking in foresight and persistence either, having struggled to find solutions for their problems for a long time. Not surprisingly, they did not present the classic menu of psychopathic characteristics on psychological or neurophysiological examination either. Psychopathic Disorder simply seemed the only classification that could be used to send them to where secure treatment was available. It was the only definition broad enough to accommodate them.

References have been made to the old hysteria category of

neurotic disorder which might have enabled these to be included within the former McNaughtan Rules and therefore to have figured in Partridge's breakdown of diagnostic groups. Case illustrations of the primary (aggressive, ruthless) and the secondary (neurotic) types of psychopathic disorder are also now needed to illustrate use of the new provision introduced by the 1959 Act.

The typical 'primary' or aggressive psychopath has been described above: impulsive, lacking in affective feeling, stimulus seeking, failing to maintain relationships or persist in employment and thereby tending to develop aggressive behaviour when thwarted and unable to get what he or she wants (the aggressive component is not necessarily part of the basic definition but a consequence of the failures resulting from the primary traits). Thus some psychopaths who encounter a favourable environment may not become aggressive. They will, nevertheless, tend to be forceful in their impatience and heedless of the distress they cause to others. In normal situations some successful businessmen or politicians may be counted in this category.

It is unlikely that aggression does not emerge sooner or later, however, simply through the psychopath's need to get what he or she wants more quickly and in larger quantities than most of the rest of us and therefore, when this does not happen, getting frustrated and resentful and hence aggressive. Unsuccessful psychopaths who sooner or later break the law do so on any of a number of fronts. The successful ones may eventually be involved in business swindles and embezzlement. The unsuccessful ones may get involved in petty theft and then gradually move up to greater crimes, more of these eventually involving violence and, of course these days, probably drug trafficking and abuse because this is where the maximum gratification is to be most quickly obtained.

At a personal level and while all this is going on, the psychopath is probably going in and out of a succession of personal and sexual relationships, simply because he or she needs gratification of these impulses just like anyone else but more quickly and at greater intensity. Abandoned, manipulated and neglected friends; jilted partners and deserted or abused families lie scattered in the psychopath's wake. All these disasters are happening on an increasingly wide front and at an escalating level until the law almost inevitably becomes involved. Here it will usually by now have become apparent that this is not a simple pattern of criminality (family and fellow criminals alike will not be so eager to stand by them as with a more 'normal and caring' offender). If some agency is prepared to find their case 'treatable' then they might be committed under the Mental Health Act; if not then prison custody is the outcome, despite this being most unlikely to result in their eventual release without the whole cycle of disaster repeating itself.

This picture of the 'primary' or 'aggressive' psychopath repeats itself monotonously in Broadmoor case material. Any individual case illustration will simply comprise a large number of the features described above.

A different picture can occur with the 'secondary' or 'neurotic' psychopath. The addition of the emotional element might seem to negate the basic definition of psychopathy where emotional response is lacking. Strictly speaking this is so and this group would simply be classified as neurotic but for the added traits of impulsivity and extraversion, meaning that fears and anxieties will be 'projected' or directed at other people and the environment in general rather than inwardly as the introverted anxiety neurotic or obsessional will tend to do. The result is that, progressively if problems are not resolved, the secondary psychopath will also tend to become aggressive, fail in work and social contexts and in personal relationships, probably eventually also breaking the law.

Case examples at Broadmoor typically include the many men who lost jobs, failed in their marriages, neglected and eventually abused, injured or even killed wives and children. Young women in this category would similarly have failed in jobs and relationships and, whilst not necessarily injuring someone, would probably have injured themselves and been destructive to either the marital or parental home, possibly setting fire to it (women more typically use self-directed aggression than outward aggression, as a man would). Other examples would include the emotionally withdrawn and isolated young men who, in a desperate attempt to obtain the satisfaction of a relationship when reaching maturity and without this element to their lives, might have made an inept and botched attempt at a liaison in a quite inappropriate context or with someone they had not yet sufficiently got to know, resulting in rejection, argument, an actual or attempted rape and probably a struggle resulting in injury or death for the victim.

SEX OFFENDERS

This last example brings us to the category of sex offender who might well also gravitate to the Psychopathic Disorder category; that is if there were no psychotic features to allow a Mental Illness classification. This group might include those whose victims were either adults or children and of either sex. There were those whose motivation might have been displaced jealous affection or who were acting out of sadistic vindictiveness. We shall look at these in more detail later on when considering categorizations and their treatments. Suffice it here to say that, although again not conforming precisely to the 'psychopathic disorder' category psychologically, they nevertheless fitted what the medico-legal nomenclature allowed and were clearly seen to be going to the right place in Broadmoor.

The last 'secondary psychopath' example provides a case

illustration of one type of sex offender. More specific to the sexual element being included in the diagnosis we need to look at those where the sexual element is the primary motivation (in the last example above it was incidental to the psychopathic problem). These would include those where an attempted sexual liaison goes wrong - possibly the initiator's attempt is scorned - and the presence of psychopathic tendencies compound the problem until a violent outcome results. It would also include those sexual sadists who have, from some early life influence or experience, grown to associate sexual gratification with violence or other deviant activities so that their partners become endangered and ultimately victims.

Why then don't all sex offenders follow a route to Broadmoor and why is there so much debate currently on the appropriate sentence and placement of such offenders? The answer lies partly in the extent to which medical evidence is sympathetic to a concept of 'mental disorder' as an underlying problem in such cases (remembering that this is the basic definition governing entry into the current mental health legislation) and partly in the opinion as to whether the condition is treatable. It will be remembered that the 1959 Act had *"requires or is susceptible to medical treatment"* in its definition, whilst the following 1983 Act removed this from the definition and placed it with the section dealing with committal for treatment. Whilst the definition of psychopathic and associated personality disorders remains medico-legal but the main thrust of research into both identification and treatment of this group of disorders has been psychological and neurophysiological, opinions of treatability have varied.

Whatever the classification and the treatment approach, there is no doubt that such offences stem from a grossly disordered orientation towards one's fellow human beings and that the best hope at present of effecting any change in such people is through a psychological programme. The argument that this is as yet of variable and unproven efficacy is often used to deny that it is the appropriate domain for considering its cause and remedy at all. It is, however, the best hope we have so far of effecting any change; simply to imprison someone without providing any avenue for change is eventually to discharge such people into the outside world as a continuing hazard to their fellow human beings.

SUMMARY

Two of the 1959 Mental Health Act's four categories of 'Mental Disorder' governed the criteria for admission to Broadmoor after 1960: Mental Illness and Psychopathic Disorder. Patients in the former category were far and away most often schizophrenic, including a large proportion of the sub-category 'paranoid schizophrenic' or simply 'paranoia'.

The affective psychoses were the next group, comprising mainly depressives but some manic-depressives and a small number of manics.

Then there were the organic psychoses which included mainly those with some form of brain damage, through injury or illness (such as that permanently resulting from prolonged alcohol abuse) and a dwindling number of epileptics.

Mental Illness accounted for between three quarters and four fifths of the patient population. Psychopathic Disorder, the new category introduced in the 1959 Act, accounted for the rest. It included the classical psychopathic type characterized by prolonged and persistent antisocial irresponsibility, impulsiveness, aggression and callousness, as well as a variable and arguable mixture of other neurotic and antisocial personality problems characterized by destructiveness to self and others. It also included some of the contentious group of sex-offenders if they had passed through the filter of courts and expert witnesses as sufficiently 'mentally disordered' and 'susceptible to medical treatment'.

This chapter has elaborated the main sub-categories of these mental illness and psychopathic categories, summarizing their main features, and with case illustrations. This has included differentiation of the neurotic groups and their blurring into psychopathic disorder which has enabled a wide range of mentally disordered people to be admitted and treated in Broadmoor who would not have been admitted under the definitions of the preceding legislation.

It is imperative to emphasize again that the great majority of people suffering from mental illnesses are not a hazard to others. Only where a specific problem or preoccupation exists within the patient's particular disorder, underlying personality, or prior life experience, will there be a violent outcome and these circumstances are the exception. Illustrations have been given of these, too, which indicate how similar mental processes can result in harmless results in some, harmful ones in others, so belying the idea that there is such a thing as an 'evil' person; there are only evil outcomes to some otherwise common variations of human motivation and conduct.

All this suggests that the psychiatric system of classifying mental disorder leaves a great deal to be desired. It is an approximate and variable process. Not surprisingly it is widely criticized. For the purposes of this history, however, it is the system that operated during the period of the 1959 Act and defined the people in Broadmoor. We shall return to it again in Part III, by which point ideas and developments arising from the operation of the 1959 Act will allow a better consideration of the form future legislation might take if it is better to accommodate the problem areas covered by this history.

CHAPTER 4

THE PATIENTS AFTER 1959: OFFENCES; ADMISSION AND DISCHARGE RATES; AGE AND LENGTH OF STAY

Having looked at the patient population before and after the 1959 Act in terms of their mental disorders, the next criterion must be the offences they had committed in order to be sent to a special, rather than a conventional, psychiatric hospital (or 'mental' hospital in those days).

DANGEROUSNESS

The essential element of the offences is dangerousness - either to society at large or to some specific individual. Later we shall have to ask the question whether dangerousness is the cause or the result of being mentally disordered or whether the two are independent. At this point it is sufficient merely to note that it is the combination of mental disorder and dangerousness that requires secure rather than conventional hospital care. What, therefore, have been the violent behaviours of the patients?

OFFENCE CATEGORIES

Partridge gives the impression that the majority of Broadmoor patients are there for murder with this being predominantly the crime of the 'pleasure' patients. In fact the figures for the two years prior to the implementation of the new Act suggest that this was not so and that 'homicide' (behaviour which has resulted in the death of another person must be the criterion for medical and psychological purposes rather than whether the court verdict was murder or manslaughter) was at a fairly constant level both before and after the 1959 Act (see Figure 1). This is despite the great increase in admissions to Broadmoor brought about by the new Act.

FIGURE 1

Proportion of homicides among male admissions

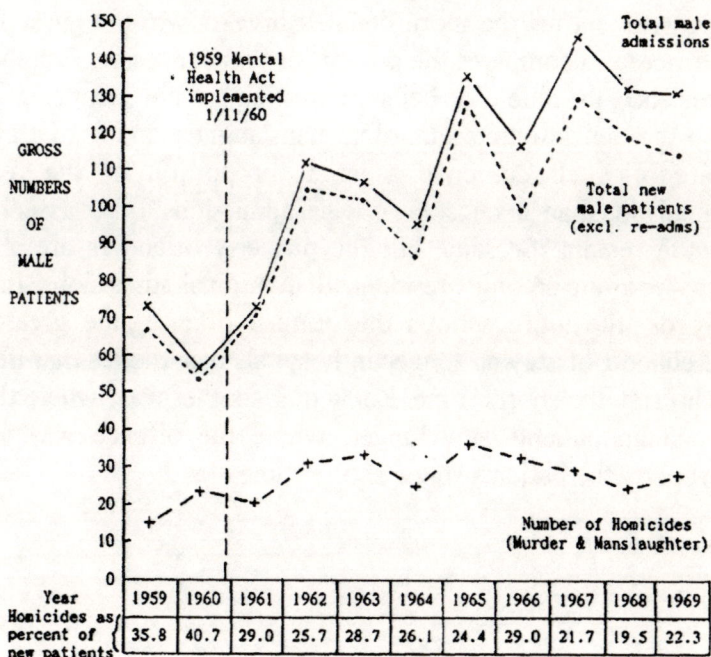

Year	1959	1960	1961	1962	1963	1964	1965	1966	1967	1968	1969
Homicides as percent of new patients	35.8	40.7	29.0	25.7	28.7	26.1	24.4	29.0	21.7	19.5	22.3

In passing we should remark upon this increase in the admission rate, which was the inevitable result of the increased range of mental disorders eligible for admission to Broadmoor under the 1959 Act's changed criteria, and especially with the introduction of Psychopathic Disorder as one of these, together with the introduction of 'diminished responsibility' in the Homicide Act a few years previously. These provided a marked contrast with the former McNaughtan insanity principles.

Whilst the admission rate for men was doubling in the space of six to eight years, from about 60 or 70 to a peak of 140 (and for women rose from 9 or 10 a year to some 12 to 15), the number of homicides admitted remained at a fairly steady 20 to 30 per annum. Figure 2 shows the more detailed breakdown of figures for all offences and compares the proportions on admission with those in residence, the difference being interesting but not surprising in that the murder, attempted murder, manslaughter and sexual offence categories all comprise a larger proportion of the resident population than amongst the original admissions; other assaults and arson remain the same but the property offenders are a much smaller group amongst residents than original admissions. In other words, the more serious the original offence, the greater the likelihood of staying longer in hospital. It is the lesser offenders who stay the shorter time. Looked at another way, where there is a victim patients stay longer, where the offence was against property the patients stay a shorter time.

FIGURE 2

MALE PATIENTS   MALE PATIENTS
ADMITTED 1963-70   RESIDENT AT 1/1/70

Mean N = 116   N = 675

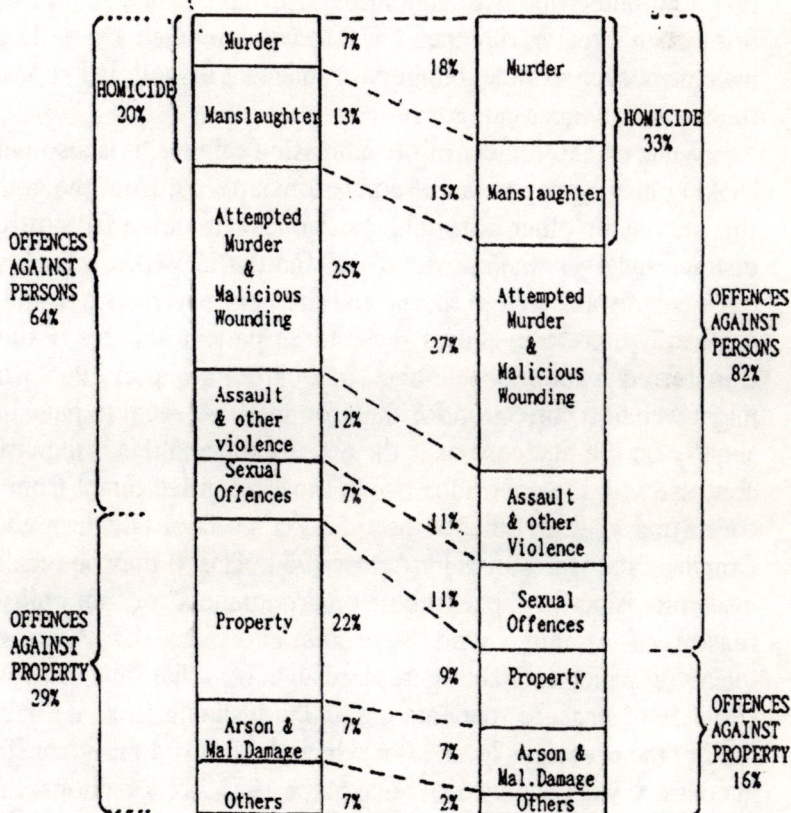

A point worth making about sex offenders, in case it should be thought that the proportions shown in Figure 2 are small at 7% of admissions and 11% of residents, is that there will be a number of sexual offenders concealed within the murder, attempted murder and manslaughter groups. These are more serious indictments and it is the most serious indictment on which someone is convicted that appears in the statistics. These will, therefore, conceal the fact that a number will have committed a sexual offence as part of or prior to a greater offence. Only those convicted on a 'lesser' indictment such as rape, buggery or indecent assault will appear in the sexual offences category.

While on the subject of the admission offence, it is also worth looking at the proportion of admissions arriving from the courts, the prisons or other hospitals, particularly in view of Partridge's distinctions over 'the convict class' and the 1959 Act's facility to transfer patients between special and ordinary psychiatric hospitals. Figure 3, therefore, shows these three patient sources. Patients transferred from prison, in fact, apart from a blip in 1965 which might well be a correction for the drop in 1964, seem to have been slightly on the decrease over the 60s decade and this is in marked contrast with the enormous rise in those admitted direct from the courts under one or other of the 1959 Act's sections or through the Criminal Procedures Insanity Act of 1964. This, it may be recalled, made provision for those 'insane on arraignment' or 'not guilty by reason of insanity' who were the equivalent of Partridge's 'pleasure' patients. Other figures available from that time, however, show the 'pleasure' patients gradually declining to some half or third of their previous level, after which they stayed fairly constant, in contrast with patients under one of the 1959 Act's sections: these became the vehicle for committing the great majority of Broadmoor's patients from then on.

FIGURE 3

SOURCES OF MALE ADMISSIONS

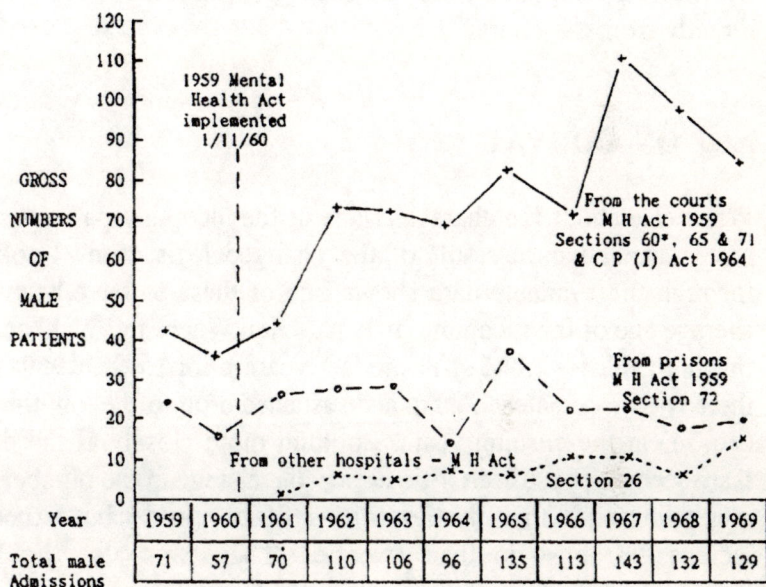

Year	1959	1960	1961	1962	1963	1964	1965	1966	1967	1968	1969
Total male Admissions	71	57	70	110	106	96	135	113	143	132	129

Chart labels: GROSS NUMBERS OF MALE PATIENTS (y-axis 0–120). 1959 Mental Health Act implemented 1/11/60. From the courts – M H Act 1959 Sections 60*, 65 & 71 & C P (I) Act 1964. From prisons M H Act 1959 Section 72. From other hospitals – M H Act Section 26.

* This will include a small number under Section 60 who will first have been sent to a local psychiatric hospital and then subsequently transferred to Broadmoor.

The result of the facility to transfer patients from ordinary psychiatric hospitals is also seen in Figure 3. Gradually increasing use was made of this through the Act's first decade, although the numbers involved were small when compared with the numbers transferred from prison and the huge growth in those committed directly from the courts.

AGE ON ARRIVAL

What else about the characteristics of the incoming patients may have changed as a result of the changed legislation? Looking through the available data shows one of these to have been the average age of the incoming male patients. Where this had been in the high thirties (37-38) in the last years prior to the 1959 Act, there was immediately a sharp and sustained drop to the low thirties (30-34) in the ensuing years. Looking more closely at the data, there seems to have been little noticeable change in the numbers of men admitted in their thirties, forties, fifties or older but rather an increase in those in their twenties. There was also the first appearance of a teen-age group from 1961 onwards. These look to have been the groups which brought down the average admission age. It is not surprising that these younger age groups are larger after 1959. Psychopathic disorder is predominantly a condition of younger people and so the introduction of this category into the new legislation was bound to increase the number of younger people admitted, so lowering the average age. The same trend appeared with the women patients.

LENGTHS OF STAY AND DISCHARGE DESTINATION

How long do patients stay in Broadmoor? Are there differences in the different diagnostic or offender categories? Partridge talks of the varying numbers to have left Broadmoor over the years, with fluctuations resulting from the different regimes under different superintendents, but in general gives the impression that the norm is for patients to stay until they die. Although the hospital population has fluctuated over the decades, sometimes increasing and sometimes dwindling (for which Partridge gives a number of reasons varying from the effects of the two world wars to the policies and outlooks of successive superintendents) the number leaving has generally kept pace with the number arriving. Often, indeed, the former seems to have been dictated by the latter and this seems especially to have been the effect of the 1959 Act. Figure 4 shows the steep rise in movements out to have parallelled the equivalent rise in arrivals during this post-1959 period of flux. However, whilst the numbers going to other psychiatric hospitals (called 'transfers' in special hospital parlance) rose sharply in parallel with the total departures (except for 1967), the numbers discharged directly into the community, in the careful way Partridge describes, changed but little - in fact decreased during the initial period of great transfer activity - and only picked up to a pre-1959 Act level after 1967.

FIGURE 4

Number of male patients leaving hospital, by each method, in the years immediately before and after the start of the 1959 Mental Health Act

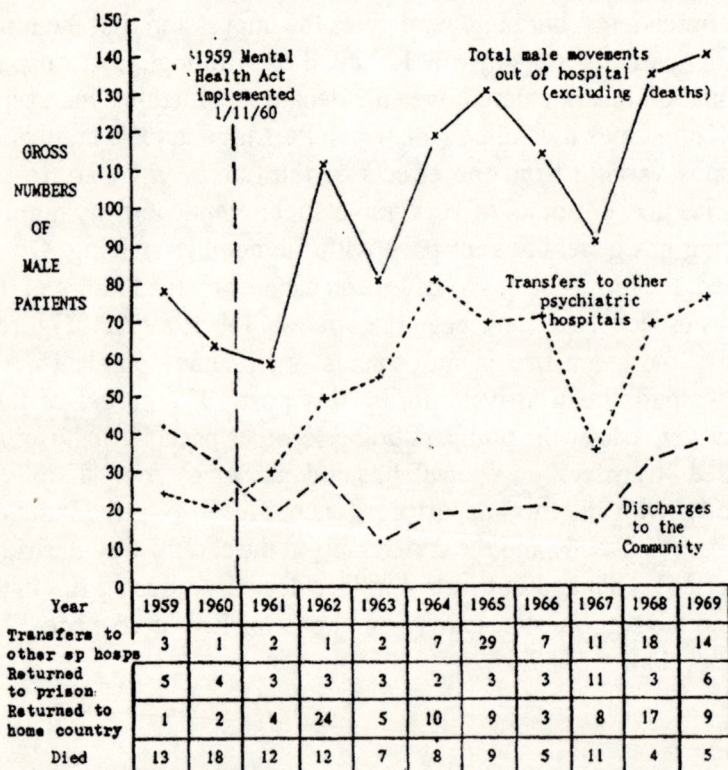

Year	1959	1960	1961	1962	1963	1964	1965	1966	1967	1968	1969
Transfers to other sp hosps	3	1	2	1	2	7	29	7	11	18	14
Returned to prison	5	4	3	3	3	2	3	3	11	3	6
Returned to home country	1	2	4	24	5	10	9	3	8	17	9
Died	13	18	12	12	7	8	9	5	11	4	5

An interesting feature occurs here and accounts for the blip in 1962. There had since the second world war been a number of patients of European origin in Broadmoor and Partridge speaks of some of these, in particular the Poles. To these were gradually added a number of people from the former British colonies that were still the responsibility of the British Government after, of course, a great many had gained their independence: the occasional patient from Aden, Gibraltar, Malta, Bermuda, Hong Kong, etc. An even larger number then began to arrive from among the growing population of immigrants from the West Indies, initially, and later from Africa, India and Pakistan. These were first generation immigrants born in their country of origin.

With these it was often thought that their mental disorders were brought on or aggravated by the stress of a new and unfamiliar environment and its pressures to adapt. They would be helped, therefore, by returning to a familiar environment. This view is epitomized by the saying that emigration is the challenge of the strong but the escape of the weak and persecuted. Whatever the reasoning, it was no doubt bolstered by the pressure on accommodation in Broadmoor caused by the burgeoning admission rate following the 1959 Act. In dribs and drabs, therefore, patients in these categories were returned to their country of origin, either to hospital or to their families.

However, in 1962 the departure figures were inflated by the chartering of an aircraft to take back a large party to the West Indies. Journeys such as these were popular with staff from whom an escort would be selected to accompany patients to their home country. This provided a chance to see exotic lands which few, in those days, would have had any other opportunity to see. The large party to the West Indies was accompanied by male nurses and Dr Cyril Perry, the Deputy Superintendent. A Cypriot patient was returned to Cyprus in the care of a nurse who had served there in the army, likewise several from Aden. The return of an Australian patient was the opportunity for Dr Boyce Lecouteur, an Australian himself, to act as escort.

With some journeys the conditions at the receiving end did not inspire confidence and some of the returning escorts spoke of their qualms at leaving their charges in what had sometimes seemed primitive and inadequate conditions where they doubted whether the patient would receive the care they had enjoyed at Broadmoor. With some patients it was not always possible to arrange for the Broadmoor escort to accompany the patient all the way home and the procedure would be for the escort to hand over the patient to a duly appointed person at the port of departure or arrival. In the case of one patient, handed over on board ship at Tilbury, it was rumoured he never disembarked at his destination. Such were the days of that cold war era and such was the pressure on keeping Broadmoor from bursting at the seams after the 1959 Act's effects.

FIGURE 5

Destinations of the 1,127 male patients who left Broadmoor in the decade 1960-69 (Average = 113 per year)

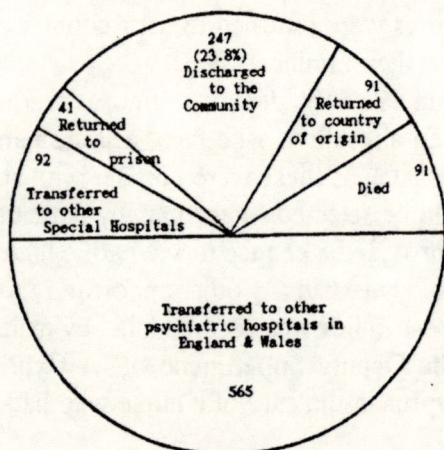

Figure 5 shows the total number of departures during the entire 1960s decade - 1,127, an average of 113 per year - of which it can be seen that half went to other psychiatric hospitals and nearly a quarter directly into the community.

How long had all these patients spent in hospital by the time they left? Figure 6 shows how long the resident population at 1.1.70 had been in Broadmoor - two thirds less than 5 years and a fifth between 5 and 10 years. Only 2% had spent more than 25 years there.

FIGURE 6
Length of stay of resident male population at the end of the decade
(1.1.70) (Total men in residence = 677)

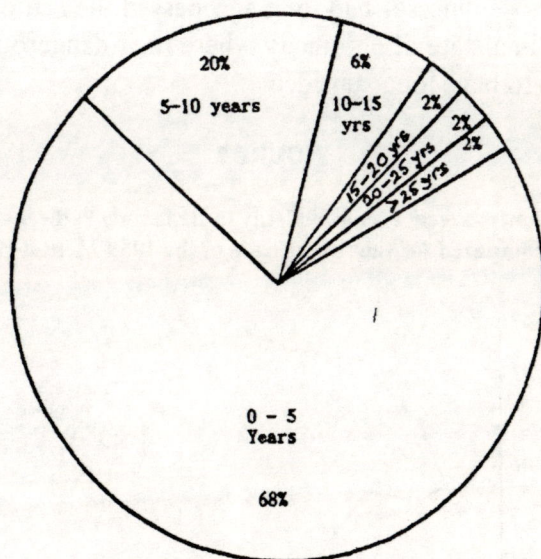

However, if we look at the average length of time spent in Broadmoor by those who left each year during that first decade of the 1959 Act, one can get another view of how the surge in new admissions was countered, using the new facility to transfer between the special and the local psychiatric hospitals. Figure 7 shows the average length of stay of those discharged to the community and transferred to other hospitals each year through the 1960s. Whilst those discharged in 1960 had been in Broadmoor an average of 10 years, by 1969 the average had fallen to under 5 years. By contrast, and whereas those transferred to other hospitals in 1960 had spent an average of only 6 years in Broadmoor, the average time quickly rose to over 15 years through the mid-1960s until falling back to around 7 years at the end of the decade. This reflects the practice of moving to local settings those more elderly patients whose illnesses had long ago passed the acute stage and who were in a state of chronicity where their dangerousness was considered to have long subsided.

FIGURE 7

Male patients' average length of stay in Broadmoor: discharges and transfers compared for the first decade of the 1959 Mental Health Act

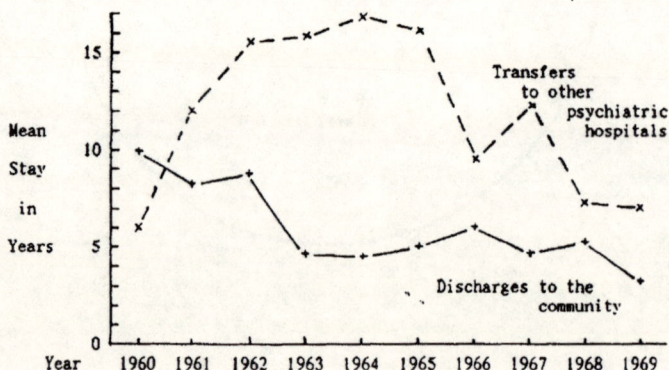

62

By the end of the 1960s, the majority of those who could be said to be fit to go had gone. The falling average length of stay of those who were transferred later demonstrates that it was becoming a younger, less chronic, group that was going. This reflects the effectiveness of the newer medicines for schizophrenia but also the experience and confidence of the consultants who had come to Broadmoor following the 1959 Act and the successful contacts they had built up with colleagues elsewhere in the NHS. Only later, as we shall see, did the doors close upon them and the whole process of transfer become a vexed and prolonged process of negotiation and reassurance.

Where the elderly patients were concerned, Partridge described how many had made their home at Broadmoor, settling into a routine of work and recreation, often having no one left on the outside to provide the necessary companionship, supervision and support. They were given a continuing home at Broadmoor out of compassion. This feeling persisted through the time of the 1959 Act but sadly the pressure on beds meant that only the dangerous could be said to need the secure care of Broadmoor. Some sad letters were subsequently received from patients who had moved out, telling how they were misunderstood as dangerous and kept locked away with far more disturbed patients than themselves.

THE WOMEN PATIENTS

Equivalent data were also collected for the female population but the small numbers meant that equivalent statistical analyses were not carried out until much later.

The total number of female patients in the 60s was around the 120 mark most of the time and the annual admission rate rose from about or just under 10 per year up to the 1959 Act to some 12 or

15 thereafter.

Offence and diagnostic categories were similar but relative numbers differed. Whilst the victims of the women as well as the men frequently featured their spouse or partner, their children were victims more often than with the men. They also tended to damage or set fire to their homes more often than the men, which is more typical than personal violence for women.

Of course, sex offenders among women were virtually non-existent. If prostitution is classified as a sex offence it would not appear as an 'index' offence in this population, i.e.: the one bringing about the admission, as it would not warrant a secure form of hospitalization. Women with a history that included prostitution might well be found in Broadmoor but that would not be their index offence: they would have done something else in addition that was dangerous. A sexual component to a woman's crime, however, would often occur, just as it would with the men, in that some sexual damage or mutilation could be inflicted upon the victim's body. Dr McGrath, drawing upon his knowledge of Latin, chose the ablative as well as the accusative case for his definition of a sexual component as: "an offence by, with, or upon, a sexual organ".

This history will differentiate between the offences, diagnoses and progress of the women patients, in contrast with the men, where information was obtained showing such differences. Otherwise it should be assumed that similar situations and conditions apply for both.

SUMMARY

This, then, in the space of two chapters, is the picture of the patient population of Broadmoor from the point of view of their mental disorders, their offences, their ages, lengths of stay and ultimate destinations. The available figures and tables are derived from the records of the male patients assembled by the Psychology Department and later the Special Hospitals Research Unit whose directorate was based at Broadmoor.

In this chapter, the figures and graphs dramatically demonstrate the large increase in numbers of patients arriving in Broadmoor, almost doubling in the space of half a decade. This was due not only to the introduction of the category of 'psychopathic disorder' to the criterion groups defined in the new Act but also to the broader definition of 'mental disorder' by comparison with the previous McNaughtan criteria for insanity. There was then also the increased facility to transfer patients from local psychiatric settings who were thought to pose a danger there. What psychopathic disorder did influence, however, was the reduced average age of patients on admission, this being predominantly a disorder of younger people.

Contrary to popular belief, not all Broadmoor patients have killed. Even before the new Act allowed a wider range of disorders to be admitted, this had not been the case. The new Act further diluted the numbers of murderers and manslaughterers, although they were clearly seen as more dangerous (or more difficult to discharge, which is not the same thing, as we shall see later), as the higher proportion of homicides in residence demonstrates when compared with the proportion amongst new admissions. This illustrates how the homicides 'accumulate' in the hospital.

In consequence of this rise in admission numbers and categories there had to be a rise in departures at the other end, both to the community direct and via the other psychiatric settings now made possible by the new legislation. The age of those transferred showed that it was the older, more chronic and, therefore, less dangerous patients who went first. When these had gone, there would be greater problems in finding patients suitable for another setting. Even so the average length of stay of those discharged also fell. Subsequent chapters will look at the consequences of these dramatic changes from a number of standpoints.

Meanwhile, and before passing on to the day to day work of the hospital, we should look at the staff and the effect on their work, numbers and professional diversity brought about by the 1959 Mental Health Act.

CHAPTER 5

THE STAFF

Partridge defers discussion of the staff until after a description of the hospital's history and its accommodation. In the present account, however, the 1959 Act brought and coincided with such changes in the constitution, structure and organization of staffing throughout the country's psychiatric services that these really should be discussed after the patients. The context in which the two interact can then follow in a more understandable way. There is, in any case, no need to repeat a history which has been so well covered by Partridge and this present update will inevitably recall significant historical events as they bear upon more recent ones.

THE MEDICAL STAFF

Partridge covers the time until Dr Hopwood's retirement and mentions that Dr S G James followed, promoted from the younger special hospital of Moss Side, at Maghull, on Merseyside (not Birmingham, as Peter Thompson erroneously locates it in his Broadmoor books. Nor to be confused with the area of Manchester by the same name). Dr P G McGrath was appointed in 1956, not as medical superintendent but as the first consultant psychiatrist in addition to the superintendent. Prior to that the rest of the medical staff were appointed at SHMO (Senior Hospital Medical Officer) or Senior Registrar level. Dr James, however, was not in good health and Dr McGrath found himself deputizing a great deal until, on Dr James's death in 1958, he was appointed superintendent in his place. Dr Cyril Perry, SHMO, was then appointed deputy superintendent. Dr Brian O'Connell was the replacement as the extra consultant psychiatrist but on a sessional basis, visiting Broadmoor from London on four days a week and spending his other time at St George's Hospital working with Sir Desmond Curran. This detail warrants a mention as the forerunner, effectively, to Dr McGrath's policy of opening Broadmoor to 'interaction' with the rest of the psychiatric world, in particular the teaching hospitals and centres of research.

When I was appointed at the end of 1959 as the first clinical psychologist, the staffing was much as Partridge describes it. In addition to the 'Physician Superintendent', as Dr McGrath preferred to be called, his deputy, Dr Perry, and Dr O'Connell as visiting consultant, there were three senior registrars in psychiatry: Drs Leife Maine, Peter Smith and Tom Bergin. That was the total of the medical staff and would have been standard for a psychiatric hospital of the time. The much larger Rainhill Hospital, on Merseyside, where I had come from, had some seven or eight full time equivalent consultant level psychiatrists for a patient population of 2,700. Although this was the second or third largest in the country at the time, mental hospitals with 2,000 or so patients were then common. Broadmoor, by comparison, was quite a small hospital with its 850 patients. Of the other special hospitals, Moss Side was smaller still, about half Broadmoor's size, while Rampton was larger at about 1,100 beds.

The distribution of responsibilities amongst the medical staff was that the SHMO and senior registrars between then covered the day-to-day medical needs of the ward blocks which, at seven male and two female, made roughly two each. Dr Maine had the female wing as his patch with Dr O'Connell giving consultant cover. Drs

Perry, Smith and Bergin covered the male wing with Dr McGrath as consultant and Dr O'Connell sharing with him the job of reviewing and supervising progress of the new male patient arrivals. Dr McGrath's special concern was Block 2, the parole block, from where most of the discharges would come as Broadmoor was then still organized on an hierarchical system of progress much as Partridge described. Male patients would be admitted to Block 4, an intermediate block of fairly acutely disordered patients, unless they were so violently or unpredictably disturbed as to warrant admission to Block 6 which was still the block housing the most disturbed patients (still called a 'back block' or 'refractory block' in those days). Dr Peter Smith was the senior registrar in Block 4 and would work up and present to a case conference all the new arrivals. Dr Maine would do likewise for new female arrivals.

OTHER SENIOR OFFICERS

In addition to their medical duties one of the jobs done by the other doctors (i.e.: non-consultants), together with the chaplain, was monitoring the incoming and outgoing mail each morning and together they could be seen doing this in an office near to the main gate sitting on tall stools at large sloping desks for all the world like a scene out of a Dickens novel. Just why the chaplain should have been involved in this work I do not know except that this legal requirement was obviously regarded as a senior staff responsibility and it must have been helpful for the doctors to have had another person on the job with them. The chaplain, in addition, would have been involved in dealing with any distressing news from home that would need to be tactfully conveyed to a mentally disturbed patient. After the medical staff the number of senior staff in those days were few and, as Partridge describes, the chaplain occupied a prestigious position amongst the hierarchy.

The other senior 'officers' of the hospital were the Steward and Clerk of Accounts, Mr Horace Dowling at that time (the equivalent of the hospital administrator or manager these days); the superintendent's confidential 'clerk' (in charge of the medical office), Mr Eric Cooper; the Chief Male Nurse, Mr Pat Bennett; the Matron, Miss Mary Osborne and the Social Worker, Mrs Helen Paton. Horace Dowling's and Eric Cooper's posts were civil service ones filled from Ministry of Health headquarters at Saville Row. They had executive and clerical officer staff supporting them and promotions meant the likelihood of a return to Saville Row. (Incidentally, Saville Row was where I had attended for interview for my appointment to the Broadmoor clinical psychologist post. It was much later that the Ministry of Health, later Department of Health and Social Security, moved to Alexander Fleming House at the Elephant & Castle.)

Professional staff also included a pharmacist. One had just left so that I and my family took over her rented house, the only one at the time which the hospital owned in the village of Crowthorne. A replacement pharmacist in the person of Mrs Muriel Gear was appointed a little later. Then there were the heads of 'works' and 'engineering' in the attached department of the Ministry of Works, respectively Mr Bill Ayres and Mr Tom Nolan. Most of these, except the social worker, lived in houses on the hospital estate, being people who were 'on call', and these houses reflected the status of their occupants. Partridge speaks of the medical superintendent's house which was situated between the male and female wings. This was the grandest although not the most attractive, this being the deputy's house on the brow of the hill overlooking the road down to the village of Crowthorne. Dr McGrath occupied this on his arrival as deputy and opted to stay there when he became superintendent, giving it his own chosen name of 'Kentigern' to reflect his Glaswegian origins. (The house is recognizable in Patrick McGrath junior's book 'Asylum', upon which he clearly drew from his childhood recollections of living there.) Not relishing a position for his young family squeezed between the two wings of the hospital, despite the panoramic views, Dr McGrath rejected the traditional superintendent's residence for which, in any case, he had other plans as we shall see later.

After the two principal medical residences in 'grandness' came the chaplain's house, reflecting the status of that post in the history of the hospital. This was half way down what was known rather obviously as 'Chaplain's Hill', the southern road out of the estate, and was then occupied by the Rev Basil James and his wife (no relation to Dr James the former superintendent). The house was occupied by several successors after Basil James's retirement but was then demolished for proposed new developments. This was a pity as it was a rather attractive house in construction and outlook and its position has not since been developed other than to straighten out the bend in the road at that point. Basil and Mrs James were well known and liked figures on the Broadmoor scene of 1959, Mrs James being a gracious but friendly and motherly figure who was always to be seen at hospital social events helping Matron and her staff with refreshments or encouraging patients to take part in whatever activity the event featured. Basil James was a robust figure who had enjoyed a notable career at cricket in his younger days. Later he had become too portly to run between the wickets and always instructed his younger, headstrong partners that there was to be "No running between the wickets; it's four or nothing!" His son had obviously inherited his talent and had not long before distinguished himself by scoring a century for Cambridge University against the Australians. Basil James, as his figure demonstrated, always enjoyed the refreshments at patients' social events and numerous people took some delight in telling me to watch out for his arrival at any of these, which was guaranteed to coincide with the appearance of the food. Sure enough, he would always appear. He was renowned for the sing-song way he greeted the arrival of refreshments: his 'ho ho, sausage rolls' was mimicked by staff and patients alike and an uncannily accurate rendering was to be heard from one of the staff messengers, Percy Hagley.

Anyway, after the chaplain's house in the hospital hierarchy came those of the other officers which were situated at various positions along the 'terrace' - the row of houses in the road facing the hospital main gate (see diagram facing and in Chapter 6). The exception was the matron who occupied a well-appointed flat over the female wing gateway. This gateway was a rather attractive structure, unlike the traditional institutional main entrance to the male side. It was later the subject of a painting by one of the occupations officers and made into a Christmas card for that year. Facing the gateway was a sunken area of garden known as the nurses' garden, although one scarcely ever saw anyone enjoying it by 1959. The area is now incorporated in the enlarged area within the walls of the new hospital buildings. But it was a peaceful spot, being at the end of a cul-de-sac and bordering on the surrounding forestry land.

(See diagram and in Chapter 6.)

SKETCH PLAN OF BROADMOOR HOSPITAL
IN RELATION TO CROWTHORNE

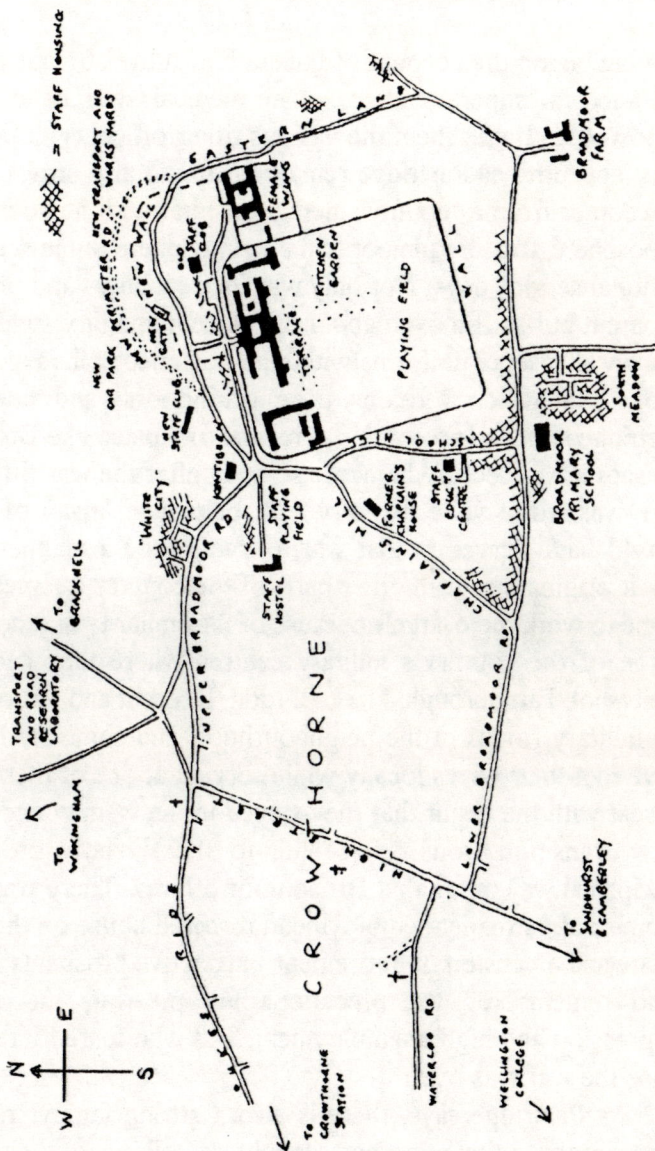

THE STAFF 'CLIMATE'

Having begun the account of the staff with the obvious person of the medical superintendent, other medical staff have naturally followed and with them the various other officers. 'Officers' is a very apt term, as Partridge remarked. It had also struck me, as a newcomer from a 'county' mental hospital with no such military atmosphere, that Broadmoor had an atmosphere reminiscent of my national service days. Not only was its cleanliness and orderliness apparent but staff moved about the place in military style, dressed in navy blue serge uniforms with high buttoned collars and peaked caps - caps which were only taken off indoors - and they saluted! Partridge seems to accept this as natural to a place like Broadmoor; perhaps it was because he wrote so soon after the war. In 1959 the war was still a vivid memory and, of course, many of the staff would have served in that war. In fact, quite a number of staff, albeit originating from other parts of the country, seemed to have come to work there largely because of its similarity and nearness to some of the country's military centres where they had served. Aldershot, Farnborough, Fleet, Bordon, Deepcut and Arborfield are all military towns in the neighbourhood and some staff seem to have met their wives locally while serving at one of these military bases, with the result that they stayed in the vicinity and made an easy transition from service life to the similarly ordered and disciplined way of life that Broadmoor offered. There was also the promise of permanent employment, a rented house on the hospital estate and a pension on retirement - attractive prospects to people who remembered the precarious life pre-war, the economic depression and high unemployment, and who feared a recurrence once the war was over.

As Partridge says, there is also a strong family tradition at Broadmoor, with sons and daughters following their parents.

Crowthorne was, in any case, a quiet village environment in those days. Other work was further afield. Only with the expansion of suburbia and the encapsulation within the yet-to-come M3, M4 and M25 did the area become engulfed in commuter country. The intervention of the war had taken many away temporarily who brought others into the area with them when they returned. The result was a cosmopolitan mixture of people from all parts of the kingdom which conveniently matched the country-wide origins of the patients. For a patient there was almost always a member of staff who knew their home town, its pubs and its football team. If the tradition of saluting the superintendent was a hangover from such a surfeit of ex-service personnel it would not be surprising.

The superintendent's position in a system that relied for its security and success on a clear line of authority made him stand out as a command figure and Dr McGrath was well known for his wartime service as an RAMC colonel in China and Burma. He projected an image of military authority. I observed this on one occasion when accompanying him across a courtyard where one of the staff, an ex-Irish Guards colour sergeant now occupying the job of ward sculleryman, was walking across the yard carrying a large wicker basket of the ward's stores. This meant that he was unable to raise his arm in salute; nor would that have been proper as he was wearing the sculleryman's 'uniform' of a brown overall and was without a hat - and, of course, you cannot salute without a hat on! So what did he do? Without a flicker of hesitation he did a smart 'eyes left' for the regulation five steps. Pat McGrath responded with an equally proper but warm 'Good morning, Paddy'. Paddy was not alone. Many of the older, ex-service staff would salute senior staff such as the doctors whom they regarded as 'officers'. They also tended to be addressed as 'Sir' and Mrs Paton and Matron as 'Ma'am'.

So the real staff, in terms of their greater number and their importance in the everyday running of the institution (and 'institution' it was until the change of name to 'special hospital' with the 1959 Act) were the nursing staff. Partridge likens them to the military 'other ranks' with the charge nurses and departmental nurses on the 'blocks' as the NCOs and the Chief Male Nurse and his deputies as the RSM and CSMs. I had this emphasized personally soon after my arrival when I had asked Jack Wilkinson, the staff nurse attached to me and an ex-staff sergeant REME and former 'boy' soldier from Arborfield himself, to be introduced to each of the blocks and their staff. Arriving on one block where the DN (Departmental Nurse, equivalent to an assistant chief male nurse) was a former Scots Guards RSM, he accompanied me around the ward to show me the accommodation and facilities. To my surprise he walked a half pace behind me, indicating where we should go, neatly falling into step with me as we went along. I don't know whether Jack Wilkinson had quietly leaked to his former DN that I had myself been a National Service subaltern, which was actually quite a useful credential in that environment in those days, but I certainly felt compelled to recall my old army habits and walk smartly in step with him, head up, no shuffling! Even the nurses on the female wing, with their smartly starched uniforms, seemed to fit in with this military atmosphere. In fact Dr McGrath clearly recognized the similarity and affectionately referred to the female wing staff as his 'QARANCS' (Queen Alexandra's Royal Army Nursing Corps) whose headquarters were also at nearby Aldershot. Other staff were also likened to attachments from other service arms, the Ministry of Works obviously being from the RE & RASC and the Catering Officer from the ACC. 'What am I, then?', I once asked. 'Attached REME' was his immediate response! Dr McGrath's service background was some years later to provide what he regarded as the ultimate 'policemen are getting younger' story when he attended an RAMC reunion at the Royal Military

Hospital at Netley, Southampton (now closed). Not surprisingly he found many wartime junior colleagues now risen to the ranks of general. "I must be getting old," he said "when the generals call me 'sir'!"

Despite all this military metaphor, however, there was no doubting that, under Dr McGrath, Broadmoor was to be a hospital, although one run with brisk efficiency and clinical accountability. Incidents were always to be promptly reported and explained on a 'half-sheet'. This was a sheet of paper from a small pad rather slimmer than the modern A5 size. The circumstances of the incident were to be reported and understood in terms of the patient's medical condition and, despite the liberal regime of Dr Hopwood, too often they would be reported in the defensive way of an incident between quarrelling people. It took Dr McGrath some years to get across that he was not looking for 'blame' but for discernment of the disordered thinking and emotions that prompted the behaviour of psychiatric patients. Of course, it was difficult entirely to eliminate the element of blame in the sense that responsibility for the incident had to be ascertained: what had triggered the patient's reactions? If some element of nursing care had been overlooked or misapplied then there was the potential for a reprimand on one's record which could go against promotion in the future.

THE NURSING STAFF

Nevertheless, the nursing staff of this somewhat militaristic institution were not unthinking disciplinarians. They knew their patients and the quirks and oblique thinking that characterized their behaviours. They knew when they were going to 'blow' and how to handle things when they did. They might not know all the 'fancy names' psychiatrists gave to these incidents or the fine distinctions of their diagnoses but they knew how to get the best out of their patients and where they could best be 'placed' in the hospital's system of employments and recreations.

As Partridge has pointed out, the nursing staff at Broadmoor have never been prison warders even though, as one-time employees of the Home Office, their Trades Union has been the POA (Prison Officers Association). They were 'attendants' of, initially, 'criminal lunatics' and now of 'mentally disordered offenders'. With the creation of the National Health Service they became mental nurses, going through the same three year mental nurse training as those elsewhere in the NHS. With the RMN certificate (Register of Mental Nurses) they were eligible for promotion through the nursing hierarchy. Broadmoor had its own nurse training school to prepare people for the RMN examinations. Others could go through a shorter and less demanding two year course of training for the SEN qualification (State Enrolled Nurse) whilst others without training would work as NAs (Nursing Assistants).

Despite Peter Thompson's concern, in his books of his experience as a Broadmoor patient, that the nursing staff were largely untrained, this was something of a misconception. Certainly the NAs were not formally trained and learned their skills beside their qualified colleagues on the ward. One would have liked to have seen more staff holding qualifications but the NAs were at least well outnumbered by the trained and qualified RMNs and SENs. SENs and NAs would not be eligible for promotion to charge nurse (male) or sister (female) and ultimately to DN (departmental nurse, the equivalent of assistant chief male nurse or assistant matron). Only the RMNs were eligible for this, so ensuring the charge nurse and higher level posts were occupied by fully qualified staff. There were always, however, RMN qualified charge and staff nurses on duty on any shift and in every ward and so skilled and qualified attention was always available if required, even though it may not always have seemed like it to the perceptions of distressed and disordered patients.

RMNs might additionally go on for their 'double training', i.e.: to obtain the SRN qualification (state registered nurse) in general nursing. This would add versatility to a nurse's position in Broadmoor, enhancing promotion chances, and there were several places where this was needed. Partridge described the insulin unit in Block 1. A photo of this appears in the edition of Broadmoor's staff magazine commemorating the 50th anniversary of the NHS and shows Percy Horton and Tom Smith, both 'doubly trained' staff qualified to supervise this hazardous treatment which was still going on in 1959 in the top ward of Block 1.

Partridge also speaks of the early provision of operating facilities. By 1959 a room opposite the physician superintendent's office in the central corridor had been equipped as an operating theatre and later a better suite was built with a 'doubly qualified' charge nurse running it. Similarly 'doubly qualified' charge nurses ran the infirmaries of Block 3 (elderly male patients) and Block 4 (admissions and acute patients) whilst there were some doubly qualified female wing sisters, too, and the main female ward also had an infirmary. However, one group of surgical treatments for psychiatric patients of that era, namely prefrontal leucotomy and related lobotomies, was not carried out at Broadmoor. Such operations had been a weekly event at Rainhill Hospital where I had previously worked. Dr McGrath's comment on this omission was typically to the point: "we have enough disinhibited people here struggling to develop control over themselves without adding to them by doing leucotomies" (the operation was essentially one for extremely tense obsessionals and schizophrenics: its effect was to disinhibit them).

Another further qualification for nursing staff to attain was that of nurse tutor. There were two nurse tutors in 1959: Len Beazer and Tom Gilmour. The Broadmoor nurse training school at that time was a couple of rooms in the corridor above the pharmacy, equipped with three long board tables. Later staff training was to blossom into a wider range of topics and a new staff education centre was built outside the walls, in the grounds. At that time, however, it provided one of the first non-patient activities of my new psychological service when I was asked to provide some brief testing of staff applicants to verify that they were capable of profiting from the investment in three years student nurse training. I used three brief tests of verbal attainment, learning potential and personality, the latter to discern emotional stability and social temperament which I thought relevant for the Broadmoor work setting. This went on for several years until replaced by the nursing profession's own tests.

Nursing duties on the 'Blocks' (three storey buildings comprising three wards) involved supervising both clinical and security aspects of patients' needs. Critics and visitors have sometimes queried why Broadmoor has never had separate nursing and security staff and this is raised by Peter Thompson in his books. Dr McGrath, who had visited similar institutions in the USA and seen this arrangement, always shunned it. A rivalry was inevitable, he said, and one or other was always unoccupied part of the time. In any case: "consider a nurse's daily routine", he said. This will include getting the patient up; seeing that dressing and toilet are accomplished; supervising meals (which, at Broadmoor includes the tallying of crockery and cutlery); seeing to medication, mail and cleaning of rooms; getting patients to workplaces, recreation or sport; sitting in on visiting; encouraging letter writing and hobbies; more meals; more medication; and finally getting the patient to bed. The degree of direct assistance as against merely watching, checking and encouraging will vary according to the patient's degree of disability but, either way, this repetitive closeness to the basics of living inevitably results in a similarly close knowledge of every quirk of a patient's personality and clinical condition. Then, said Dr McGrath, and only then, was a member of staff able to fulfil the requirements of both nursing and security: he or she would then know not only what the daily care needs were but also what the likely hazards and risks were. For him the care of the patient and the security of those around him were fulfilled by one and the same person - the mental nurse - whose duties could not be separated.

This closeness might be too close for those who, in later philosophies, are primarily concerned with a patient's privacy and individual freedom. However, these are patients who have been responsible for some of the country's most horrific crimes. Until they are understood and their mental states return to normal, staff who care for them must be expected to stay close and keep careful observation. This was the dual role of special hospital nurses and they knew and fulfilled it to the letter. It might not always have been easy then to obtain from them an account of what they knew. There is often a difference between what someone knows and what they are able to report, especially if there are also misconceptions about what is expected of them. Such were the changes taking place after the 1959 Act, the pressures of the escalating army of doctors and other specialists, and the concerns of their staff union, that the perception of what was required could become confused and distorted. On the ward, however, and with their patients, if you could get inside and gain their confidence, most of Broadmoor's staff very well knew what their patients' problems and needs were.

THE OCCUPATIONS STAFF

Parallel to the nursing staff and equivalent to them in their knowledge of their patients, and second only to the nursing staff in numbers, were the Occupations Staff. Around the hospital were various occupational centres and workshops, which were extended and renovated over the years. Their staffs were referred to erroneously by Partridge as 'occupational therapists' and gradually over the years this is what they have become through recruitment and training. At that time, however, they were not so trained and qualified. But they were far from being 'unqualified'. They were recruited generally as having some relevant trade skill and qualification. These would have included carpentry, metalwork, upholstery, shoemaking, tailoring and, on the female wing, needlework, dressmaking, laundry work and handicrafts. The 'occupations' provided, therefore, were far from the 'sewing mailbags' sort, thought of publicly as the occupations of prisoners. Partridge has described them. They were still there in 1959 and grew and developed thereafter.

The Occupations Staff were ostensibly there to teach and supervise patients in the various crafts and trades of their workshops. The variety of trade skills were wide and useful. Later we shall consider how these were dovetailed into the individual treatment needs of patients but in 1959 that was a thing for the future. Many of the hospital's needs were met through the work of these shops: tailoring the uniforms; making and repairing shoes; cleansing and remaking mattresses; repairing utensils, furniture and upholstery around the hospital; printing forms and programmes; and, of course, doing the hospital's laundry. Then, and although these were not in the charge of occupations officers, there were patients working in the hospital kitchens and stores, supervised by the kitchen staff and the stores clerk. Several parole patients worked in the hospital shop, run by an outside contractor, and which supplied the daily sundry purchases of patients and staff alike, from the inevitable cigarettes, tobacco, sweets, stationery and greetings cards to the gifts patients might want to send out to their friends and families or the items they might want to enhance their own lives in the way of food and clothing. If they weren't stocked they could be ordered from outside.

In all these workplaces the staff, like their nursing counterparts, would come to know their patients and their characteristics inside out. As well as the daily routines of getting up and going to bed, seeing to one's dressing and toilet, eating meals and interacting socially with one's fellow patients, the routine of work and recreation provides similarly important information. The way one receives and reacts to instruction, learns a new routine, handles materials, responds to colleagues and rivals, deals with accomplishment and failure - all these are pointers to personality characteristics and the progress of any disabling illness or disorder. The occupations staff knew their patients from these activities just as the ward staff knew theirs from their daily routines.

They would also use the workshop situation to observe and test out their patients. On one occasion I visited the main Handicrafts Centre just after a patient had sawn in half a table he was making. "Why didn't you stop me?" he had accused the staff. "We wanted to see whether you'd really do what you'd threatened and how you'd deal with the result" was the response. This was a bit of aggression that they could see did no harm to anyone else, so they had let it go ahead and then made use of it. The patient was a well-known psychopath, given to impulsive outbursts but highly intelligent. He was angry with himself and everyone else about the table but Jim Gale and Jack Barber, the occupations officers in the Handicraft Centre, thought he would learn something from the experience and helped him through it.

Doctors and other specialist staff were always well advised to consult occupational as well as nursing staff for basic, corroboratory, supplementary or contradictory information about the patients on whom they were reporting and making crucial decisions. Personally, I would always defer doing this until I had made my own required assessment of a case, so as not to be influenced by what I was told. I would then set the information from staff alongside my own findings and either draw attention to the agreements or try to account for the discrepancies; nothing could be discounted, it had to be resolved and was an invaluable means of expanding one's understanding of the patient's problems and progress.

WORKS AND DOMESTIC STAFF

Other staff about the hospital often also provided interesting and helpful insights into patients' behaviour and progress as well as often providing personal support. These were principally the Ministry of Works (MoW) staff, porters, messengers and, later on when patient labour ceased, the domestic staff. There were also later 'pool men' (nursing staff who had passed retirement age, which was 55 under 'Mental Health Officer' conditions, but then who stayed on at NA level to perform the many escorting duties that were increasingly needed). The MoW men were referred to as the 'little green men' because of their green overalls (a deliberately distinguishing feature in a setting where everyone needed to be identifiable; contractors of outside firms were provided with red overalls; patients working outside the walls wore yellow-beige corduroy trousers and, in winter, grey serge jackets). The MoW men, always being about the place and involved in jobs where patients might also be present, were obvious targets for conversations from patients and learned to deal with the sometimes odd course these could take. Friendships would develop with certain of these staff so that a patient might feel they understood and 'related' to them better than the traditional staff.

There is, of course, no telling what chemistry might make for a successful relationship and this has been recognized in more recent times in identifying specific members of the clinical team to be a patient's personal contact. At Broadmoor it was always as well to inquire who was the staff member who knew a patient best. That was the person to whom to go for information or through whom to establish contact with a patient for a particular purpose, such as planning and carrying through a treatment programme.

OTHER PROFESSIONAL STAFF

This chapter mentioned at the outset the people regarded as the hospital's 'officers'. The medical superintendent and his immediate medical and allied professional colleagues in effect constituted the 'management' and the providers of specialist services were to grow over the years. What were then singleton Psychology and Social Work services grew into distinct 'departments' with roles in the eventual 'clinical teams'. They will be discussed more fully later, together with the Education Department which didn't exist at all in 1959. A library and librarians were also to arrive later, as were psychotherapists and research staff. The chaplaincy has already been mentioned and continued, though not occupying the prominent position in late 20th century thinking that it had in Victorian times, as other staff groups grew to swell the staff complement. Chaplains from other denominations were drawn from local churches on a part-time basis. Later the increase in patients from other religions meant that these also needed to be catered for, and were. A single pharmacist had been increased to three by the end of the 1959 Act. There was a dental surgery and a local dentist visited one day each week, later two days. Occupying this post in 1959 and for some years afterwards was Mr Abraham. Specialists in other branches of medicine visited regularly or when needed, and an optician visited monthly. An anaesthetist was also available, not only for any operations but also for giving the anaesthetic for ECT. We shall hear more of some of these as the new Act took effect and the hospital developed.

THE 'LAY' STAFF

There remains what was always called the 'lay' staff, so-called because they were not medical, nursing or other clinical staff directly concerned in day-to-day patient care. It goes without saying that any organization needs administrative back-up. The 'steward and clerk of accounts' and the 'medical superintendent's confidential clerk' have already been mentioned as 'officers' of the institution and they, in effect, headed the two sectors of the lay administration at that time: the 'front office' and the 'top office'. The first of these was so-called because it was near the front entrance, the main gate. It was, of course, actually the back and not the front of the hospital which, in common with most mental hospitals of the time, had its grand frontage looking on to the best view but had its access for what were 'tradesmen's' deliveries at the drabber back of the building. The 'front' office housed the small group of staff involved in the housekeeping functions of the hospital: salaries, staff recruitment, supplies and accounts and was adjacent to and to the right of the main gate. The big main gate itself opened on to a courtyard around which were stores and offices. Further round the courtyard to the right of the 'front' office were the main stores.

The staff entered the hospital by a doorway to the side of the main gateway where arrays of hooks held all the keys. Nursing and occupations staff exchanged their number tag for a set of keys appropriate to the needs of their rank. Other staff's keys were kept on named hooks in sets of small boxes with windows, observable at all times by the gate staff. Gate staff would then always be able to monitor security and know if staff were in or out of the hospital by whether keys were on their hooks or not, just as they knew who was on duty on the wards or in a work area by the disc number on the relevant hook of the main board. Behind and to the left of this gateway, a mirror image of the 'front' office, was the nursing administration with its tabs on the nerve centre of the gateway. As you walked through this entrance, up the left hand side of the centre courtyard, you passed the grocery stores with its humming 'fridges. On the fourth side of the centre courtyard, facing the gate, were the similarly humming 'fridges of the kitchen complex and the kitchens themselves. Either side of this the paved pathways under colonnades ran from the main gate to doorways (again locked - all interconnecting doors were kept locked) into the transverse corridor which, on one side, gave access to the kitchens and on the other to the central hall. On either side of this hall were further rooms: to the left the patients' shop and to the right the superintendent's office and the 'top office' which housed the medical administration. (For diagrams, see next chapter.)

This 'top' office was in those days one large room with the confidential clerk's desk partitioned off in one front corner by the window, looking on to the hospital terrace and gardens, and the typist's desk in the other corner. In the centre of the room were large tables for the two clerks concerned with patients' documentation and records. These latter were kept in filing cabinets and cupboards around the outer walls with an archive section of former patients' records in another room elsewhere. It could now be seen why it was called the 'top' office: you were now 'up' at the 'front' of the building looking out over the descending terraces and gardens. There was one typist for the front office and another for the top office.

I have gone into this detail to provide comparison with the situation today. How did the whole panoply of running Broadmoor get done with these two small office areas - 'front' and 'top' - and the equally small nursing office? Yet, at the time, people pointed to what they saw as an unnecessary amount of administration and asked why it was all needed when "it had originally all been done by one person." There are several answers and it is not just a matter of life being simpler then. For one thing, a great deal of what is now a local responsibility was then carried out at the Ministry of Health in London. Typing was needed less because, strangely by today's customs, most paper work was hand written, with carbon copies. The case notes consisted of handwritten entries with only special reports typed. These were gummed or stapled on to manilla sheets, coloured according to the specialty with which they dealt. Documentation dealing with the admission of a new patient was on handwritten forms, with carbon copies, printed in the patients' workshops. The only significant correspondence generated was from the medical superintendent, the medical office and the steward and clerk of accounts. As new disciplines joined the staff and departments grew, and as responsibilities were devolved from the Ministry of Health in London to local level, so did administration expand. The lay staff were civil servants of clerical assistant (CA), clerical officer (CO), or executive officer (EO) grade, headed by a Higher Executive Officer (HEO) in each office and a Senior Executive Officer (SEO) overall - the steward and clerk of accounts.

Nevertheless, these so-called 'lay' staff would also have contact with patients, with potential beneficial effect. Patients worked in the kitchens and parole patients in the stores and patients' shop. Above the central hall was the hospital chapel where a parole patient was organist. Parole patients could visit the shop unescorted and might stop to chat with staff. All these would be in daily contact with 'lay' staff. These staff would also often attend the social functions, dances, sports days, etc, which Partridge describes, and intermingle with patients. Some would play in staff teams which had matches with patients' teams - football, cricket, table tennis, bowls. Eric Cooper, originally the medical superintendent's confidential clerk, who later became the steward and clerk of accounts, was captain of the staff cricket team and, indeed, had become familiar with Broadmoor and interested in a post there from visiting with the Ministry of Health headquarters cricket team. Other lay staff might have contact with patients through singing with the patients' choir; indeed this would be augmented not only by staff but also by families of staff and local villagers. So opportunities existed for many people, in addition to the traditional clinical professions, to exercise an influence on the careers and progress of patients.

STAFF ACTIVITIES

The Broadmoor estate constituted a close knit community. This not only arose from its nature and function but because it was outside the main village centre of Crowthorne. With two day shifts and a night shift many staff were off duty and around and about during daytime hours. The position is the same today but the way of life has changed. Mobility and increased local facilities mean that staff and their families find their recreation at a distance in a way that was not available and did not happen in the immediate post-war years. So the social life of the hospital in the 1960s still reflected the great deal of estate-based activity that had grown up over the years and the hospital grounds provided facilities for this.

Clinical and lay staff alike participated in staff sports teams and these interacted with patients when the teams played each other. The staff recreation club was a social centre, with a bar, which provided opportunity for staff to meet and relax when off duty, fostering *esprit de corps,* sustaining morale and providing contact with the rest of the outside world. Matches with outside teams in various local leagues were the pattern for the football, cricket and bowls teams and, later on, further sports and pastimes were added. For a time there was a thriving badminton club in a hall behind the staff club where activities for staff families also took place. Alf Lister, then a staff nurse, ran a judo club for children of staff and there were regular staff dances and socials. The Christmas draw and the New Year's Eve dance were big attractions. For a number of years, however, Broadmoor staff's most prominent sporting asset was its tug of war team which reached the level of national champions and represented Great Britain in international championships in Sweden. Jack Wilkinson, the staff nurse attached to work with me, was the tug of war team's secretary so I was kept fully informed!

Jack Wilkinson was succeeded in his secondment to me by Roy Clarkson who had been an assistant golf professional as a young man, with a handicap of eight. On discovering that I had played some golf off and on during my life he suggested we enter for the London Area Mental Hospitals annual golf competition, as Broadmoor was geographically situated just within the North West Thames NHS Region, so making us eligible. The competition was for pairs from the competing hospitals. As my golf had never been much good and his was rusty, our main concern was to avoid coming last! As the years passed, however, others became interested and a number of very good golfers emerged so that our team became regular winners of the competition. The LMHSA, as the sports association became, developed leagues and championships at many games and sports in which Broadmoor teams took part over the years, often very successfully. The athletics section sometimes used the Broadmoor estate for its cross country run, being well suited to the purpose with its woods and hills.

Broadmoor's location within the NW Thames Region of the NHS, geographically though not administratively of course, was due to East Berkshire being in that region, although the boundary was very close and, in fact, ran through the middle of the Crowthorne area, a matter of considerable inconvenience at times. The SW Thames Region lay within sight, just over the Surrey-Hampshire border to the south, but the western half of Crowthorne was within the Oxford NHS Region. Living in that part, one's NHS services were in Reading whilst, in the other half, they were in Ascot, with some even as far as Slough. There was a small NHS unit just outside Crowthorne in those days, Pinewood Hospital, which had been a military hospital during the war and a TB unit afterwards. It was now a chest hospital. Dr McGrath was asked to attend an emergency there on one occasion that resulted in the patient having to be admitted for psychiatric treatment. Some care was taken in ascertaining whether it would be more convenient for the patient to be in the nearest NW Thames psychiatric hospital for this, or the nearest equivalent in the Oxford Region. I forget now which was decided but it did necessitate moving the patient's bed to another ward so that the committal could be authorized in the catchment area of the hospital chosen. The boundary ran through the middle of the hospital.

Broadmoor staff social activities were not confined to the

sports field. As well as the Christmas and New Year socials and dances there were other social activities in the staff club and the new premises built later (see Chapter 14) had greatly improved and extended facilities for these. Two of the activities, however, did not involve the club premises. One was the Staff Horticultural Society which put on its annual show in the staff club; but where the work was done, of course, in people's gardens. This now bygone activity generated sharp rivalries between the dedicated growers of giant vegetables and ravishing blooms. The name of Arthur Pearce, one of the two assistant chief male nurses at that time, always featured at the head of the prize winners' list.

The other activity was the Staff Concert Party which, in 1959 and for some years afterwards, performed its revues on the stage in the hospital's central hall. Called 'Broad And Moorish', this was something in which I enjoyed taking part and it ran for a number of years before dwindling support caused it to wind up. A talented group of staff used to put together humorous topical sketches, alternating with musical scenes based on some theme such as Robin Hood, New York, or a South Sea Island, which allowed appropriate songs, dances and linking dialogue to be strung together rather in the style of the Black and White Minstrel Show, which was popular on TV in those days. For the Broadmoor Centenary year in 1963 the revue was called "That Was The Century That Was", borrowing from the popular Saturday night TV satire of that era: "That Was The Week That Was". As with the patients' drama group (see Chapter 9), staff shows were presented on Wednesday and Saturday evenings over a period of some six weeks and were open to the public, who could write in for tickets (which were free, although a collection for charity was made). This resulted in parties attending from a distance, by coach. Whether they appreciated which shows were given by patients and which by staff is debatable!

A staff feature which calls for comment is the 'lead payment' which staff received on top of their national salary scales. This has often been referred to as 'danger money' but it was not introduced for that reason. It was intended to be an incentive to employment in an unpopular and more demanding area of the psychiatric field, a recognition of the extra skills required and a compensation for the restrictions imposed, like being available for emergencies when off duty. The nursing and occupational staff received the full rate and other staff half the rate, except medical staff who were not included. Recruitment was certainly difficult during most of the period of the 1959 Act, due to full employment. This restricted choice in staff selection. Staff representation and negotiating procedures have not been raised in this chapter which simply describes the range of staffing services available. These will be discussed in Chapter 19, which looks at the management issues which arose as a result of the changed nature and demands of the work described in the intervening chapters.

Another staff feature that should not go without remark, and which began in the time of the 1959 Act, was the introduction of staff from a wide range of ethnic backgrounds. The ethnic backgrounds of the patients were, of course, similarly widening during this period and staff recruitment followed the same pattern. This was just as well, given the understanding of cross-cultural factors that the broadening population demanded.

All in all, Broadmoor was a close-knit community, its full range of work and play on a well developed and maintained estate testifying to its stability and integration. At the same time, it was a community separate in many ways from the outside world, both geographically, as it was up the hill, away from the adjacent village of Crowthorne; and socially, in that it endured public ignorance, misunderstanding and criticism. It tended, therefore, to defend itself with an attitude of dogged determination to do its appointed public duty come what may.

SUMMARY

This chapter has described the staff of the hospital, not just for the record but because of two main features. The first of these was the obvious increase in both numbers and variety of professional disciplines that the new Act brought in its wake. The second was the change brought by the greater variety and more particularly by the advance from the pre-war and wartime culture, with what now seems its quaint ways, to the busy impersonality of more modern times. Broadmoor's geographical isolation on its hill was gradually eroded by the encroachment of surrounding suburbia and the interaction which this brought with an increasingly mobile world.

The basic staffing in 1959 was, of course, medical, nursing, occupations officers, administrative staff and staff of the attached department of the then Ministry of Works. Only two of the medical staff were consultant psychiatrists, one being the physician superintendent. The four other medical staff were a senior hospital medical officer and three senior registrars. The chaplain, pharmacist and social worker were singletons, as were the new arrivals, the catering officer and myself, the first clinical psychologist. The nursing staff numbered between five and six hundred, however, and there were some 30 to 40 occupational staff and 20 or so attached Ministry of Works staff. There were a dozen or so administrative staff, on secondment from MoH HQ and liable to return there on promotion, headed by the steward and clerk of accounts, a civil servant of senior executive officer rank.

The nursing staff were headed by a chief male nurse on the male side and a matron on the female side, both with their deputies, and each ward block was headed by a DN or DS (Departmental

Nurse or Sister) who was of assistant CMN or assistant matron rank. Each ward was in the charge of a charge nurse (male) or sister (female) of whom there were two on opposite shifts.

This compact organization, compounded by the hospital's isolation, its tradition, the closeness of the recent war and the many ex-servicemen on the staff, gave the place a military air which it was interesting to see gradually dissipate as the staff grew and diversified, the surrounding world grew closer and the war further away. The staff estate, its club and the many sporting and recreational activities, however, still preserved its close social identity.

CHAPTER 6

THE BUILDINGS AND SECURITY

BUILDINGS

Victorian hospital buildings might all seem much the same. In updating the history of Broadmoor Hospital, however, and in considering how the patients and their lives changed when legislation changed and clinical practices developed, the buildings are a constant factor underlying everything else. Their size and security impose a pattern on life within. Misconceptions and errors have arisen about them and they did begin to change during the 'interacts' period. The big changes happened later but began to be seen towards the end of the life of the 1959 Act. Partridge only describes the hospital buildings in passing but they are the place where everything happened and their character has a lot to do with the nature of those things.

The first thing to say, which may seem odd, is that the brickwork is red - a bright 'brick' red - with courses of yellow. The significance of this is that one can often tell if a lurid article has been written by someone who has never visited Broadmoor by use of the phrase 'grim, grey walls'. Unimportant, perhaps, but one of the many irritations that reinforce the belief of those who work there that 'the media' likes to miss no chance to put the place down and maintain the mystery of a distant impregnable fortress. Of course Broadmoor looks forbidding on a cold, wet winter's night - it is large and the walls are high - but most of the time its warm red bricks and squat mass give it a comfortable, somnolent air. Of

96

course, this description will be thought equally biased in the opposite direction: after all, didn't I work there for more than a quarter of a century? However, in support of this view I recall Dr McGrath's telling of his surprise at how well one woman patient settled in. A cultured woman and a Cambridge graduate, he put this to her and was surprised by her reply: "well, you see, the buildings remind me very much of my student days at Girton". My own wife, also a Girtonian, volunteered a similar comment.

It will be interesting to see if the attitude to Broadmoor's appearance and location changes at all as a result of the new relief road that has been built to by-pass Crowthorne and allow a quick link-up between the M4 motorway spur to Bracknell and the M3 at Camberley. This now passes behind Broadmoor and allows a glimpse of it through the heathland nature reserve and the Crown forest land, nestling into the adjacent skyline. Previously this heath and forest land to the south and east was empty countryside whilst the hilltop screen of trees to the north and west hid it from view on the Crowthorne side. "Out of sight; out of mind". Attitudes probably won't change, however. The mystery and awe that the media like to invest in Broadmoor seem likely to persist no matter how much it tries to open itself to public view. Long experience of the steady flow of articles and broadcasts about the place, which have had no perceptible effect on the public image, suggests that human beings best maintain their equanimity and hopefulness in life if they can shut out the worst aspects of themselves and pretend they are not there.

One thing a visitor will notice about Broadmoor's exterior wall is that its top six feet or so are a different shade of red - or were before they mellowed. This is because the height has been changed several times, again reflecting, no doubt, society's changing attitude to Broadmoor, for the changes have not always been upwards. Three feet were added to the original walls, they say, then three more feet; then three feet were taken off before, some years later, being put back on again. One of the Block 6 staff is reputed to have remarked around this time, Block 6 having one of the small semicircular airing courts for patients of particularly unpredictable dangerousness, that patients would soon be taking their exercise at the bottom of a well. A newly arrived patient with a dangerous reputation, being put into the selfsame small airing court, is said to have asked where was the twenty mile vista that the judge had told him Broadmoor enjoyed. "Straight up", said the ever resourceful staff man, looking skywards.

Broadmoor's three storey ward blocks (see sketch plan) are built in pairs with Blocks 3 and 4 in the middle, either side of the central hall and what was the administrative area. With the chapel above the central hall this presented a symmetrical appearance with this central building running along the scarp side of the 'broad moor'. Blocks 1 and 2 were then at right angles to this at the eastern end and Blocks 5 and 6 similarly at right angles at the western end, although the latter had an 'L' shaped extension, parallel to the front exterior wall. Block 7 was added on what remained of the western plateau some fifty years later, beyond Blocks 5 and 6. It was the last to be built and the first to go in the rebuilding. With Blocks 1 and 6 behind their companions they were, as Partridge says, known as the 'back blocks', whilst the remainder were known as 'front blocks'. Blocks 2 and 5 on each end of the terrace opened on to gardens dropping down the hillside but the gardens to Blocks 3 and 4 in the centre could only be reached by crossing the terrace and this meant patients' recreation at specific times, escorted and supervised. The back blocks, with no access to the terrace and gardens, had only their own 'exercise areas', although these were quite large and, despite being asphalted, with some large mature trees, provided quite an agreeable area for recreation.

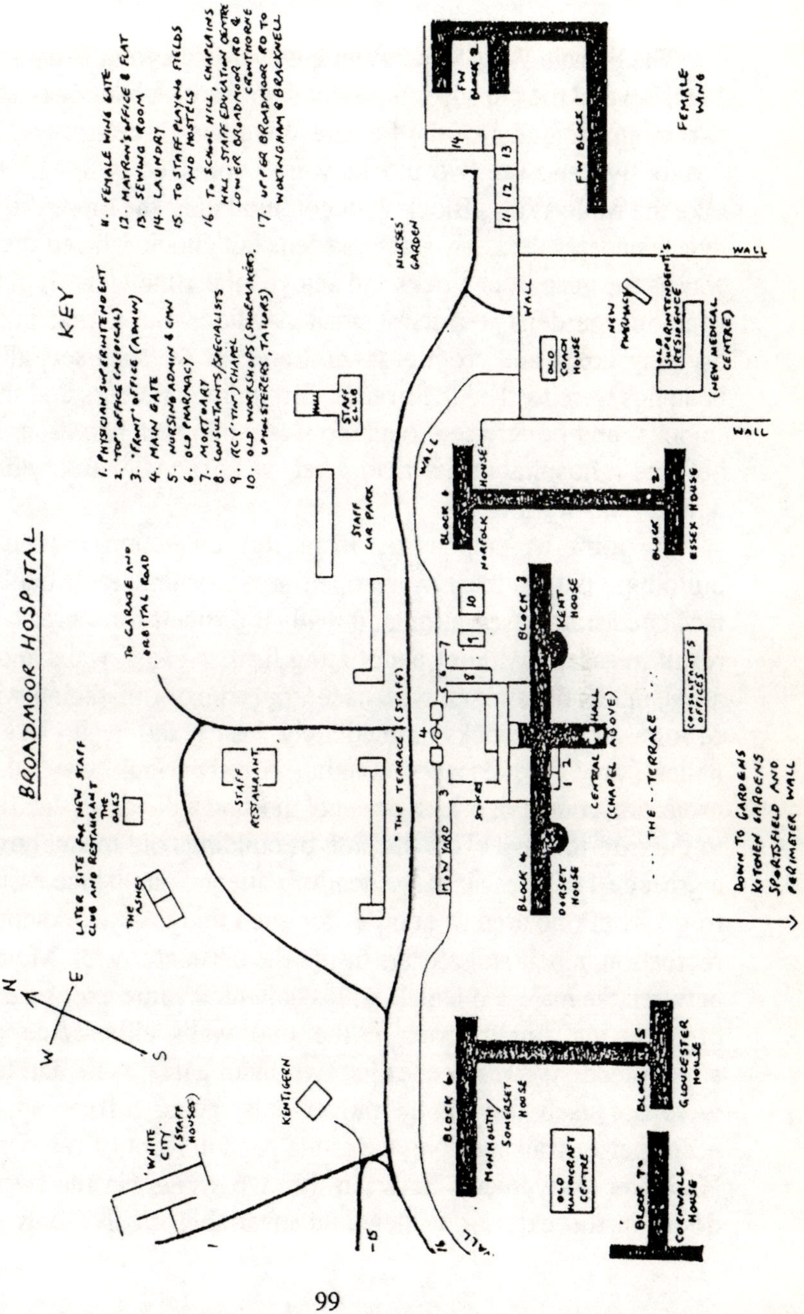

BROADMOOR HOSPITAL
KEY
1. PHYSICIAN SUPERINTENDENT
2. 'TOP' OFFICE (MEDICAL)
3. 'FRONT' OFFICE (ADMIN)
4. MAIN GATE
5. NURSING ADMIN & CNW
6. OLD PHARMACY
7. MORTUARY
8. CONSULTANTS/SPECIALISTS
9. RC ('TIN') CHAPEL
10. OLD WORKSHOPS (SHOEMAKERS, UPHOLSTERERS, TAILORS)
11. FEMALE WING GATE
12. MATRON'S OFFICE & FLAT
13. SEWING ROOM
14. LAUNDRY
15. TO STAFF PLAYING FIELDS AND HOSTELS
16. TO SCHOOL HILL, CHAPLAINS HILL, STAFF EDUCATION CENTRE LOWER BROADMOOR RD & CROWTHORNE
17. UPPER BROADMOOR RD TO WOKINGHAM & BRACKNELL
N
E
W
S
LATER SITE FOR NEW STAFF CLUB AND RESTAURANT
THE OAKS
THE ASHES
TO GARAGE AND ORBITAL ROAD
STAFF RESTAURANT
STAFF CAR PARK
STAFF CLUB
'WHITE CITY' (STAFF HOUSES)
KENTIGERN
NURSES' GARDEN
'THE TERRACE' (STAFF)
MOW YARD
STORES
WALL
BLOCK 6 MONMOUTH/SOMERSET HOUSE
BLOCK 5 GLOUCESTER HOUSE
BLOCK 7 CORNWALL HOUSE
OLD HANDICRAFT CENTRE
BLOCK 4 DORSET HOUSE
CENTRAL HALL (CHAPEL ABOVE)
BLOCK 3 KENT HOUSE
BLOCK 1 NORFOLK HOUSE
BLOCK 2 ESSEX HOUSE
... THE ... TERRACE ...
CONSULTANT'S OFFICES
OLD COACH HOUSE
NEW PHARMACY
OLD SUPERINTENDENT'S RESIDENCE
(NEW MEDICAL CENTRE)
FW BLOCK 1
FW BLOCK 2
FEMALE WING
DOWN TO GARDENS KITCHEN GARDENS SPORTSFIELD AND PERIMETER WALL

The Female Wing was further eastwards, beyond Blocks 1 and 2 and beyond the old superintendent's house which lay between the two wings. Block 1 of the Female Wing had three storeys, Block 2 only two and the two blocks were connected in an 'L' shape. Like the Male Wing, Block 2, accommodating the more disturbed female patients, had only small gardens but Block 1 faced the same way as the male front blocks and enjoyed the same view. It also had spacious gardens, terraces, small pavilions for sitting in and a bowling green and croquet lawn. Later, as we shall see, all these buildings were to shed their rather forbidding numbers and the title 'blocks' and be referred to as 'houses' and given names, as better befitted a hospital rather than what was originally an asylum and later an 'institution'.

A point to emphasize, from this collection of separated buildings, is that there were open areas around each one which facilitated staff observation and made it difficult for a break-out to result in escape without negotiating further gates, walls and open areas, unless the attempt was made from an exterior-facing window of one of the blocks immediately inside the wall. Even this necessitated the escaper making a precarious way along a projecting course of brickwork until meeting a dividing wall that led to the exterior wall. This division of buildings did mean, however, a great deal of open air movement of patients, and hence escorting, to go from one area to another for such things as workshops and recreation, albeit still always inside the perimeter wall. Movement between the male and female wings did entail some exposure to the outside, via small doors in the two walls either side of the superintendent's residence (the two main gates, male and female, were not used for patient movements, being further apart and necessitating walking along the estate road in front of the hospital). However, movements between the two wings via the two small doors in the exterior wall would invariably involve only parole patients, established as being more reliable, and would still be well escorted.

In front of the 'front' blocks the ground dropped steeply and, with dividing walls marking off the area of each block, provided terraced areas that were, in 1959, a mixture of paths and gardens. These were tended by patients, as Partridge describes. Along the top, however, there was the terrace which runs the full width of the 'front' blocks and its lawns were prepared as bowling greens. The 'back' blocks had no gardens but their asphalted areas with trees and seats allowed patients to sit, walk or play games. The other thing to emphasize, once again, is that between each of these buildings and around the various 'airing courts' of the back blocks, large and small, with trees or bare, were inner walls. As with the hospital as a whole, any escape bid would invariably have more than one wall to negotiate; the main peripheral wall was not the only security for the outside world from the patients inside. Moreover, not only were the external and internal doors of each block locked (except Block 2, the parole block, during daytime) but each area was locked off from the next. Even Block 2's parole patients were only able to walk between their block and the next locked door, except that they were able to walk the whole extent of the front terrace and could go out into their own block's garden freely. Other blocks' patients could only do this at prescribed 'exercise' times when staff unlocked the doors, counted them through, and supervised the area.

With the increased height of the walls over the years, the existence of internal walls and locked doors, and the supervision of all internal areas, the risk of a patient climbing the wall was extremely slight. When it happened, as it inevitably and occasionally did, this was usually with the aid of some lapse of vigilance, the leaving of an available ladder or cable, and not as a result of some shortcoming of the wall itself. Later, of course, the now familiar bulging plastic coping was added, making it wellnigh impossible for any gripping device to hold. Partridge mentions several climbings in the pre-1959 era as if this was a simple matter. First one had to get out of one's block and all windows were, of course, barred as well as internal doors locked. After that there would be more locked doors and more walls. The walls were too high to climb without ladders, rope or some similar assistance and these, too, were kept away from patients except, again, under supervision or as a result of some lapse. Climbing one wall would almost always only lead to another to be climbed. To escape over the wall, therefore, a patient would need both assistance and an opportunity when unobserved.

Most escape attempts, therefore, despite being referred to in staff jargon as "going over the wall" tended to be either opportunism, planned by a route other than 'over the wall', or an abuse of a privileged status such as working on an outside party. Even so, the escape rate was exceptionally low and, despite the public view (and that of many judges too) of a hospital, even a secure one, being less secure than a prison, Broadmoor's record is exemplary. In my 27 years, there were no more than some half dozen escapes in all. This astounded many foreign visitors, especially Americans, who sometimes asked what was our annual (or even monthly) escape rate and were then surprised by our explanation that it could not be easily expressed in that way as it would result in a decimal or fraction less than one.

Below the terrace and the 'front' block gardens, where Partridge describes first the kitchen garden area and then the sports field, was the football ground doubling as a cricket field in summer. This must have had one of the largest sightscreens in the country, comprising a length of peripheral wall, painted white. Later some tennis courts were added. Walls and locked gates again separated this area from the rest.

Outside the walls there was the farm. Farms were a common feature of the old asylums and were worked until after the war, providing a means of occupation and exercise for more able patients and, of course, farm supplies of meat and vegetables towards the asylum economy. After the war their use for occupying patients died out as belief in fresh air and exercise as a treatment for mental disorder also died out and was replaced with the plethora of sophisticated medications. Broadmoor's farm was similarly obsolete by the time of the 1959 Act and was rented out to a private farmer who ran it as an independent business. This seemed a pity. Although there were now more sophisticated treatments for mental disorder these were long term patients staying in hospital for an average of 6 or 7 years, often much longer, and the opportunity to spend their days in an active way outside the normal confines of the walls seemed as relevant as the well-developed workshops. Dr McGrath's and Dr Udwin's comment was that there was now little opportunity for farming skills to be used outside Broadmoor. This seemed to miss the point. It was the opportunity to do something that reflected the wider world outside that seemed to be the point: getting used to a daily routine, often for the first time in their lives, in the company of other people, staying reasonably active, and so building upon the effects of their medication. Too many patients, under the effect of their medication, unless they went to work areas, would tend to just sit and doze. I often commented upon the lack of a gym, for instance, and the PT instructors that featured in the life of my previous hospital.

This covers the buildings and land, together with the ground below the ward blocks where the gardens, kitchen gardens and sports fields were located. Behind the frontage looking across the terrace were all the administrative areas which were described in the previous chapter.

Another aspect of the buildings worth observing at this point, however, is that of the area enclosed by them. These days the received wisdom is that special hospitals should be closed down, like their large former psychiatric hospital companions, and be replaced by small local units. There is no doubt that there should be such small local units. In fact, a great many already exist in each NHS region and some regions have several. Probably more are needed but that is another question. The question of size, however, has arguments in favour of both small and large and there is probably a need for both. In the context of the present chapter, it is probably already apparent, even before we have begun to talk about what goes on inside these buildings, that the scope for activity is far greater inside a wall enclosing 40 acres (and with grounds outside extending to several hundred acres more) than it can be inside a small unit. I have referred to gardens and terraces; playing fields and a kitchen garden; recreation areas and workshops; a central hall and chapel; whilst later on there was to be an education centre and a library and greatly improved occupational facilities. At the same time the patient numbers were large enough for teams to be constituted for inter-block competitions and to run a hospital team for competitions in outside leagues (all home matches, of course!). A small unit does not have the numbers for this.

Whatever advantages there are to small units and whatever disadvantages there are to large institutions, the large ones can at least provide their own self-sustaining 'communities' in which to provide their own form of 'community care'. When society understandably expects that it should be protected from its mentally disordered offenders, at least there are alternative 'communities' within which to try to build or rebuild normal social behaviour in such people. The criterion is what one does within these large institutional communities and how one avoids routine declining into neglect. It is this, and the changes that took place in the time of the

1959 Act, that we must examine over the rest of this history.

ACCOMMODATION

The inside of these tall, Victorian buildings comprised long corridors overlooking the hilltop vista. Down one side of the corridors (called galleries in Broadmoor parlance) opened the patients' rooms, their windows unfortunately not enjoying the vista but the drab internal landscape. One supposes that this would have been irrelevant in 1863 (and much of the time in 1963 too) when patients were only in their rooms at night or, if in daytime, only when they were so disturbed as to need seclusion. This latter is arguable, of course: it might have been helpful for a secluded patient to be able to look out at the distant countryside vista. This was the view, however, afforded to patients walking along the galleries or while in the day rooms, which comprised the much greater proportion of their daytime and so presumably was originally intended to give the greater benefit for the greater amount of time.

Accommodation was entirely in single rooms for the patients in the 'back blocks', for security purposes, and for the majority of patients in the parole blocks, 2 and 5, for privilege purposes. The 'in-between' front blocks, as it were, of 3, 4 and 7, had many more patients in dormitories than single rooms. The latter were a privilege for the more reliable patients who tended to be the 'ward workers', some of whom were later accorded parole status, even though not in Blocks 2 or 5. Ward workers did not go out to the occupational centres and, despite their designated name, had many privileges on the block. They were free to come and go around the block when their cleaning, fetching and carrying duties were done, having access to their rooms during the normally closed daytime hours, and would often sit, talk and play cards with the staff for whom they made tea. They looked after the ward kitchen, known as the scullery, from where the meals were served, carrying in the insulated food containers which were brought on trollies (later motorized) from the central kitchens. Meals were served by the staff, who were responsible for checks such as counting of cutlery, but the 'ward cleaners' would clear up after meals and so were then able to enjoy sitting in the warm scullery environment when their job was done.

Apart from the small number of single rooms along the ward galleries, the bulk of the accommodation in these central blocks, 3 and 4, and 7 too, was in dormitories. The 1863 concept was for almost entirely single room accommodation. The dormitories were, therefore, often created from what had been intended as daytime, recreation, rooms and therefore restricted recreational activity within the wards. Not only that but these dormitories had also become very crowded with the increased demand for accommodation. Indeed, there was a short time when beds had to be put in the galleries themselves. Although the hospital population in 1959 had fallen to about 850, it had been over 900 a few years earlier when only intended originally for some 500. By the 60s the spaces between dormitory beds had been reduced to the bare minimum, sufficient for a patient to be able to squeeze himself into and out of bed ('herself' is not relevant here as the overcrowding was confined to the male side). This obviously ruled out any privacy and, worse, aggravated the problems of disturbed patients' outbursts during the night. Dormitories were locked at night, for security, although toilet facilities were available within the dormitory, unlike the single rooms. Even so this was a highly unsatisfactory situation from sanitary, security, clinical and aesthetic standpoints. It was repeatedly reported upon during the inter-acts period, especially when any breach of security arose or an incident occurred between patients as a result of dormitory friction, and was the constant irritant that eventually contributed to the building of a further special hospital (Park Lane) on the Moss Side site and to the recommendations for Regional Secure Units from the 'Butler' Committee (Chapter 15).

Patients in dormitories had little privacy or room to keep personal possessions. The latter were restricted for security purposes, anyway, but at least extended to a drawer or shelf for clothing, reading and writing materials and some keepsakes. Even these were withdrawn from the patients in single rooms in the 'back blocks', whose isolation was necessary for their own and others' safety, so that their rooms were restricted to the basic minimum for sleeping, toilet purposes and a drink of water. However, in contrast with patients who were secluded for their and others' safety, who might have their mattress on the floor and be in canvass bedding and clothing, as described earlier, other patients in Blocks 1 and 6 would normally at least have a proper bedstead, normal bedding and bedclothes and probably a paperback book, newspapers and magazines, in addition to the basic mug of water and a pot. As progress was achieved through the hospital to other blocks and when this had reached the point of moving from a dormitory to a single room, more personal effects were allowed: storage for more clothing, a table to write at with writing materials, books, pictures and probably a radio or record player. Later these became quite sophisticated with advancing technology, to include tape recorders and TV sets and it was arranged for these to plug into a socket rather than be solely dependent upon batteries. Even in the 60s, however, there was a reasonable range of personal belongings allowed for the single room patient all over the hospital up to the level of the long stay parole patient whose room would be the equivalent of a university student's bedsit. Patients exercised their own choice of a rug, bedspread, and pictures on the walls. Some of the women patients' rooms became highly admired works of art. This minority of patients, however, contrasted with the majority who lived in cramped conditions which restricted the amount of personal possessions they were able to enjoy.

Amongst this distribution of patients' rooms, dormitories, toilets, day rooms, store rooms, scullery and dining room, there were staff rooms on each floor and a ward office adjacent to the entrance. Staff rooms, where staff took their breaks and ate their meals (which would be taken in turn during the shift), also stored their personal effects. The ward office was that of the CN or sister, whilst on the ground floor there would be an office for the DN or DS who organized his or her duty rotas for the whole house and from which liaison took place with both staff and patients.

The day room, or rooms, for there were usually more than one, even with the number given over to dormitories, would comprise a collection of easy chairs, some card tables and upright chairs, cupboards of books and invariably a small snooker table. The degree of sophistication varied with the level of security of the ward - the back blocks being inevitably more spartan - and the function of the room. Where there were several in a ward, different activities would go on in each. The female wing's wards were inevitably more homely and decorated. In the early days of TV there was only one set in each ward and a collective decision had to be taken on the channels selected during an evening's viewing. The parole blocks, however, permitting free movement between the three separate wards, had separate day rooms allotted for the, then, two channels. By the time more channels had come on stream there was also a greater distribution of personal sets so that choice on the dayroom set became less of a battle. Even so, the day rooms were sufficiently large that viewing was mostly confined to one end, so enabling other activities to proceed in other parts of the rooms. Chess and bridge were popular pastimes, as described by Peter

Thompson in his account of a patient's life. Later, musical and artistic pastimes extended from the formal activities of the handicrafts and OT centres to the wards themselves and rooms were created, usually from former small dormitories, for patients to practise, say, their guitars (a popular growth activity following the rise of the Beatles) or for drawing and painting (paints had to be carefully vetted to ensure they contained no poisonous element).

SECURITY

As discussed in the previous chapter, ensuring security was part and parcel of the nurse's role; an inevitable result as well as requirement of getting to know one's patients and catering for their needs. Nevertheless, this dual role would not be possible without a secure perimeter and secure buildings within it. Close nursing observation and knowledge of the risks any one patient presented was achieved according to the degree of environmental security within which a particular patient was situated. The security requirements of every area had to be understood and observed by every member of staff. Some years later a specific appointment of a 'Security Officer' was made, at nursing officer level, and an induction course for new staff instituted. This has become legendary with its culmination in a demonstration of the collection of macabre memorabilia looked after by the security officer, including weapons and keys fabricated by patients out of cutlery and pieces of tin cans, wood, stones, ball-pens and whatever could be purloined when unnoticed. Dr McGrath told of interviewing a patient one day, early in his superintendency, when he expressed scepticism about the feasibility of escaping, whereupon the patient took out of his mouth, hidden in his cheek, several pieces of metal and a sardine tin key which he then assembled into a key which unlocked the ward door! Memory fades where the outcome of this story is concerned, except that the patient was persuaded to hand over the handmade key and security was thereafter tightened. Patients were well known to be able to memorize the shape of a key from repeated observation of a nurse's use of one and did not need surreptitiously to take an impression, although this, too, had happened.

Most doors had provision for double locking, either at night or for certain doors at all times. Until the arrival of the modern Chubb key now familiar to all watchers of TV prison soaps and newsreel reports and which afforded a double turn facility, certain staff had to carry two keys: one for the normal lock and the other for the, second, 'top' lock, used at night or for special security doors. Furthermore, in 1959, different doors were of different levels of security categorization: the basic M1 or F1 key was for the male and female ward doors. The M2 and F2 were the charge nurse's and sister's keys giving further access to medicine cupboards, whilst M3 and F3 were the Departmental Nurses' keys and M4 and F4 the doctors'. M5 and F5 were the select privilege of the physician superintendent, whose office needed the M5, the chief male nurse and matron, and the steward and clerk of accounts. Each key also opened all doors opened by a key of a lesser number. If a sister or charge nurse had to leave their post for any reason, such as lunch break on a full day shift (which in those days occurred twice in every shift cycle sandwiched between two afternoon shifts and two morning shifts) the senior staff nurse on the ward would 'act-up' and the two would exchange their bunch of keys for that period.

All internal ward doors, for example of patients' rooms, opened outwards. This was a cause of some argument, there being those who held that this made it easier for a patient to burst it open into the face of the person opening it. The reason, however, was the more important one that it prevented the patient from barricading it from within using, say, a bed to prevent it being opened. Rooms in the 'refractory blocks' had their beds secured to the floor and their doors also had the extra security of bolts top and bottom to prevent them being burst open. Even so, the occasional exceptionally strong patient managed to do so, whereupon a carpenter from the MoW yard would be promptly called to repair the damage. There was a small glazed spy hole at eye level to observe the patient inside as well as another lower down for shining in a torch at night (see diagram). This was in addition to the long vertical slit in the adjacent wall, covered with a lockable narrow glazed door, no more than six inches wide, through which conversation with the patient could take place, and medicines and some limited food could be passed without requiring the main door to be opened. As the latter could only be done, when a room was occupied by a high security or 'secluded' patient, with a minimum of two staff present (which would always be the case when the meals or medication trolley was being taken round for patients who were not 'up and in association'), the slit window beside the door was essential for unaccompanied staff to observe or speak to a patient or to hear what a patient might want. This was especially important at night when most wards, except in the 'back blocks', had only one member of staff on duty. Dormitories and individual rooms were then, of course, locked. If some incident required the opening of the door to a patient's room then the nurse on duty would have to phone the night superintendent for a second nurse to attend.

DOOR TO PATIENT'S ROOM

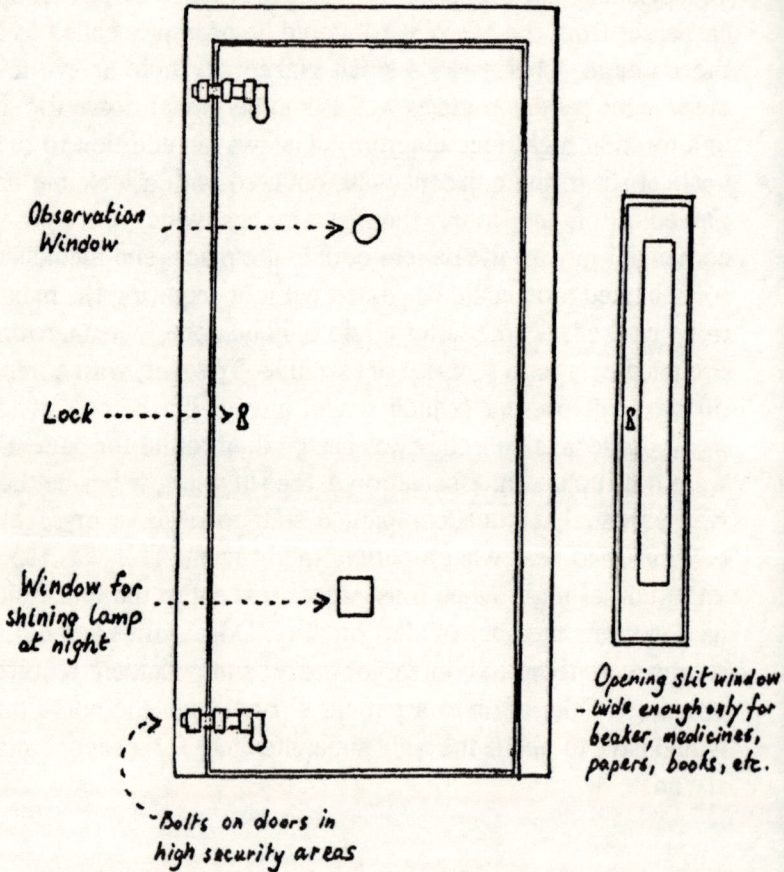

Observation
Window

Lock

Window for
shining lamp
at night

Bolts on doors in
high security areas

Opening slit window
- wide enough only for
beaker, medicines,
papers, books, etc.

There were no interview rooms on the wards in 1959. Doctors saw patients in the charge nurse's office, nursing staff always also being present anyway. The two consultants had consulting rooms in a small corridor near the main gate to which patients would be brought by an escort. A third such room was used as a clinic for visiting specialists and became the psychologist's room. I had to arrange to be elsewhere in the hospital when a specialist visited. The parole block - Block 2 - had a small library and a writing room and the Female Wing Block 1 also had several small sitting rooms, some with shelves of books, and from amongst these there could usually be found an empty space to interview or assess a patient when required. Later, and especially with the reduction in patient numbers, all wards had interview rooms where specialist staff could see patients. The point about these rooms so far as security was concerned, however, was that all the access doors had windows allowing the staff to see in, although not hearing what was being discussed. There would always be someone assigned to duty 'on the gallery' who would look in at random intervals.

In this way both security and confidentiality were achieved at the same time. A simple but invariable rule, however, was that the patient always sat nearest to the door, across the table from the interviewer. This not only meant that the patient was not distracted by anyone looking in or passing by and the specialist could see and respond to such a person but that the all-important principle could be observed of the patient being immediately accessible in the event of an 'incident', unobstructed by the interviewer.

When a room was specifically allocated for interviewing new patients in the eventual admission ward it was fitted with a button under the interviewer's side of the table which could sound an alarm in the ward office to alert staff of any sudden incident. I never once had any occasion to put this procedure into use. Most patients, even the most disturbed, saw a session with specialist staff as an important event, especially as it did not happen often, and were too concerned to get across whatever might be preoccupying them, or to comply with whatever seemed to be required. Even the antagonistic patients would usually control their hostility and scepticism when interviewed by specialist staff, such was their awareness of the uniqueness of a hospital order whereby discharge depended upon their being regarded as having recovered from whatever disorder had brought about their initial admission. They might react afterwards, to the ward staff, which was always useful to discover, but rarely to the specialist staff who saw them only on special occasions and in whose reports so much importance was vested where their futures were concerned. Of course, in a treatment context, the session might include some strategy that was deliberately intended to provoke, when an outburst was more likely, but my own patient contacts were for many years confined to assessment purposes and, later, my treatment work was carried out in a group context or with other staff involved.

Nowadays, security observation has the benefit of modern technology and the universally available video camera. After a visit to the USA Dr McGrath returned having observed widespread use of these and was opposed to their introduction in Broadmoor. He shunned anything having a prison aura. He also observed alarms triggered by movement which he and his consultant colleagues also rejected at Broadmoor. The fear was that technical unreliability might mean too many false alarms: a bird might perch on the wall and set it off. Broadmoor had a rich variety of bird visitors. Most numerous were the pigeons, constantly bobbing and pecking, and the jackdaws with their upright walk, grey and black plumage and piercing eyes. These, therefore, were often referred to as the reincarnations of past patients and staff, forever re-enacting the roles of their former lives.

Common security provisions so far as the old mental hospitals around the country were concerned, included strait jackets and padded rooms. These were used to control the very unpredictably violent patients, prone to outbursts destructive to themselves or others. They were, of course, also held to be a mark of an earlier, primitive, age. Dr McGrath always proudly told visitors that neither of these had ever featured in Broadmoor. Opinion might hold that this was unkind and that damage might have been avoided if they had been in use. Dr McGrath's view, however, was that such destructive behaviour should be avoided by full clinical knowledge of the patient, so that alternative strategies could be used that were not restrictive. Of course, with the immense strides in pharmacological treatments that marked this post-war era, the incidence of sudden violent outbursts was greatly reduced but it was of considerable interest that, even in Broadmoor's early days, no provision was made for these common features of asylum life.

Strong bedding, however, was used as a security provision for the very destructively disturbed patients. It was the only way to enable such patients to occupy and sleep in their rooms without constant attention. These were patients who, despite modern medication and every available nursing attention, would still tear up normal bedding and night attire, possibly using these to strangle themselves. They would, therefore, be in a room without anything other than basic essentials, to avoid them using anything with which they might damage themselves. These basics would comprise a plastic mug of water and a plastic chamber pot (rooms did not have built-in toilet facilities in those days). There would be no bed, the mattress, for safety, being on the floor. This was covered with stout canvass and the sheets and night gown, too, were of canvass. Observation of these special and fortunately few patients had to be recorded at regular and frequent intervals.

ESCAPES

Despite all the safeguards of buildings and security procedures, and the low incidence that surprises official visitors, escapes still happened, of course. Dr Hopwood's otherwise successful and forward-looking superintendency was sadly not to end without being marked by the tragic escape of John Straffen in April 1952, the year of Dr Hopwood's retirement. Partridge's book, published a year later, refers to this escape in the concluding chapter where he points out that this is the first escape in what was then ninety years of Broadmoor's existence to have resulted in a further killing. Straffen had been in Broadmoor for less than a year when he escaped, having been found 'insane on arraignment' and committed for the murders of two little girls. Another little girl was killed in the short time he was at large, a terrible tragedy for her and her family, the village neighbourhood which was not far from Broadmoor and, of course, Broadmoor itself. Nearly thirty years were to elapse before another escape was to occur entailing a fatality, this time in another country which the patient had managed to reach, and not until a year later when he shot a policeman who was about to apprehend him. This patient had used his parole status to acquire the means to scale the wall and to do so when the area of wall was unobserved, and he had arranged help from outside to get well away from the hospital quickly. Ironically, 1981, the year of this next fatal escape, was the year of Dr Patrick McGrath's retirement, the man who, after Dr Hopwood, had done so much to advance the hospital and the life and prospects of its patients.

In the thirty years between these two escapes the escape total barely reached double figures. This would have produced a figure of about 0.3 per annum for the inquiring Americans. There were, of course, a great many attempts with varying degrees of purposefulness, but they still had to be officially logged, even though they might actually have been a quite hopeless dash for an open gate or door, or the feeble assembling of bits and pieces of string, torn clothing and other bric-a-brac intended to achieve the climbing of the wall or the making of a key. Many attempts merely indicated the degree of mental disorder of the perpetrator. Even the more realistic ones, products of more orderly minds, would have had little chance of actual success. A few, of course, would always succeed. Anthony Barber, when Minister of Health, was paying the traditional visit of a new government minister when, on seeing a large laundry basket in one of the corridors on his tour, remarked to Dr McGrath accompanying him that this was the way he had escaped from a prisoner-of-war camp. "Not so loud", urged Pat McGrath, "you'll give the patients ideas!"

Of the escapes that reached the outside world in the 'inter-acts' period, all ended in recapture, some very quickly, and none resulted in the tragedies that followed the escapes of John Straffen and Alan Reeve (his name, too, can now be mentioned, not least because he published an autobiographical book which included the events of his escape and life in Amsterdam afterwards). The first was quite soon after my arrival, on New Year's Day 1960 (not a holiday in those days). This was of a man on an outside working party who was discovered, but embarrassingly not for several days, hiding in the loft of the chaplain's garage. The embarrassment was that this should have been searched and he found much earlier. Another escape involved a very small man who managed to squeeze between the bars of a gate. He was also found in a few days. Another man took a run at the heap of coal piled up against the wall which enabled him to grasp the coping and heave himself over. His time out was numbered, not in days or even hours, but minutes. The hospital escape siren is tested for five minutes every Monday morning at 10, so it was inevitable that someone would eventually attempt an escape at that time. One woman patient successfully

117

scaled the female wing wall in this 'interacts' period but broke an ankle in dropping down outside so that she was not able to make any great distance before being discovered and brought back. Another man who absconded from an outside working party had done so on being distressed about news from home but his state of mind prevented him from making any significant progress and he was eventually found wandering in the Forestry Commission's woodlands only a mile or two away from the hospital. This is probably an example of a situation that should have been anticipated had it not occurred after routine monitoring of mail had ceased. Thereafter only certain patients, who were known to be plotters or nuisance writers, would have had their mail scrutinized. Thus the event was missed.

The escape siren was situated on the hospital scarp, on the far side of the staff sports field. It gave out an intermittent warning signal and a continuous all clear, but quite unlike the wartime air raid sirens. As the neighbourhood grew and residential estates sprang up in the areas between Crowthorne and Bracknell, Wokingham and Camberley, more 'satellite' sirens were established to meet the requests of local people who were told to stay indoors; not to answer the door to strangers; report any suspicious incidents; and to fetch their children home from local schools. School staff were instructed to keep and look after any children until collected. An escaping patient would know that there was a great deal of forestry land in the vicinity and that he or she should stay hidden among the trees for as far as possible. However, roads had to be crossed eventually and so escape search procedures always involved posting a group of police, always with a member of staff who could recognize the patient, at key junctions and intersections. Traffic was stopped and vehicle occupants informed and questioned.

The staff club became the escape co-ordination centre where

the Thames Valley Police would set up their headquarters. All off-duty staff were expected to report to the staff club for search duty on hearing the siren. Later a well-oiled procedure was perfected enabling descriptions and photographs to be available, and these were sent out to all the check points, but on that first escape after my arrival I remember that, being very new and not familiar with what was expected of me, and since I was able to type, I spent the initial hours typing out descriptions of the escaper. This was before photocopiers. Also later, there was a system devised whereby there was always a duty consultant and a duty senior member of the administrative staff readily contactable (the chief male nurse's office was always staffed, of course, if not by himself then by one of his deputies or, at night, the night superintendent). The next escape after the New Year's Day one in 1960 must have been in the summer of 1961, for my family and I had not long moved out of the rented hospital house and into one we had bought in the village and we were having a housewarming party. The 'phone rang. It was the hospital main gate switchboard asking for Dr McGrath whose response immediately told the story: an escape. That was the end of the party.

Before this 'inter-acts' period but sufficiently recent in 1959 to be much talked about at the time of my arrival, was the escape of Frank Mitchell, who can again be named because his escape and subsequent career was widely reported. Mitchell was reputed to have been a member of one of the well-known East End gangs. However, it is commonly said that such gangs reject any member who gets sent to a mental hospital rather than a prison: a 'nutter' may do something unpredictable and therefore cannot be relied upon. Mitchell was recaptured but, on the inevitable trial that follows any escape, he was sent instead to prison, in this case Dartmoor. However, he managed later to escape from there, too, whereupon he was never heard of again. The explanation that went around was that, despite Dartmoor, his Broadmoor 'nutter' status remained and, therefore, he had been 'eliminated'. The M4 Chiswick flyover was in course of construction at the time, so he was confidently said to be encased in one of the pillars. It must be apocryphal. Surely modern scanning procedures would be able to reveal if this were so. But that would spoil the story. Mitchell was a man of a very well developed physique which he cultivated while in Broadmoor. Jack Wilkinson, the staff nurse first attached to my department, had been one of the staff of the block where Mitchell resided. Jack would open up in the morning and, on reaching Mitchell's room, would find him stretching and flexing his muscles in the open doorway. Mitchell always gave him a friendly welcome and boasted of his intention to get out of Broadmoor but added: "Don't worry, Mr Wilkinson, I won't do it when you are on duty; I wouldn't embarrass anyone who has treated me right." He didn't. He escaped the day after Jack was posted to another block. He had managed gradually to loosen a window bar which he removed at the opportune time, accomplishing quite a physical feat from the second floor to manoeuvre himself along ledges and pipes, and then several intersecting walls, to reach the outside.

Despite the rarity of escapes, the siren was heard frequently, every week in fact, when it was tested. This took place at 10 am on Mondays, as mentioned above, and happened week in, week out, even on bank holidays and when Christmas Day fell on a Monday. It would be sounded for three or four minutes, then would change to the all clear signal for a similar period. The testing was necessary, of course, to ensure that all the various satellite sirens that were spread over the surrounding countryside, more of them as the local townships and residential estates expanded, were adequately heard and were not faulty. Nevertheless, it left no one in any doubt of what lay in the midst of what has now become a very desirable residential neighbourhood. So much so that I once suggested that the testing day should not be a Monday; in fact any weekday but Monday. It seemed to me to be an unnecessary infliction upon local people's feelings to have the siren sounding on every bank holiday when people were at home and in their gardens; it could at least be restricted to what were usual working days. The suggestion, however, was peremptorily rejected. Yet I couldn't see that it mattered which day the testing took place and it would have been a nice little gesture of neighbourliness.

INTERNAL ESCAPADES

The buildings not only presented a challenge to get out of but a challenge inside for climbing. Several rooftop incidents occurred in the 'interacts' era, usually as a form of protest against continued detention in Broadmoor or the failure of an appeal, and especially as the introduction of the psychopathic disorder category brought in more active, young, antisocial people.

As described later in Chapter 15, the late 60s and early 70s was the era of social protest movements. A group of patients adopted this philosophy and a rooftop escapade was an ideal way to both demonstrate physical prowess and protest against what they felt was Broadmoor's unfair and repressive regime. The book published much later in 1983, by Alan Reeve after his escape in 1981, clearly illustrates this outlook.

Some of the roof climbing incidents did considerable damage to the roof, slates being torn off and thrown down. Some lasted for several days, with food and water being passed up during the altercations and negotiations by the consultants in their strategy for dealing with what was obviously seen as a manifestation of their psychiatric disorder.

A particularly sad rooftop incident involved a young woman

patient who climbed on to the roof of the female wing. She was one of the more notorious self-mutilators. She would often ask for a course of ECT, although this was not the treatment indicated by her psychopathic condition, even though it was complicated with anxiety and tension. Her reason for wanting ECT, however, was the buzz she got after being given the pre-ECT muscle relaxant medication. (Self-mutilation has more recently been recognized as another way of obtaining a buzz, especially in deprived or negative surroundings, lacking stimulation.) Her rooftop escapade, however, ended in tragedy. She had injured herself quite severely and was losing blood until she eventually lost consciousness and fell, suffering injuries from which, sadly, she died. She had been an intelligent and lively young woman with a great deal about her that had endeared her to the staff and other patients.

SUMMARY

Its buildings, then, tell a great deal about Broadmoor, embracing the activities within: providing sanctuary, protection, replenishment and order to some; activity, opportunity and challenge to many; but an unacceptable and repressive restriction to others.

This chapter has examined, therefore, how these buildings have been designed and used specifically to incorporate all these activities although inevitably irking many of the residents. The likelihood is that it will not have been the buildings, however, that were irksome but what they stood for and the inevitable restrictions upon movement that their locked rooms and barred windows imposed.

Within these inevitable restrictions the size of the whole campus and the internal design and layout were nevertheless intended to enable a great variety of activity to take place, in accordance with the Victorian principles of 'fresh air and useful pursuits'. The occupations, pastimes and recreations of the 20th century were thereby also afforded scope, enabling as far as possible the hospital to function as a community, as the next chapter describes. It would be the smaller rooms to provide opportunity for individual and small group therapy discussions that would prove to be lacking at the end of the 20th century, together with offices and workrooms for the large increase in specialist staff and their equipment. These were only provided, initially, by using what had been patients' rooms, thereby temporarily reducing patient accommodation.

This chapter has also outlined the security procedures which operated within the primary security of the 'bricks-and-mortar' and referred to some of the escapades to which these inevitable restrictions gave rise. These reflect the changing times as well as illustrating some of the problems of the patients for which Broadmoor caters.

Next we must start to examine what went on inside the buildings and how that changed after the 1959 Act. Was this, and can this be, a therapeutic community?

CHAPTER 7

A THERAPEUTIC COMMUNITY?

'Treatment at Broadmoor is being there'. This has been a common introduction to countless talks on Broadmoor by generations of staff. It is, of course, both partly true and partly misleading. It was more often true than not in days gone by, although the extent of its effectiveness was not always realized, especially as modern medical treatment took over from the essentially social rehabilitation of the old days. It is still true as a groundwork or an ingredient to the more sophisticated and especially individualized treatments that have developed in recent times.

From the comments in the previous chapter about the land and buildings being large and extensive enough to constitute a 'community' within which a great deal can be devised and arranged to the benefit of those who live there, it follows that the Broadmoor community can likewise achieve a structure and functioning for itself to meet the requirements of its residents. This is what all communities do when they adopt rules and devise a system with which to order their lives. The variations in national laws, constitutions and practices throughout the world illustrate the variety of different perceptions and developments of the human species in this respect.

Broadmoor, of course, is not a democracy. Even though a great many of its activities are chosen, devised, organized and carried through by its residents - the patients - their arrival and departure are not theirs to choose, nor is a great deal of the daily routine in between. Neither, of course, is the life of a patient chosen by him or her when detained under a 'section' in a local psychiatric hospital. Even the 'informal' (voluntary) patient, who can choose to come or go as and when s/he pleases and whether or not s/he accepts the treatment offered, is not altogether free. There are, in effect, contracts. These may be entered into with varying degrees of willingness but, once done, the sequel is a chain of events one must accept at each juncture or else leave the contract and risk jeopardizing one's progress. Nevertheless, the informal psychiatric patient has greater freedom than a child, who must accept what its parent or teacher decides; no contract here. A good example, this, for there are those who argue that children should have the benefit of such contracts just as there are those who argue that no psychiatric patient should be forced into treatment s/he has not chosen.

Anyway, it is not the purpose of this history to take a position on the issue, whether or not its author holds one. Its purpose is to describe what happened at Broadmoor and, by analogy and comparison, to illustrate the problems it faced. Its campus is large, comparable with a school, factory, business headquarters or barracks, all of which create their own 'mini-environments', cultural ethos and ways of life, with their inevitably varying degrees of freedom and requirements for compliance. Within its remit of containing several hundred people who have behaved violently whilst suffering from what was accepted at the time as a mental disorder, so that they were not held fully responsible for their actions, it affords as much freedom of choice to its residents as it can. This may change over time and, as told by Partridge, has done. It changed again between the 1959 and 1983 Mental Health Acts. The justification for the restriction of freedom is not knowing whether someone who has behaved violently will do so again.

The case histories of many Broadmoor patients, as with other special hospitals and, indeed, the people who pass through our criminal justice system generally, are replete with abuse, brutality, crisis, deprivation, exploitation, fear, greed, humiliation, injury, molestation, neglect, pain, persecution and so on through the alphabet. "We all have to cope with these things" say many people. Indeed we do. But some of us are better equipped to do so than others or don't have them inflicted on us so severely or totally. We are all different. We may be born better equipped to cope or we may have been brought up in a way that better enables us to cope; probably both.

There are, of course, people who have apparently been born and brought up normally and who unaccountably develop some physical or mental disorder which impairs or distorts their judgement and behaviour. I recall having a man referred to me at my previous hospital who was suffering a severe neurosis but who presented none of the underlying personality characteristics or family background features that would be expected in such a neurosis. But what he had experienced was a mining disaster where he was trapped underground and lost a number of friends and workmates. He had reacted normally to an extreme situation. Nowadays we recognize this in providing support and counselling for the victims of disasters - road accidents, air crashes, etc. We are even looking back to the first world war and re-examining what happened to 'shell-shock' victims who are now often recognized as cases of PTSD (post-traumatic stress disorder). The man who experienced a mining tragedy was too early for such automatic recognition and was too stoical to seek it. Only when its disruption of his life and his inability to keep going fortunately brought him to where the problem was finally recognized did he receive the treatment that helped him to cope again. Not all who suffer from a mental disorder which results in outwardly destructive or self-disabling behaviour readily reveal twists and turns to their previous lives which can be held to account for this. Fortunately, it is not always vital to probe their lives to unearth such influences, although it almost always helps. Medication can do a great deal; and psychotherapy, to promote confidence and new life strategies, may do the rest. Nevertheless, if it can be discovered, there is invariably an explanation in early experiences, or in congenital variations of neurological functioning, or both, that accounts for the way a mental disorder manifests itself.

Not all Broadmoor patients will slot neatly into any single one of these categories as the earlier chapters will have illustrated. All will have been categorized as suffering from a mental disorder, as defined in the Mental Health Act, but will demonstrate a variety of symptoms, underlying personalities and environmental circumstances. A large number, however, whatever their legal or psychiatric classification, turn out to have a chaotic, catastrophic and disintegrated life history. 'Being there' provides a number of palliatives, reassurances and encouragements that many patients need, whatever else they need in the way of medicine or other therapy. Above all it provides, or should provide, an ordered, fair and consistent life, the like of which many have lacked hitherto. A daily routine; warm bed; regular meals; the means to keep clean; companionship and the 'parental substitute' emotional support, advice and discipline of the staff, can all provide something that has been inconsistent or lacking in the lives of many Broadmoor patients. Until one reads or listens at case conferences to the catalogue of woe that characterizes the lives of many of these, one can easily underestimate the significance of this new experience. The fair and consistent discipline that characterizes the approach of most of the staff is new to many patients and gradually introduces them to a way of life that they have not met before but which most of them gradually appreciate is basic to a successful, satisfying, enjoyable, trouble-free and, above all, self-controllable life. The introduction new patients receive on the ward often includes the comment that this is 'day one' of the rest of their lives and their past record is not going to determine the way they are treated: they are now starting again with a clean sheet and will be treated according to the way they behave from now on, not according to their record.

'Pull the other one' some will say to this idea of Broadmoor as a form of environmental or 'community' treatment and, indeed, the role of the hospital must not be overplayed. At the same time, however, and especially in the context of the changes we encounter as the effect of the 1959 Act is felt, it would be a serious omission to ignore it. In any case, it is there, whatever else is on the treatment menu, and its effect must be taken into account. There is no such thing as a 'neutral environment'. Everything and everywhere exert an influence. 'Doing nothing' can be harmful. When prisons are referred to as 'universities of crime' it is worth contrasting this with the concept of a 'university of living' which, within its obvious limitations, is what Broadmoor effectively is. This is also in contrast with other psychiatric hospitals which function on a time-scale nowadays of being places of 'time-out-for-treatment' rather than a 'way of life', even though it is often a change in way of life, or the acquiring of a hitherto lacking way of life, that is what many psychiatric patients really need. Enabling someone to change their way of life, or develop a new emotional view of it, so that conflicts and disasters are eliminated or avoided instead of always tripping them up, is much more the approach of modern psychiatric settings, with or without the help of medication to ease the process.

This is still not fully apparent or made fully explicit, however. The process is carried on within the medical setting of a hospital or clinic where the notion persists of an 'affliction or illness' which can be treated and removed in the same way that a general hospital or a GP treats an infection, repairs damage or removes something harmful or diseased. The problem is seen as within one's body but somehow 'outside' one's 'self'. With psychiatric problems, except for the minority arising from physical illness or injury, the problem *is* oneself.

This is not to infer that mental functioning arises from non-physical events. We are not invoking here the spiritual or the paranormal. As discussed earlier in Chapter 5, when describing the domain of psychological practice in contrast with medical, we are dealing with the 'process': the perceptions, awareness, information, knowledge, emotions, meaning, skills, attitudes, drives and habits, and the interpretations of these with experience. All these go to differentiate one individual from another and mark out his or her distinct personality. They are still material events, but in the form of stored and transmitted physiological data akin to the stored and transmitted digital, magnetic or chemical data of the computer, cassette or film. They are processes; and stand in contrast with the skeleton, musculature, heart and blood vessels, brain and nervous system, which are vehicles for processes. Some of these can give rise to similar symptoms when they go wrong just as a faulty replay mechanism or a blank tape may give rise to symptoms similar to a programming fault. And as neurological and physiological research progresses, more abnormalities can be traced to such sources. Experienced practitioners are needed to tell the difference, just as experienced engineers will do so for technical equipment. Just so long as both possibilities are recognized and scrutinized for solutions, we shall stand a chance of finding answers and explanations. To restrict the search to only one domain is to handicap the endeavour before it has begun.

Personal 'programmes' are acquired over a lifetime as a result of innate and acquired characteristics interacting with environmental experiences. They are the codes and images stored on the human equivalent of the computer disk, the cassette or the film, and referred to in Chapter 5. It seems likely to be these processes that are awry when we are confronting personality and neurotic disorders - of which psychopathic disorder may be thought of as one instance - and which have over the centuries caused agonies of argument as to the degree to which they disable the 'mind' and may be held to 'diminish' responsibility. Increasingly they appear amongst Broadmoor patients after 1959 because the new Act's concept of Mental Illness has been interpreted to allow them to; because it has also explicitly introduced the classification of Psychopathic Disorder, and because case histories demonstrate with monotonous regularity the chaotic 'programming' of life that has given rise to them.

What of the 'psychotic' mental disorders then? There are increasingly those today who hold that these, too, are totally or largely a matter of acquired 'malprogramming' of the human system. Majority professional opinion so far, however, tends to prefer some kind of more physical (i.e.: 'hardware') explanation but probably of a metabolic or neurological kind. That is to say that explanations are thought more likely to be found in what is travelling around our bodies in our bloodstreams or nervous systems or is functioning differently in some part of our brains. Odd constituents or conditions of these have not yet, however, been consistently demonstrated except in a minority of 'organic' states where damage or infection is known to have altered some aspect of brain, nervous system or metabolic functioning. This still leaves the bulk of the psychotic disorders without clear explanation except by analogy. We know that medication can help alleviate the effects of many of these so the 'hardware' basis for them may eventually emerge. Alternatively, it may be that a medicine is merely facilitating a better flow of the 'software process' or removes some hindrance to it. It is just as likely, therefore, that some 'software' approach to treatment will be needed instead of, or in addition to, whatever medicine or surgery can provide. After all, absence, loss, or damage of a limb, organ or faculty, as in deafness, blindness, paraplegia or amputation - all quite clearly 'hardware' faults - nevertheless require 'software' solutions in the form of rehabilitation and retraining of alternative skills to enable the individual to cope with life as normally and self-supportingly as possible.

Whatever the explanations which eventually emerge for the mental disorders defined within the Mental Health Act, it is likely that a 'software' programme will continue to be required, at least for the forseeable future, in addition to whatever 'hardware' solution is forthcoming. Why stress what now seems obvious then? Because in the recent history of mental disorder and in this 'Inter-Acts' period especially, it doesn't seem to have been obvious. Even now, people still talk of mental disorder in terms of 'curing a disease or illness' and look to a medicine to do it, instead of the more basic requirement of wiping the mental tapes clean and putting in a new programme. This requires, not medicine, even though medicine might help and might eventually provide a means of doing the job better. Essentially, however and at present, it requires the disentangling and understanding of the emotional turmoil arising from unsuccessful life strategies and the developing and practising of new skills and strategies for dealing with what life presents. Sometimes it also requires the elimination of inappropriate, inefficient or harmful ways of dealing with those situations. If someone has never learned how to cope with something, it is usually simpler to start from scratch than if one first has to eliminate bad habits. Anyone struggling to learn a skill at a sport or musical instrument, say, knows this. A lot of hard practice is required to do well and it is harder if one has to eliminate bad habits first.

Emphasizing all this is only to add a corrective to longstanding thinking on the subject and to enable us to recall what might have had therapeutic value in the 'social rehabilitation' ethos that typified Broadmoor and our other Victorian asylums before the 1959 legislation arrived. The 1959 Act was, indeed, a piece of revolutionary legislation which brought much needed current medical knowledge and wisdom to the aid of the inmates of our asylums. Medical advances were what characterized the post-war era. Now that we have undergone the 'Information Revolution' and are into the 'Information Era', we can envisage the processes that define the behaviour of human beings because of the example of the complex equipment we nowadays use. As a result we can view the 1959 Act as having progressed services by means of a 'knight's move': one step forward and two sideways. It helped considerably but at the same time it moved our thinking off at a tangent and into something of a cul-de-sac. If the developments described in this book seem to be along predominantly psychological ('software') rather than medical ('hardware') lines then, of course, the writer would say that, wouldn't he? He is a psychologist. But also it is because that is where the quantum leap of progress was made and from where so much of the new thinking came, as the publications demonstrate during this 'Inter-Acts' period.

Returning to the practicalities of running Broadmoor and the 'way of life' represented by the organization and activities of the hospital community, of course there are inconsistencies in this way of life, there always are. It does not work faultlessly. Not everyone operates an appropriate system or operates it appropriately all the time. It was always so, everywhere. Experience of all life's 'institutions' tells you this: school, university, industry, business, the armed forces: all have their flaws and their bad apples. They also have their erroneous assumptions and practices. Sometimes these erupt into something which requires corrective action but, contrary to what the media would have us believe, this is seldom as often or as severe as they like to make out: the insatiable appetites of the newsrooms demand constant feeding and, if starved, will manufacture or magnify events to meet their gluttonous needs. But in case anyone should think that writing about the experience of working at Broadmoor means that malpractices or patient abuse will be revealed, risking the accusation of a 'cover up' if one doesn't, this is not so. Reports and rumours inevitably abound but nothing is likely to be seen by someone who visits many wards and none regularly or for long enough to know what goes on only in the private corners or the quiet moments of the evening or early morning. Only if you are present there all day and every day can you be aware of that. The occasional and non-routine visitor to any one ward would never be likely to see anything other than the conventional and acceptable. This is not to imply that anything does or did 'go on', just that a peripatetic specialist member of staff will not know.

Of course, the terms of employment for special hospitals' staffs bar one from reporting such things publicly anyway. Any information one might obtain would be reported internally. But the daily chat and feedback that came my way rarely led me to believe there was anything happening that was out of the ordinary. The patients were a principal information source, of course. A parole patient once told me: "Of course some abuse goes on, it goes on everywhere I've ever been, but it's not a problem. If it ever becomes one I'll let you know." He never did. So I assume it didn't.

A fundamental difference, and a lack by comparison with the outside world, was the mingling of the sexes. As Chapter 9 will describe, a great many mixed recreational events took place. With the evolution of accepted practice during the lifetime of the 1959 Act, more mixed events took place, as well as mixed therapy sessions, as this history will record. But this is still not the same as normal life. Mixed sex households where people live, eat and sleep together, did not happen in Broadmoor. Same sex nursing staff also characterized each side of the hospital, male and female wings, until well into the lifetime of the Act. Even then, the numbers of each that were introduced to the other were small. Security and possible hazard was the concern where women were introduced on the male side; sexual misbehaviour, or allegations of it, were the main concerns with the introduction of men to the female wing.

Conjugal visiting was a further subject that arose during this period. It was argued that a patient's spouse or permanent partner should be allowed to visit in a private room, for a substantial part of the day, even if not overnight. Dr McGrath, his medical colleagues, the DHSS management and probably a large number of the rest of the staff (I don't think there is a record on this) all ruled out the suggestion. The grounds were not only the safety of the visiting partner and the risk of pregnancy, as one might suppose (although there were those who argued that this was part of returning to normality and the responsibilities of normal life). A further factor raised was the creation of a division between those patients who had partners and those who hadn't; and another was the exacerbation of the problems of those who had difficulty in relating to the opposite sex. In both instances resentments could arise, friction occur and treatment be put at risk.

SUMMARY

Broadmoor was a community, then, as far as it could go within its obvious constraints. It provided, within these constraints, a great deal within its walls that went on outside and, to many previously deprived people, a great deal that had never previously been available to them.

This chapter has looked at these community aspects of 'Old Broadmoor', contributing a vital socio-psychological element to treatment and standing in marked contrast to a prison culture. Whilst not the whole treatment story, which will include other psychological strategies as well as psychiatric, or medical, treatments, it was always a hallmark of the original Broadmoor concept in 1863. With the advances following the 1959 Act, especially pharmacological, there was a tendency to lose sight of the benefits of a well planned and run institutional community.

The discussion of the hospital environment, for a population usually spending a good many years there, has led to some explanation of the diversity of therapeutic methods, introducing a 'hardware' and 'software' analogy for the medical and psychological approaches involved. This led to reference to the phenomenon of gradual variations in behaviour where critical deficits and excesses might constitute the root of, or at least a critical element in, the behavioural problems confronting first the court and then the hospital. These are discussed later on, especially in Part III of this history.

Also raised by this topic is the problem of managing 'institutions' of all kinds, social, educational or commercial. It becomes well-nigh impossible to monitor everything that goes on in such settings so that, human nature being what it is, there will inevitably be mishaps, mismanagements and abuses of the system and the people in it. Nevertheless - and a peripatetic specialist is unlikely to be present in the remote corners of the hospital at the exact moment when incidents occur - the signs and the gossip in the Broadmoor system never rose, during the time of the 1959 Act, to a level where specific official intervention resulted.

Whilst the elements of treatment introduced in this chapter will be developed later, it has been thought important to raise these issues now, because of the criticism that has been levelled at closed institutions in recent years. The numerous benefits of modern treatments should enhance existing ones rather than necessarily always replacing them.

The next step in this history is to describe the treatments which typified mental hospital life up until the 1959 Act, upon which developments built. This is the subject of the next chapter.

CHAPTER 8

TREATMENT - THE WAY IT WAS

MEDICAL

The medical treatments described by Partridge were still going strong when the 1959 Act started. It is not within a psychologist's professional competence to explain medical treatments, nor would such explanations be appropriate for this kind of book. A layman's analogy will be more appropriate.

Physical

Electro-Convulsive Therapy (ECT) was in its heyday. Its mechanism of working was not understood nor, I believe, is it fully understood today. It induced a seizure or 'fit' and was supposed to have cleared the neural circuits of whatever was clogging them, as it were. It was the treatment of preference for depression, especially the 'endogenous' (or psychotic) variety rather than the 'reactive' (or neurotic) type although a persistent case of the latter might also be regarded as likely to benefit from ECT. Many schizophrenics also received ECT, especially people characterized by a withdrawn or lethargic state akin to depression (catatonia) and it might even be given to other types of schizophrenic (simple; hebephrenic; paranoid) if they persisted and failed to respond to the fast expanding number of drug treatments becoming available. A course of ECT usually consisted of six or eight treatments at, say, two a week and this might be repeated after a few months until improvement was achieved, or to maintain equilibrium if there were relapses.

Surgical

As was said in an earlier chapter, no brain surgery of the lobotomy or prefrontal leucotomy type was carried out at Broadmoor in 1959 or afterwards. It was typically, in its heyday, used for relieving the inhibitory tension of some obsessional neurotics and schizophrenics but the resulting additional disinhibition of some normal functions was considered unwise for some people whose problems included an inability to have controlled their aggressive impulses in the first place.

Insulin Coma Therapy

Partridge describes this as commonly practised before 1959 and it was going on for a while thereafter. It was a risky procedure, however, with variable results, involving putting someone into a coma with insulin and, with the rapid advances in pharmacological treatments during the 1950s and thereafter, it was soon brought to an end. The top ward of Block 1 was the 'insulin ward' and, after its ending, Dr McGrath turned this into his new Admission Ward.

Pharmacological (Medication, i.e.: Drugs)

This was where the big advances were to be seen after the 1959

Act. Indeed, it had been the beginnings of this advance in the 1950s that partly accounted for the introduction of the Act and its recognition of a predominantly medical basis for lunacy, so changing the concept to one of 'mental disorder'. Drugs were developed for the various psychotic illnesses to alleviate the confusion of schizophrenics, even out the mood swings of manic-depressives, and increase the activity levels of depressives; whilst there were also drugs for the many variations of neurotic disorder to calm the fears of anxiety neurotics, lift the mood of depressives and relieve the tensions of obsessionals.

PSYCHOTHERAPY

This was virtually non-existent at Broadmoor prior to the 1959 Act. Of course, psychoanalytic therapies had been going on for a long time in the sphere of mental illness treatment world-wide, especially of the neurotic kind, but were very time consuming and individualized, and expensive in terms of therapist availability. A visiting consultant had been appointed at Broadmoor some years previously to provide some psychotherapy sessions but the continuity in this role was fitful until later. Of course, the superintendent and some of the other medical staff would provide some psychotherapy to some patients sometimes. This would depend upon their assessment of its appropriateness, the patient's need and the availability of their time. The numbers of patients in each one's care and the large amount of documentation that came with most Broadmoor patients, and was required thereafter for legal as well as medical purposes, all worked against being able to provide much more than physical and pharmacological treatment for patients' mental disorders. Indeed, these virtually constituted psychiatric treatment in the post-war, pre-1959 Act era. One should not decry them.

Expensive individual psychotherapy of the psychoanalytic kind, which was the predominant therapy available, was provided either by the smaller, mainly private, hospitals and clinics or privately on an individual basis. The NHS mental hospital service, comprising a country-wide network of large hospitals deriving from the former county asylums, was never able to afford the time or cost of individual psychotherapy and certainly was not likely to explore such an avenue when the arrival of 'psychotropic' ('mind influencing') medicines in large numbers promised to do the job of emptying the old asylums. Papers abounded in the psychiatric literature evaluating this drug or another for this mental disorder or another whilst other papers examined the mechanisms by which the drugs worked and the light they threw on the disorders. Psychotherapy on a larger scale, therefore, awaited the development of briefer psychiatric alternatives to psychoanalysis and of the psychological therapies which were to grow from the newly developing profession of clinical psychology. Both figure in the era of the 1959 Mental Health Act.

OCCUPATIONAL ACTIVITIES

As said in Chapter 5 on staff, occupational therapists were not employed prior to the 1959 Act, nor for a long time afterwards. The workshops around the hospital and in some of the wards themselves, therefore, could not be said to provide 'occupational therapy' in the true sense, where a referral would be made of a patient's needs and the occupational therapist would devise a programme which would contribute to meeting these.

The Main Workshops

The various workshops around the hospital, however, effectively provided therapeutic work for perhaps a couple of hundred patients. The main 'shops', as they were called, were located behind Block 3 and were a set of single storey original buildings housing the shoemakers', upholstery and tailors' shops in the charge of Messrs Wells, Caplin and Fraser respectively. There was also a small tinsmiths' shop in one of the rooms off the central courtyard. The work, as the names imply, were essentially part of the internal economy of the hospital, as was said in Chapter 5 when describing the staff. Tailoring included staff uniforms and some patients' clothing, likewise shoemaking, whilst upholstery comprised chiefly the making and repair of hospital furniture and especially the cleansing and remaking of fouled bedding. The staff in charge were qualified at their trade. Nevertheless, they also became effective therapists as their experience of the ways of their patients accustomed them to what to expect of them and how to manage their sometimes odd ways. A number of patients here would be in process of gaining a trade qualification which would stand them in good stead when discharged, in many cases enabling them actually to follow a formal trade in what they had learned in Broadmoor.

The Handicrafts Centre

The larger 'Handicrafts Centre' was a modern prefabricated building behind Blocks 5, 6 and 7, in the charge of Messrs Gale and Barber but with other staff in support. Again there were trade skills employed, a great deal of the work being with wood in one way or another, including formal items of furniture or toys and other recreational items. Again, much was done for the hospital's internal

141

needs, especially cabinets for enclosing the growing number of televisions which, during this era, were appearing in each of the blocks and were eventually to constitute the focal point of every ward. TVs had to be in lockable cabinets for their safety when switched off - they weren't on continuously as would tend to happen today.

Toys were popular items both for patients' relatives and friends and for staff who would place orders for them. The quality of these was particularly good, made from quality wood, not hardboard or chipboard. In fact, some years later when the chaplain decided it was time to replace the old chapel pews with modern chairs, there was a good supply of solid pew wood for remaking into furniture and toys. Popular lines were toy garages, forts, dolls' houses and cots and the ingenious ramifications of these which resulted from the exercise of patients' imaginations led to a constant popular demand from staff and the local populace of Crowthorne. My small sons had a splendid solid wooden toy garage emblazoned with the name: 'Black Brothers' Garage' whilst my daughter had a rocking dolls' cradle made from an old pew. These items were costed for sale purposes according to the cost of the raw materials.

The main Handicrafts Shop also had a printing and bookbinding section, emphasizing once again that, like the main 'shops', their function was economic as well as therapeutic for the patients. The printing section produced much of the hospital's printing needs in the way of forms, and programmes for staff and patients' social events like sports days, dances and menus. The report forms for psychology and other department's reports were printed in these shops for many years. The bookbinding section repaired many old books from hospital and private collections and later, when I was given the task of setting up the hospital's first clinical library, all the journal runs were bound in annual volumes in the Handicrafts Centre. One patient was particularly good at inscribing the titles on the spine in a fine copperplate hand and could be said, therefore, to be 'undergoing a therapeutic experience' through this outlet. However, whether this rather quiet, obsessional work was what he needed or whether instead he would have benefited from something that took him out of such introspection and counteracted his ruminating, is another question. Such refinements were to come later.

Ward Occupational Facilities

As well as the Workshops and Handicrafts Centre there was a small handicrafts room within Block 6 for what were then still called 'refractory' patients. This was not part of the internal economy and was much more like the handicrafts associated with OT (occupational therapy). In other words it involved drawing, painting, modelling: 'handicrafts' in the traditional sense. There was also the ubiquitous rug making so widespread in mental hospitals of that era.

Female Wing Occupations

Rug making was also done in the Female Wing and handicraft activity was much more common around the ward areas too, no doubt reflecting the feminine outlook to life. The main work areas for the women, however, were part of the hospital economy again, like the male wing. Here was a sewing room where staff uniforms and patients' clothing were made and the array of sewing machines was reminiscent of 'The Rag Trade', a TV comedy series of that era. Many women patients left Broadmoor adept at a sewing machine if they weren't already so when they arrived. The other part of the hospital economy run by the women patients and a team of staff was the laundry. This was a major requirement for 850 patients, especially as some were likely to soil their bedding. This was not always because they were incontinent, although some were, but because they would foul their rooms and possessions as a result of either the regressive behaviour that characterized their illnesses, or the hostility deriving from their personality problems.

Occupational Placements

The various sections of the workshops were used effectively as therapy and the choice of patient to fill a vacancy was, before the 1959 Act, a matter for the ward staff when notified by the shop in question. The decision was, in fact, that of the DN or DS (departmental nurse or sister), i.e.: the (wo)man who was in charge of the Block. S/he would confer with the staff of the actual ward but would have done this continuously anyway and would know in advance who were the next patients in line for vacancies, on the basis of ongoing knowledge of the progress of all the patients on 'their block'. A DN/DS would know what was required in any 'shop' and would choose accordingly. There would be less input from the man or woman in charge of the shop or section who would reckon it their job to accept whoever the wards felt needed to be placed there. If it didn't work out then the patient would go back and another one found but the challenge was to accommodate whoever the ward sent across and make something of him/her. In any case, the DN's/DS's knowledge was usually sound and his/her decision rarely failed, either from the hospital economy point of view or the eventual welfare of the patient.

This sort of procedure characterized much of Broadmoor's life prior to the 1959 Act and was one of the reasons the Act was so traumatic for Broadmoor's way of life. The Act designated the consultant psychiatrist the 'responsible medical officer' (RMO) who was in charge of the patients' treatment. After 1959 the number of consultants gradually increased and responsibility for the hospital's ward blocks was divided between them. Their decisions therefore replaced many of the decisions previously made by the chief male nurse, matron, their deputies and the DNs/DSs. Perhaps some of the newly arriving consultants had not fully appreciated what had been the extent of the staff's responsibilities and autonomy up to that time. At any rate, there was some considerable friction after 1959 in the running of the wards and with regard to decisions such as to which workshop a patient was to go. I remember being drawn into this when, as I have said already, I could see the usefulness of a work situation to a patient's clinical needs in terms, say, of learning to persist at a task, to accept instruction, or to work with a team, whereas the criterion operated by the consultant might be quite different such as, say, in simply getting a patient out of the ward environment and activated.

The resolution of such difficulties awaited the creation of clinical teams many years later and the availability of a wider range of occupational activities where the production economy of the institution was not affected. We shall return to this again later. For the moment, it will be enough to note that this was one of the areas of conflict and dissatisfaction with the new Act and the basis of some staff antagonism to the newly appointed consultant psychiatrists. I recall a conversation with Pat Bennett, the chief male nurse at that time, in which he expressed his sadness at retiring when the hospital's equilibrium had received such a jolt. Dr McGrath himself was fairly new in the hot seat and people had not yet got used to him. They would say: "Oh, for the days of Dr James" just as years later, after his retirement, they would say "Oh, for the days of Dr McGrath". With other new consultants also arriving the change was magnified and the senior nursing staff felt their authority and influence threatened and reduced. Neither the 'super' nor his new consultant colleagues seemed entirely to have grasped this situation or to have seen the need to overcome the tensions and resentment it raised.

Work in Hospital Departments and Grounds

A number of other work-places used patient labour and were, again, regarded as contributing to their treatment. These included the kitchens and stores, the patients' shops on both wings (known as 'canteens') and, outside but within the walls, the grounds and kitchen garden. The latter was a large area below the buildings which was reached down a long flight of steps (described by Partridge in his chapter on the hospital sports day). Running the entire width of the hospital, i.e.: the length of the top terrace but beneath the bottom wall, was this area for growing vegetables, with its associated greenhouses. Work parties went down here each day. Above, on the terrace itself, were lawns for playing bowls, with paths and flower beds in between. All these provided work for patients. Not all these work-places required a 'parole card' to work there, parties of various kinds of patient in varying phases of their illness being escorted to the place of work. Groups from each block, or later 'house', would be gathered together on their way to the gardens, grounds or workshops and would peel off at the appropriate point, the procedure being reversed on the way back at lunch time or the end of the day. It was quite a co-ordinated operation. Many years later there would be co-ordination by mobile phone but not in 1959.

One work-place, however, did require parole patients and this was the hospital grounds outside the walls. Several parties of half

146

a dozen, each in the charge of a member of staff, would emerge through the main gate each morning, dressed in their distinctive yellow corduroy trousers and, in winter, navy blue serge jacket. They would work on the paths and verges along the estate roads, garden areas, staff sports field, and one group would tend the garden of the superintendent's house. As time went by the 'outside' parties were reduced to only one. Dr McGrath's view was that, if a patient was fit to go outside the walls he was fit to be discharged and ought no longer to be in the hospital. I always felt this was debatable. If he was fit to leave the hospital it might be a good idea to test him out and accustom him to the outside world with a period working on the grounds. There he would see men, women and children of the staff and the general public, visitors and vehicles, in fact the normal world again. I felt this would be a useful transition experience and was rather confirmed in this by the *cris-de-coeur* of some discharged patients. They would tend to phone the hospital, asking to speak to the staff man or woman with whom they had felt most at home while in hospital, telling of their fears and seeking reassurance and encouragement.

Instances of other kinds of separation anxiety and patient dissatisfaction arose as the 1959 Act took hold and more patients were transferred to other psychiatric hospitals rather than to the outside world directly. They would often find themselves in the 'back wards' of such hospitals, being regarded with suspicion and wariness, whereas they had probably been parole patients at Broadmoor with the freedom of the grounds. So they felt restricted and not understood. They would also have little scope for, say, conversation or playing cards or chess when they were placed with people whose mental disorder was more acute and more impairing of their social capacity. They still needed to regain confidence in coping with the outside world, however. One example of this arose was when a discharged patient called from a 'phone box in

Piccadilly tube station. He was intelligent, capable and had done responsible jobs in the hospital but had apparently been overcome by the noise and bustle of the tube station. He needed reassurance from the man he had known and trusted in order to get out of the station and continue on his way. So I always felt that an outside work party (and indeed a great deal more, although that was much longer coming) was helpful preparation for rejoining the real world. One of the commonest comments of discharged patients was how noisy and crowded they felt the outside world to be.

There was no equivalent of the outside work party for the women patients even though they also worked in the gardens of the female wing inside the walls. However, small groups of parole equivalent women patients (the Female Wing was too small to run a proper parole system) would go out on shopping trips to the nearby towns. They had gone to the local village shops in former days but this was later regarded as too obvious to prying press as well as embarrassing for off duty staff and their families. Larger, more anonymous towns a little further away were chosen instead. Later still, recreational outings for both sexes to a seaside or country resort took place.

SUMMARY

This chapter has reviewed the range of treatment approaches available in the days up to the 1959 legislation. Formal treatments mainly comprised the physical and pharmacological aspects of medicine, psychotherapy being confined to whatever the psychiatrist could fit into his demanding time schedule (where a patient was thought likely to benefit from it) and a few sessions from visiting psychotherapists.

Physical treatments included principally ECT (electro-convulsive therapy) and insulin coma therapy as surgical approaches such as leucotomy were thought likely only to aggravate the already impulsive traits of many offender patients (surgical interventions invariably decreased inhibitory controls and therefore made an already impulsive patient's condition worse). Pharmacological treatments, however, were on the increase with the rapid strides beginning to be taken at that time. The sites in the brain associated with different behaviours were becoming better known and the effects of various chemical substances better charted, to the better advantage of a patient's mental equilibrium.

Aside from these more formal aspects of treatment, however, and to take account of the large amounts of time available to the long-stay patient, the occupational facilities of the hospital were of paramount importance and could also contribute usefully to a patient's mental stabilization, not to mention the possible gaining of an occupational skill. This chapter has, therefore, described the wide range of these facilities that were then available.

Formal psychiatric treatment, then, was limited in 1959 and a great deal depended upon the rehabilitative effect of work and recreation. The latter was sufficiently extensive that it has the next chapter to itself.

CHAPTER 9

RECREATION

The previous chapter has recapped, updated and carried on where Partridge left off in his Chapters 13, 15 & 16. In looking at what constituted treatment in Broadmoor, both medical and social, at the outset of the 1959 Act, however, it is necessary also to look at what went on outside the normal working day. If Broadmoor is a community and everything that goes on within it is potentially 'treatment', we must look at what was available in the way of recreation. In doing so we will be spanning aspects of Partridge's Chapters 4, 8, 10, 11, 17, 18 & 19, but not necessarily in that order, and this must be done before embarking on the innovations and developments that followed the 1959 Act.

Any large community will organize for itself, and indulge in, a large range of recreational activity. Unless it is a prison when it is likely to be limited. Broadmoor is not a prison, however, despite its security, and this is no better demonstrated than in its recreational activity, which mirrors that of any normal community. This can be seen in both its communal and individual activity.

INDIVIDUAL RECREATION

Take first the situation of individual patients in the wards. These, of course, varied considerably according to the nature and degree of the disorders which any one block or ward catered for but the basic level of normal living was maintained as far as possible by means of books, newspapers, magazines, writing materials, games, radio and television. Some of these were available in individual patient's rooms if the patient was fit to cope with them without damaging them or using them to damage himself or others. In particular these would be the norm for parole patients (who occupied the whole of Block 2, most of Block 5, one ward in the Female Wing as well as being scattered individually throughout the other blocks). In fact, as a patient's condition improved and s/he moved to a better ward, his/her room would come to look more like any bedsit outside. This meant that, in addition to the hospital furniture provided, a patient might buy or have brought in by relatives: small tables, rugs, curtains, knick-knacks, photos and so on. Parole patients would have their own radio and hi-fi and, especially as time went by and they became more prevalent, eventually TV. In 1959, however, TVs were still only available on a one-per-block basis and then later one-per-ward. Patients who had a particular hobby might also have, say, drawing and painting materials or a musical instrument. Original pictures from the 1860s show a patient with a violin but, post-1959, guitars were more the mode.

As described in Chapter 6 on Accommodation, every block had individual rooms whilst most also had dormitories, some of them holding 30 or 40 patients, some smaller for 6 or 8 patients. These rooms, by the way, were never known as cells - another way of emphasizing the differences from prisons. What is the difference? A cell is a room and a room may be a cell if it is perceived that way. Some of the bare, shuttered rooms of the 'refractory patients' might have looked like cells, though they were never called this. Rooms of other patients didn't look like cells, being furnished to a lesser or greater degree, according to the progress the patient had achieved and the ward block he or she was in.

Again as already said but worth re-emphasizing in the present context, single rooms were for patients at the two extremes: an achievement for those who had made progress and were able to look after themselves; or a security measure for the most disturbed who might damage themselves or others. In the latter case the room would have the bare minimum for safety described in Chapter 6. Within this kind of room recreation would, indeed, be a euphemism, limited to newspaper and paperback and the occasional conversation from staff through the observation window in the wall adjacent to the door. This was openable and lockable, with a strong frame, some 2-3 feet in length and about six inches wide, making an observation space of about two inches (see diagram, Chapter 6). When unlocked this slit window would swing outwards to allow either conversation or the limited passing in of food, drink, mail, newspaper. Meals would be brought for those who were too unfit to come to the ward dining rooms and would be handed in through the open door. This meant at least two staff, one to open the door and observe while the other put the tray on the floor. Patients would be told to stay in the opposite corner of their room while this was done, or might be in bed anyway, and the observation windows in door and wall enabled staff to ensure this was so. Even then, it was not uncommon with the more disturbed patients in the 'back blocks' to have a patient try to rush out or throw their pot and its contents at the staff. Although all windows were barred and the glazing was gradually replaced with toughened glass, the most secure and minimally furnished rooms for the most dangerous were also provided with secure shutters over the windows, leaving only a small ventilation grille. They could, therefore, get very foul smelling.

Fortunately, this basic level of minimum provision, because of maximum security being required, only affected perhaps a score of patients at any one time. Most patients, even in the 'Back Blocks'

1 and 6 and, in the women's wing, the bottom ward of Block 2, were up and about during the day and able to make use of the ward day room facilities. Patients in the other blocks, especially the parole Blocks 2 and 5 and the Female Wing Block 1, had more means of recreation in their rooms - a choice of books, papers, radio - and would not, in any case, be spending their day time in their rooms like secluded patients but in the ward day rooms or the hospital occupational centres.

This account might seem to belie the assertion that, within this hospital 'community', life and the amenities provided for it approximated the normal world outside. But Broadmoor is a secure hospital and a few of its patients are, of course, extremely disturbed much of the time, some of them most of the time. Despite all of them having done something violent to have been admitted in the first place, however, only a small proportion are violent continuously and not more than perhaps a half are violent even intermittently. Most violent crimes are one-off or intermittent anyway, as we shall discuss more fully later. Away from whatever provoked the offence in the first place, and with continuous monitoring, very few psychiatric patients, even at Broadmoor, actually behave in a hazardous way very often. The basics of a humane community are provided for everyone; a great deal more for those who are able to behave normally within the constraints of the hospital.

Individual rooms, dormitories and day rooms vary, then, between the bare basics for the extremely or continuously disturbed few, through the level of a comfortable hostel up to the top level of perhaps a modest commercial hotel. All the usual means of off-duty enjoyment, reading, hobbies, games and entertainment are available, these being under maximum supervision for the most disturbed but minimal supervision otherwise. As well as the individual facilities for hobbies such as music and painting already mentioned, there were tables for writing and for card games, chess, etc and in some wards, such as in the parole block, rooms were set aside for these or for a full size snooker table. Block 2 had its own library. For the remainder the county library van would be brought in through the main gate and parked on the terrace once a week in the days before a hospital library was created, with groups of patients attending from each block in turn.

Meals were taken in each block separately, each ward had its own kitchen and dining room, except that the whole of each parole block ate in one ground floor dining room at separate tables, rather like a university refectory. In 1959 the other blocks had long board tables. However, the food was all cooked in the central kitchens and brought to the blocks in insulated trolleys. A member of staff (the 'sculleryman') and selected patients, as mentioned in Chapter 6, would carry these through to the ward kitchens from where a serving hatch would open on to the dining room area. In the parole blocks (2 and 5) patients would often cook their own evening meals, or extra meals, in the ward kitchen, buying in what they wanted from the hospital shop.

Ward cleanliness was also the responsibility of the staff and patients on each block. Only much later were domestic staff employed. All patients were expected and encouraged to keep their own rooms clean and the first job on getting up, after checking security, would be cleaning rooms and making beds. Cleanliness of corridors, day rooms, dining room and reading rooms was either a corporate activity, shared on a rota basis or, in the case of a ward where most of the patients went out to work in some other part of the hospital, one or two patients would be appointed as ward cleaners and stay on the ward all the time (Chapter 6). These might actually be the sole parole patients on the ward, reliable enough to have free movement for cleaning, making tea, helping bring in the insulated food containers, serving, washing up. For all this and as parole patients, they would then be able to go off the block during the afternoon to visit friends in other blocks, go to the shop or take part in an afternoon game of bowls, before coming back for the evening meal and going on to some parole patient activity in the central hall.

A droll variation on the ward cleaning theme was current in Block 7 (later Cornwall House) in 1959. In those days patients in the 'ordinary' (non parole) blocks would keep their clothing and personal possessions in stout wooden boxes about two foot square. These stayed in their rooms during the day but were put outside at night when they would exchange day clothes for pyjamas. This allowed an inspection before going to bed when they were undressed, but before putting on their pyjamas, when they stood briefly naked, to ensure that nothing hazardous or that might assist an escape was being taken into their rooms. On cleaning days, charge nurse Tommy Warns (a former naval chief petty officer) would marshal all the patients outside their rooms with their storage boxes, under which were placed pieces of old blanket. The wooden floors with their strips of lino up the centre would then be polished, on Tommy Warns command, by all the patients pushing their boxes along the corridor in line ahead. The floors of this ward always gleamed brightly and everyone was then required to walk along the plain boarded edges and keep off the lino to maintain the polished surface in the centre. Some wards were said to be considerable fire hazards by Ministry of Works staff (the green men) who had to go underneath the flooring for electrical or plumbing maintenance and who were concerned at the curtain of floor polish 'stalactites' hanging below the floorboards. Nowadays, of course, the corridors have wall-to-wall matting or carpeting.

In the pre-1959 Act, pre-TV days, gardens were also a popular activity. All the 'front' blocks had garden areas below the terrace. The occupants of Blocks 2 and 5 could reach theirs directly out of their back doors and, as parole patients, would do so at their own initiative. The doors from Blocks 3 and 4 opened on to the terrace itself and, without parole, parties of patients were escorted across the terrace and down through the big iron gate to the gardens where those with gardens would work in them and those without would merely watch, sit, walk around or organize some pastime for themselves. Each level had a row of garden plots in which patients would grow flowers, vegetables, or both, probably entering them for prizes at the patients' annual show. Such was the competition for plots, especially in the parole blocks, that a new arrival on the block would have to wait his turn for a plot to become available. Gradually, as TV and other activities took hold over the years and interest waned, plots became fewer and more neglected. Some were retained or other features built for those few still interested, otherwise they were grassed over and the terraces became merely exercise or games areas. An ornamental pond was made in Block 2's garden (by then 'Essex House'), which eventually attracted a pair of mallards. Ducklings have been a spring feature ever since.

Creativity at an individual level was not confined to the gardens. A great deal of creativity was exercised indoors - inevitably with the British climate. Many patients wrote, both prose and poetry; others played musical instruments and, later, a room was set aside for guitar and other instrumental practice in one of the upper wards of Block 2, Essex House. Others again were artists and both drew and painted, sometimes exhibiting at the annual show (described later). Both wings of the hospital featured murals by patients. One, at the end of the middle ward gallery (corridor) of Block 1, Female Wing (later York House), gave a vista effect apparently elongating the gallery whilst another on the end wall of the bottom ward dining room in Block 2, male side (later Essex House) gave a similar vista effect of looking on to a harbour scene.

Finally, on a personal level, all patients were and are

encouraged to maintain links with family and friends outside through correspondence and, more recently, phone calls. Visits, which Partridge intimates were limited, actually became virtually unlimited on any day of the year except Christmas Day. Visits for most of the hospital took place in the central hall (small hall-cum-dining-room in the Female Wing). Only for the 'back blocks' were visitors taken across to the relevant block for a visit in the ground floor day area.

In the central hall and Female Wing hall tables were put out so that patients and their visitors could sit, talk, look at correspondence, photos, etc, and have tea or coffee and snacks. These were ordered from a parole patient orderly who worked in the patients' 'canteen' (shop) and brought in on a tray. Observation was undertaken by three or four staff (more at busy weekends) posted around the periphery of the hall. They were able, therefore, to observe but not overhear conversations. Observation at that distance was not perfect, of course, but this arrangement was considered an acceptable balance between security and privacy. In any case, patients' visitors were checked through the main gate and had to leave any gifts or packages for patients to receive back in the blocks. These were placed in sealed boxes and opened later in the patients' presence. In summer time or good weather, parole patients were able to have their visits take place outside so that they could walk along the terrace and have their tea and buns on a seat in the sunshine enjoying the grounds and the view. From the terrace, unlike the small semi-circular exercise yard in Block 6, this really did extend for twenty miles on a good day, across the Berkshire border into Surrey and Hampshire. The immediate vicinity was thickly wooded, the Crown land being worked largely by the Forestry Commission, so that the adjacent Sandhurst lands could not be seen. When there were exercises involving firing, however, they could be heard, which more than once gave rise to the comment from visitors: "that's how you keep the numbers down!"

COMMUNITY RECREATION

If individuals could pass the working day and their evenings and weekends as nearly as possible like the world outside, what activities were available on a corporate basis? As described by Partridge, there was a concert party/drama group; a chapel choir and choral group; an institution magazine; sports days; a flower, vegetable and handicrafts show; parole dances; concerts in each of the blocks; a weekly film show in the central hall; and team sports with matches against outside teams (all games were at home and the corny joke was frequently cracked that the pole vault was not allowed!). All of which sounds rather 'between-the-wars and Miss Marple-ish'. Certainly in the post-war era it had that flavour about it and, after all, it was in effect a 'village community'. Gradually the atmosphere changed and a more modern air characterized the social events, so that 'parole dances' became 'discos', film shows gave way to pop concerts (TV was, of course, available later on every ward and in many parole patients' rooms as well) and block concerts became patients' gigs. With the decrease in garden produce the 'flowers and veg' aspect of the annual show gave way to more handicrafts, furniture, modelling and patients' art exhibits. This was greatly encouraged by the annual Koestler award for artistic enterprise in prisons (with which Broadmoor managed to get itself permitted to be associated).

Co-ordination of patients' recreation in those days was the job of the chaplain in conjunction with the musical director who, for many years, was a charge nurse, Luther Brittain, always affectionately known as 'Britt'. He had to carry out his many entertainment duties in addition to charge nurse duties on the wards, however. There was also a patients' recreation committee, as described by Partridge. The core group were parole patients but a representative of each block was also appointed and the whole was presided over by a member of staff. Originally, in 1959, this was Dr Cyril Perry, the deputy superintendent, but eventually it became the Nursing Officer in charge of 'Activities'. It is worth having a closer look at some of these activities.

'The Broadhumoorists'

This was the name adopted by the patients' concert party and drama group and remained largely unchanged, not only from Partridge's time but onwards through the 'interacts' era. It was, however, less a concert party and more a drama group by this time, putting on a play each year, on the small stage in the central hall.

The 'concert party', by contrast, was a staff enterprise at that time which put on an annual revue 'Broad & Moorish' written by staff members but with borrowed music, until the hospital's centenary when a play was also produced. Then plays took over from revues which had become difficult to maintain through dwindling numbers. I remember these well because I took part and was also producer for a while. The staff concerts and the Broadhumoorists ran for about six weeks and two months respectively, but not nightly, only on Wednesday and Saturday evenings, the former through November and early December, the latter through March and April. They were open to the public who could write in for (free) tickets. Collections were, of course, taken during the interval and both the staff and patients' productions raised welcome funds for the Patients' Benevolent Fund and for other charities of the participants' choice.

Such was the reputation of both patients' and staff shows that coach parties would come from surprisingly far afield, not just Camberley, Aldershot and Reading but also Slough, Basingstoke or Portsmouth. Each coach load was escorted through the main gate and central court-yard, across the central corridor and into the main hall. Productions were chosen by the patients that often turned on some criminal or macabre theme, as if there was some expiation of feelings facilitated by laughing at the whole enterprise. Scenery and costumes were constructed, sewn and assembled in the patients' Handicrafts Department and the Female Wing sewing room with the redoubtable Jim Gale, who was the Chief Occupations Officer, also fulfilling the job of Stage Manager, assisted by such staff stalwarts as the young Brian North, Johnny Waldron and Mick Ball.

The Broadhumoorists had some accomplished actors and actresses, whom staff and ex-staff may not name, but one had become very much the successor to Ronald True. Partridge names him because he had by then just died and he describes him as the central force in organizing patients' activities. The stage in the central hall was not an easy place on which to act, because two of the eight iron pillars which supported the chapel above went through it. It helped if they could be incorporated into the plot or scenery as happened when a local company, The East Berkshire Operatic Society, brought their production of *The Mikado* to entertain the patients. Koko, in his Act II duet with Katisha, whose embraces he is trying to avoid, managed to do this on the Broadmoor stage by climbing one of the pillars!

Comic incidents in stage productions might bring excessive or quite different reactions from a patients' audience than from the public; patients would be less inhibited in expressing themselves, especially in the non-public atmosphere of Broadmoor. Any reference to criminal activity would usually bring whoops of delight whilst any slightly effete gesture from a male actor would also bring hoots from the male section of the audience. Reactions could, however, be quite unexpectedly different. In the 60s each block would have a special Christmas film show combined with a special meal brought in from an outside caterer. I was invited to attend one of these in the parole Block 2 where the two films chosen by the patients were 'League of Gentlemen', about a smoothly operating group of gentlemen criminals plotting the perfect crime, and 'Saturday Night and Sunday Morning' about a rather tragic husband-wife relationship. Whilst the first of these was enjoyed with, again, whoops of enjoyment, the latter was watched in total silence. Too close to home? At the end of this history (Chapter 25) there is discussion of the novel enterprise of introducing several of Shakespeare's tragedies to a Broadmoor patients' audience. In 1959 and the early years of the 1959 Act, stage activities were much more restricted and traditional.

Acting was paralleled by other artistic accomplishments in painting and music which enabled life in Broadmoor to be greatly enriched, as demonstrated by the range of talent exhibited at the annual show. Would any eight hundred or so residents in a community outside demonstrate this level of creative activity?

Chapel, Choir and Choral Society

Broadmoor has a fine chapel, above the central hall as has already been said. In days gone by the men patients occupied the ground floor whilst the women sat in the balcony. By 1959 they all sat in the main body of the chapel, but in separate groups, and the balcony was used to store stage props until it was demolished some years later. Attendance was voluntary. On the left hand side sat staff and any villagers who wanted to attend services. The choir comprised patients, staff, their families and villagers, which provided a means of enabling patients to meet and mix with people from the 'normal' world. It was ably conducted by the redoubtable 'Britt' - Mr Luther Brittain - throughout the bulk of the 'Inter-Acts' period. He was a former military musician who presided over all musical activities in the hospital. He had the help of a number of, mainly, ex-service musicians who played in the hospital orchestra for parole dances and other entertainment, such as sports days and the staff revues. He was also the chapel organist, although later there were a number of patients who played piano and organ and shared these duties. Conducting the chapel choir and the hospital choral society, which also encouraged staff, their families and villagers to take part, were his main accomplishments.

As well as choir recitals there would be an annual patients' choral concert which also ran for several weeks on Wednesdays and Saturdays. For all these performances and their months of rehearsals there would be the benefit for patients of taking part, developing new skills and interests (or maintaining existing or rusty ones) and mixing with other people, many of whom were not only not patients but were of the opposite sex: another of the rare occasions when the men and women were able to mix. 'Britt' managed all this with his own special brand of tradition, gentle discipline and humour. Some of his favourite arias and operettas, such as 'Maritana', became very familiar to all his loyal singers who might groan at their repetition but who nevertheless wallowed in their nostalgia. Every concert performance opened with 'Let the People Sing' which the regulars in the audience knew they were expected to join in singing.

The Broadmoor Chronicle

This monthly magazine was produced by a small team of parole patients in a specially designated magazine office using contributions from patients throughout the hospital. In 1959 it was produced on a Gestetner or Roneo duplicating machine, using wax stencils. This was fairly straightforward for typing the articles and poems but to see the illustrations and cartoons produced by this system made one wonder at the level of accomplishment involved, and in colour. I still have my collection of issues from 1960 onwards, somewhat musty now. Again, the level of contribution, as well as the production technology, was of a remarkably high standard and, of course, many of these were extremely poignant, knowing from whom they originated. They also managed to be up-to-the-minute topical as fresh government legislation, green and white papers, or just critical publicity, emerged about mental disorder, criminality and so on. The magazines enjoyed a wide distribution, being displayed at the main gate and the central hall for sale to patients' visitors and later on when it was formed, the League of Friends, at its canteen. Three old pence per issue or three shillings for an annual subscription.

The Parole Dance

As well as being used for plays, revues and choral concerts in the evenings and patients' visitors during the day, the Central Hall was the venue for a number of other hospital events, like any village hall. As I have said, before the advent of TV in every ward there were weekly film shows involving, again, major movements of patients under escort from their blocks (later 'houses'). However, this time, women patients did not make the journey from the Female Wing, which involved traversing an area outside the main walls from a small door in the Female Wing wall, across the front garden of what had been the superintendent's house, and through another small door into the Male Wing via Block 2's asphalt tennis court. Instead the weekly film had separate showings in the Male and Female Wings. Also in the central hall table tennis took place with contests between each block, against the staff and against some outside teams.

One of the other main events in the central hall, however, was the 'Parole Dance', a prestigious event that took place at roughly quarterly intervals to coincide with some national holiday or similar event, such as the conclusion of the Broadhumoorists' run. The New Year's dance was one of the major occasions, although it took place on 30th December so as not to clash with the staff New Year Dance in the staff club on the 31st. The staff claimed precedence.

Parole dances were greatly looked forward to as one of the few occasions when men and women could get together and, in contrast to its later development (some would say 'decline') when 'anything went' in the dress direction, much preparation was given to dress and appearance. One elderly man would always turn out immaculately in full evening dress. A very 'Miss Marple-ish' occasion.

The protocol was also quaint. Patients no longer sat in long lines, each sex separately down opposite sides of the hall, which was often the pattern of the post-war era in village 'hops' throughout the land. Nevertheless, it was the custom for attending senior staff to sit in a semi-circle in the bay window at the end of the hall. The 'super' and his wife sat in the centre, flanked by his deputy, the matron, chief male nurse, the chaplain and any other senior staff, together with their spouses. This tradition very much reflected the time-honoured ranking of the senior staff. Other grades of staff also attended, with a cohort of nursing staff to provide the 'escort' element. There was also a member of the Ministry of Works staff present, and the fire officer, for any emergency that might arise. With this August assembly my wife and

I were graciously invited to take our place.

For all the attending staff, however, this was not an entirely 'off-duty' event. With attendance went the expectation that you would dance with a full range of patients. The men were expected to invite a number of women patients to dance whilst their wives, the matron and her deputies were expected to accept invitations to dance from male patients. One had to be scrupulously fair in all this. No favourites. And there were always patients who had to be brought on to the floor who might otherwise get neglected. At the same time one had to exercise tact in not inviting to dance someone who was clearly in great demand from other patients. The exception to the convention that the men did the asking was in respect of the 'super' who might be asked to dance by a woman patient, and the matron and social worker by whom male patients were happy to be asked to dance. There were some very accomplished ballroom dancers amongst the patients (for ballroom dancing was still the vogue in those days) and the staff wives often enjoyed a better dance with them than they would from their own husbands. However, none surpassed Wilf Bagshaw and Alf Lister, then staff nurses, and their wives, who could always be relied upon to set the tone with their immaculate ballroom style.

Of course, the ballroom dance era also featured a number of collective dances like the palais glide, the conga and the hoki-koki which allowed people to join in *en masse*, whilst a barn dance, if progressive, would allow the changing of partners. By and large it was the dancers among the staff who were relied upon to volunteer for parole dance duty. As the night staff came on duty at 9.30 pm and the dances would not end until 10 pm, the staff would have to stay on to see the groups of patients back to their wards. The appearance of the night superintendent at the door of the hall, holding his lamp, was always the sign that the evening must be coming to an end. Traditionally, the physician superintendent was asked to grant an extension for an extra dance, which he invariably did. I expect this had been taken into account in scheduling the time-table for the evening! 'Britt' and the orchestra would then always observe the convention of those times by finishing with the last waltz and then the National Anthem.

The Annual Show

Again in the central hall, this had originally been the annual flower and vegetable show, giving an opportunity to all those who had patiently and keenly tended their gardens during the year the opportunity to display the results of their efforts and the chance to win a prize. A splendid display of blooms and of vegetables rather than fruits (fruit trees were in short supply inside), that would stand comparison with any village show, went on display and great pride resulted from the prizes won. There would be cups and certificates, of course, and a token to be redeemed at the hospital shop. Money was, of course, not available in the patient community so a system of book accounting in the 'patients cash office' enabled gifts, earnings and benefits to be credited and spending to be set against this through a system of 'chits'.

The annual show had always featured a section for Female Wing handicrafts, as the women patients did not have the same opportunity to compete with flowers, fruit and vegetables in their limited gardens that the men did. They had nicely tended decorative gardens and would submit some flower arrangements, but not on the same scale of individually tended plots. So the work from their sewing room, and needlework, knitting, crochet, rug making and patchwork done in their ward day rooms would feature in the annual show. From this, and as the men's workshops and handicrafts burgeoned, the section in the show for these things grew, eventually virtually taking over as interest in flowers and vegetables declined. Gradually, also, the artistic element increased as more patients made use of the greater facility and encouragement to paint, draw and model in their rooms and on the wards. So all these also featured in the annual show which eventually became more an art and handicrafts show than a horticultural show. It ran for several days so that patients could view it, block by block, as could staff, and then it was open to the village and public to attend.

Sports Field Events

Partridge has well described the main event of the year on the sports field, the annual sports themselves. The weekly football matches in winter and cricket matches in summer were also well attended by patients who stood or sat along the touchline or boundary cheering or politely applauding as appropriate (life was conventional in those days!). Tea was also an attraction in the pavilion afterwards or at the interval. Groups were gathered from each of the blocks with their escorting staff, numbers were tallied and counted through the gates down the steps as Partridge has described. All was reported back by 'phone to the chief male nurse's office from where the exercise was co-ordinated, with the assistance of a 'phone down at the sports field. Nowadays there is the luxury of the mobile 'phone. An early limited version of this by the 70s was allocated to selected staff who co-ordinated movements through it and to a central control. As these staff 'roamed' the hospital areas they inevitably became known as the 'Romeos' and their call signs were Romeo 1, Romeo 2, etc. I had particular cause to remember the flights of steps between the main terrace and the cricket field as I played on one occasion for the staff against the patients. I was struck on the foot by the patients' main fast bowler but, thinking it was not significant, went on playing, only to be embarrassed later, while fielding, by the foot swelling up so that I was unable to stand or walk on it. The patients took particular delight in carrying me up the entire flight of steps back to the main building, victim of the patients' demon fast bowler.

The main event of the year on the sports field, however, was the annual sports day itself. Large numbers turned out for this, not just for the races but for the festival atmosphere: flags and bunting; music from the hospital band; buns, sandwiches and cakes; tea and lemonade; the competitions and sideshows; the doctors and other senior staff who could be seen and spoken to in relaxed mood; the hilarity as 'Steve' once again fell into the water jump in the obstacle race, confidently predicted by Dr Cyril Perry, and contrived to lose his shorts; and, again, the chance to see and chat up the patients of the opposite sex. This was the climax of the year and, if the sun shone, would be remembered and talked about until the next year. The races and jumps, straight and novelty, mostly handicapped for the benefit of the older or the more disordered patients, were a minor part of the day, serving merely to justify the afternoon happening at all. Still it was good to see a tolerant spirit, so that the feebler, struggling patients were encouraged and applauded. Sadly, as the years went by, this occasion slipped down the scale of prestige events. Run now by the staff activities department and the patients' recreation committee, fewer senior staff attended, their time apparently commanded by other pressing duties. The Broadmoor 'community' declined and became more a disparate collection of specific locations, activities and therapeutic 'events' (see Chapter 19). Parallelling the world outside, no doubt, fractured and fragmented, drifting away from its community roots and turning into itself and its teledependence. In 1959, however, this had not yet started. A community spirit still prevailed.

The Female Wing events equivalent to sports day were the

women's bowls and croquet finals. Progressing through the summer on a knockout basis until the last two emerged, they were made a social event where, once again, the parole patients came over from the male side and tea, sandwiches and cakes were served. Britt and the hospital band played in one of the conical shelters which were just as they looked in the old engravings from the Illustrated London News of 1864, reporting Broadmoor's first year. A scene straight out of Kipps on the Folkestone sea front. The winners were politely applauded; the trophy awarded; and everyone moved into the small hall for the inevitable evening dance. This hall had an even smaller stage than the central hall, but no pillars. It did, however, have a splendid backcloth painted by a patient artist of years before. Not Richard Dadd (the famous artist who had been a Broadmoor patient in the 19th century), but quite a masterpiece. Some of Richard Dadd's paintings had been on the frontage of the central hall stage at one time but were removed later for safety. His paintings had been on sacking, on windows and anything he could find that the staff would let him paint on. His London figures (road crossing sweeper, wooden legged sailor, street fiddler) hung in the super's office and for years provided relief when meetings or case conferences got boring. Anyway, the small hall stage in the Female Wing just about managed to accommodate Britt and the orchestra. The croquet lawn and bowling greens may now have gone but not the memories of the finals and their dances - frozen in time.

Events on the Block

Apart from the chapel, the central hall, the sports field, the gardens and the little room where the Broadmoor Chronicle was produced (later moved into part of the new handicrafts complex), there were some corporate events on the blocks. I've already mentioned the

Christmas dinner and film show. Blocks also had their own concerts at Christmas where the aspiring performers who did not have a parole card and could not attain the level of the Broadhumoorists could nevertheless get up and give vent to their own brand of singing, playing, joke telling or reciting, entertaining themselves whether or not they entertained their fellow patients. As time went by and amplification equipment became more readily available, it became more feasible to mirror the entertainment seen on the box and feel in touch with the evolving world outside. Back in 1959, however, it still had the ring of the village hall about it, still in the age of Miss Marple.

Schizophrenic thought disorder didn't prevent many patients from giving vent through voice and instrument to their musical talents. Dr Patrick McGrath was very insistent that I attend one block concert to listen to a particular patient who, chronically schizophrenic, exemplified thought disorder in music. A competent pianist, one could listen with admiration to his playing but, gradually, one realized it didn't quite fit together. Not as obvious as the wrong notes of Les Dawson, it nevertheless emerged subtly off key. You had to listen carefully to discern it and it could be quite entertaining. If it had been his own composition it would probably have been much admired, just as are the apparently off key compositions of some established modern composers. But this was his own rendering of traditional composers. The bizarre paintings of many psychiatric patient artists are familiar and, indeed, can both fascinate and impress with their imagination and quality. Like dreams, they are often interpreted and art is often used in therapy, increasingly so nowadays. I had not before heard the equivalent on a piano.

Corporate activity at block level didn't need to wait for an organized concert, however. Regular and frequent activity was organized by the ward staff to include beetle drives, bingo, whist drives, quizzes, snooker and table tennis.

SUMMARY

The corporate and individual activity of a large community like Broadmoor, whether intentionally therapeutic or merely attempting to maintain as normal a way of life inside the walls as outside, is as important a component in this history as many of the more formal clinical activities. It defines the setting in which everything else took place, and in which the effects of change after the 1959 Act would have to be understood, but it also exerts its own not inconsiderable influence.

Although the most disturbed patients, which at any one time were only a minority of the patient population, were restricted in the recreational activities they could safely undertake, even they had access to reading and writing materials much of the time and would come out of their locked rooms whenever possible, under supervision, to listen to radio, watch TV, play games, go into the outside recreation area and interact with as many staff and other patients as possible. Compare this with the residents in many of our prisons, not ostensibly disordered, who spend up to 23 hours a day in their rooms.

At an intermediate level, patients on the way to recovery, or who had reached a chronic level of stability, or whose mental disorder did not take a continuously disruptive and aggressive form, would all have access not only to reading and writing material but to the ward radio and TV, to snooker and table tennis, to numerous card and board games, and to the physical activities of the outside recreational areas and gardens. They would also be able to attend the chapel, weekly film shows and periodic concerts and socials in the central hall, and go down to the sports field to watch the weekly football or cricket matches. This in addition to some half of the total patient population going to work areas, as described in the previous chapter, during the working day. Not a bad approximation to the outside world and, for many, a more congenial, varied and hassle-free one, albeit restricted, than they had often experienced hitherto.

For the (internal) parole patients, mostly in Blocks 2 and 5, almost all of whom were at work areas during the day, there was also more scope for recreation in the evenings and at week-ends. These were the patients who were doing much of the organizing of the activities for the rest, in terms of sports and other recreational events. They produced the patients' magazine: 'The Broadmoor Chronicle'. Because of their ground parole and freedom of movement inside their ward blocks they could follow creative artistic, writing and musical hobbies. They could have their own room furnishings including radio, record player and, later on, television, although more bulky items like artists' easels and musical instruments tended to be used in the larger recreational rooms specifically set aside for them. Apart from the barred windows and locked external doors, this life certainly approximated that of the outside world.

Even so, before going on to describe what changed after 1959, it will be useful to describe how the 'clinical team' of that time functioned; who they were, how they assessed new patients, reassessed existing ones and finally decided whom to discharge and when.

CHAPTER 10

CLINICAL PRACTICE

Chapter 5, in describing the staff, has already said something of their functions. These may also be expected to be reasonably well known from common knowledge of what a nurse, a doctor or a social worker does in general medicine. In mental health, however, it is not always so clear. Giving medicines may be obvious in any setting but just what does a nurse additionally do to care for a mentally disordered person and how does a doctor (who in this setting is a psychiatrist) evaluate and report a patient's progress so that decisions are reached, first, about diagnosis and treatment, then about what constitutes recovery and, finally, about readiness for discharge and the aftercare requirements? All these have 'special' significance in a 'special' hospital where the penalties for a mistake can have dangerous consequences for many people.

THE CONSULTANT PSYCHIATRIST

In 1959 the new legislation operated in a context of medical hegemony. New disciplines and new specialties of old disciplines had not yet blossomed to the extent of requiring a 'clinical team' approach. Such specialisms as there were took referrals from the medical consultant responsible for a patient and reported back their findings for the consultant to incorporate into a diagnosis and a course of treatment. The nursing profession carried out the requirements of such treatment at the day-to-day ward level and were the vital channel of communication between doctor and patient of the hour-by-hour treatment effects. A doctor could observe the signs and symptoms a patient presented and reported at a psychiatric examination but would also incorporate information from nursing staff about other fields of patient activity beyond the consulting room, just as the results of X-ray and other specialist investigations would be incorporated. A patient's activities in leisure time or when coping with the essentials of getting up, keeping clean, dressed and fed, and organizing his or her daily routines, would all be grist to the mill of understanding how his or her mind worked and how mental illness or disorder might be impairing the free flow of daily routines. Workshop staff could comment on the patient's reactions to a new work pattern: the ability to learn, persist, receive instruction and co-operate with others in the work setting. A social worker could supply information about a patient's home, family and work circumstances from home visits and, on discharge, would visit potential employers and accommodation to find a suitable situation in which the discharged patient might re-establish normal life or develop a new life.

The consultant was, therefore, the gatherer and co-ordinator of all this information, incorporating it with his or her own in arriving at a diagnosis and course of treatment. Even if a colleague, medical or otherwise, carried out some or all of this treatment, the consultant remained responsible and in overall charge. This situation persists to this day, even though other specialties might now carry through their own analysis of the problem in alternative terms and use procedures that are not medical. Whilst other services may now be independently consulted in a community care context and a GP may make direct contact with any of them, within the context of a secure hospital the medical consultant, in this case a psychiatrist, remains, in the terminology of the Act, the 'Responsible Medical Officer', or RMO, and therefore in overall charge of the care and treatment of the patient. Parliament, in taking evidence in 1982 for the amendment of the 1959 Act, considered the case put by other professions about formulating and carrying out alternative modes of treatment, but retained the existing system of according overall responsibility only to the medical profession. It was said that MPs were ever reluctant to accord responsibility for people's lives to anyone other than themselves and lawyers (and Parliament is the overall lawyer) so that its departure from this to accord the medical profession such power was quite sufficient an innovation for one century. Anything more would have to await the millennium![1]

THE CLINICAL CONFERENCE

Meanwhile, in 1959, Broadmoor had one consultant psychiatrist in the person of the Physician Superintendent, Dr Patrick McGrath, and another part-time one in Dr Brian O'Connell. Whilst the other non-consultant medical staff might prescribe medication for routine physical needs and renew the psychiatric medication prescribed by

---

1. Since this chapter was drafted a new century has arrived, together with a new millennium, and with it yet another Government White Paper with proposals to amend the next Mental Health Act after the one which is the subject of this history. Surprisingly, and somewhat unexpectedly so soon into the envisaged 'millennium', the white paper includes a proposal to change 'Responsible Medical Officer' into 'Clinical Supervisor' and, with it, the restriction of the role to the medical profession. Clinical psychologists are specifically named as one of the professions that might undertake this expanded role. The white paper is hotly debated and has many vociferous critics (in respect of this as well as many of its other proposals), so the proposal may not be enacted until further into the millennium, if ever. If it is, watch out for a further footnote.

the consultants, and whilst they would also supervise the giving, for instance, of ECT (electro-convulsive therapy), the consultant remained the 'RMO' (although this term did not come in until the new Act) with overall responsibility for decision making and recommendations which, in Broadmoor's and the other special hospitals' cases, went to the then Ministry of Health for onward liaison with the Home Office.

In 1959, then, a weekly case conference sufficed to keep pace with the admission of new patients. This was held in the physician superintendent's office: an august, spacious, wood-panelled room hung round with Richard Dadd paintings and the tangle of wires crossing the floor to the several telephones on Dr McGrath's desk. Sat around a large table to one side were the members of the case conference, headed by Dr McGrath. To his left, Dr O'Connell; to his right his confidential secretary, Mr Eric Cooper, the head of the medical office, who would take notes and report the conference. Dr Cyril Perry, the deputy superintendent, would also be present, together with others of the medical officers who were available and the social worker, Mrs Helen Paton. Dr Peter Smith, as MO in Block 4 where new patients were normally admitted, was responsible for presenting the conference case. To this august assembly I was invited when I began the psychology service at the end of 1959 (when, as I have already said, the 1959 Act had not yet been implemented: that did not happen until November 1960).

A case conference began with a presentation of the case from Dr Smith (or Dr Maine for the far fewer female admissions). This would trace the patient's life history in terms of childhood, development, health, education, work, home and family, traumas and past offences, etc., and any oddities or abnormalities of any of these, finishing with a detailed synopsis of the events of the offence which had been the cause of the patient's admission to Broadmoor. Mrs Paton contributed social work information from her visit to the home and family, amplifying from first-hand observation what Dr Smith might already have described, particularly describing the views and attitudes of any family she had met, and the home circumstances. I presented the findings of the psychological assessments I had carried out.

Introducing Psychological Assessments

Since this was an innovation and may still be obscure to those who otherwise understand what doctoring, nursing and social working is all about, a little detail may not go amiss at this point. Devising a psychological assessment programme for new admissions clearly had to be one of my first tasks. This would enable an opinion to be available at the outset and a base line to be established for future comparison and assessment of change. It had to be a standardized procedure so that comparisons could be made between newly arriving patients as the numbers accumulated and any trends observed as they emerged. It also had to be both comprehensive and practicable so that all the basic indicators were available but without taking up so much time that other functions for the new service became excluded. From standard psychological practices of the time and my previous experience at Rainhill Hospital I had assembled a range of assessment procedures and materials which I was keen to use in this new situation both to answer the standard questions a psychologist was expected to answer and to see what results would emerge from this different patient population. One of the key roles that had been included in the specification for the new post I was to fulfil was the assembly of a body of research information that would gradually build a picture of the clinical variations to be found at Broadmoor. This should then enable a better understanding of the factors associated with the offences and diagnoses of the patients and the consequent development of a more effective service.

Three procedures were adopted. The first was the comprehensive intelligence test of the time. This was not primarily for the purpose of estimating intelligence, although that was also useful to know. Its principal usefulness lay in its ten or eleven component parts (known as 'sub-tests'). These rarely produced an even set of scores because most people's individual abilities varied over the component tasks involved. Certain patterns that commonly occurred were well documented and these, of course, included those associated with the impairments in thinking and reasoning that were associated with certain mental disorders. It was, therefore, helpful to see if a newly arrived patient showed a pattern typical of any of these. If so then there was some corroboration of the disorder; if not then there was information suggesting a modification of the diagnosis, its severity, or progress. Either way there was a base line against which to chart response to treatment: improvement or deterioration. Meanwhile strengths might suggest where a patient could usefully work in the hospital, or receive training which would capitalize on these strengths for eventual discharge; weaknesses might suggest where treatment or workshop training should be concentrated (a formal education department was yet to come to the hospital).

The second procedure was a maze tracing task. Again success or otherwise was only part of this test's usefulness, equally important being the manner of tackling the task, a set of 'qualitative errors' being scorable. A markedly poorer performance than on the first test would alert one to the possibility of certain kinds of brain damage or a temperamental variation of the psychopathic type - a principal reason for selecting the test. The qualitative errors would then be tallied for characteristics of the impulsive and careless kind. Absence of these and characteristics instead of the hesitant, uncertain kind would conversely suggest an alternative personality type which, again, would be important to relate to the other information, psychiatric and social, that had been gathered on the patient.

Thirdly and finally, a comprehensive questionnaire was included in world-wide use and with well attested personality and clinical 'profiles'. Again, the individual's results could be compared with these to discern similarities and differences which might confirm or modify the other diagnostic indications available from other sources and highlight problem areas which would be important to address in subsequent assessments and treatment. This questionnaire took some time for a patient to complete (an hour or two) but time was not, of course, a limiting factor for patients in Broadmoor and there was scarcely ever a complaint. The circumstances of the patients were, furthermore, hardly those to encourage a complaint but many patients said they were glad to be doing something with their time that they saw as relevant to their progress: they could see that the questionnaire gave a comprehensive coverage of the problems that they might be experiencing whilst enabling them to rule out those that they saw as irrelevant. Validity checks were built into the questionnaire which indicated the degree of frankness, exaggeration, concealment or defensiveness in the patient's responses. These were later to contribute to the psychology service's early research endeavours and to give rise to some intriguing ideas and theories as well as to the development of new assessment methods and, later still, to treatment innovations. Of course it is part of the psychologist's role and training also to interview the patient about significant life events which would be expected to have influenced thinking, emotions, attitudes and behaviour generally but undue repetition of what the patient had often already been subjected to *ad nauseam* was to be avoided at this point and the process was generally confined to what was required to establish rapport and to explain the reasons for and likely outcomes of the procedures which were to follow. It was interesting (and relevant) to observe a patient's reaction to this explanation. Many were intrigued and appreciative and the majority welcomed the explanation. A few were disinterested and simply wanted to press on and get the procedure over with, sometimes saying so impatiently. Either way, part of the skill in administering these procedures was to try to ensure interest and motivation and maintain the patient's co-operation.

The Patient Interviewed

With the case conference primed with all available information from the attentions of the various disciplines involved (the nursing contribution was to follow) the patient was brought into the room, accompanied by a nurse escort who, as a member of the relevant ward staff, was able subsequently to comment from the nursing angle on the patient's clinical state since arrival in the hospital. Dr McGrath would explain the purpose of the conference and reassure patients that it was in their interests for staff to understand the reasons they were there, what they might be suffering from and what might be done to help them whilst in the hospital. He would then take them through the circumstances of their offence and their state of mind at the time, seeking comments and reasons for what they had done in order to establish the basis for a psychiatric diagnosis. Dr O'Connell would follow Dr McGrath and was adept at drawing out inconsistencies, irrationalities and bizarre aspects of thinking that would demonstrate a psychotic mental disorder. Others would follow with further questions.

The case conference would be taking place some six to eight weeks after admission in order to allow the patient to settle in, the nursing staff to have adequate time to observe the patient's pattern of behaviour and symptoms, and the other disciplines to have carried out their various procedures. (This had the disadvantage, of course, that the full impact of the patient's disorder might have passed and not be clearly seen. This might well have accounted for the lack of gross disturbance indicators on psychological assessment that was sometimes noted, although other explanations eventually turned out to seem more likely.) Finally, the patient would be asked if he or she had anything they wanted to say or ask. They were usually too overawed to do so, although a common question was "how long am I going to be here?"

The patient would then be taken back to the ward and the accompanying nurse would be asked to return, when the nursing observations of ward behaviour would be recounted. A general discussion would follow, often with arguments over whether clear diagnostic pointers had been established or not. My own contribution, I have to say, was often the discrepant one as I was not always able to find the evidence of psychosis from the assessments I had used (in terms of impairment of reasoning functions or endorsement of questionnaire items typical of the usual disorder categories). Of course, as has been said, the patient's condition some six to eight weeks after admission might not by then be in the extreme or florid state that it was at the time of the offence and that, in addition, would have taken place a long time previously to admission, taking into account the period on remand awaiting trial, the time of the trial itself and then the delay awaiting a decision on place of committal.

Psychological assessments prior to my own were sparse, although an IQ test had usually been done in the case of men who had come via Brixton Prison where, as a remand prison, there was a psychological tester (Len Fost) and contact was soon established to have the results of these routinely passed on to us. Even so, differences, disagreements and inconsistencies still occurred and were the source of concern until a body of data began to accumulate to illuminate the range of results we were obtaining and the possible explanations for them. At that time, however, this was still in the future.

INITIAL TREATMENT

Conclusions from the admission case conference determined where the patient would then go for what was the initial phase of their treatment. Up to that point any treatment other than to maintain some equilibrium in very disordered patients was avoided in order to have as clear a picture as possible of the disorder which had brought about the admission to Broadmoor. This would by inference be the disorder responsible for the offence although one of the questions awaiting research was precisely this: was the mental disorder the cause of the offence; the result of the offence; or the state of mind that allowed an offence to be committed which otherwise might have been inhibited or dealt with differently; or nothing to do with the offence at all?

The majority of the male patients would, in fact, begin or continue their initial treatment in Block 4 (later Dorset House). This was because it was a large 'general purpose' ward block whose three wards catered for the great majority of conditions. The other main alternative was Block 7 (later Cornwall House) although this was selected for the rather more difficult patient or one whose condition was already becoming chronic. If the patient's behaviour was particularly violent most of the time, or with unpredictable violent outbursts, then the more secure wards of Blocks 1 and 6 (later Norfolk and Monmouth Houses) would be where the patient went. Those who were extremely violent on admission would be admitted direct to Block 6. These were not so much smaller ward blocks as blocks which housed fewer patients because they were almost all in individual rooms, not dormitories, for security reasons. Block 3 (later Kent House) was for older and/or physically ill patients whose condition had usually passed the acute and was instead in the chronic stage and where the infirmary catered for many ailing, bedridden men. This just left Blocks 2 and 5 (later named Essex and Gloucester Houses) which were for the specifically improving male patients, so were inappropriate for placement immediately after the admission conference.

The options in the Female Wing were fewer, with only two blocks, but these divided into five wards, so a similar gradation was possible with the smaller number of patients there and only the women's equivalent of Block 6 patients started in FW Block 2 (later Lancaster House), most starting in the bottom ward of Block 1 (later York House).

Even someone who, by the time of their arrival, had passed the acute stage of illness, or was in remission, or perhaps had never demonstrated very abnormal behaviour apart from their offence, would not go immediately to one of the parole blocks. Broadmoor in 1959 was still organized on the hierarchical system of progress being assessed partly in terms of degree of mental disorder and partly on acceptability of social behaviour. This had always served it well in the days of very different legislation when treatment was limited and progress measured largely by social behaviour. The effects of the 1959 Act were yet to be felt, with its growth of medical and psychological concepts and expansion of staff to deal with the new legislation. Block 4, Dorset House, was therefore where the bulk of the initial and acute treatment of the male patients took place, and Ward 1 in the Female Wing.

The treatment regime envisaged by the admission case conference would generally be formulated initially in terms of the appropriate pharmacological treatment for the diagnosis at which the conference had arrived. Largactil was the principal medication for schizophrenia in that era and remained so for many years. ECT (electro-convulsive therapy) was still in its heyday and would, as described in Chapter 8, be specified particularly for the depressed or those whose schizophrenia took a withdrawn and retarded form. Psychotherapy had not yet become routinely available except what the medical staff might be able to fit into their heavy case loads, although if this was thought particularly important it might be recorded as necessary and some means of providing it sought. As someone who had been involved in some pioneering use of behaviour therapy at my previous hospital, I was sometimes asked whether I thought this had anything to contribute but, at that time, I was neither confident that I knew the forms of mental disorder I was seeing sufficiently well to offer such a strategy, nor did I feel that this was a priority for my new service at this stage. It would be taking time from what I saw as the first priority, namely to assemble as soon as possible a bank of data from the assessment of all incoming patients and gradually the entire resident population by means of group testing throughout the wards. Only with this foundation did I feel there would be adequate basis for tackling the greatly more time consuming work of individual treatment programmes. If the admission case conference was dealing with one of the 1959 Act's newly categorized psychopathic patients then a psychological approach would have been particularly appropriate but at that time neither the theory nor the practice had been developed.

Apart from the growing range of psychiatric medications or ECT (insulin treatment had virtually ended by 1959 and brain surgery was regarded as counter-productive, as already said) there was, of course, the treatment environment of the hospital itself, which has been discussed in some detail in the immediately preceding chapters. Partly because large closed mental hospitals have had such a 'bad press' and partly because of the limited availability of any other forms of treatment, this treatment aspect has tended to be disparaged. As described in the preceding chapters, however, it was much more comprehensively organized at Broadmoor than in the 'county' hospitals where, in any case, patients tended to be less 'long-stay'. The initial case conference would therefore often try to foresee what area of workshop, ward-based or recreational activity might be developed or encouraged to provide benefit to a patient. This would not necessarily be in terms of the actual skill or accomplishment involved but would be looking to the opportunity to develop motivation for a return to more normal daily routines, something often conspicuously lacking in a patient's recent or even prevailing life experience. Response to instruction, assimilation of new knowledge, response to surrounding co-workers or environment and adjustment to routines and targets were, therefore, the aims of a work placement. Similarly, the identification of potential to contribute to or derive benefit from leisure opportunities might also be foreseen and encouraged. These would be particularly relevant for the psychopathic category of patient whose ability would often be high but whose persistence and application might be brief, or whose capacity to co-operate and respond to instruction might be minimal.

CONTINUING TREATMENT

In the days before the implementation of the 1959 Act when the consultant cover of Drs McGrath and O'Connell could not extend much beyond the processing of new arrivals and, at the other end, discharges, the continued monitoring of progress 'on the blocks' was up to the other medical staff (at senior registrar and SHMO level, it should be remembered) together with the DNs/DSs (departmental nurses and sisters) and other nursing staff. As has been said already, however, these staff would be in a good position to get to know their patients, seeing them continually in all their daily pursuits. They were, therefore, able to spot changes in individual dispositions; responses to new arrivals and departures; visits from friends and family and so on; enabling judgement of progress towards dischargeability or, conversely, relapse and deterioration.

ASSESSING PROGRESS

Between the long-serving nursing staff and medical officers on the one hand and the newcomers resulting from the new Act on the other, the business of monitoring and reporting patients' progress through the often lengthy duration of a patient's stay gradually took its course. The regular reviews required by later legislation which entailed the patient's discharge unless firm evidence of mental disorder could be demonstrated were not the procedure of pre-1959; nor, in fact, of the 1959 Act either. This was to await the 1983 Act. The 1959 Act, however, did require reviews. These, rather than requiring evidence as to why a patient should stay, required a case to be made as to why they should go. Entries in case notes, therefore, followed a pattern of reporting progress but rarely expressed a positive, enthusiastic recommendation for discharge. This awaited the arrival of a male patient in Block 2 (later Essex House) and the granting of parole. This was Dr McGrath's house. In the two blocks of the Female Wing it would be the progression to Wards 2 and 3 of Block 1, later York House, where Dr O'Connell was the consultant. It was these two senior medical staff, at consultant level, who took the responsibility of recommending discharge and they, therefore, tended to make the majority of referrals for a psychological report on whether there were still signs of remaining disturbance that might go against a discharge recommendation.

Right at the outset, then, in parallel with the assessments of mental state on admission, there arose the unusual task of assessing 'normality'. For most clinical psychologists normality was accepted in the absence of a need to assess abnormality. At Rainhill we had been occupied with assessing degree and type of abnormality and when a patient was ostensibly recovered there was never felt any need to refer for confirmation; a patient would go out and normality would be confirmed by his or her successfully coping with the outside world. If they failed they could return. At Broadmoor, however, normality could never be assumed. In the interests of public safety it had to be proved. This was a new task. A set of normal assessment results might be obtained but how did we know if these were relevant to the abnormal behaviours that had brought the patient into Broadmoor in the first place? To those who tended to criticize psychological assessment work at Broadmoor, especially a little later when, in the treatment boom of the 70s, 'testing' became a dirty word associated with 'labelling' and 'pigeon-holing', we became weary of explaining this important difference in the Broadmoor work. Not for us the luxury of assessing only abnormalities, needs, assets and potentials. When someone seemed well, or claimed they were, we had to assess that too, to substantiate or refute it.

The other area of assessment related to departing patients came by referral from Mrs Paton, the social worker. She was concerned with the placement of patients in work, as well as their accommodation, and was often asked by potential employers about a patient's abilities and aptitudes, especially if a patient had no particular educational qualifications. To any assessment related to discharge suitability, therefore, it proved helpful to add a specific aptitude test and one of vocational interest which Mrs Paton came to find useful and to rely upon in meetings with potential employers or hostel wardens.

The new psychology service was therefore quickly into a twofold task of assessing and reporting newly arriving patients on the one hand and readiness for discharge of long-standing patients on the other. To enable comparisons and to build up a body of research data, the same basic tests were used in the assessments of potential discharge as were used for the new admissions. For the discharge assessments, however, and precisely because the issues were of specifically targeted aggression and not just of the degree and type of disorder at which we were looking in the admissions, there was the need to go further. Ideally we would have been looking at this in the arrivals, too, but this had to await the expansion of the service. In any case, it would be advisable to identify what one was looking for in the potential discharges and from this develop something for use with admissions. Moreover, the extended assessment of admission problems would be taking place in the next phase of a patient's stay when the response to initial treatment had achieved a mental state where such further assessment could be better undertaken.

'Going further' in the case of the potential discharges enabled the selection of any of a number of other tests which were already in the repertoire of clinical psychologists in the 1950s and were, furthermore, being published and reported in the literature with each new book or journal issue. There were 'cognitive techniques' for assessing the kind and degree of reasoning deficits or disorders; there were questionnaires for differentiating symptom-clusters and personality characteristics; there were rating scales for use in conjunction with nursing observations to compare the presence and relative strengths of symptom clusters again; there were varieties of tests which differentiated people's manner of performing the various daily tasks that life presented and which could, therefore, suggest differences of a developmental or pathological origin; and there were the 'projective tests' of much argued repute but which had the merit of presenting someone with an open-ended or possibly quite ambiguous set of circumstances into which they 'projected' their own ideas and feelings and from which preoccupations and personality deviations might be inferred.

The range of validatory populations, from which all these techniques and procedures had been derived, varied but were rarely specific to a patient population the like of Broadmoor's. Whilst their results might not initially produce the certainty with which a discharge recommendation needed to be made, they all had potential, and needed to be used to accumulate a data bank from which variations could be related to outcomes. All this would take time. For the moment, however, there was at least a variety of measures which could demonstrate the basic abnormalities, or their absence, which were relevant to the range of mental disorders defined in the 1959 Act, and which could, therefore, help to answer this first question. Whether or not they could also answer the further question, of future likelihood of violent behaviour, was another matter.

DATA STORAGE AND RETRIEVAL

The assembly of a bank of information on patients arriving in the hospital, comprising social, criminal, psychiatric and psychological factors, obviously called for a data storage and retrieval system which would facilitate research. One needed to be able to relate the categories of diagnosis and offence to each other and to background factors in patients' lives and circumstances. Their relationship to the new Mental Health Act categories of mental disorder was also vital whilst, of course, my concern was also to relate them to the information being assembled from the psychological assessments. These were the days before computers, or at least the sort of widely available and easily usable computers we have today. We had had in the army ponderous old valve operated computers for linking and controlling guns and radar; and both universities and industry were beginning to acquire equipment using the new wonder marvel - the transistor - but the microchip was as yet unheard of.

There were, of course, punched cards. Hollerith was the main one, although requiring a machine to read the results. However, the psychology department at our sister special hospital, Rampton, had acquired a different and novel punched card system which could be sorted by hand and read by eye. Each card catered for a 'variable' - an item of information or set of characteristics - rather than an individual. Sets of cards could be assembled for each of many variables, catering for the variations between aspects of those variables. These might be only two, as in 'present' or 'absent'; 'high' or 'low'; or they might be numerous, as in ages, offences, diagnoses, former occupations, education and, in the case of my psychological interests, IQ and other test scores. We therefore obtained sets of these cards and set up a system for recording the relevant information. All the patients resident on 1st January 1960 were numbered from 1 upwards, 1 being the man who had been longest in Broadmoor and had the oldest hospital number. Similarly for the women patients. One to about 750 catered for the male patients whilst the women began at 2000 and went up to about 2120, leaving plenty of room from 750 to 1999 for new male admissions yet to come and above 2120 to the limit of the 2500 spaces on the card for female admissions yet to come.

A HOSPITAL SURVEY

Finally, in the implementation of a new clinical and research service, and to tap into the great mass of the patient population who were neither new arrivals nor being assessed as potential discharges, a survey was undertaken, block by block, of general ability and its impairment, together with a brief questionnaire assessment of emotional stability and personality. Each ward was visited, at lunch time when all the patients were together, to explain what was to happen and why it could help them all to take part. The staff nurse in the psychology department was trained to administer the procedures and worked his way through all the wards, some half-a-dozen patients at a time, taking an hour or two on one or two days a week. It took a couple of years to complete the male wards, a rather remarkable achievement for our 'one psychologist and a nurse' service, by which time demands had escalated to the point that an extension to the Female Wing had to be deferred.

The results with the male patients proved valuable and somewhat surprising. What was not surprising was the degree of impairment in many of the patients of the 'back blocks', assessed in terms of how far present reasoning ability was below their past attainment as measured by their acquired vocabulary level (a 'recall' task unaffected by the impairment which accompanied many psychotic disorders). However, the surprise was in the levels of present reasoning to emerge. Almost all ward blocks showed a level above the national average and the results from the parole patients in Block 2, Essex House later, were well above. This threw light on the possible criteria that might have brought them to notice for selection for Block 2: their degree of competence and attainment would have tended to lead to greater involvement in useful hospital activities. Of course, to some extent it was not surprising that Broadmoor had a population of considerably above average intelligence when the patients classified under the new Mental Health Act as 'mentally subnormal' or 'severely mentally subnormal' (later referred to as 'mentally handicapped' and in the 1983 Act as 'mentally impaired') were sent to Rampton and Moss Side, the other two special hospitals for England and Wales. This left the intake to Broadmoor 'skewed' in an upward direction.

CONCLUSIONS

This chapter, detailing the range of clinical practices and especially the procedures for assessing patients on arrival and in preparation for discharge, has dwelt extensively upon psychological work not merely because the writer was the psychologist concerned but because this was a new service. It represented the main addition to the existing routines of a mental hospital at that time. Psychiatric procedures were already well established, using direct clinical observation and interview and the medical history. Mental nurses, as they then were, similarly acquired skills of observation of patterns of mental activity and physical behaviour, but from a different standpoint. Social workers compiled information derived from observation of personal, family and social background and circumstances and tended, therefore, to interpret problems and requirements in terms of their sociological significance. Psychologists, however, were introducing different and novel methods involving a person undertaking tasks which either replicated or drew upon aspects of things done and abilities used in the course of everyday activities. Reasoning out some problem, recalling something learned, assembling the components of some common object, finding a route, or reporting a personal characteristic, preference, habit or opinion; all these kinds of thing were the bases of the procedures being developed by psychologists at that time. They analysed the normal variations in performances on these tasks and noted where significant differences emerged which could distinguish between diagnostic categories or sub-groups.

Some of the psychologist's activities might replicate the questions asked by other observers, but psychologists were adding the element of measurement to these, assessing performance on a range of standard problems and tasks, graded in order of increasing difficulty, always the same and in the same sequence, which therefore allowed objective comparison. Additionally, questionnaires used items of personal information and opinion, where the answers could be clustered, classified and validated by comparison with large groups of other individuals, standardized according to age, sex, occupational group, educational level, diagnostic category, etc.

These, therefore, allowed a much more systematic and accurate comparison to be made between the individual being assessed and the range of data accumulated on the assessment procedure in question. The procedures sometimes had the disadvantage of seeming to be rather impersonal and covering matters that would be irrelevant for some patients and therefore irritating. But they were comprehensive and objective. Psychiatric interviews, although with the potential to be more relaxed and informal, were inevitably and intentionally more selective and subjective, not constant between one individual and the next, and so would not permit quantifiable comparison. They were directed at the discovery of some one or more signs or symptoms associated with a diagnostic condition. Comparison was therefore possible only at a 'nominal' or categorical level and not at an 'ordinal' or quantifiable one.

Different professional practices were, therefore, complementary and cumulative, avoiding unnecessary replication. With the arrival of clinical psychology, another dimension to the understanding of a patient's condition was in prospect. Later, new methods were to be available to the several professions, and further new specialities within them, and yet other new professions would be arriving on the scene. Some of these will figure in this history of Broadmoor. For the moment, and with the arrival in 1959 of new legislation and a new profession, this chapter has aimed to set the scene for the clinical development that was to take place through the 1960s, 1970s and up to the arrival of the next Mental Health Act.

SUMMARY

This chapter has described the way patients' mental disorders and offences were assessed on arrival in Broadmoor and the information derived by the several clinical disciplines presented, discussed and integrated by the RMO (responsible medical officer), i.e.: the consultant psychiatrist, by means of a clinical conference. This has included some explanation of the role of the clinical psychologist who was the newcomer to the clinical scene at that time and whose methods were therefore unfamiliar, as they probably are to many even now.

The dispersal of patients to the various parts of the hospital was then made on the basis of type and degree of disorder and the '$64 thousand dollar question' then became that of assessing, invariably a number of years later, the response to treatment and eventual readiness for discharge. This entailed answering questions of a quite different order from those of psychiatric hospitals generally, dealing not merely with diagnosis and treatment but with verifying normality. This is usually assumed when 'good health' has returned but that is not enough with those who have behaved violently and whose normality has to be 'vouched for' before they can be allowed to return to the outside world. 'Prognosis' has a quite different connotation in this context.

The role of the new psychological service was, therefore, augmented by this need and an assessment programme on arrival was devised to provide a base line against which future reassessments could be set for comparison. The existing resident population was also the target of a group assessment research programme to derive further information for identifying both the immediate needs of the population and some basis for assessing their readiness for eventual discharge. Both endeavours, the initial base line assessment and the hospital survey, together with the pre-discharge assessments which also gradually accumulated and could be set against the arrival assessments, called for a data storage and retrieval system. In those pre-computer days this consisted of a punched card system. The assessment priorities meant there was no time for treatment activity but this, where psychologists were concerned, was in its infancy in those days. A thorough research-linked assessment programme, however, would establish a better basis for a future treatment role when it eventually developed, as it inevitably did. This features later in Broadmoor's modern history.

PART II

THE WAY IT WENT

CHAPTER 11

CLINICAL DEVELOPMENT

With the clinical resources and routines described in the previous chapter, therefore, Broadmoor braced itself for the arrival of the new Mental Health Act. My arrival at the end of 1959 gave me just long enough to observe life under the old legislation before the new Act came into effect at the end of 1960. In fact, Broadmoor's character as a century-old establishment, familiar with its duties, showed little immediate response. There would still be the same patients with the same requirements of care and security. Changes in the new legislation, however, did bring changes in the numbers and nature of the incoming patients. The old-style patients were still there but gradually they became less prominent amongst the growing numbers and types of new patient arriving as a result of the new legislation. These increasing numbers and varieties of patient inevitably imposed changes upon the hospital's procedures and practices. Chapter 3 has described how the 1959 Act brought changes in the types and proportions of mental disorder to appear at Broadmoor, whilst Chapter 4 has described and illustrated the changes in the other defining characteristics of the population such as their offences, ages and lengths of stay, together with the effects of the Act on rates of admission and discharge. What were the associated clinical consequences?

The basic job of the hospital had to continue: to treat, in conditions of security, mentally disordered patients from the courts direct, or by transfer from the prisons, or now by transfer from other hospitals. Either because of a court verdict, or mental disorder manifested in prison, or dangerous behaviour arising in another hospital, its patients were considered to need their care and treatment in secure surroundings where the public or their particular victim would be safe from them. Their usually copious documentation would arrive with or shortly after them and then a case conference would establish a diagnosis and treatment needs. They would make their way through the wards of the different 'blocks' receiving whichever of the treatments of the time was thought relevant to their needs, and participating in whichever of the occupational activities was available and suitable to them.

Life was inevitably institutional but of a generally benign kind enabling participation in a personal and community life approximating to that outside, except for the security to ensure that they remained where they were and did not endanger each other or the staff. According to the philosophy and personality of the departmental nurse in charge of their ward block and of the staff on each shift and, of course, the security level of the block in which they found themselves, they might sit, read, talk, play games, exercise, go out to a workshop and generally interact with other patients and staff. Most staff would encourage activities and many would themselves take part, although this was still only emerging from a philosophy that required them merely to station themselves at various vantage points and observe, intervening only in a crisis: counting numbers as patients moved to and from exercise, workshops or recreational pursuits; counting cutlery after meals; counting bed linen, towels; checking stores, mail; accompanying patients to wherever they might be going - workshops, visits or recreation - counting them through each door and relaying the number to the next member of staff along the way; counting and checking constantly.

CONVICT OR PATIENT

One of the first changes following the new Act which affected the status of patients arose from the use of the 'hospital order' authorizing their detention. As explained in the opening chapters, all the patients in residence on 1st November 1960 had either been detained under the old 'Her Majesty's Pleasure' conditions or been transferred as time serving prisoners. 'Pleasure' patients were either GBI (Guilty but Insane) or IOA (Insane on Arraignment) and these were accommodated within the new Act (in Section 71). Later the Criminal Procedures (Insanity) Act of 1964 more specifically addressed these. By 1970, hospital research statistics showed that over a quarter of those still in the hospital were in this category although only a little over a tenth of the decade's admissions had come in with this classification: such was the reduced use of the 'insanity' plea by comparison with the new nomenclature but the slowness with which existing patients moved out. The status of these 'Section 71' (or subsequently 'CPI Act') patients was, therefore, of people who had not been convicted. They enjoyed various privileges not available to a convicted person, such as inheriting from their victim if, as would often be the case, their victim had been their next of kin. Under the new legislation, however, the old insanity procedures fell into increasing disuse. The more flexible 'mental disorder' criteria were easier to establish as was, of course, their intention. However, this meant that the outcome of the trial was a conviction followed by a hospital order for treatment, not an acquittal on grounds of insanity. They were now 'convicts' under a hospital order, not 'pleasure patients'. The differences in legal status caused some misunderstandings and grievances.

THE NEW MENTAL DISORDER CATEGORIES

The change bringing far wider consequences, however, especially to the running of the hospital, was a double one: first, the arrival of this much broadened category of patients classified 'mentally ill' who would not have met the former 'McNaughtan insanity' criteria and, second, the arrival of patients under the new classification of 'psychopathic disorder'. It was not until some time later, when the admission rate had steeply increased and pressure on accommodation became severe, that the significance of 'dangerousness' was emphasized and merely to be a mentally disordered offender became insufficient to warrant high security care. Many of these patients could have been treated in conventional psychiatric settings and did not need high security care. By then, of course, local services had greatly changed as a result of the new Act, advances in psychiatric treatment and the public and political mood. It became more difficult to persuade local services that hospital order patients from the courts should be accommodated locally, when local mental hospital walls were being knocked down and wards unlocked. The provision in the new Act to be an 'informal', i.e.: voluntary patient, meant that most in-patients were in hospital under these conditions rather than by the old 'certification'. Compulsory orders under a 'section' of the new Act were less often used. Meanwhile, the special hospitals were the sufferers of these changes in taking increasing numbers of 'hospital order' patients who did not actually need high security care: they had been convicted of lesser offences of the nuisance rather than the dangerous kind but were, nevertheless, increasingly rejected by the newly emancipated local psychiatric hospitals who saw themselves now fulfilling a different role.

The changes did not introduce categories of patient whose mental disorders were unknown to the staff. These 'lesser' offenders presented similar kinds of disorder; it was only their offending behaviour that differed. They did bring about a change in the *proportions* of the different disorder categories, however. There were more neurotic type disturbances which would not have been classified as 'insane' under the old McNaughtan procedures. As remarked earlier, they might have been 'squeezed' into a McNaughtan classification by a sympathetic court in the case of a sad domestic homicide, so the type was not unfamiliar. They arrived in larger numbers now, however, and with lesser offences to their name. Alternatively they might have been classified under the new psychopathic disorder category, especially when the offence was a greater one and seen as part of a long standing personality disturbance as, for instance, in the case of the sex offenders. Psychopathic disorder also enabled a larger range of very disturbed people with aggressive offences on their record to be sent to the special hospitals. These, again, were not new to the staff's experience, but arrived in larger numbers and were, in fact, now properly placed as an intended result of the new legislation. It is interesting to emphasize this at this point for, years later with the changes introduced to the procedure with psychopaths in the 1983 Act and with the far greater use of care in the community, it has become more, rather than less, difficult to place these psychopaths in the special hospitals. The result has been that they are too often left with no alternative but to be sent to prison, contrary to the intentions of the legislation. Treatment conditions there are the exception rather than the rule, are different, and are not part of a 'continuum of care' through the system of secure hospital, medium secure units, open residential facilities and ultimately supervised community care. The 1959 Act, for all its radical changes from its predecessor and the need to 'top-and-tail' it with the 1983 modifications, had some tangible advantages for effective treatment and public protection with this vexed category of patient.

EFFECT OF ABOLISHING CAPITAL PUNISHMENT

A category of patient which gradually dwindled, especially after capital punishment was abolished in 1965, was the murderer who might have been regarded as insane by a sympathetic court despite lack of evidence of this at the trial. This was not because of a change in court procedures or jury attitudes but because there was no longer the need for a defendant to seek ways of avoiding 'the drop', as capital punishment by hanging was known. It was preferable to accept the prospect of a life sentence from which, with good behaviour, parole might eventually be achieved than to face an indefinite stay in hospital and carry the stigma of mental disorder for the rest of one's life. Of course, if the crime had bizarre or inexplicable features to it the question of mental state might still be raised. However, it was often difficult to persuade some defendants to plead this and, after the risk of the death penalty had been removed, there is no doubt the number of these cases in Broadmoor dwindled.

THE FACILITY TO TRANSFER PATIENTS BETWEEN PSYCHIATRIC HOSPITALS

The factors making for a rising admission rate, however, outnumbered those reducing it. One of these was the facility under the new Act for psychiatric hospitals around the regions to transfer their more difficult patients to a special hospital, on the grounds that such difficulty represented dangerousness. This tendency increased as local hospitals enjoyed the freedom to provide their treatment under less restricting conditions and doors were increasingly unlocked for the growing proportions of 'informal' patients. Those who attacked fellow patients or staff, were destructive of hospital property or who were thought to be a public risk when they absconded, were all inclined to find their way now to a special hospital. Numbers went on increasing.

Of course, requests for the transfer to Broadmoor of a patient who had behaved violently in a local hospital could be met with a corresponding request to take a patient from Broadmoor in exchange. This was undoubtedly a factor in the growth of the interchange between Broadmoor and local psychiatric hospitals, which is discussed below, but the problem here was one of 'catchment areas'. Patients at Broadmoor at that time came from the whole of England and Wales, even from some of the remaining overseas territories still administered from Britain. Only Scotland had its Broadmoor equivalent (in the State Hospital at Carstairs, which also took patients from Northern Ireland). The other two English special hospitals of that time (Rampton and Moss Side) were for mentally subnormal patients, as they were then known. Only as the 1959 Act gave way to the 1983 Act did all the special hospitals take all kinds of mentally disordered patients and become in any way regional in their 'catchments'. This meant that few, if any, of the patients ready to leave Broadmoor at any given time were likely to originate from a catchment area where the local psychiatric hospital had someone needing to be transferred to Broadmoor. Conversely, any local hospital that did want to transfer a patient to Broadmoor would be unlikely to be in an area of the country where Broadmoor had a patient ready for transfer.

INCREASED NUMBERS OF STATUTORY PROCEDURES

In addition to the pressure from increased patient numbers, the new Act introduced new procedures which increased the amount of time spent reviewing and reporting on patients, once in residence. The new legislation required more periodic reports by the RMO (the 'responsible medical officer' or consultant psychiatrist). There was also the increased reporting and responding entailed by the introduction of 'Restriction Orders' and Mental Health Review Tribunals (MHRTs). Restriction Orders, imposed by the court in the most serious cases and requiring the Home Secretary's consideration of any discharge recommendation or request for home visit or temporary leave, took more time and paperwork than a discharge which could be effected on the authority of the RMO alone. The new procedures with new legislation took some time for staff to become used to, especially with the influx of new senior professional staff that was arriving.

MHRTs, of course, were an innovation and occurred with great regularity as patients reached the specified time intervals under their respective 'sections' when an appeal could be made. An appeal naturally required a response by the RMO as to why he (they were all men at that time) did or did not think it allowable but it also took further staff time, principally on the part of the RMO again, when the tribunal's medical member visited to make a prior assessment and when the tribunal hearing actually took place. The RMO invariably needed to be available to discuss the case on both these occasions. If the MHRT entailed a public hearing, as sometimes occurred, or the patient had legal representation, more work and time would obviously be involved. All this was, of course, to the benefit of the patient and the proper and detailed review of his or her case and was the new legislation's intended purpose. With the increased numbers of admissions and, therefore, throughput of patients in residence, however, the pressures upon staff, especially the RMO, were greatly increased.

WAYS OF LEAVING BROADMOOR

Limitations of Discharge

'Throughput' brings us to the question of leaving Broadmoor. An increasing admission rate, as illustrated in Chapter 4 and doubling in the space of five years, naturally called for an increase in those going out. Bed numbers were limited and not infinitely expandable. Even so, there were times when some wards had to put beds in corridors (known as 'galleries' at Broadmoor) after beds had already been crammed ever more closely together in those blocks which had dormitories. As Dr McGrath was known to emphasize to visitors: "The special hospitals are the only hospitals which cannot refuse to take a patient. We are the end of the line. We take whomever the Home Office and Ministry of Health decide to send us." The picture is different today under the next Act.

If discharges were to increase, however, this could only mean that either:

(a) the previous discharge procedure or policy had been too cautious;
(b) discharges would now be taking place that might put people at risk; or
(c) there were now more kinds of patient in Broadmoor who were not there previously and who could be more readily discharged.

The first of these, (a) was an unknown; (b) was unthinkable; and (c) was likely to yield only limited results. Alternatively, other destinations must be found for patients who, although they might still need some kind of in-patient or supervised care, might no longer need it in the high security environment of a special hospital. Psychiatric hostels and day hospitals were rarities then whilst medium secure units were not yet in existence, although suggestions were inevitably raised as to their desirability and probably contributed to their eventual realization.

Kinds of Transfer

Local psychiatric hospitals (the former county mental hospitals) did exist, however, and it was to these that attention was principally directed for the transfer of patients under the new facility of the 1959 Act. Although these have been described as resistant to the reception of special hospital patients, they had not yet developed this resistance in those early years of the 1959 Act. It was only as time went on and they became more open that the difficulties arose. In the meantime there was a large reservoir of long-stay patients in Broadmoor who had responded to treatment but were not yet thought suitable for discharge, or who had become non-violent with the onset of a chronic, more passive stage of their disorder. Old age was an obvious further factor. These patients were more readily seen and accepted as suitable for transfer and this accounts for the graphs in Chapters 3 and 4 showing the large increase after 1960 in both the numbers of patients transferred and the lengths of time they had been in Broadmoor - upwards of 12 years - which stood in marked contrast with the fall to around 5 years for the lengths of stay of those discharged. Even so, it took hard work and much persuasion for these transfers to be achieved and Dr Edgar Udwin, the first of the new RMOs, spent a great deal of his time on that task.

Other forms of transfer which had to be examined to avoid the escalating admission numbers from overwhelming the hospital were: (a) to return to prison those transferred from there who had recovered or stabilized under treatment; (b) to transfer to one of the other special hospitals (where overcrowding was less of a problem with the 'subnormal' patients), any who might not be too out of place there, especially if their home area was nearer to Rampton or Moss Side than to Broadmoor; or (c) to return to their country of origin any of those who had arrived here because of the war and whose families still lived back in their home country, or who were first generation immigrants again with families in their home country.

In the case of (a) a patient could not be sent back to prison who had not come from there in the first place. The large number of patients still in the 'Pleasure' category at the outset of the new Act were not convicted so could not be sent to prison. Those arriving under the new 'hospital orders' were likewise ineligible for prison having been found to be suffering a mental disorder for which treatment was required and who had not been sentenced. Those 'time' patients who were recovered would probably have been returned to prison in any case to derive benefit from any remission due to them. Few were to be found who could take this route, therefore, but some could be argued to have reached the limit of their treatment progress so that return to prison was defensible.

In the case of (b) it was not impossible to transfer someone to the other special hospitals who fell outside the formal limits of mental subnormality so long as the margin was small and it could be argued that their behaviour was in significant respects tantamount to that of a subnormal person so that they could derive benefit from the treatment programmes available at the other special hospitals. Nearness to their homes and families was, in any case, reckoned to be tantamount to a treatment bonus where better contact and ease of visiting was involved.

In the case of (c) and as mentioned already in Chapter 4, there was in 1959 still a group of Europeans, mainly men and mainly

Polish, who had arrived in the UK to fight for their country's freedom forces during the war. Their mental disorders were now mostly chronic and non-dangerous and arrangements were made to return many to their families in Europe. Then there was a handful from former colonial areas with families still back in Malta, Gibraltar, Aden, Cyprus, Hong Kong, etc. Lastly there were the newly arriving West Indians and, later, Indians and Pakistanis. Most were still solitary representatives of their families in the Caribbean or the Indian subcontinent and had developed mental disorders, perhaps, as a result of the stress and strangeness of the emigration experience. Returning them to establishments for care and treatment near to their families was considered the best therapeutic strategy for them. This helped the Broadmoor accommodation problem as well.

EFFECT OF MORE PATIENTS AND EXTRA PROCEDURES ON STAFFING

Medical Staffing and Training

All these changes represented a great deal more work, not only in terms of the greater numbers arriving in Broadmoor but also in the assessments, reviews and reports now required. The responsibilities of the new RMOs have already been mentioned. It was not long, therefore, before further consultants were recruited to share the extra work with Drs McGrath and O'Connell. First to arrive, as has been said, was Edgar Udwin and others to join during the 60s were Arthur McQuaid and Robert Reeves.

Changes inevitably took place at the senior registrar level, too, as some moved on to vary their experience and others joined. The new Act brought training obligations and Broadmoor became a training venue for all the various professional groups which worked there. A training link for senior registrars in psychiatry to take what was then the RMPA membership examinations was formed with the Institute of Psychiatry in London from where Dr Peter Scott brought groups of visiting trainees and where placements were organized. One early senior registrar was Boyce Lecouteur, an Australian with a name deriving from the Channel Islands - who came and stayed, later becoming one of the growing group of consultants. This enabled a much more equitable division of medical responsibility and workload to be achieved, each consultant taking responsibility for, roughly, the equivalent of one block.

The workload was a heavy one in terms of the evaluations and reports already described but new consultants and senior registrars also enabled greater treatment activity to be achieved, above and beyond the prescribing of ECT and medication and the placement of a patient in one of the occupational centres. With the new Act's designation of the consultant psychiatrist as the medical officer responsible for the care and treatment of the patient, the new 'RMOs' responsible for the 'intermediate' blocks (Dr McGrath retained responsibility for the men's parole Block 2 and Dr O'Connell for the Female Wing) naturally saw this as extending to decisions on the placement of patients in the various workshops around the hospital.

As mentioned earlier, this quite abrupt change of responsibilities and roles was a cause of distress and disagreement in the hospital where the departmental nurses and sisters (DNs/DSs) had always had the responsibility of deciding on workshop placements. They not unnaturally saw their knowledge and experience as spurned as well as their status downgraded. Whilst no doubt the new consultants would be discussing their evaluations with their nursing staff, they would often be operating different criteria: they were concerned with the treatment of the psychiatric condition of their patients; the criteria of the DNs/DSs would have had more to do with their patients' social functioning and reliability and the interests of the workshops. The new 'pecking order' meant the RMO's decision held sway and the DN or DS was overruled.

A New Department for Patients' Education

An education service was also begun during the 60s, the first teacher in charge being Ieuan Williams but with visiting teachers being recruited from local authority services. This not only provided basic literacy and numeracy for those who had never managed to achieve competence in these but also offered opportunity to take what were then still known as GCE 'O' & 'A' levels and, as time went by, even university degrees. This was seen as especially relevant to the large number of younger patients now arriving who included many of good intelligence, but poor achievements, whose eventual discharge success would be greatly improved if they could obtain some qualifications. An increasingly wide range of educational opportunity grew from this small beginning with four full-time teaching staff by the time of the 1983 Act and numerous sessional visiting teachers. Programmes included vocational and recreational subjects as well as traditional career subjects. Allocation to an educational programme, being an innovation not previously figuring in the daily routine of the hospital, was a matter of agreement between the patient, his or her RMO and the educational staff and was not, therefore, a matter of tension between the newly arriving RMOs and the DNs or DSs.

Creation of a 'Medical Centre'

As well as more medical staff and an education service, the clinical pressure also resulted in the appointment, first, of an additional social worker, Mary Gatt and, a couple of years later, another clinical psychologist, Margaret ('Paddy') Bennett. The inevitable expansion of clinical services brought about by the new Act gradually led to other innovations, one of which Dr McGrath had wanted to see at the hospital since his arrival. This was a 'medical centre' where all the specialist services could be located. The small operations theatre in 1959 was opposite the superintendent's office, whilst the pharmacy was a corridor and a courtyard away with a further corridor down to the mortuary (post mortems were routine in those days for a death within a mental hospital). Other services were similarly scattered or missing.

As mentioned earlier in another context, Dr McGrath had first arrived as deputy superintendent and occupied the deputy's residence, actually a rather fine building outside the perimeter wall at the crest of the hill above Crowthorne. He and his family had settled there and liked it so they decided to stay there when he eventually took over the superintendent's post. This left the old super's residence vacant and unused, itself a fine building but rather 'four-square', in the manner of the ward blocks, and plumb between the Male and Female Wings of the hospital. This was the place Dr McGrath had identified for the medical centre. It was a relatively simple matter to run a new wall across the front of its grounds, linking the male and Female Wings' walls, so enclosing it within the secure perimeter. Its spacious rooms lent themselves to clinical purposes and it only needed an extension to accommodate the operating theatre suite. This was done.

'Medical Centre' was a somewhat all-inclusive term for what was then only a nucleus of some clinical and support services but these included a visiting clinics room, an X-ray suite, the pharmacy and its store, a dental surgery and waiting room, the photography and dark room facility, a new clinical psychology suite with tiny laboratory, and consulting rooms for Drs. O'Connell and Udwin. Photography was, of course, required because all newly arriving patients had their front and side-view 'mugshots' taken, as with their prison counterparts, and these had to be routinely updated as age took its effect and as fashions changed, such as the one shortly to arise for long hair and beards. In the event of an escape an accurate photo had to be immediately available.

A charge nurse/sister's post was eventually located in the Medical Centre to take charge of the operating theatre and clinics. Previously responsibility for theatre work and any post-operative as well as sick nursing was undertaken by the charge nurses in the sanatorium wards of Blocks 3 and 4 and Ward 1 in the Female Wing. These wards continued with the rest of their former functions but immediate pre- and post-operative care became the responsibility of the charge nurse in the Medical Centre and was provided in the clinic room suite where there was a bed for this, although security required that a patient return to an infirmary ward in one of the blocks as soon as possible.

The surgical procedures which were carried out in the Medical Centre's theatre were not specifically psychiatric, leucotomy and similar brain surgery having already been described as 'taboo' in Dr McGrath's plans. However, in a population of some 850 patients at that time the need for a certain amount of minor surgery was inevitable, such as hernias and appendices. Another need in a psychiatric population was for the occasional removal of things swallowed and the repair of self-injuries such as slashed arms. These tended to come and go in 'phases' and were avoided as far as possible by the constant checking and counting of things likely to be used for self-injury. For instance, staff had always to be sure they left no papers around held by paper clips whilst magazines with stapled pages were not allowed without first removing the staples. Nevertheless, it was well-nigh impossible to avoid everything potentially harmful and patients determined to injure themselves were likely to find the means of doing so somewhere, from as casual an occurrence as a twig from a tree or bush in the grounds or a splinter of wood from a floorboard or furniture, which could be secreted on the person for future misuse. There was one very sad case of a woman who, after an operation for the removal of something swallowed, would then tear off her dressings and reopen her wound, necessitating further surgical repair, of course. This eventually happened so many times that the surgeon doubted he could effectively repair the abdominal wound much longer.

The reason for operations being done inside Broadmoor rather than at the nearest outside hospital, of course, was security. Later in this 'interacts' period, during the 1970s, surgery within the hospital was to dwindle to the very minor, most being transferred to the local NHS Region at Heatherwood Hospital, Ascot, Wexham Park Hospital, Slough, or the Royal Berkshire Hospital in Reading. This required nursing staff escorts to go with the patient but was still more economical because the surgeons, during the time they spent travelling to and from Broadmoor for maybe only one operation, could be doing several at their normal hospital base. It was also inefficient to raise the theatre to full operational standard for only one case. Cost efficiency had finally prevailed over security! A list of small, non-urgent surgical cases might be accumulated for an entire half-day theatre session and this was also the procedure for the clinics such as Eye, ENT or general medicine.

ECT, however, continued to be given on the ward where the patient was situated, being a regular treatment running to, usually, twice a week for some six or eight weeks and involving a number of patients on any one ward at any one time. This was a physical treatment not involving surgery and the equipment was portable on a trolley around the wards involved. Each block had its 'ECT day'. It was a procedure within the competence of psychiatric medical and nursing staff although with the attendance of a peripatetic anaesthetist. A recovery room was available on each ward block where ECT was given. Patients in the parole Blocks 2 and 5 were reckoned to have reached the stage of not needing ECT. In the rare event they did, and for physical illness or surgery, they would be transferred to one of the infirmary wards in the other blocks. Here was another instance where the Broadmoor 'community' reflected very much the pattern of the community outside.

Release of the Central Courtyard Accommodation

The Medical Centre developed and changed, as we shall see in due course, but at its inception it did indeed represent the nucleus of Dr McGrath's ambitions for a better developed hospital service. Its opening freed up the small existing suite of modern rooms which had been tacked on to the old pharmacy corridor near the main gate. The one room for psychology had already been exchanged for a bigger one in the corridor above the original suite as a result of it being vacated by the nurse training school which moved into new premises. These were in No.2, The Terrace, outside the hospital walls, which had in turn become available as a result of Eric Cooper, by this time the Hospital Steward and Clerk of Accounts, moving with his family to a house in Crowthorne village. The nurse training school had far more room for its expanding activity and its two rooms inside the hospital went to the psychology service and to the second social worker, Mary Gatt.

With the move to the Medical Centre building a couple of years later, together with Dr O'Connell, the original rooms provided a far better suite of offices for the nursing administration, whilst the removal of the pharmacy enabled a better gatehouse, security and porters' suite to be constructed adjacent to the main gate. Changes were also taking place in the nursing profession with a clutch of national reviews, such as the Salmon Report. The departmental nurse or sister category disappeared and nursing staff became nursing officers, senior nursing officers, acting and deputy chief nursing officers with, ultimately, a chief nursing officer replacing the old chief male nurse category. No sooner had common Broadmoor parlance got used to DN and DS instead of PA (principal attendant, which was still heard in use out of habit on my arrival) than it had to abandon it in favour of NO. However, at least nursing officer had a more acceptable ring to it for a security hospital whose staff were members of the POA than had departmental nurse. Meanwhile, however, chief male nurse and matron persisted, Tom Sands replacing Pat Bennett in the former post and Mary Osborne continuing in the latter.

The removal of the psychology service's furniture and equipment to its new quarters in the Medical Centre turned out to be an event of great hilarity and ribaldry, bordering on 'music hall'. The limited hospital transport system of an official limousine and a lorry turned out to be urgently required elsewhere on the actual day. The only alternative was the hospital farm tractor and trailer, normally used for shifting fodder and manure. The ensuing scene could have come straight out of a 'Carry On' film. Many people, of course, thought it very aptly summed up the status of this still relative newcomer to the hospital's services!

CREATION OF A SENIOR COMMON ROOM AND LIBRARY

Expansion and dispersal of key people and services to the four corners of the hospital broke up what had been a compact corridor of people, with Dr Pat McGrath giving up his consulting room and Dr O'Connell moving his. Dr Udwin decided not to use the one allotted to him in the Medical Centre but to be 'peripatetic' around the ward blocks for which he was responsible. The psychology service and the pharmacy had both moved to the Medical Centre. Yet the superintendent's office and associated services remained in the central administration area. The departure of Dr Bergin and his wife, the anaesthetist, who had occupied a flat above the superintendent's office, prompted Dr McGrath to turn this suite into a senior staff common room. Here his growing but dispersed team could meet and exchange news over a coffee break or lunch time. It already had kitchen and toilet facilities which needed little alteration to make facilities for senior staff to have lunch and use as a sitting room area. Whilst this would now smack of élitism, there was in those days no proper staff restaurant, merely a small dining room at the bottom of Block 6 where the few single staff who lived in rooms within the hospital could have a meal. The nearness of the hospital estate meant that most staff went home for meals, especially as nursing shifts changed mainly at meal times. There were also facilities to eat in the staff rooms on the wards during breaks.

The nature of the hospital as one of the country's only three places for mentally disordered offenders and its administration by the Ministry, later Department, of Health also meant that there were increasingly now ministers, officials and specialists visiting to see for themselves how the new legislation was working. They needed somewhere to eat during their day's visit. There were also the visiting Mental Health Review Tribunal members regularly every week and, increasingly with the new Act, members of the mental health fraternity from around the world. A senior common room-cum-dining room had become imperative. A 'mess-man' was found in, first, Max Dewdney and, later the much-loved Fred Spring, who donned starched apron and 'buttled' busily and devotedly, fetching lunches up from the kitchens in the corridor below to set upon the starched white linen of the dining table. There were still collections of old Broadmoor crockery: massive white plates, dishes, tureens and sauce boats, all embossed with a crown and 'Broadmoor Criminal Lunatic Asylum', and heavy silver-plated cutlery bearing the same insignia (where have all these gone?). Sometimes there might only be some half-dozen at lunch: Drs. McGrath, Udwin and Perry, Eric Cooper, Ieuan Williams and myself; at other times a larger gathering augmented by a visiting tribunal or visitors from the Ministry of Health or the Home Office, possibly including a Minister of State. We were all 'on parade' to supply information for people who often had little idea of what Broadmoor was like, what it was for and how it carried out its duties. The bay window afforded a good view of the terrace and, as lunch time was 1 o'clock but the patients' ate earlier, by 1.30 one could observe the parties of patients walking in 'crocodiles' from their wards to workplaces or recreation. There was a kind of rivalry in being able to identify patients and to know the details of their offences and mental disorders.

The senior common room development inevitably involved someone ensuring supplies of coffee, tea, etc., and it was not long before Dr McGrath conceived the idea of keeping a bottle of sherry in the cupboard for visitors. Someone clearly had to act as common room secretary, collect subs and make purchases. Dr McGrath homed in on me, announcing that I was the most obsessional of those present and therefore the obvious one to do the job! He also said it was time to start a hospital library and he wanted me to do that, too. I could take over the existing books and journals which turned out to be a few old tomes of Hack Tuke on the Victorian asylum system and some tattered back numbers of the *Lancet* and

217

British Medical Journal, all in one small, old, glass-fronted cupboard. I was to compile a list of books we should acquire and journals we should take and liaise with him on their purchase. We would have a set of shelves put on the walls of the ante-room through which one entered these dining and sitting areas. The hospital's Ministry of Works department put up shelving and a run of appropriate medical, psychiatric, legal and psychological journals was begun, together with some of the basic texts of the day. Consistent and frequent use was made of this by staff who used the common room, as well as visitors, and it provided a warm and comfortable place to read, write and study for those who had no offices.

The enterprise was a great success from which the official staff library eventually developed. As annual volumes of journals accumulated they went over to the handicrafts department where, as mentioned in an earlier chapter, a particularly talented patient made a highly professional job of the binding and titling. Volumes from this era are still readily identifiable in the present library from this patient's immaculate work. The later 'lettraset' never proved as durable. The front pages from Daniel McNaughtan's case notes were copied and framed to go on the wall, together with reproductions of some prints of the hospital from the Illustrated London News of a year or two after it opened in 1863. These again provided a talking point for visitors.

SUMMARY

Having described, in Part I, the hospital, its legal context, its staff and patients, its therapeutic resources and its clinical procedures, Part II of this history has taken up the story of how all these responded to the changes brought by the 1959 Mental Health Act.

This chapter first looks at the clinical consequences of the changes described in Chapters 2, 3 and 4. Patients were now convicted under the new Act, not technically acquitted as under the old McNaughtan 'Not-Guilty-by-Reason-of-Insanity' criteria (changed at Queen Victoria's insistence to 'Guilty-but-Insane'). A wider range of clinical types arrived within the four new categories of mental disorder, however, especially with the introduction of psychopathic disorder as one of these. The introduction of diminished responsibility in 1957 and the abolition of capital punishment in 1965 further widened the range of patients within the murder and manslaughter categories (more conveniently and concisely referred to as 'homicides', to borrow an American term).

One result was the almost immediate doubling of the admission rate. This obviously put pressure on all resources and inevitably resulted in a greater number going out. Fortunately, the new Act greatly facilitated the transfer of patients to local psychiatric hospitals and units and this is where the majority initially went, until the greater informality of the new Act and local 'open door' policies led to this avenue virtually closing.

Other results of the new Act, with the increase in specialist staff and in review, appeals and reporting requirements, were the creation of a patients' education department and the expansion of other clinical facilities, such as a medical centre and a library.

A beginning had therefore been made for adapting the century-old buildings and services to the radically changed requirements of the new legislation. New staff and procedures, with their related service and accommodation back-up, were in place to tackle the growing numbers and types of incoming patient and their discharge or transfer when ready. How it all turned out is the continuing topic of Part II of this history.

CHAPTER 12

RESEARCH BEGINNINGS

Research papers had been published by clinicians, that is to say mainly the medical superintendent of the day, over the lifetime of the hospital. Partridge refers to some of these. They were intermittent, however, not part of a continuing and integrated programme and derived from an era very different from that of the 'inter-acts' period with its radical changes and sweeping professional advances.

Dr McGrath had gradually accumulated clinical material on his chosen subject of 'maternal filicides' (women who had killed their children) whilst Dr O'Connell was working on the rather similar sounding but quite opposite subject of 'matricide' (people who had killed their mothers). A research programme had been developing for a few years at Rampton Hospital at the initiative of the clinical psychologist there, Dr John Tong, and the superintendent, Dr G W Mackay. Otherwise most of the research derived from around the rest of the country, especially the Institute of Psychiatry, and was undertaken by forensic psychiatrists and medico-legal academics, mainly on the problems of identification and appropriate placement of mentally disordered offenders, or of the medico-legal problems associated with these, such as the concept of 'criminal responsibility'.

Active departments of criminology existed at several universities (this was before the university growth boom in the 1960s and 1970s) whilst some prominent forensic psychiatrists of the day were Peter Scott, Trevor Gibbens, Desmond Curran, Dennis Hill and Donald West. With the new mental health legislation and the Royal Commission that preceded it, all had been engrossed in the problems and definitions of mental disorder in succession to the old McNaughtan insanity definitions and, in particular, the issues of mental capacity and responsibility that were entailed.

It was not surprising, then, that new research initiatives and professional bodies sprang up. The RMPA (Royal Medico-Psychological Association) was not to become the Royal College of Psychiatrists for another decade, let alone form a forensic section, but its forensic members were an active group within it. Forensic pathology in that era had the redoubtable Francis Camps at its head at the London Hospital. Associated with it were the Home Office forensic science laboratories. Many lawyers, too, were active participants in the debates, especially over 'responsibility' and fitness to plead. Frank Lawton was one, whilst Sir Roger Ormerod was one of a small group of medically qualified judges active in this direction. Like Sir Roger, many of these prominent figures were, or became, knighted.

A natural consequence of all this activity was the formation, in 1961, of the British Academy of Forensic Sciences which specifically encompassed the three disciplines of "Medicine, Science and the Law" (and this became the title of its journal). Professor Leon Radzinowicz, head of the Institute of Criminology at Cambridge, where the library is named after him, was the first president and Dr (later Sir) Francis Camps was its first secretary, then president for a year, and then 'Secretary General' in perpetuity. Sir Frank Lawton was an early president, a post which rotated around the three core professions. Sir Desmond Curran at St George's was one of the prime movers in all this activity and so Brian O'Connell, who worked with him on his non-Broadmoor day, brought news of all this activity to the senior common room at Broadmoor and both he and Dr McGrath were frequent attenders of scientific and planning meetings. The three of us all joined the British Academy of Forensic Sciences and I began to attend an increasingly broad range of meetings and to get to know some of the famous names of the time.

BROADMOOR CENTENARY MEETINGS

Dr McGrath was very keen to put his evolving clinical service at Broadmoor on this national (and indeed international) medico-legal 'map'. We all had his support to report work at meetings and conferences of our various professional bodies. An appropriate occasion for this was the imminent hospital centenary celebrations in 1963, when various events were very naturally held to mark the date. One was a meeting of the RMPA, held at Broadmoor. Dr McGrath was to speak, not on his maternal filicides, but on the work and development of the hospital as a result of the changes brought by the 1959 Act. Dr O'Connell also gave a paper, if I remember rightly, on the problems of amnesia in offender patients. The rest of the speakers were people prominent in the forensic psychiatry field from around the country. However, with only a day or two's notice, one scheduled speaker was unable to attend, too late to arrange a replacement. Knowing of the results of our survey of the wards around the hospital, which had been displayed on our office walls in the form of graphs and pie-charts, and the trends emerging from assessments of incoming and departing patients, Dr McGrath asked if I would like to fill the gap. This seemed too good an opportunity to miss and the punched cards were quickly scanned and compared to yield some hand-outs of tables and graphs for the occasion.

The findings of an above average patient population where intelligence was concerned caused some surprise to the RMPA audience whilst the combinations of intellectual impairment and psychiatric disorder did not, and the reduction in impairment levels in the discharged groups was reassuring. All these augured well for building a wider base for descriptive, and especially predictive, work where admission and discharge decisions were to be made. The types of disorder shown on the clinical questionnaire also aroused interest, especially with respect to the various offender categories and the still new Mental Health Act disorder categories. Fairly marked differences emerged between the groups overall, although individual variations, of course, were wide and prevented confident allocation to a group on such criteria alone. Nevertheless, they suggested degrees of probability and facilitated more accurate descriptions of patients' conditions and their requirements. Whilst the picture emerged more clearly later and was intensively investigated by people not yet on the scene, it was interesting to report at this early stage that the 'time' patients and acquisitive offenders showed a greater prominence of psychopathic disturbance; the 'homicide' group (murder and manslaughter) showed more depressive features, whilst the non-homicide aggressive offenders, especially where the victim was a stranger (grievous bodily harm [GBH], wounding-with-intent [WWI] and assault) showed the greatest incidence of schizophrenic symptoms.

Superimposed upon all this, however, but interestingly not obscuring the differences, was a phenomenon which was reported without surprise but which was seen as needing new strategies to penetrate, and this was the distorting attitude to the questionnaire revealed in the profiles of many patients. Whilst the 'exaggeration' effect was already familiar from psychiatric populations, resulting in inflated scores across the board, and was to be expected, especially amongst floridly psychotic patients still in the acute stage of their disorder, the large number of opposite response patterns, i.e.: defensiveness, had not been so commonly seen. However, it seemed an obvious expectation amongst a population who would quickly have come to realize, if they hadn't already, that eventual discharge depended on their achieving normality. The incidence of this pattern was high, therefore, amongst those assessed on leaving (this was a routine research exercise at that time and the discharge did not depend on the outcome). More surprisingly, however, it was also frequent amongst incoming patients, especially the 'homicide' group. Whatever the defensiveness was concealing, the fact that an incoming patient was able to respond in this controlled way at least suggested that whatever mental disorder had existed at the time of the offence must have quickly resolved itself. Such a defensive attitude would be expected to be beyond the capacity of an acutely psychotic person to operate consistently. The trend was most commonly encountered amongst the 'homicide' group, moreover, where clear evidence of mental disorder had often been sparse but where many of the offences had shown such bizarre features that a court had had little difficulty in reaching a mental disorder conclusion (e.g.: sexual mutilation or dismemberment of the body, concealment of its parts in odd places, wandering off in a confused state for hours or even days, and later a tendency to be unable to account for the offence or to deny it altogether).

This clinical questionnaire picture often presented by patients gave rise to considerable scorn at case conferences in the hospital and the questionnaire was derided. Nevertheless, it became a common pattern and was often accompanied by unimpaired cognitive test results. In any case, the tests were so often 'spot on' in other cases. I had, therefore, had to suggest that there might be some alternative explanation for the pathology in these cases and that they might not even meet the 'mental disorder' criteria although, at that time, an alternative explanation did not come easily to mind. Before the abolition of capital punishment, for instance, one would have expected the opposite tendency in people concerned to avoid it: they would more likely to have been "putting-on-the-pot", as the Broadmoor saying went, not pretending normality. For the audience where I was a stand-in at the RMPA conference, however, this seemed to provide a 'topping' to a cake that was sufficiently different from the usual conference fare that it provoked considerable discussion. There were sufficient findings that made sense and were to be expected that the audience did not reject the novel results as errors in the validation of the questionnaire, which was of international use and standing anyway, but instead saw them, as I had, as something to be accounted for. Dr McGrath was very pleased that one of 'his team' had held the attention of the conference and attracted commendation, especially when it was such a last minute offering. I had apparently enhanced the reputation of clinical psychology and of Dr McGrath's research initiatives at Broadmoor at an opportune time.

Later that year another meeting was held at Broadmoor, in conjunction with the centenary, this time of the British Psychological Society's professional division. Again the attenders were able to tour the hospital and see for themselves what it comprised and some of the activities going on within it. Again I presented some of the early findings from our assessments of incoming and outgoing patients, rather more fully organized with the benefit of more time for preparation, and more technically oriented for a psychologist audience. This was a rather new and different field from that in which most psychologists worked so that polite bemusement might be described as the predominant response, rather than the enthusiasm of the psychiatrists. Nevertheless, it served to publicize that psychology was now being applied to problems of mentally disordered offending and an awareness was aroused in the profession of the potential significance of this field of work.

ON THE ABOLITION OF CAPITAL PUNISHMENT

Two years later, in 1965, capital punishment was abolished. By then, Paddy Bennett had joined me in the psychology department and we decided to present some of our results, developed from the 1963 RMPA conference and including some further material as well, at the annual conference of the British Psychological Society, that year in Aberdeen. Paddy was then going on to Glasgow to join Boyce Lecouteur in presenting at a conference there some work done with him with the women patients.

Our chosen context was the abolition of capital punishment and the likely pressure on the system from the increase over the years of people in prisons, as well as special hospitals, who were under the new alternative of a mandatory life sentence for murder and would, therefore, eventually present the problem of having to have their suitability assessed for parole and possible release. The two of us presented our material in two parts, followed by a discussion session where we hoped to get some answers to the assessment problem. We also hoped to challenge our colleagues in the psychology profession with an alternative kind of problem to the usual one of assessing types and degrees of abnormal function. Reflecting the indefinite length of both life sentences and hospital orders, we called our double session in the conference programme: "Detention Unlimited or When Should 'Life' End?"

We were allocated a small lecture room accommodating, perhaps, fifty or sixty people and were somewhat disappointed at the scheduled time to have an audience of only two or three. Just as we were wondering how to run a discussion with so few, however, a session at an adjoining lecture theatre ended and many of the audience there began to fill our empty seats. Then a session in another lecture theatre ended and more people poured into our, by now, cramped little room, cramming themselves on to window

226

sills and gangway steps. A novel, punning title was unusual at a learned society's conference in those days, although almost overdone nowadays, and clearly ours had aroused some curiosity. From dejection our mood changed to hysteria within the space of a few minutes.

Somehow we got through our presentations and enjoyed the obvious intrigue that we had created in our audience. We had already anticipated some of the ways of overcoming the distorting effects of abnormal test attitudes - exaggeration and its opposite, defensiveness - and had accumulated a sample of some fifty or more records from one of the 'projective' techniques of the time: the Rorschach Ink Blot test. Even though I had been trained in a school critical of this approach the problems of assessing this new and unique patient population demanded that no stone be left unturned. Presenting a task where the requirements weren't obvious would seem to be a way of obtaining helpful clues as to a patient's condition and problems. Even this, however, proved unsuccessful and many patients, clearly wary of something where they could not see what might be required, had responded in a very limited way with only a few obvious and mundane responses. At the other extreme were people who couldn't stop responding and went on interminably providing more and more. Despite this apparent failure of a method that we had expected the audience to have seen as a way of penetrating someone's defences, they responded spiritedly and a few ideas were brought away for further thought. Interestingly for future work, there was a correlation between restricted responding on the projective test and defensiveness on the questionnaire and, on the other hand, of copious over-responding on both tasks.

Paddy Bennett went on to Glasgow to join Boyce Lecouteur at the further conference. Sadly she had neglected, in order to do her bit at these two conferences, the appearance of a lump in her breast and, by the time she returned home this had enlarged alarmingly. Secondaries were quickly apparent and she went downhill rapidly, despite devoted extra medical and nursing attention from Boyce Lecouteur and volunteers on the Female Wing staff who attended her home round the clock. This is the affection and loyalty she had engendered in a very short space of time and is typical of the Broadmoor staff when they accept someone as 'one of us'. Her death left a sad and tragic void and there was an inevitable hiatus before we could begin to address the problem of future staffing or find time for further research.

STUDENT PROJECTS

A phenomenon began to be seen then, however, that was common later, i.e.: the attachment of a student for the long summer vacation who could assist with research. Several Reading University students had already carried out projects with us for their undergraduate theses, giving rise to some intriguing new methods and apparatus for assessing various mental functions. One, by David Gibbons, had involved the building in the handicrafts department of a small but simple mechanical device known as a tachistoscope which enabled words to appear briefly in an aperture on a screen. This enabled investigation of what were known as 'perceptual errors' whereby, if inadequate time is available properly to take in a word, people will put their own interpretation upon what they see. This was postulated to reflect personal preoccupations which, in the case of Broadmoor patients, might comprise some element of their offence or attitude to it. As such, of course, and being a quick-fire test requiring an immediate response, it might contribute to the problem of penetrating the exaggerative and defensive tendencies already encountered.

Another student, Vincent Crowley, made use of a maze task which had recently been developed by Alick Elithorn at the Royal Free Hospital. This was intriguingly different from the standard kind of maze, which itself had already yielded relevant indicators of 'motor-style', or the way people go about tackling problems in their surroundings and planning their solution. Elithorn's task involved tracing through a maze with a series of binary choices but collecting target 'blobs' at a number of the intersections. Success depended upon planning and foreseeing the route by which the most 'blobs' could be acquired. Elithorn later worked on a computerized form of this test and it represented the potential for a rich development of this kind of research and, ultimately, use in clinical assessment. We had yet to enter the era of 'anti-test' when the escalating movement into the new therapies led to assessments being scorned and, more relevantly, their validity as reflectors of real life behaviour challenged. For the present, there was much opportunity for wider description and analysis of whatever could be revealed about a patient's thinking and emotional state. Whatever happened in the rest of the clinical world, this seemed always likely to be needed at Broadmoor on account of the vexed problem of assessing discharge readiness and collecting information on admission, and at intervals thereafter, to reflect change.

A student who came much later, in the 1970s, but who should be mentioned here because she also undertook a research project during her stay, was Cathy Widom. Many people later undertook projects but, as an American who went on to prominence in the forensic psychology field in her own country, it is pleasing to be able to record that she undertook her PhD project at Broadmoor.

The project involved an interactive 'game' called the "prisoner's dilemma". This involved making a choice between the co-operative option 'A', which would result in a large gain if one's opponent made the unco-operative choice 'B' but a much smaller gain if both made the co-operative choice; and the antagonistic option 'B' which would result in a larger gain if one's opponent made the cooperative choice 'A' but a large loss if one's opponent had also gone for the antagonistic option 'B'. This was, in essence, what was entailed in the interrogation of prisoners, hence the name. Keeping quiet could bring gains, albeit small, if one's accomplices could be relied upon to do the same but much greater loss if they confessed. Confessing, or 'grassing', could bring much greater gains, but only if one's accomplices didn't, when it would bring greater loss.

Cathy Widom used this investigative 'game' procedure in conjunction with the usual questionnaires and, a novelty, the relatively new "Repertory Grid" technique which is described more fully in the 'Psychological Initiatives' section of the next chapter. She had been introduced to this by Don Bannister, her PhD supervisor in Britain who, at the time, was busy with colleagues Fay Fransella and Miller Mair exploring it in connection with applying Kelly's Personal Construct Theory to the understanding and treatment of psychiatric patients. In the course of all this she had to make careful translations of American prison slang into their British equivalents, especially when told that her phrase for 'grassing' on an accomplice translated into something sexually unpleasant in English. Nevertheless, she just could not believe that 'grassing', was the term used over here. She returned from her first patient encounter overjoyed, however, exclaiming; "They understood it - they understood it!"

EQUIPPING A LABORATORY

The first of the students who came to work a long vacation was Alan Howe, a meticulously careful annotator of records, who spent his time cataloguing the data from our punched cards, cross-tabulating test data with all the diagnostic, social, criminal and Mental Health Act category information therein. Another student was Frank Adams who had already spent a vacation at Rampton building some equipment for John Tong, the psychologist there. Frank had been a Post Office telephone engineer at one time and was therefore adept at building apparatus that worked on Post Office relay-type equipment. With these he had made a machine that could switch a series of lights on a screen through a sequence. The lights appeared on either the left or right of the screen and the operator had a lever to be moved in the direction of the light. The task could be made more difficult either by speeding up the sequence of lights or by adding further green or red lights which indicated whether the lever was to be moved in the direction of the lights or the opposite direction. A relay was triggered all the time the lever was off centre, so indicating how long the operator spent responding and how much more quickly he did so when the sequence was speeded up, under several levels of task difficulty. It was a simple concept but quite an exacting task, especially when the confirmatory or countermanding meanings of the greens and reds had to be taken into account as the task speeded up.

The apparatus derived from some similar work done during the war by psychologists with the training of RAF pilots where they had found that the degree to which trainees increased their speed in accordance with the speed of the changing lights, especially when the task became more complex, varied quite widely. Three broad groups were identified: over-reactors, under-reactors and moderate reactors. Subsequent performance in flying their aircraft, and in battle conditions, showed that the most successful pilots turned out not to be the excessively quick, or over-reactors, who were presumably prone to impulsive errors, nor to the under-reactors who might be thought to be the phlegmatic type, cool under pressure, but who were presumably too slow to avoid trouble. The most successful pilots were, in fact, the ones in the moderate reactor category. Applied to a pre-discharge group of patients at Rampton and related subsequently to success or failure of discharge (in terms of a further offence or return to Rampton) Tong and Adams had found the same trend as with the trainee pilots: the most successful were the moderate reactors.

Frank Adams's equipment therefore went into action as part of the selection of assessments given to patients prior to their discharge from Broadmoor and which were intended, no doubt with refinements and substitutions being required along the way, to establish criteria of dischargeability. On notification from the office that a discharge was pending, patients would be approached and asked if they would undertake a number of tasks for research purposes, the results of which would not necessarily help them but might help people coming after them. Frank Adams's apparatus was known as the 'Psychomotor Stress Test' but it was always referred to by Dr McGrath as the "demented pianola". Still, he couldn't have been totally sceptical as he would invariably bring any VIP visitors to our department on his tour of the hospital, typically with a remark to the effect that "you've got ten minutes to explain the work of your department and show our visitor the demented pianola!"

Envisaging research developments of a laboratory kind which would gradually feed into and sharpen the effectiveness of clinical assessments and treatments, the new psychology department in the Medical Centre had had one room fitted with two test cubicles, with an interconnecting observation window. Both were fitted with benches and entered only from the main room, where the staff nurse would be located, so that both security and privacy were ensured. For the Psychomotor Stress Test the control unit was in one cubicle and the 'demented pianola' in the other. A 12-volt DC electricity supply was brought up to the control room from the Medical Centre's basement where the hospital's emergency batteries were situated. Both cubicles were sound-proofed and one was painted black to allow for perceptual experiments to be done using sound and small light sources. (The idea was not altogether successful on account of the tramping of feet in the corridor outside when the adjacent dental surgery was in session. Male staff tended to wear boots. We had to try to avoid Tuesdays and Thursdays, the dental surgery days, for laboratory work!) Perceptual phenomena were another area of investigation that had shown promise in experimental psychology elsewhere, with such phenomena as the critical interval between two pin-point light sources being switched to produce the illusion of apparent movement (the principle behind the illuminations at Piccadilly Circus or Blackpool). The time interval required for perception of the apparent movement again varied slightly among people, some requiring a longer and some a shorter delay. The phenomenon, again, looked as if it was one that might fall into the over-reactor, under-reactor and medium-reactor categories and be correlated with stability on discharge. This work did not, in the end, develop, being squeezed out by other demands, but the cubicles remained and were much in use for later experimental work.

EXPANSION OF STAFF, FACILITIES AND PROFESSIONAL COMMITMENTS

All this new work took place with the improved facilities and equipment in the new Medical Centre and with the assistance of students although, with Frank Adams's departure at the end of the vacation, putting his apparatus into use became my particular interest, in discussion with John Tong at Rampton. In any case, during this period Dr Michael Craft, a consultant psychiatrist working with mentally subnormal offenders in North Wales, involved me in compiling a contribution for his new book on psychopathic offenders and the library version of this included an appendix from me on the usefulness or otherwise of all the available psychological tests and experimental procedures where the problem of psychopathic behaviour was concerned. My available spare time was, therefore, entirely taken up with this compilation for a while.

The pressure for clinical appraisals and opinion on a reduced service, and in an environment of growing activity and patient numbers and movements, in time forced action to expand the psychology service. Dr McGrath was also now pursuing the creation of an actual research department and making representations on this to the Ministry of Health. The special hospitals are never for long without some event giving rise to publicity and a combination of one of these with one of the succession of inevitable government commissions and working parties that always seem to be taking place, this time brought success (1968 Second Report from the Estimates Committee: the Special Hospitals and the State Hospital, London, HMSO).

First, however, in 1967 the psychology department was expanded by the creation of a senior clinical psychologist post, with my own post upgraded to principal. A probationer grade post was also created so that a trainee could take part in the regional training that was now characterizing most parts of the country and would therefore in turn bring a mix of trainees on work attachment to our own service, thus widening the knowledge of our work. Shortly afterwards we also had a clerical officer post created for the growing amount of this work which had hitherto been done, inappropriately really, but very efficiently, by the succession of attached staff nurses: first Jack Wilkinson, then Roy Clarkson followed by Jim Cass. The additional clerical officer post was seen as a great privilege for us as such posts had hitherto been restricted to the 'top' and the 'front' offices. Typing services, however, were still confined to these offices and all our handwritten reports were sent over there to be typed. Eventually, of course, dictaphones appeared and Mrs Helen Paton, the senior social worker, was an early user because of the great deal of time she spent away from the hospital, carrying around a large wooden box made in the carpenters shop to accommodate the cumbersome machine. When we had them, too, it made drafting reports much quicker. Eventually we had a clerical officer-typist for the department as a whole but this was not until we were a larger number yet and, in all my 27 years, I never had a secretary, an omission I was never able to remedy and which I always felt considerably restricted my work output, especially where research reporting was concerned: this was always the first thing to be shelved in the interests of the day-to-day clinical work.

Appointed to our new senior clinical psychologist post was Ron Blackburn, who came with impressive credentials. He had followed his first degree at Cambridge with clinical training in Leicester and then an MSc in comparative physiology at Birmingham. He already had publications to his credit, being particularly concerned with use of the new 'factor analysis' for distinguishing the components of a person's responses to questionnaires. These were yielding fresh insights into measures of personality characteristics and of emotional stability, amongst others, which were relevant to the body of data we had now accumulated on all successive incoming and departing patients. Ron was attracted by the opportunity to draw upon this data bank for research and to apply his existing experience to the assessment and reporting work of the department.

With Ron's arrival we were able to split the incoming patient assessments between us and were both able to develop research activities. His were in questionnaire factor analysis and personality typology whilst mine were in the refinement of assessment methods from the large array I had trawled through for use in the special problems of Broadmoor. Ron made much more headway than I did, which was no doubt largely due to his greater application but was also partly because my spare time was becoming increasingly absorbed by professional developments nationally. I had been continuing my activity with the BPS after the centenary symposia as it had seemed to me to be important for someone on this unusual fringe of conventional clinical work to remain in contact with the mainstream of the profession, both to keep abreast of developments and to try to maintain the interest of others in our work. Additionally, the BPS was finding it useful to have someone in this unusual corner of the applied field to whom to refer the queries that were increasingly arising about the 1959 Act, services for mentally disordered offenders and related professional development issues. Inevitably I found myself on committees and working parties. Dr McGrath had again encouraged this kind of involvement as helping to maintain awareness of Broadmoor's active participation in advancing research and clinical work.

The BPS had had a division for professional psychologists' interests which, as it grew, split into independent divisions for clinical, educational and occupational psychologists. Others were formed later. I became assistant honorary secretary for the new clinical division on its formation in 1966 and, a year later when the secretary took up a post in Canada, I succeeded him. A new division entailed much work. Additionally, the Zuckerman Committee was set up by the government to review and report on the work of scientists in the NHS. This called for the usual carefully drafted submission on how clinical psychologists saw their own role, a task undertaken by the clinical division committee whose secretary I was. So maintaining the clinical service was all I could manage at Broadmoor and I was relieved that the research baton was enthusiastically and competently taken up by Ron Blackburn who had, after all, joined us with that particularly in mind.

THE 'OVER-CONTROL' CONCEPT

Nevertheless, in 1969, we had submitted, and had accepted, papers for a forensic sciences conference in Canada. Dr McGrath and the Ministry of Health decided that only one of us would be funded to attend and, as the senior, I was selected (Ron made up for this later in an illustrious academic career). My paper was yet a further development of the demographic information which our routine assessments were accruing. A wider range of psychological information was presented, related to different aspects of the patient population, e.g.: age, diagnosis, offence, Mental Health Act categorization, length of stay and so on. Ron Blackburn's, which I was to read for him in Toronto, detailed his work on his factor analytic studies so far, and especially as they related to those patients whose offence was manslaughter or murder ('homicide'). This was a seminal paper marking the development of personality typologies amongst mentally disordered offenders which he continued to develop and extend to other groups. Basically, however, he had distinguished four types, two of which were predominant amongst homicides whilst the two others were more predominant amongst non-homicide aggressors. Where the latter were concerned, this was to give rise to work describing, defining and explaining the phenomenon of psychopathy as, basically, the two groups predominant amongst the non-homicides were distinguished by impulsivity and acting out tendencies. Where the former group, the homicides, was concerned, the other two types predominated and were characterized by inhibition, social

237

conformity and absence, or denial, of symptoms. Thus links had been made and elaborated with my earlier reports to the RMPA and BPS conferences on defensiveness and its opposite response tendency of exaggeration.

Blackburn's work tied in with some parallel work being done in the United States by Edwin Megargee upon similar groups of homicidal and other aggressive offenders where he had observed similar typological differences and described the two contrasting pairs of types as "over-controlled" and "under-controlled". The reason the under-controlled got into trouble was obvious but the reason for the over-controlled was not. This is not the place for complex phenomenology and theoretical discussion and the interested reader will have to look in the now copious literature if he or she wants more (see Bibliography and Appendix). However, to provide the continuity essential for this account of how services developed, a brief resumé is necessary.

The explanation for the over-controlled group's violence broadly turns upon their inability to recognize and deal with crises within their own personalities and especially the relationships dependent upon such recognition. Over a period of time and if subjected to continuing stress, as would occur in a disastrous personal relationship, strains build up which the repressive-denial system eventually fails any longer to cope with, when a catastrophic reaction may occur. This is an over-simplification and the explanatory theory has undergone revisions and refinements since Megargee coined the terms "over- and under-control" and Blackburn made his initial discoveries in the Broadmoor population. Basically, however, it began to address the puzzling phenomena we had been observing from our assessments up to that time and to offer some kind of explanation for the behaviour of perhaps the most prominent, although minority, group of Broadmoor's patients, the 'one-off', domestic homicides (murderers and manslaughterers).

By contrast, and looking at the opposite typologies, it also began to spell out criteria and provide explanations for the behaviours of the psychopathic disorder group and it is in this direction that Blackburn's work predominantly continued, with a rich succession of papers, chapters and books on the subject. The terms "over-control" and "under-control" became part of Broadmoor terminology, and indeed beyond, although not always correctly used, any more than 'paranoia' or 'psychopathy' are correctly used.

DR R.P. BRITTAIN'S SEXUAL SADISM RESEARCH

Rob Brittain was at Broadmoor during the 1960s, as a senior registrar in psychiatry, although he had had a previous career as a pathologist, reaching consultant level. He had given this up, partly as a result of having contracted tuberculosis through his work, but also because he had developed an interest in finding out more of the circumstances and motivation for some of the strange deaths he had had to investigate. These had seemed to be suicides. The men (they were always men) had usually died by asphyxiation, for example as a result of self-strangulation or putting a plastic bag over their heads, or else through inhalation of a toxic spray or vapour. They were frequently naked or near naked and often tied up. Bondage and sado-masochistic activities were, of course, well known but these were cases of men who had apparently been alone and not part of a consenting pair or some group sexual activity. The 'buzz' produced by partial consciousness was not then the well known phenomenon which it now is and certainly not when practised as a solitary, self-stimulating activity. The credit for initiating the current knowledge of this phenomenon, therefore, is largely Rob Brittain's. The suicides proved not to have been intentional, of course, but usually the accidental outcome of going too far with a procedure where, as it had been used in a solitary context, there had been no one to provide revival.

Rob Brittain had, therefore, moved from pathology to forensic psychiatry. His interest at Broadmoor led him to search for any patients who might have indulged in the kinds of sexual self-stimulation which he inferred had been at the root of the deaths he had seen as a pathologist. Although this would not have been the reason for their being there, it was a good guess that, if they existed, they might have indulged in other sexual or violent activities for which they could well have found themselves at Broadmoor. This indeed proved to be the case. One case even arose from the Broadmoor consultants running out-patient clinics in the local health district, an initiative that Dr McGrath had felt was good for both his medical staff and the district, cementing closer professional ties. Rob Brittain was the doctor who picked up this case and, as a registrar, had to invoke Dr McGrath's co-operation on the appropriate next step. Broadmoor admitted only 'sectioned' patients. The out-patient, however, agreed to be sectioned, on being persuaded that his pathology was at any time likely to lead to some injury or even fatality to himself or a victim, and he subsequently spent several years as a Broadmoor in-patient.

Rob Brittain was a painstaking clinician and in his typically thorough manner he carried out comprehensive psychiatric examinations and gathered information from all available sources, which meant he was always concerned to have a thorough psychological assessment made. The result was his paper: 'The Sadistic Murderer', published in *Medicine, Science and the Law* in 1970, and a later book.

This group has frequently since then been referred to as 'the sexual psychopath', which is understandable but a misnomer. There is an over-inclusive tendency to categorize any violently callous person as psychopathic, just as there is to call every suspicious person 'paranoid'. This is where the medico-legal classification, intended to be broad, is at odds with the psychological one. Psychopathic disorder does not merely define an unfeeling person who might also be violent but one who is impulsive and fails to profit from experience. Psychopaths are not usually socially isolated, unless shunned, but generally seek company. Sexual sadists, by contrast, are generally careful planners, often persistently and obsessionally so, and not impulsive. They often also prefer their own company, sometimes to the point of isolation. Psychopathic and sadistic behaviours are not mutually exclusive, in fact they do occur together but for different reasons than the ruminant sadists' reasons. However, they are not closely correlated either. Each may sometimes display some characteristics of the other. They are often lumped together erroneously because of their common tendency to violence and a ruthless lack of feeling towards their victims.

Psychopathic disorder is discussed in Chapter 3. It is difficult to define precisely because it depends more upon psychological than medical criteria. Its possible neurological basis, influenced by psychological and developmental factors, also distinguishes it from sadistic behaviours. Psychopathic problems will invariably lead to failure to deal with relationships, and this will invariably also involve sexual adjustment, but this will not always lead to violence. Not all sexual pathology is sadistic. When it is, however, it is not necessarily accompanied by, or the result of, psychopathic characteristics. As has been said, the definitive feature of impulsiveness in psychopathy is usually lacking in the sadist, who plans and ruminates. His aetiology (causation) usually lies in trauma associated with early sexual development, this being mishandled or even punished by significant adult role models (parents or parent substitutes) resulting in failure to deal with sexual drives when these ultimately develop. There may simply be inept failures in attempted sexual relationships or these may be used violently to vent frustration and anger. Rob Brittain's work described the way sexual arousal could become associated with a range of perverse activities, in attempts to achieve both emotional as well as physical satisfaction, when this activity had been inadequately modelled, distorted or punished in childhood and adolescence.

This period of Broadmoor's development was, in my recollection, relatively settled and happy for both staff and patients. It may seem strange to say this of an institution which housed patients responsible for terrible tragedies. Nevertheless, there was an atmosphere of hope and optimism that the developments of the 1959 Act had now settled in, and the staff developments with them. The new legislation was now familiar to everyone. Dr McGrath was no longer a newcomer. There was overcrowding and pressures on admission and discharge but these were tackled with enthusiasm and the hope of continuing new discoveries. Rob Brittain was an example of this *esprit de corps*. He was energetic and stimulating, with a rapid, staccato Scots accent, and threw himself into everything he did. This was the era when World War II ex-servicemen were numerous and he still had much of his army kit. On the occasion of an escape during this period, and before the careful organization for such eventualities that characterized later eras, he surprised everyone by donning his belt, holster and pistol and recruiting a few picked staff to help him patrol the entire outer wall of the hospital. Needless to say, this did not meet with official approval, but it endeared him to the staff and was a great boost to staff morale. Sadly, not many years later but after he had moved on from Broadmoor, and having already survived tuberculosis, he succumbed to cancer. He had been a heavy smoker. He was sadly missed.

'SHRU' - THE SPECIAL HOSPITALS RESEARCH UNIT

Where the psychology department was concerned, an era ended as the 1960s ended, for Ron Blackburn moved on to restart the psychology service at Rampton Hospital in 1971. John Tong had emigrated to Canada some time before and been followed by Dan McKerracher before he, too, went to Canada. This was the era of the 'brain drain'.

For Broadmoor, however, another era was beginning as Dr Pat McGrath's pressure for a specific research department was rewarded. Appointed as director of the new 'special hospitals research unit' (known as SHRU) was Dr Gavin Tennent and the directorate covered all three special hospitals, with clerical and research assistants at each. The demographic coverage of Rampton and Moss Side hospitals was begun and at Broadmoor replaced the punched card system of the psychology department, which it greatly extended, although without the psychometric data. This was the start of the 'case register' to log all available information on patients and their backgrounds, including their criminal records and psychiatric histories. Thus an invaluable and ongoing record was begun by which to answer the numerous questions likely to arise over the ensuing years. Elizabeth Parker was appointed specifically to run this project, operating from SHRU's London office, at that time in the Camberwell Road. This was an ambitious, long-term undertaking for it was not merely a paper record as the psychology department's early attempts had been. It involved interviews with patients and their nearest or other relevant relatives. It also included data from CRO (Criminal Records Office), of previous offences, and from the Mental Health Register (MHR), of previous psychiatric events. This, therefore, required further staff to carry out the visiting, interviewing, and record searching. The interviewers had to use as much 'hard' data as was possible to obtain (dependent on facts with minimal risk of misinterpretation) which entailed careful and thorough training of the unit staff. This was initially provided by Dr J A Baldwin and Dr D J Hall of the Aberdeen case register.

A case register is, of course, built up slowly as patients are admitted and pass through the hospital. Information coming out of it would only have accrued gradually and its usefulness for inquiries, other than annual statistics, would therefore be limited until some years had passed. To start with, therefore, it had to put up with criticism from those impatient to see quicker results. To be worthwhile it must be guaranteed long term funding. Fortunately it received this and gradually provided increasingly valuable information to many inquirers from inside and outside the hospital. The Special Hospitals Research Report No.15 detailed its first five years work, including triennial statistics for 1972-74 by Dell and Parker; a census of patients with a five-year length of stay by Susanne Dell and a paper on identifying types of sex offender by Elizabeth Parker. Elizabeth had already published two earlier reports in the series, on the reliability of special hospital case records where previous criminal and psychiatric histories were concerned, and on the incapacities of mentally handicapped patients at Rampton and Moss Side. SHRU was well under way and proved an invaluable resource throughout the years of the 1959 Act. Its value will probably only increase as the years pass, as legislation and practices change, and as comparisons will come to be made with past generations of patients.

Other work done in the early years, under the aegis of SHRU and published in the monograph series, dealt with chromosome abnormalities in special hospital patients whilst a controlled trial was reported of a new drug for control of libido (sexual arousal). This demonstrated the usefulness of the drug for sex offenders, which was thereby put into use for their treatment. As we shall discuss later on, however, there is more to sexual dysfunction and abuse than physiology and biochemistry. As regards chromosome studies, significant differences were demonstrated in the incidence of some chromosome abnormalities, in particular the occurrence of an extra Y chromosome in males in the special hospitals (known as the XYY phenomenon). Unfortunately, the differences were significant because the small incidence of the phenomenon in the special hospitals was significantly greater than the extremely small incidence in the population at large. It was not enough to account for all sexual offending and only provided one small ingredient in a rather large recipe for such offending. But such is often the nature of research.

Publication of these reports in mimeographed form in the SHRU monograph series allowed people from a number of professional backgrounds at all the hospitals to make known their findings quickly, and for other researchers and practitioners to know what was going on, about work that might not necessarily have gained publication in a recognized journal for some time, if at all. Blackburn's paper: *Personality Types Among Abnormal Homicides*, discussed above, was No.1 in the series and his and others' papers on the development of various kinds of scale for identifying problems of special hospital patients are sprinkled through the successive publications. Blackburn published here one of his early papers on the classification of psychopathic disorder. Christopher Treves-Brown published a regional analysis of referrals to the special hospitals. Later a number of useful bibliographies were published of work relevant to the problems of special hospitals' patients.

The Special Hospitals Research Unit (or just 'SHRU', as it was known, pronounced 'Shrew') needed accommodation and this was found in the Medical Centre but only by transferring the pharmacy to a prefabricated building specially erected in the grounds in front of the centre. Actually, this suited the pharmacy better as it was more accessible for the portage of the many boxes of medicines that were always being delivered. They no longer had to be laboriously carried upstairs. As the majority of Broadmoor patients were on some medication, except for most of the parole patients, the weekly throughput of medicines was enormous. Many of these were in syrup form, the better to ensure that patients had swallowed them. A pill could be hidden in the mouth so that it was either not taken at all or was accumulated with other pills over a period of time for a suicide attempt or to 'sell' to other patients. ('Selling' in Broadmoor was not done with money, of course, but in kind, usually cigarettes or 'roll-up' tobacco.)

One of the problems of medicine in syrup form, however, was the sugar content and this contributed to tooth decay, much to the dentist's concern, and to putting on weight. A sedentary life-style characterized many patients, either because they did not make use of the facilities available to them or, more likely, because the effect of much medication, especially for schizophrenia, was drowsiness. It always seemed a pity that Broadmoor had no PT facility, although there were several ex-service PT instructors among the staff. My previous hospital had had some half dozen PT staff organizing activities from basic movement, for the most regressed patients, up to full-scale games and sports. Broadmoor had an annual sports day, as has been described in Chapter 9, and hospital and ward cricket, football, bowls and table tennis, but no gym or regular physical activity for the rest of the patient population other than what the staff might organize informally in the 'airing courts'.

The role of SHRU, apart from the case register, an enormous enterprise, became very much that of facilitator for others' research work. Gavin Tennent found that responsibility for all three special hospitals, each more than a hundred miles apart, meant that he spent a wasteful amount of time on the road between them.

Projects were initiated that collectively involved the staffs of each individual hospital's research unit and Gavin Tennent worked his way round them, contributing supervision and advice to them all. He also became involved in reporting and discussing research results and requirements at meetings and conferences around the country, so becoming a kind of 'travelling ambassador'. One significant area of work to develop involved the installation of an electroencephalograph service (EEG). This is not a treatment, as many mistake it to be, but is a form of assessment. Whilst the EEG was an essential part of the growing clinical service resources of the hospital, it also comprised a vital element of much research. This will feature later, in Chapter 17.

SUMMARY

Research marks the next stage of this history because of the great increase in medico-legal activity following the legislative changes of the late 1950s and early 1960s. Data were accruing on the results of these changes. The Royal Colleges and the associations of other disciplines (which were gradually spawning forensic sub-groups) held meetings to learn of the results. Broadmoor's centenary was celebrated with just such a series of meetings. Capital punishment was then abolished. The changing times posed many questions and the professions concerned wanted to know the answers.

This chapter has therefore described the results of the first data analyses from the new psychology service, detailing the characteristics of the patients being assessed and treated in this new context: their thinking impairments and their clinical and personality features; and what was different about them by comparison with their predecessors. What, in particular, were the features of the new 'mental disorder' categories?

Students came and contributed through their research projects. The creation of a Medical Centre in the former superintendent's residence facilitated the creation of a small laboratory, expanding opportunities further. New staff arrived, one of whom specifically researched the characteristics of sexual sadists and another the characteristics of murderers. The latter replicated work recently carried out in the USA, with the same results, and this brought the terms "Over-control" and "Under-control" into common usage over here. Importantly, this also tied in with and made sense of the puzzling results obtained in the early psychological assessments described in Chapter 10. Exciting times!

Finally Dr McGrath achieved his ambition of creating a specific research unit. This quickly began undertaking projects and accumulating data throughout the three special hospitals, including a case register, which was increasingly able to provide vital information for the important questions of the day.

Now it is time, with the arrival of the 1970s, to look at the expansion taking place in the therapeutic activity of the hospital.

CHAPTER 13

TREATMENT EXPANSION

As the 1960s moved into the 1970s, then, Broadmoor had a research service, albeit shared with the other special hospitals, and an enlarged professional staffing to enable it to cope with the demands of the 1959 Act and the larger 'throughput' of patients that resulted. Where consultant staff were concerned, Dr Brian O'Connell, Dr McGrath's only consultant colleague at the outset of the 1959 Act, had by now moved on to a new unit in north London. The consultant ranks had increased and post-holders had come and gone. Dr O'Connell's spacious first floor office in the Medical Centre had been vandalized to make two smaller rooms for the growing numbers in that building.

Office space was made for the growing numbers of consultants and their secretaries (one shared between two), together with their duplicators and eventually the photocopying equipment which followed. A prefabricated building was, therefore, horror of horrors, erected along the scarp of the hospital's main terrace, one of the only spaces available but quite vandalizing the beautiful outlook. This was partly enabled by the decline in use of the terraced gardens running along and just below the scarp. (See sketch plan, Chapter 5.) Few patients any longer tended gardens in the face of the TV onslaught and, to be fair, the considerable expansion also in other alternative occupational, educational and recreational facilities. The remaining gardens were nurtured by a few patients in the parole Blocks 2 and 5. Also in the new terrace suite was a conference room, the superintendent's office being no longer big enough or sufficiently often available for the increased numbers of meetings now taking place.

NUMBERED BLOCKS INTO NAMED HOUSES

At long last the ward blocks were no longer 'blocks' but 'houses' and were named. A competition was announced in the patients' magazine, *The Broadmoor Chronicle*, to choose a set of names. The criteria were that they should all start with a different letter of the alphabet, to facilitate marking equipment and clothing with a differentiating initial letter, and that their abbreviations should not lend themselves to rude, disparaging or embarrassing inter-pretations! A flood of submissions resulted but the temptation was too great for some bawdy variations and abbreviations not to be submitted, based on notorious people or places. The final decision was that county names would be adopted, reflecting the hospital's countrywide catchment area, and the choice, within the constraints set (e.g.: avoiding Beds, Bucks, Wilts, etc.), broadly accorded with the hospital layout, so that Cornwall was in the extreme west and Essex and Norfolk in the east. The suggestion that the Medical Centre, between the Male and Female Wings, should be named Middlesex, however, was rejected! The outcome was as follows:

Male Side		*Female Wing*	
Block 1	Norfolk House	Block 1	York House
Block 2	Essex House	Block 2	Lancaster House
Block 3	Kent House		
Block 4	Dorset House		
Block 5	Gloucester House		
Block 6	Monmouth House (later Somerset)		
Block 7	Cornwall House		

Individual wards still remained numbered, although some years later they were given names of towns in the county after which their house was named.

AN ADMISSION WARD AND AN 'ADOLESCENT' UNIT

An admission ward was first made in the top ward of Norfolk House instead of mixing new patients with the large population of Dorset House, the old Block 4. Staff were selected who would work up the admission cases for presentation at a case conference - which particularly involved student nurses - and these took place some eight or ten weeks after arrival, after which the patient would be moved to another house as soon as a vacancy arose.

The middle ward in Monmouth House was made into a so-called 'adolescent unit' for the increasing numbers of young men now accumulating, although 'adolescence' described their level of maturity and psychological needs rather than actual age. There were certainly young men of 18 and 19, and even the occasional one of 16 or 17, but most were in their twenties. The ward was organized on a 'bedsit' basis, with individual rooms, not dormitories, and the occupants were able to choose interior decor, the habitual posters, etc, and have radios, record players and later TVs, like their parole counterparts in the renamed Essex House. Needless to say the occupants were specially selected and not all young men were considered well enough to be in this ward. To distinguish it from the rest of Monmouth House, it was named Somerset House. The top ward was also later included in Somerset House, with only the bottom ward remaining Monmouth and continuing to care for the very disturbed patients characteristic of the old Block 6. Finally, the entire house became Somerset when the only accommodation for very disturbed patients that was needed could be assimilated within Norfolk House, the other old 'back block'. The growing range and efficacy of pharmacological treatments for combating psychotic disorders was responsible for this.

With all the highly disturbed male patients now in Norfolk House, the admission unit was moved from its top ward to the top ward of Somerset House. The idea of an admission unit being Dr McGrath's, he ran this for some time himself but eventually, when Dr David Tidmarsh joined the hospital as a consultant, he took over this job. It was very much suited to his meticulous method of record keeping and compiling patients' case histories, and his research interests. (By then Dr Tennent had moved on. 'SHRU' was next directed by Dr Malcolm MacCulloch from Park Lane Hospital, the new 'Broadmoor of the North' on Merseyside, before being run from the Institute of Psychiatry in London by Professor John Gunn.)

PSYCHOTHERAPY

Psychotherapy had begun to figure more largely in Broadmoor's treatment programme about this time, the first visiting consultant psychotherapist being Dr Dougal McPhail. He worked on an individual basis, however, and it was not until later that several more sessional psychotherapists visited and some ran group therapy sessions. Outstanding as a charismatic character among these was Dr Murray Cox, a former GP turned psychotherapist who enthused both staff and patients with his energy and commitment. A speech therapist, Mrs Jenny France, was recruited, again on a sessional basis and, like Murray Cox, devoted many years to the service of Broadmoor. Speech therapy had seemed a relevant need for the many shy young men, especially, who seemed to have difficulty articulating their thoughts and ideas. Actually, this phenomenon was to provide the basis for a great deal of subsequent work by the psychologists but there is no doubt that the acquisition of specialist therapists of all kinds was a great step forward for the many patients who badly needed to be able to talk about their lives and problems with someone who could offer an understanding ear and constructive suggestions. I recall vividly when I was spending a great deal of time in one of the Female Wing wards (for reasons I will come to) a group of women patients approached me with the plea that I should organize a discussion group for them to 'get things off their chests'. I had to disappoint them at that time, much though I would have liked to have complied, by saying that not only was my time fully occupied but also that the request had to come from the RMO. This was in the days before clinical teams although, of course, I passed on the request.

THE CHAPLAINCY AND RELIGIOUS LIFE

As well as the augmented medical staff, other staff disciplines were also increasing. The chaplain in 1959, Basil James, had retired not long afterwards to the country parish of Ufton Nervet in West Berkshire. The chaplaincy was then held by a number of successors who were responsible for various initiatives to develop their therapeutic as well as spiritual role.

One of the avenues for arranging supervised discharge for patients, for instance, was to use the Church Army's and other organizations' hostels, such as those of the Richmond Fellowship. Church Army chaplains and other hostel wardens would therefore visit, to review and discuss with patients their future. Chapel activity expanded into discussion groups. A group of Franciscan monks figured in these at one point. The chaplain at this time, Ion

Davies, facilitated the wider activity of the chapel by having the pews replaced with chairs.

The chapel had always been an active centre for choral presentations, as well as the regular Anglican services and special events for the various Christian festivals, but its role was now greatly expanded as a resource to occupy, stimulate and minister to the psychological as well as spiritual needs of patients. Ion Davies's wife and young children were to be seen in chapel each Sunday and family activity was always a 'draw' for patients who welcomed any chance to talk with staff and their families in an 'off-duty' setting. Dr McGrath had set a pattern on his very first arrival of going round the wards on Christmas Day with his young family, which was a greatly welcomed 'normalizing' influence and augmented the other intermittent occasions when patients could meet staff and their families on sports days, parole dances and at social occasions such as those described in Chapter 9. Even so, these were rare occurrences at long intervals apart. Chapel services, therefore, were a regular and welcome occasion for patients to meet staff families and villagers, who augmented the congregation and the choir.

Dr McGrath and his family attended mass on Sundays in the hospital's RC chapel which was a small, corrugated iron building in the area beyond the central courtyard squeezed between the back of Kent House, the workshops and the peripheral wall. Dr McGrath would describe with amusement the effect of his family's arrival when RC chapel attendance promptly began to swell. However, he let it be known that he expected a higher standard of behaviour from practising Roman Catholics, whereupon congregations fell back to their former level!

With the development of the main Anglican chapel as a facility for wider activities of a cultural and devotional kind and with the demolition of the old corrugated iron RC chapel for building the new workshops, the main chapel was consecrated for use by all denominations. A local Free Church minister also visited patients and conducted non-conformist services. Patients of other religious denominations increased over the years, especially as more were admitted from amongst the various immigrant groups then settling in the country, so arrangements had to be increasingly made for their spiritual needs to be met.

OTHER STAFF GROWTH

Other staff to increase in numbers at this time were the social work, psychology, patients' education and staff education services. Nursing staff numbers also increased, especially as more were allocated for new duties and off-ward activities and as the hours of the working week were reduced and shift systems had to be rescheduled. However, when nursing staff numbers were in excess of six hundred whilst medical staff could be counted on the fingers of two hands and other professional groups on one, the effect is distinctly more noticeable in the smaller groups.

In social work, Helen Paton retired and Mary Gatt left to get married. (A year or two later she surprised and delighted everyone by becoming a mother - the surprise being that she was by then 48 - and this was in the days before the assistance of hormones and test tubes.) In place of these two popular and warmly regarded ladies, Newman Hooker was appointed to run the social work service and Peter Bowles his deputy. Others were gradually added through the 1970s until a department of over half a dozen was achieved, reflecting the growing demand for social and family histories to be compiled for the newly arriving patients and for liaison with the outside world for all the many other patients' concerns which affected them while they were inside Broadmoor, not to mention the continuing task of arranging work and accommodation after discharge. This was still the time of full employment when these were two of the Home Office-cum-Ministry of Health conditions for sanctioning discharge. Student social workers also became a feature, just as psychology students were doing in the psychology department, and training attachments were arranged for many courses around the country, and indeed abroad, in both disciplines so that their trainees could obtain benefit of experience with mentally disordered offenders and the British system of secure care.

NEW WORKSHOPS

Messrs Fraser, Wells and Caplin, tailor, shoemaker and upholsterer respectively in the original Victorian, red-brick workshops, had repeatedly laughed to scorn the suggestions that new and enlarged workshops would ever materialize, certainly in their lifetime. Nevertheless, with the advances of the 1970s, they duly appeared. With the going of the RC 'tin chapel' and the old workshops, there arose in their place a set of modern workshops which were to house all the occupational activities from the former shops and the handicraft centre. There was sufficient space for this larger complex, with the old shops gone, and so occupational facilities were concentrated together. Even so, their use still awaited some kind of co-ordinated planning where patients' needs were concerned and they continued to be used on an *ad hoc* basis to accommodate the patients the RMOs thought needed to be there.

The new centre for handicrafts and workshops was still staffed predominantly by people with a trade skill and qualification who, as has been said, had nevertheless developed considerable therapeutic skills with their patients. Arguments continued on whether occupational therapists should be introduced but, as the system seemed to be working satisfactorily as it was, the principle: "If it ain't broke, don't fix it" prevailed. Even so, the satellite occupational activities on some of the wards, especially where the patients lived who were too disturbed to attend the central handicrafts and workshops, were known as 'occupational therapy' and provided activities of drawing, painting, modelling, rug-making and similar 'handicrafts'. By the 1980s, occupational therapists were beginning to appear but then so were many other people.

THE GROWTH OF NEW THERAPIES

New forms of group therapy and of 'behavioural therapies' were beginning to be practised around the country at that time and some nursing staff began to want to be more actively involved in such treatments. A series of informal discussion groups was started, largely on the initiative of Fred Furber, a nursing officer and former local secretary of the Broadmoor branch of the POA (Prison Officers' Association), and his wife Gwen, a staff nurse, later sister, in the Female Wing. Several medical, social worker and psychologist staff were invited to attend and explain the developments. All these staff were involved in the curriculum of the nurse training school, for the three year student nurse training, but students were finding it frustrating to learn about new approaches which were then not known about or practised on the wards. The more the small staff group learned, the more they tended to think that 'behavioural treatment' was what they did themselves anyway. (I cut out for my pin board a little *bon mot* from a journal of that time which went: "First they tell you that you're wrong and they can prove it; then they tell you that you're right but it's not important; and then they tell you it's important but they've known it all along!")

It was undoubtedly true to some extent that nursing staff operated a system of rewards and sanctions, and this was the prevailing philosophy of the pre-1959 Act Broadmoor 'Institution', before 'medicalization' and the arrival of numerous 'responsible medical officers'. Such rewards and sanctions were not, however, systematically applied with the consistency and comprehensiveness required for success. Too often natural responses were of a 'put down' kind. I recall once working a nursing shift on one of the wards so as to be conversant, first hand, with the procedures and opportunities that might be used for a behavioural treatment programme I was planning in the 'disturbed ward' of the Female Wing. The staff on that shift were competent and encouraging to their patients, whom they treated well, and they were liked. Even so, the greeting for many of the patients on opening their rooms first thing was "Good morning Janie" (or Julie or Jenny, or whatever); "how are you this morning? Are you going to be good today?" The envisaged possibility, indeed expectation, that someone might NOT be good, tends to be self-fulfilling and should, of course, never be raised if one wants to treat each day as a 'clean sheet', only expressing disapproval or imposing sanctions if required. It is, of course, a natural remark. But it illustrates that the 'natural remark' is not always the 'right remark'.

Careful training and self-discipline are needed, in a treatment environment where mental disorder involving antisocial behaviour is involved, if a patient is to be enabled to feel valued and appreciated for what they can do, however limited. The disapproval and, possibly, sanctions for what is antisocial then stand in contrast with this and does not become the only response someone obtains from the people around them. Whilst antisocial and uncooperative behaviour would be reprimanded, too often helpful and constructive behaviour would be ignored, taken for granted, when it needed noticing and encouraging. This is because we are not accustomed to giving encouragement in normal circumstances; it is not reckoned to be so often needed with normal personalities or is shown in more subtle and intimate ways; we become used to being told only of our faults.

For damaged personalities who have learned that the only way to get a response from other people is to do something dramatic or harmful, however, there is a continual need to pay attention to, and show appreciation for, any and every little manifestation of normality and helpfulness that is forthcoming. Nursing staff would make the understandable point that bad behaviour could not be ignored if it risked the safety of others and indeed this is so. However, it proved surprising for them to discover in discussion the many behaviours that were not risky, merely rude, uncooperative or insulting, which could safely be ignored (a potent but seldom recognized motivator), whilst there were many other occasions, so trivial as not to get noticed, of positive and helpful behaviours that could have received an appreciative comment; which is all that is needed to establish the contrast and provide the encouragement known as 'positive reinforcement'. Much of this is well known for handling children. Whilst adult psychiatric patients are not children and need responses which are appropriate to an adult context, what often seemed overlooked was that the learning or relearning of normal behaviour patterns, previously neglected or absent, is a similar process, at whatever age.

A TRIAL RUN FOR BEHAVIOUR THERAPY

The specific problem for which I was asked (perhaps 'challenged' would be the appropriate word) to suggest a treatment was of a woman in the 'disturbed' ward of Lancaster House who was confined to her room round the clock because any attempt to get her to come out prompted a violent outburst from her.

Seclusion in a side-room was a recourse used for aggressive, disruptive outbursts that had injured staff, other patients or the patient herself, or had caused damage to the ward environment. A room devoid of furniture in which no damage could occur would be available on most wards, particularly of the 'back blocks'. Where a patient was of a tendency to continual aggressive outbursts the side-room would be the patient's own room, appropriately stripped of dangerous contents. In this case the patient had been living in these conditions for a long time because of her immediate aggressive response to any attempt to bring her out of her room.

I suggested we try a strategy that assumed she actually now only felt safe in her room and reacted violently to the prospect of facing the outside world. Whether this was a correct analysis or not, a strategy based on it would soon shed further light on the problem. The suggested programme for which I was given the go-ahead to proceed was, therefore, to visit her every few hours each day encouraging her, on the first few occasions, just to come to the door of her room and look out. If this were successful, i.e.: accomplished without any aggressive outburst, then she would be encouraged to step over the threshold for a moment but then immediately go back inside. Next she would be asked to take a few steps down the corridor when no one else was about but immediately to return.

And so the pattern would continue, any advance on the time and distance out of her room being dependent on aggression-free success at the previous venture. She would be told what was to happen each time so that she knew she would always be near her room and out of it for only as long as she could tolerate. (This strategy is essentially what is known as 'desensitization' and is widely used for the treatment of irrational or excessive fears such as heights, crowded or open spaces, spiders, etc: the frightening circumstances or object are faced in what is known beforehand to be going to be for only as long a time as can be managed and in a form that can be coped with. The first step is such an easy one that it often seems to be ridiculous, which is useful: something ridiculous is less frightening.)

Talking through the plan with the patient met with her agreement, no doubt largely on account of the novelty and attention, and that it was a man involved! Never mind - we would use whatever it took to enable that first foray without violence. The strategy worked remarkably well and, in fact, the patient progressed faster and further than had been expected, to the point that the frequent short visits by me became unnecessary because of the longer periods she was spending out of her room, even to attending the OT (occupational therapy) in that house for several hours at a time. Her response raised doubts in my mind that the problem was what I had originally thought it was but, never mind, she was now 'associating', as the term went, and not violent. This allowed more conversation and the chance to discover what really were her reasons for secluding herself. Unfortunately this revealed little. Her ability to converse was limited, she could give no explanation of why she wanted to stay in her room or why she kicked and hit people. She vacillated between happiness at her new way of life and misery at what she saw as her hopeless situation in Broadmoor.

Eventually, of course, there was the inevitable relapse when she once again kicked a member of the staff and was promptly returned to her room. It was to no avail that I pointed out that this was a normal pattern for any behavioural programme and that we needed to understand more about the precipitating cause. People progress and fall back, then progress a little further and fall back again, but each time building on previous progress and eventually achieving an acceptable level of competence, freedom from fear, or whatever may be their problem. I explained that patience had to be exercised in starting again lower down the 'hierarchy' of activities outside her room before longer periods of sustained success outside would be achieved. As far as the ward staff were concerned, however, I had had my chance and it had failed. Never mind that more and longer success had been achieved than at any previous time. Having one's varicosed legs kicked was a potent disincentive to continuing. I was told to abandon the project.

These were early days of any new behavioural treatment endeavour and I had gone into it with my eyes open, glad to have the chance of demonstrating a different way of looking at patients' behavioural problems. As time went by there were more opportunities and these methods became better known and more widely practised, on a firmer basis, with patients whose condition and problems were better understood and whose treatment programmes were better planned. This, by the way, was the programme, involving me visiting one particular ward on a regular daily basis, that led to the incident of a group of women approaching me to run a discussion group for them.

PSYCHOLOGICAL INITIATIVES

In the psychology department a considerable turnover of staff had by now taken place. Ron Blackburn had moved on to run the Rampton psychology service. Pat Clancy was appointed to replace him and took over the running of the library which had flourished in his care. She was a welcome recruit to our still small service, with an 'unfazed' attitude that greatly helped to deal with the 'psychologist baiting', as Dr McGrath called the banter over lunch in the senior common room, especially if there were visitors to entertain (Ron Blackburn, a similarly 'unfazed' person, had always gone home to lunch, so Pat's arrival constituted 'reinforcements'!).

There continued to be a probationer trainee post but a further basic grade post was established, to which Kevin Howells was appointed. After post-graduate training he had spent a year working at Atascadero, the state hospital which fulfilled for California a similar function to Broadmoor's for England & Wales. He had worked with Richard Laws, the psychologist there, who was pioneering new explanations and treatments for sexual offenders. A couple of years later Kevin's post was made senior and two further basic grade posts were established, when David Crawford and Roger Paxton were appointed. David had been our probationer trainee and later he, too, spent a year at Atascadero during a period when there were several staff exchanges between Britain, the US and Canada.

Patients' Perceptions or 'Attributions' About Themselves and their World

Ron Blackburn had gained a PhD from his work on the study of personality characteristics of mentally disordered offenders at Broadmoor and the gist of his work has already been described. Our probationer trainee at the end of the 1960s, Rachpal Singh Randhawa, also gained a PhD on work with a particular psychometric procedure. In the 1970s both Kevin Howells and David Crawford followed with PhDs from their work. These two, however, based their theses on the new treatment methods that characterized the 1970s. It is worth trying to explain their work in general terms, to illustrate the kind of advance and new thinking that was taking place at that time.

Kevin Howells had started looking at the motivations of Atascadero patients and continued this at Broadmoor, in what was called an 'attribution theory' framework. He was concerned with the thinking processes used by sexual offenders to justify their behaviour and he extended this work at Broadmoor to include the hostile and paranoid 'attributions', or interpretations, made by some patients about their victims to justify their illogical reasoning about their own motives and behaviour towards their victims.

In this he was helped, as we all were, by the development and publication of a new kind of approach to assessing such motives and 'attributions'. Courses were being run in the Repertory Grid and Semantic Differential methods, deriving from the work of Kelly and Osgood in the USA, and mentioned in the previous chapter as used by Cathy Widom. They need further mention here because they not only led to a new treatment approach but they largely overcame the distorting effects of test-taking attitude described in the previous chapter.

Whilst trying to avoid too much technical detail, it will be relevant to describe the basics. They represent a conceptual shift in the treatment developments of this period of Broadmoor's history. They involved obtaining, from interviewing the patient, a list of people significant in their lives and then comparing and contrasting these people to obtain another list, this time of the key qualities that the patient uses to account for the significance of the relationship, positive or negative.

A 'repertory grid' was thereby constructed with people along one side of the grid (known as the 'elements') and qualities along the other (the 'constructs'; see the Figure below). Each construct could then be 'attributed' to the list of people and a score or rank given to them. The grid could then be analysed statistically to discover the degree to which people were alike or where there were associations between any of the constructs a person used in their understanding of their personal world. Because this assessment technique used qualities about people that the patient had supplied, it was 'projective' (i.e.: not imposed by the assessor) but it was also 'objective' because it yielded data amenable to statistical analysis and graphical display to show the degree of either association or independence of the 'constructs'.

EXAMPLE OF A REPERTORY GRID

ELEMENTS	Likeable	Helpful	Respected	Clever	Sexy/passionate	Frustrating	Provokes me	Soft/tough etc.
Mother								
Father								
Sibling								
Friend								
Enemy								
Partner								
Teacher								
Victim								
Me as I was								
Me as I am								
Me as I would like to be								
Me when I was doing my crime								

CONSTRUCTS

The Repertory Grid method could show how far a person's ways of evaluating their surrounding world, and the people in it, were typical of people in general, and concordant with the meanings of the constructs used or, conversely, whether they were idiosyncratic and indicative of conflicts or deviant motivation. Further, and intriguingly, because its comparisons of the people (elements) and the qualities about them (constructs) that were important to the patient were relative and not dependent upon some absolute 'score', it side-stepped the problem of 'response distortion' that had beset the earlier work on admission and discharge assessments.

Finally, it led to formulations of treatment needs. Where patients do not always realize the basis or source of their problems or that they have treatment needs at all and where, additionally in the case of special hospitals patients, there may be an element of intentional misleading in order to impress, this further quality of the 'repertory grid' approach was a distinct bonus. It could, for instance, show how some people (comprising the elements) were construed similarly. The victim or circumstances of the offence were always included in the grid so that the question of the motivation could be probed. For example, Kevin Howells might be able to demonstrate that a patient's use of violent or sexually abusive behaviour was associated with perceptions of their ideal self involving, say, their sense of achievement or self-worth, or with feelings of anxiety relief, personal security or sexual status (to name but a few). One young male patient showed a close association between his ideal of himself and the offence of poisoning, although this was not his own offence. It transpired that his 'ideal person' was a former patient who was a poisoner.

Treatment, of whatever approach, with this as with other sorts of problem, would need to include strategies for dissociating the violent or antisocial components from the ideal person and enabling more normal, healthy concepts to take their place, thus reinstating a more normal set of 'constructs' about their personal world and their relationships within it. In this way a patient would be helped to avoid the violence that had characterized their behaviour in certain specific contexts in the past; they would no longer see that context as provocative or threatening in the way that had previously acted as a violent stimulus. A repeat of the grid assessment would then show how far this separation of previously morbidly or negatively associated evaluations (constructs), or the people giving rise to them (elements), had succeeded.

The 'Social Skills' Approach

By the time David Crawford, following on, had formulated his own ideas for a PhD thesis on treatment initiatives, 'social skills' had arrived. Common parlance now, this was a novel idea in the early 1970s. It derived from the observation that many people's problems seemed to stem from, or be accentuated by, a noticeable lack of competence and confidence in conversing, and thereby forming relationships, with other people. They seemed shy, hesitant and unable to express themselves.

This approach actually arose initially from work in the rehabilitation of chronic schizophrenic patients at a number of hospitals around the country. Such patients characteristically lacked, or else had presumably lost, the ability to relate to, or communicate with, the people with whom they came into contact. From whatever cause, and once the condition had become chronic, the requirement seemed to be that they needed help to restore this capability.

The restoration of 'social skills', therefore, seemed to be where the treatment action needed to be directed. The complex system of social behaviour was broken down into its component parts and patients were coached in each of these in turn, gradually building up a composite of appropriate and competent behaviours.

Thus, a start might be made with simply encouraging a patient to look another person in the eye, a prerequisite for making any kind of personal or social contact. Because it would be fatuous simply to require someone to do this in silence, saying something very simple, undemanding and non-threatening needed to be the reason for doing so. Saying their name was the most obvious strategy. Some very shy or regressed patients had great difficulty looking anyone in the eye, and then only for a brief moment and, if they managed to do so, they would then rapidly mumble their name. The initial treatment sessions using the 'social skills' method would concentrate on lengthening the time a patient was able to look one in the eye and saying their name more clearly.

Once this had been achieved the therapy, or 'social skills training', could move on to further aspects of personal relationships such as posture, facial expression, gestures, intonation and expression, and so on.

Actually, and where posture was concerned, a further attribute of the use of this form of treatment quickly emerged, with Broadmoor patients perhaps more than the chronic schizophrenic patients with whom the method had begun. This was the need for learning to relax. The posture of many patients was tense and unnatural and they were clearly anxious. This was so in all their social relationships, not just with the therapist. It was essential, therefore, to train patients in how to relax. Then the steps in the social skills training could more readily be undertaken, probably with spells of further relaxation required before and during each session. Finally, and probably only after many sessions over a period of months, the patient might be encouraged to walk out of the treatment room and go down the corridor to the office where there would be a clerical officer who was a stranger to the patient, and ask if he or she might be allowed to put on the kettle to make a cup of coffee.

David Crawford and colleagues in the psychology department at that time would then often go to social events on the wards or in the central hall in the evening to observe and encourage a patient's progress in the activities taking place there.

The Arrival of 'Video'

The march of technology lent a hand at this time. The psychology department acquired one of the first generation of portable videotape recorders, camera and monitor; black and white at that time, of course. Although rather cumbersome it was at least portable and the department's staff nurse, who was present for security purposes but was inevitably and sensibly also incorporated into the treatment programme, adopting various social roles as required by the therapy, supplied an additional pair of hands in the equipment's transportation to various wards. The great asset of 'video' was not only that a record could be kept of a patient's progress but that its playback, immediately after a treatment task had been completed, provided a potent demonstration of how a patient was doing. Patients were able to see how stiff and gauche they appeared initially and how much better their attempts at eye contact and conversation looked on the video as they progressed. This also acted as a further stimulus to better achievement as they strove to improve their video 'performance'.

Video became a facilitator for various kinds of psychotherapy. Social skills spawned 'assertiveness training' for shy and uncertain people and, conversely, 'anger control' for the opposite kind of problem: patients with hostile attitudes and an aggressive manner of dealing with problems. Just as video graphically demonstrated, better than any therapist could explain, how inept, rude or aggressive a patient's conversation and interactions were, it also facilitated group work. Once again, in enacted sequences of imagined conflicts and arguments, the comments of fellow members of a group were a more potent influence on a patient's realization of a need to change than anything a therapist might urge. The therapist could then concentrate on planning the contexts of further treatment sessions and open discussions of why the group members might have felt the need to react in the way they did and how they might have reacted differently with different, and less disastrous, consequences. The video, in effect, provided the 'reinforcing feedback' to patients' efforts at resolving, in their enactments, the sort of problems they had failed to resolve in real life.

Video-recordings, in fact, provided an essential basis for the presentation of the number of standard settings used by David Crawford in his PhD research. It also provided the means of measurement of patients' responses. Whilst the agreement of a number of judges of a patient's response to a video sequence was obtained as the 'measurement', which is a notoriously 'soft' measurement of low reliability, this was greatly enhanced by the facility to count objective responses such as the numbers of smiles and gestures and measure the lengths of sentences used by a patient.

The 'Multi-Method' Approach to Therapeutic Problems

Just as social skills training had soon revealed the need to combine the method with relaxation training, as used in such other widely varying contexts as pre-natal classes and 'desensitization' for phobias, other needs also soon became apparent. For instance, social skills were found to be useful with some forms of sex offender, in particular the shy, inept young man who had never developed the ability to make a social relationship, let alone a sexual one. Relaxation training then became necessary in conjunction with desensitization of the man's fears of meeting and talking with a mature woman in a potentially sexual situation. (These fears, together with ineptness in dealing with relationships, often underlie an adult sexual offender's choice of a teenage partner, or even a child, who seems less threatening and more accepting to such an uncertain adult.)

It then emerged that many of these young men had little or no knowledge of basic sexual anatomy and physiology or of the basic elements of courtship, living together, sexual intercourse, childbirth and child rearing. The consequence was that basic information of this kind had to be prepared and used as the final phase of a multi-modal programme of treatment which had perhaps only begun with social skills. It had had to be taken on to incorporate relaxation and desensitization. David Crawford published an important paper detailing this multi-faceted treatment approach to complex problem groups.

The development of these new treatment methods was not without its critics. Years before, when developing the original assessment methods and drawing conclusions for treatment, Dr McGrath had commented: "If personality traits are permanent, what is your behaviour therapy changing?" By the time Ron Blackburn, Kevin Howells and David Crawford had completed their researches and given us new perspectives on the typologies, explanations and treatments of a number of Broadmoor's problems, it became clear that it is not the personality traits which change but the strategies people develop for using their traits in dealing with life's events. Shaped by their environments and experiences, they can vary and be changed again and again: for a new job, a sport, a hobby or, in the case of a Broadmoor patient, a relationship or a way of dealing with provocation. People don't change but their behaviour can.

This in turn gave rise to further criticism, this time from Dr

Udwin who maintained that social skills training merely "taught rapists to say please!" What we did not seem able to get across was that, if patients became able to relate to their fellow human beings and learn to deal with their fears and their ignorance, then they *would* become able to conduct their lives normally, *without* having to rape, or injure, or set fires, or kill. They would be able to "say please" and accompany this with similar socially acceptable actions. Violence would no longer need to be on the behavioural agenda. This was a big leap, however, and a challenge to the understanding of human motivation and social adaptation. A lot more work would be needed yet.

INTRODUCING MORE STAFF TO NEW TREATMENTS

Fred and Gwen Furber's early initiatives in post-qualification training for nursing staff, after the treatment developments described above, led to a more systematic attempt to establish a multi-disciplinary base to the expansion of treatment methods. At the beginning of the 1970s a group was very active in Belfast running a behaviour therapy based treatment programme for sexual disorders, dysfunctions and deviations. The team of Quinn, Harbison, McAlister and Graham - a psychiatrist, two psychologists and a social worker - accumulated an impressive series of publications on their work which received international publicity and acclaim. Both the method and the target of the work seemed to be squarely within Broadmoor's terms of reference. The Belfast group organized a series of conference-workshops each year for several years in the early 1970s so it seemed relevant to go and find out what they had achieved, and how.

The first conference was missed but a couple of us attended the next one, when it had become 'European'; Professor J.C.

Brengelman attended and spoke on his work at the Max Planck Institute in Munich. Because of the 'troubles' by now besetting Northern Ireland, the event was held in Eire, in Wexford, for several years, with great success. The methods were generally within the area of those sketched out earlier in this chapter but ranged over a wide spectrum of people and problems, from which a similarly wide range of assessment methods had also been developed for monitoring the problems treated.

Our attendance both gave us new ideas and bolstered our confidence in applying new methods to the problems of Broadmoor patients. The following year some half dozen staff attended and the year after that an even larger group went: several nursing staff, social workers, occupations officers, psychologists and a psychiatrist. Thus more seeds were sown of variations and developments in treatment that might eventually sprout and flourish to the benefit of the patients of Broadmoor, as they were doing elsewhere.

SUMMARY

Having described the new legislation, its effects upon the mix and numbers of incoming patients, the need to move patients out at the other end who no longer needed secure care, and the consequences for staffing and research, attention has turned to the question of treatment.

After describing the changes of attitude and moves forward made by naming the ward blocks, rebuilding workshops, creating a young men's ('adolescent') unit, introducing more psychotherapists and expanding the role of the chapel, a first attempt at 'behaviour therapy' has been described.

Staff expansion led to some important initiatives based on

advances being pioneered world-wide at that time. This involved developments of psychological methods that were more direct and less time consuming than the traditional psychodynamic and psychoanalytic ones. Some space has been given to explaining these 'attributional' and 'social skills' approaches and their monitoring, both because of their mould-breaking importance and because they are probably, even now, relatively little known, despite some of the terminology having passed into the vocabulary. Their development was greatly helped by the arrival of the new technology for video recording.

Psychotherapists were also appointed and increasingly used group methods. As with the group-based behavioural approaches, this greatly increased the number of patients who benefited from specific problem-focused treatment.

CHAPTER 14

REBUILDING - MOVES AND CHANGES

THE HOSPITAL REBUILDING PROGRAMME

Way back during the centenary celebrations in 1963 the then Minister of Health, the Rt Hon Enoch Powell, well regarded in the NHS as a vigorous supporter of its needs, had announced the intention to rebuild the hospital. This eventually came about - although with many fits and starts, changes of plan and, ultimately, a trimmed down version of the original. The result today, long after the end of this 'Inter-Acts' period, is essentially the preservation of the central core of the original with an expansion into additional buildings around this core to provide new wards, clinical service areas, administration buildings and gatehouse. (See sketch plan, Chapter 5.)

This extension has used the rest of the Broadmoor plateau so that the new car park is down the hill and reached from the main gate by a series of footpaths. The roadway to this main entrance gatehouse is a *cul-de-sac* and the peripheral road around the entire estate runs from the brow of the hill, past the new staff clubhouse, down past the car park and up the next hill to the new works yard and transport buildings. Transport has come a long way from a 'limmo and a lorry' and acts as a central resource for several other government departments in the Crowthorne vicinity.

During the period of the 1970s now reached, however, the rebuild was, if rather more than a twinkle in the Minister's eye, chiefly a set of evolving plans, a planning team and some preparatory works. In 1963 the celebratory lunch during the RMPA conference, attended by so many big names in the world of psychiatry of the time, was held in the recreation hall behind the old staff club. This was a typical, prefabricated, village hall kind of building, difficult to heat but warm enough when full of badminton players, dancers at a staff function, the Christmas draw or, as at the centenary, tables full of celebratory lunchers. It was at this lunch that Enoch Powell announced the Government's intention to rebuild the hospital.

The old staff club was the end building of the row of houses opposite the main gate (see sketch plan, Chapter 6) which ran the entire length of the hospital's back wall (or 'front' if you regard the way the hospital is approached as the front; as I have said before, the true 'front' is the southern aspect from the string of buildings overlooking the terrace and the distant countryside beyond). The old row of staff houses originally catered for the senior and essential staff who needed to be on hand for any eventuality inside the hospital. A row of Victorian red-brick cottages between the staff club and the rest lay back a little from the road to provide a car parking area, with a painted line at the end nearest the club to indicate where the police parked when there was an escape. Then the staff club became the escape headquarters from where the search and retrieval operation was run. The little row of set-back cottages had, apparently, been much admired by John Betjeman as a classic example of a Victorian bijou terrace.

Anyway, all these frontage buildings had eventually to go to allow the plateau area to be developed and bit-by-bit during the 70s and 80s they did. The staff club could not go until a replacement was built - the staff looking after themselves, the cynics said but, of course, there had to be a continuously functioning escape headquarters throughout the rebuilding programme. The building at the opposite end changed functions several times and after the nurse training school moved out to the new staff education centre, which we shall come to later, housed the social work department. On Dr McGrath's retirement in 1981, Kentigern, his home, rather sadly became an office block and the social work department moved in there, together with the entire hospital administration. Only the medical office stayed inside the walls, overlooking the terrace next to the superintendent's office. Half way along this string of cottages, opposite the main gate, midway between the nurse training school and the staff club, and right opposite the main gate, a small road ran to some doctors' houses. To the side of this, another prefabricated building was erected to house a new staff canteen which provided all staff, at last, with the opportunity to get a meal or coffee break at any time of the day.

THE LEAGUE OF FRIENDS

One of the cottages in the row opposite the main gate, along the stretch towards the nurse training school, was turned into a facility for the League of Friends. A hospital League of Friends had been formed some years previously on Dr McGrath's initiative, with the aim of bringing the hospital into line with the general trend for hospitals nation-wide and providing a facility that would draw local people, otherwise unconnected with Broadmoor, into contact with the hospital. This way a wider understanding of the place would grow and a further rebuttal be made of the allegation that Broadmoor was a secret and secretive place, closed to the outside world.

What went wrong with the creation of the League of Friends was never quite clear but unfortunately the staff union, the POA, saw the initiative as a threat to their status, as the guardians of both patient care and public security, and vigorously opposed the idea as undermining their authority. They envisaged yet more people 'coming in to tell us how to do our job'. There was indeed, and continued to be, a stream of government officials, ministers, commissions and committees of inquiry which visited the hospital at monotonously regular intervals and, fearing some adverse report no doubt, they were greeted by staff with wary suspicion. Most visitors, of course, were simply ensuring that they had a proper knowledge of their area of government responsibility when they were elected or appointed to office, and discovered, often to their surprise, that Broadmoor featured on their list of these. Sufficiently often, however, some group or other would be charged with making a report and recommendations and this was often enough to make staff want to give all visiting officials a wide berth. So a League of Friends was formed without the help and hospitality it might have expected from the staff. It was left to Dr McGrath and his immediate professional colleagues to maintain the contacts.

Lady Monckton, widow of Viscount Monckton of Brenchley who had held numerous cabinet offices during and immediately after the war, and herself a patroness of hospital leagues of friends nation-wide, became President of the Broadmoor League of Friends and brought a great deal of goodwill and expertise to the task, not to mention helpful contacts from around the country. Local people did join and formed the necessary committee. Money-raising events took place which enabled some extra facilities to be provided for patients and some more prizes to be given for entries in the annual handicrafts and produce show.

However, the major initiative, and one which was particularly necessary at Broadmoor, whose patients came from all over the country, was the provision, first, of a rest room and canteen for patients' visitors and, second, of a transport service to ferry visitors to and from the local bus and railway stations. The hospital is a mile

278

and a half from Crowthorne station, on the line from Gatwick and Guildford to Reading, with connections to North, South and West, and four miles from Bracknell for trains to London and the East. Buses in the village only ran hourly; and it was then a half mile's steep uphill walk to the hospital. Patients' visitors had often come from the other end of the country by rail or long distance coach and this final wearisome lap of the journey was the last straw which seemed to emphasize the isolation and ostracization their loved ones were experiencing. Once there, a visitor would usually stay all day and some would come for several days, staying in the vicinity, visiting each day. Visiting was from 10 am till 12 noon and 2 till 4 pm, so a canteen where sandwiches and rolls were available, and a warm sitting room, was a welcome innovation. A car to take them to and from the station was an added help.

Eventually, the League of Friends and the social work department assembled a list of local people who were prepared to provide bed and breakfast for those visiting from a long distance who needed to stay over. Whilst the provision of perks and prizes for patients did little to assuage the suspicions of the staff association, the POA, the help to visitors with transport and a canteen was gradually seen as an asset, creating happier visitors and therefore happier (i.e.: more settled) patients. The canteen, like the car service later, needed a co-ordinator to see to the provision of supplies and a rota of helpers and the first was Anne Maine, wife of Dr Maine, the second Dorothy Cooper, wife of Eric Cooper the 'clerk and steward' (hospital secretary) and the third was my own wife who did the job for 14 years. For this our phone number was in the patients' magazine, the *The Broadmoor Chronicle*, for all that time, although many staff insisted on having ex-directory numbers. Despite this, we never had a nuisance phone call, either in those 14 years or at any other time.

The League of Friends canteen, being in what had formerly

been a domestic residence, had a back garden in which was a prolific damson tree. After it was no longer a private residence there was no one to gather the damsons so the canteen co-ordinator would gather them and distribute them to helpers who would make jam or pies with them for subsequent sale for League of Friends' funds. Later, with the creation of the car ferrying service and a growth of helpers from the locality, more events were held in the village itself. A fête was held in the summer on the village recreation ground whilst 'wine-and-cheese' evenings were held in one of the halls of Wellington College, courtesy of League of Friends members at the college. Jimmy Saville, well known supporter of hospitals and charities, became involved in Broadmoor's League of Friends, too, and was able to draw upon his large reservoir of support to provide a disco for the patients and visits from many pop groups. With his long-distance running passion he also organized a number of sponsored runs, usually around the grounds of Wellington College or of the hospital itself (outside the walls!). He would often stay overnight in one of the hostels and came to rely on the hospital's transport manager - Don Bennett - to garage his car. His association with the hospital thereby became a two-way one as Don saw to his car maintenance and even used to spend his leaves accompanying Jimmy on some of his long distance money-raising runs, driving the back-up-cum-overnight camper wagon. Jimmy also sat his 'entrance test' to Mensa in the hospital, insisting on doing this locked in a bare 'side-room', i.e.: a room devoid of furniture or fittings such as a disturbed patient would occupy when in a destructive phase. He passed with flying colours!

Later the League of Friends initiated a patient visiting service for patients who had no family or friends to visit them. On advice from the RMO, social workers and nursing staff, patients were identified who were thought to need and be likely to benefit from such visits and League of Friends' volunteers were recruited who were willing to give time to this. Some of these initiatives turned out not to work - visitors either became too emotionally involved or, the opposite, found they could not maintain an equable, friendly relationship. As it was the patient who suffered a 'let-down' (the League of Friends member was reckoned to have a home and family to sustain them in their failure) a training programme was set up, carried out by the social work department, to ensure that potential visitors were fully aware of what they were taking on and were enabled to carry through the task.

NEW STAFF HOSTELS

As staffing expanded and attachments took place of visitors or trainees from all over the country, and sometimes from other countries, Broadmoor needed more staff accommodation. Whilst the grounds of the estate had had staff housing from day one, and more had been added over the years, these catered for staff with families and there was no flat or bedsitter accommodation for single staff and visitors. Several detached and semi-detached houses were built in the 'inter-acts' period for the growing number of medical and other professional staff although, unlike Dr McGrath who had to live on the estate as a requirement of the job, such staff were able to live in private accommodation of their own choosing if they wished.

Crowthorne was becoming a desirable residential area itself and popular with personnel from the expanding Heathrow Airport; from the Meteorological Office when it moved to Bracknell; the Road Research Laboratory when it similarly moved to Crowthorne; the RAE (Royal Aircraft Establishment) in Farnborough; and people working in the growing Bracknell New Town. Wokingham was also expanding and the whole area was popular, with good facilities and, of course, the nearby university town of Reading.

Still, the hospital estate was popular, convenient and with a reasonable rental, especially for staff likely to remain only a few years such as senior registrars. In keeping with the wooded nature of the moor (surrounded by Crown Forestry land), residences tended to be named after trees. The first occupiers were able to choose their own tree and Dr Lecouteur, from Australia, of course chose 'The Ashes': while he and his family lived there, Australia would always hold the ashes! The blocks of new flatlets and bedsits were built on the south side of the staff sports field, overlooking the steep drop down to the old chaplain's house, the Lower Broadmoor Road and the Broadmoor Primary School. There are three of these three storey blocks which have greatly improved accommodation. (See sketch plan, Chapter 5.)

PARK LANE HOSPITAL AND THE REBUILD PLANNING TEAM

A planning team for the rebuilding of the hospital was eventually sited in portacabins on the western edge of the plateau outside the hospital walls, past the row of original Victorian cottages and the new staff canteen. Its work, however, was prefaced by the building of the new 'Broadmoor of the North', Park Lane Hospital, on the site at Maghull, Liverpool, part of which was already occupied by the existing 'mental subnormality' special hospital, Moss Side. The new hospital, however, was to be staffed and administered separately from Moss Side. Its planning involved a team which drew a great deal on the knowledge and experience of the staff at Broadmoor who, with Broadmoor's own rebuild in mind, were concerned to remedy what were seen as faults at Broadmoor with improvements at the new establishment. As well as the usual security provisions of locked doors, there were now new window designs which incorporated the security bars in the lattice pattern of the window. Siting and switching of lighting, radiators and inspection windows to the rooms were all factors to be designed afresh, whilst the new hospital would have rooms with their own adjoining toilet and washing facilities. Size, length and layout of corridors (galleries) and their lines of sight were also crucial, together with the siting of the staff observation room. Then there were the specific clinical services to be accommodated, including the many new developments that had had perforce to be incorporated piecemeal in the old Broadmoor.

Park Lane Hospital was to provide a valuable chance to set up what was thought to be needed for the coming era. For instance, improved laboratory facilities were planned by Dr Tennent and myself that juxtaposed the EEG and psychology services to enable a link-up of equipment if required, and with a one-way observation screen on one side to enable both clinical and teaching observation to take place (discussed in Chapter 16). With the advance work at Park Lane accomplished some initial appointments were made of key people who would take the planning forward on the next stage. Dr Richard Neville was appointed to be the first medical director and spent some time with a clinical caseload at Broadmoor to familiarize himself with the work that lay ahead. Several senior nursing appointments were made and Broadmoor staff naturally filled some of these.

For the rebuild of Broadmoor itself a team was created that seemed to an onlooker to spend an inordinate amount of time researching and discussing the pros and cons of all the available resources for a brand new concept. Boyce Lecouteur, by now a long-standing Broadmoor consultant (RMO), and Gerry Sharpe, a nursing officer, were the spearhead at the Broadmoor end of things whilst a team of planners, architects, draughtsmen and civil servants operated from the Ministry of Works end in Croydon. The Ministry of Works, of course, no longer exists, having been absorbed into the Department of the Environment which itself was later transformed. The Ministry of Works section at Broadmoor fulfilled the role of other hospitals' engineering and works departments (as said in an earlier chapter). Government departments are always being regrouped and changing their names and, before its absorbtion into the DoE, one transformation was to the 'Ministry of Public Buildings and Works', shortened to MPBW and referred to by Dr McGrath as the 'Ministry of Public Bloody Works'.

The rebuild planning team would periodically come to something that was within one's own area of knowledge, when there was the opportunity to expound one's ideas. The team, understandably, became sceptical of individual's recommendations, suspecting them to comprise a great deal of 'empire building'. Nevertheless, when Park Lane was eventually operational, grumbling arose from our opposite numbers there about the inadequacy of facilities we had proposed. Much later, in the late 1980s but within a year or two of the completion and opening of the first phase of the new Broadmoor buildings, an extension had to be added to the psychology department. My 'over-the-top' forecast had been rejected or trimmed, only to be proved correct by the time it was eventually built. Equipment forecasts aroused similar disbelief. I had foreseen the development of computers but not to the degree or at the rate that actually happened. I knew our slow and cumbersome machine-code programmed dinosaur would give way to quicker and easier-to-operate equipment, but had not anticipated the universal desktop facility that so rapidly materialized. Where closed circuit TV and portable cameras and recorders were concerned, colour was also obviously just around the corner but it was very difficult to persuade the planning team to make provision for this, constrained by their budgetary limits. If this was happening all around the hospital it was not surprising that the planning team was taking a long time to produce their final plans. By the time they had worked their way round to a department or service again, they discovered some fresh development or innovation had arisen and they had to revise their plans yet again.

THE LIBRARY

In 1975 the appointment of a full-time qualified librarian was finally made, the library and its growing runs of journals having by now outstripped its senior common room premises and the abilities of its three successive volunteer psychologist librarians conveniently to manage. Alison Farrar was the person appointed and she immediately brought good humour to the job. Whilst the staff library had to endure a little longer in the common room, a patients' library was set up in part of the new buildings that housed the handicrafts centre, workshops and education department. Gone was the county library wagon which had squeezed its way through the main gateway and the double doors of the central courtyard to park itself on the front terrace. Patients now could visit a proper library and discuss their needs or hobbies with a proper librarian. There were still 'library days' for each house (no longer 'blocks') but these were in a more spacious, congenial and helpful library environment. Parole patients were able to visit at any time and one was actually employed as an assistant librarian, giving rise to the novel answer, when phoning and Alison was elsewhere: 'Patients' Library, patient speaking'.

With the completion of the building of the new staff education centre (see below) the staff library was transferred there and greatly improved. There were tables at which to read and study and this was greatly facilitated by the positioning of the education centre outside the walls, on the hospital estate. Off-duty staff and students could visit at any time during the working day. Study cubicles were provided where a student could work in peace and use microfiche projectors to look up material (and later, desktop computers, of course, but not in the 'inter-acts' period). There were easy chairs in which to read newspapers, journals and reference books. There was a card index system to search for a book by title or author and the books were now arranged in a classified order. Above all, there was Alison herself or, later, one of her colleagues or assistants (they had to spread their time between the staff library at the bottom of 'School Hill' and the patients' library within the walls) to consult for advice and help to find what was wanted. Later, and again after the period of this account and some years after his retirement, the library was formally named: 'The Patrick McGrath Library' in honour (and now memory) of the driving force in its foundation. It has now become a recognized national (and international) reference centre for information and publications in the field of forensic psychiatry and mentally disordered offenders, with information on all the subjects that impinge on this by way of the law, medicine, psychology, sociology, social work, hospital administration, public policy, ethics, and so on.

THE NEW STAFF EDUCATION CENTRE

The staff library was situated on the ground floor of the new education centre. This spacious, modern, light and airy building was situated half way down 'School Hill' and greatly improved the facilities for many kinds of activity. It was a far cry from the little room near the main gate with its three long board tables. However, training had expanded. As well as the three year student nurse training for the RMN qualification (registered mental nurse), the equivalent of the SRN in general nursing, there was added the two year pupil nurse training for the SEN (state enrolled nurse) qualification. Various other courses were held from time to time, for instance in fire training, the new Health & Safety Regulations, a staff retirement course, etc.

Then there were two major new nursing developments. The first was a pair of courses under what was then the Joint Board of Clinical Nursing Studies (JBCNS), one for nurses in any situation, dealing with aggressive incidents (which was happening increasingly in, for instance, casualty departments) and the other specifically for nursing in secure settings (and we have yet to come to the government initiatives that set up the new regional secure units; next chapter). These were the JBCNS Courses 955 and 960, respectively of two and six weeks duration. There were no more than half a dozen of these courses countrywide but the special hospitals were an obvious location for some of them. A curriculum had been carefully planned and I was asked to join the JBCNS national planning team responsible, with David Palmer, by then the SNO head of nurse education at Broadmoor.

My involvement had been partly with the idea that some form of pre- and post-course assessment of attitude change might be incorporated. This led to our adaptation of a questionnaire that Ron Blackburn had developed from his earlier studies of the Broadmoor patient population, focusing specifically on those measures that he had found relevant for discriminating aggressive and hostile tendencies, emotionality, and various aspects of social development. I also devised a specific 'repertory grid', like those mentioned in Chapter 12, having as its 'elements' the various topics in the course and as its 'constructs' the possible gains or changes that the course might be expected to achieve. These assessments were given at the start and the end of the course when it was hoped than any changes might throw light on the effect of the course.

They therefore served two purposes: to try to meet the JBCNS planning team's wish to reflect changed attitudes as a result of the training; and to provide an illustration of some of the ways available for assessing the personality characteristics and behavioural tendencies relevant to the patients the course attenders were there to learn about. A briefer version was used for the shorter 955 course but for the longer 960 course, who returned for a follow-up day some weeks later, there was time to process the results of the assessment procedures they had undertaken and give them the feedback when they returned. Use of these procedures was well received by the course attenders and feedback was thereby obtained for the further development of the course by its tutor, Trevor Walt. Unfortunately, the other aspect of the venture, to research the effects of the training, has sadly joined other shelved projects for which there has never been the time nor the resources to complete them.

The 955 and 960 courses were very popular and in great demand, due to the growth of regional secure units (RSUs) in the late 1970s and the 1980s. As well as specialist speakers the course tutors were able to draw directly upon the experience of Broadmoor staff to teach about the problems and practices of dealing with the range of hostile, aggressive and violent patients the course attenders were likely to meet in their roles in the new RSUs. These courses have given way now to new and revised courses for the purpose and, indeed, the JBCNS, too, has been superseded. The training goes on, however, whatever the name or the organizing body.

The other development was an internal course (which, again, became a wider resource) for training staff in dealing with physical violence safely. One might have thought that a special hospital, of all places, would already have had training for this vital and presumably frequently needed capability. In fact it never had. The way violent incidents were handled had always been a skill that one generation of staff had passed down to the next, which is not a bad way of learning, providing the procedure is sound. No doubt a century after its inception the staff now had an effective way of doing things and could pass this on to newcomers. Where the original staff derived their experience does not seem to be recorded but, if by trial and error, by a century later it was obviously working. Nevertheless, the many new kinds of patients and their behaviours that the 1959 Act had brought, the quicker throughput, and the attempt to create a more open and active treatment environment with more off-ward facilities, clearly increased the risk of violent outbursts. When the subject had arisen in the 1960s it had been rejected: Dr Udwin, in particular, had feared that any training in what would have been construed as 'unarmed combat' would have given rise to a 'bad press' and was, anyway, not a skill he wanted Broadmoor nurses to acquire. A decade and more later, however, it cropped up again and, this time, there was greater awareness country-wide which, with the existence of new forms of training, required that something be done. Urban violence was on the increase; riots, sieges and hostage taking were commonplace; street muggings were perturbing people. 'Control and Restraint' courses were therefore begun.

Essentially, these turned upon 'unarmed combat' as practised by some of the other uniformed services, by which the impetus of the attacker is itself used to disable and restrain him or her, effectively and non-violently 'disarming' the attack. There was then the crucial matter, once under control, of how to restrain someone safely and non-aggressively. This procedure, of course, is then emphasized to be merely the start of a process of understanding the cause and dealing with it so that a further outburst is averted. 'Non-provocative containment' was the accepted phrase. In principle it was what a special hospital was all about, in part and in the first instance. Initially, outside trainers ran the 'C and R' courses but soon some of those who underwent the initial courses took on the training themselves, notably Clive Bonnett, and Broadmoor again, became the venue for those courses sought out by other organizations that wanted to learn the same principles and skills.

The JBCNS 955 and 960 courses and the C and R training were not in existence when the new staff education centre first opened but the building was more than filled initially with the activities of RMN and SEN training, together with other *ad hoc* educational activity. For instance, all disciplines used the several small and large lecture rooms for their own training when courses or conferences were held or when professional groups visited and committees and working parties met. In particular, there were periodic seminars in forensic psychiatry and the course at the Maudsley Hospital in London would invariably include a day's visit and seminar at Broadmoor. Eventually, student and pupil nurse training was ended, which was a pity. This was because Broadmoor was reckoned to be unable to provide training that adequately covered the basic range of psychiatric nursing experience. It was too security-biased. At first this was overcome by combining the nurse training school functions with those of others in the neighbourhood, such as Park Prewett, near Basingstoke. In the end, however, this was still considered too untypical for general qualification and the RMN and SEN training was ended. The decision was widely resented and is arguable. A valuable resource in basic training was lost. However, an expansion in post-qualification training has taken place throughout the nursing profession and the staff education centre now has a leading place in this and has become a resource for a wider range of training. It is now a busy centre for many professional groups and the Patrick McGrath library is bigger and better than ever.

THE MAIN REBUILD PROGRAMME

It is impossible to describe new buildings without digressing into their intended and actual use - or at any rate it would be silly not to say what they were for whilst describing them. Likewise, it would be silly to leave a chapter on further building without completing the story, even though it means backtracking later when returning to other topics.

Building on the plateau thus far had been preparatory to the main rebuild programme. Anyway, the staff education centre is off the plateau and therefore unconnected with the rebuilding of the hospital itself. Departments and services were shunted around the existing buildings, both inside and outside the walls and temporary buildings came and went. The main redevelopment had essentially arrived with two enterprises: firstly, the building of the new occupational and educational centre and, secondly, the extension of the wall to enclose the rest of the plateau within the hospital itself. Neither of these had been completed by the time the 1983 Act arrived but their early development irrevocably changed the layout and character of the original hospital, so we should look at them.

The new complex to house all the occupational and educational activity of the hospital was to be sited on that part of the row of staff cottages that ran southwards from the main gate (see sketch plan, Chapter 6), including the League of Friends (LoF) canteen and the former nurse training school-turned-social work department. These last two, as has been said, had moved into the new staff education centre and Kentigern respectively. To accommodate the LoF canteen and rest room there needed to be sufficient of the new gate complex built for the canteen to move into its intended new premises there. This was a large complex compared with the former gatehouse (always known as the 'main gate') to accommodate a whole new security and communications system, with 'airlocks' (double sets of doors with a waiting area between) for staff, visitor and vehicle access. Previously all used the same door and narrow passageway. This complex was not yet operational but sufficient of it was built to ensure that the visitors' waiting room, canteen and LoF office were functional when the former premises had to be demolished. And a very nice facility, too, right on hand for visitors' access on arriving or leaving the hospital. This allowed work on the new occupational-cum-educational complex to proceed. The perimeter wall would eventually have to be extended around it but for the present this was not necessary and anyway there needed to be access to the existing main gate. The wall would be a continuation of the one now being built from the other direction to enclose the entire plateau within which new wards, medical centre and administration were being built. This wall came off the Female Wing wall on the north side of the hospital and wound its way round the western area of the former matron's garden, staff club and associated cottages (see sketch plan for Chapter 5). All had to go.

The outcome was that the new gate complex opened on to a large quadrangle around which was the new nursing, medical and lay administration block. Past this, one reached the buildings of the original hospital but to its left one would now reach the new wards and medical centre, sited roughly where the old matron's garden used to be. At the south end of the plateau, towards the top of 'School Hill', a gap was created in the main wall, with a new security fence built within, and Cornwall House was demolished: built in 1907 this was a case of 'last to come, first to go'.

With the demolition of the old buildings facing the main gate, including the old staff club, there had to be a new staff club, as has been said, and this very much improved facility was built on the edge of the western plateau, beyond Kentigern and before the road plunged down to the staff car park and up again to the transport department. A principle feature of the new staff club was that the building also accommodated the new staff restaurant, a much improved facility allowing all staff ample room for all meals. The temporary staff canteen in the road opposite the main gate had already meant that the former senior common room could finally be abandoned and put to other uses, and now the temporary canteen could be demolished to allow for the building of the new education/occupation complex which would be inside the extended hospital walls. The staff club and restaurant building now had an improved functions room for socials, dances, discos and entertainments and a games area for snooker and table tennis whilst its bar was much larger and had patio doors on to a terrace for summer time use. This facilitated 'bar snacks' as an alternative to the staff restaurant.

A proper escape room facility was now operable from a dual function room which could be quickly converted and wall flaps opened up for map displays, etc. A flatlet was available for the resident staff club manager, Brian Gale, and his family, who had seen the facility develop from its cramped beginnings at the end of the old row of staff cottages. So the site was ready for the renovations and additions of the final version of the rebuilding plan. Would it be further modified before it was fully built? Would it be abandoned altogether if special hospitals were to be wound up? Or put to some other use? So far, it is still there, but the story is not finished.

SUMMARY

Building plans and changes might seem tedious and superfluous to a history but are outlined here in order to illustrate the improvements to services that were the object of the enterprise.

(Reference back to the sketch plans of Chapters 5 and 6 will help here.)

The planning for the new 'Broadmoor of the North' on the site outside Liverpool (later named 'Park Lane Hospital' and, later still, 'Ashworth Hospital' when it was amalgamated with Moss Side Hospital) enabled lessons to be learned for the replacements and extensions planned for Broadmoor itself.

The chapter describes a number of functions and services which arose or were developed in conjunction with rebuilding: the League of Friends; a new staff restaurant and hostels; the staff education centre (SEC) and the 'Patrick McGrath' Library, as well as the rebuilding enterprise itself.

For a hospital whose patients came from countrywide, the League of Friends innovation provided a much needed refreshment and transport facility for the relatives who had often travelled great distances and needed to stay locally. More diverse staff, not necessarily living on the hospital estate, more official visitors, students and attached temporary staff meant that improved hostel and restaurant accommodation were essential. The SEC gradually accommodated a wider variety of training courses which fulfilled a countrywide role and the functions of these are described. The courses for staff who were to work at the new regional secure units or who otherwise had to deal with violent patients were among these. The library, initially a collection of journals and books for staff to consult who used the common room, became an altogether more ambitious project, comprising a specialist reference source on the entire field of mental disorder and violence and the law relating to these, and was housed in the staff education centre where all could have access.

The main rebuilding project eventually began, improving the century-old facilities and extending the perimeter wall to enclose the enlarged and increased number of new buildings. A comprehensive clinical services building, with admission and specialist wards adjacent, was early amongst these, together with improved office buildings for the now greatly increased number of support staff. Less than two decades after the old workshops had been finally rebuilt, a new occupational and educational complex was to replace them. And a new entrance gate complex would announce to arriving staff and visitors what was to greet them inside.

By now we have moved forward some way and must backtrack to see what was going on clinically and how this was affected by events on the national scene, for it was these that greatly influenced the next phase of work.

CHAPTER 15

GOVERNMENT COMMITTEES AND A CHANGING SOCIAL CLIMATE

Dr McGrath had always referred to the fact that no patient, recommended for discharge, had gone on to repeat a murder. If it happened, he had said, his resignation would be on the Secretary of State's desk the next morning. Of course, it did happen; and his resignation was duly tendered; and, of course, it was not accepted.

The first repeat murder was by the most unlikely of discharged patients, a frail elderly woman, committed originally for killing her son, who had led an exemplary life in Broadmoor over many years, conscientiously attending chapel and all the other worthy events. She returned to what should have been a quiet old age in the company of a devoted husband to whom she was also devoted. Unfortunately, during a domestic argument, she had struck her husband on the head with a saucepan and he, also now frail and elderly, failed to recover and died a week later. So the first patient to spoil the clean record was not one of the new category of psychopaths, as so many had feared.

MISHAPS AROUSING PUBLIC CONCERN

Nevertheless, other mishaps occurred, as was probably inevitable with the doubling of the 'throughput' of patients and the spreading of the job of discharge evaluation amongst an ever wider group of

RMOs. Whilst the incidence of further homicides was very small, and other kinds of failure were far fewer than the successes, and mostly summary offences at that, the very fact that some serious failures were occurring at all was a matter for serious concern over which the press lost no opportunity to castigate the hospital.

When two repeat murders occurred in close succession, and one by a high-profile young poisoner, the government of the day decided it had to take action. The overcrowding at Broadmoor had been a growing complaint, part of the phenomenon, discussed earlier, of the 1959 Act's 'open door' and 'informal patient' consequences. The Department of Health and Social Security (as the former Ministry of Health was now called) was under increasing pressure from public opinion and the number of awkward parliamentary questions it was getting. Through the 1970s and under both Conservative and Labour governments green and white papers were appearing, discussing the needs of psychiatric patients and the problems of the ever increasing numbers clogging up the special hospitals. When one of the solutions, the discharge of greater numbers of patients, was resulting in some dramatic 'news headline' failures, it was clearly time for something to be done.

What was done was to set up one committee and bring forward another which had been under consideration for some time. The first was the Aarvold Committee; the second was the Butler Committee. Meanwhile the DHSS was publishing its own 'Glancy' Report, named after one of its own senior medical officers who chaired it and who worked in the division responsible for special hospitals.

THE 'AARVOLD' COMMITTEE

Sir Carl Aarvold, a judge, chaired the first which also had a senior psychiatrist and social worker on it and was set up in June 1972, immediately following the conviction, on 29th June, of Graham Young for 'murder and other grave offences committed by poisoning, while on conditional discharge from Broadmoor Hospital'.

Its remit was to advise whether any changes, within the existing law, were required in the procedures for the discharge and supervision of patients subject to special restrictions (under Section 65). It took evidence from a wide field, including all the relevant professional bodies. The Royal Medico-Psychological Association had become, since 1970, the Royal College of Psychiatrists, and submitted its evidence, informed by its forensic members. Likewise the Royal College of Nursing and the nursing unions, including the POA for the special hospitals. The Committee visited both special and conventional psychiatric hospitals.

The Aarvold Committee reported quickly and briefly, in January 1973, basically recommending that cases which were anticipated to present particular difficulty in assessing discharge suitability should be identified as soon as possible after admission as requiring 'special care in assessment'. They would thereafter be given extra attention where their assessment was concerned. The Aarvold Committee also recommended that there should be a special Advisory Committee created to assist in reaching decisions in such cases.

Although such a procedure sounded reasonable and, from a psychological assessment point of view there were factors emerging from a decade of research that now seemed relevant to such a classification purpose, there was reluctance on the part of the RMOs to apply such a procedure at the early stage envisaged. In any case, there was the more pressing need to identify those patients who were further on in their Broadmoor careers and for whom the problem of a discharge recommendation would be looming, long before any 'difficult-to-assess' admissions now arriving. Being 'Aarvolded', as the procedure was inevitably called, hit the Broadmoor patient population of that day when they were therefore well into their hospital stay, many nurturing hopes of imminent discharge. Not surprisingly, therefore, the procedure was seen by the RMOs as a further imposition upon them and by the patients as a further 'hoop-to-be-jumped-through', on top of the 'obstacle course' towards discharge already created by the 1959 Act's new categories of disorder, its Restriction Orders and its Mental Health Review Tribunals (MHRTs).

THE COMMITTEE ON MENTALLY ABNORMAL OFFENDERS (THE 'BUTLER' COMMITTEE)

The longer term inquiry was the 'Committee on Mentally Abnormal Offenders', known as the 'Butler Committee' after its chairman, Lord (RAB) Butler. It comprised a much larger membership of some sixteen prominent medical, legal, academic and local government people. It was set up in September 1972, a few months after the Aarvold Committee, and reported in August 1975: nearly three years' work. Its report ran to over 300 pages, including detailed reviews of a number of the problem areas within its terms of reference, which were as follows:

(a) To consider to what extent and on what criteria the law should recognize mental disorder or abnormality in a person accused of a criminal offence as a factor affecting his liability to be tried or convicted, and his disposal;

(b) To consider what, if any, changes are necessary in the powers, procedure and facilities relating to the provision of appropriate treatment, in prison, hospital or the community, for offenders suffering from mental disorder or abnormality, and to their discharge and aftercare; and to make recommendations.

The Interim 'Butler' Report

In April 1974 the 'Butler' Committee took the unusual step of issuing an interim report specifically to 'recommend the provision, as a matter of urgency, of secure hospital units in each Regional Health Authority (RHA) area'. The DHSS's own 'Glancy' Report had made similar recommendations just previously, in 1973. To avoid local financial difficulties 'Butler' recommended that this provision should be financed by a direct allocation of central government funds to the RHAs. Clearly the committee recognized that, whatever else they might eventually say, this matter was of such unanimously agreed urgency that it should be effected as soon as possible, without waiting for whatever else they might recommend.

Certainly ISUs/RSUs, as these interim/regional 'medium-secure' units later became known, should have provided immediate relief to the special hospitals' overcrowding problems without jeopardizing public safety through former mentally disordered offenders being discharged either directly into the community or into non-secure hospital accommodation. Central government funding, rather than regional, would overcome local objections about lack of money. Unfortunately, the funding that government did promptly make available was 'capital' and not 'revenue', i.e.: provided for the units to be set up but not for their subsequent running costs (following the final 'Butler' Report this had to be remedied).

Whilst the NHS regions were struggling with the next problem, i.e.: where to put these units and how to reassure an anxious local population about their security, the capital provided was being spent elsewhere, for other more immediate projects: it was intended to be repaid later out of subsequent funds. Unfortunately, once used, funding stringency and the demands of more publicly popular projects made for great difficulty in retrieving this money. It was all very vexing; the resulting ISUs/RSUs were few and far between and very delayed. Virtually all, or at least a significant country-wide service, was envisaged by the Butler Committee to be up and running by 1977-78 but by that time only three 'interim' units were operational, on existing psychiatric hospital sites. The first purpose built unit did not open until late 1980 and by 1983 there were only a further three. The stress, hassle and overcrowding at the special hospitals therefore continued.

The Full 'Butler' Report

The full Butler Report covered a great deal of ground and remains a seminal document on a great many issues. It reviewed topics that had not received such close and comprehensive attention since the 'Percy' Commission in the 50s which had wrought the changes from the pre-war legislation and brought in the 1959 Mental Health Act in the first place. Many of its recommendations were incorporated in the subsequent, 1983, revision of the 1959 Act, *in toto* or in adapted form.

As well as its critical examination of the existing facilities it went into detailed discussion of the concepts of dangerousness and psychopathy and of the problems of discharge and aftercare. These occupied the first eight chapters. The remaining twelve chapters dealt with legal issues including:

* pre-trial action;
* 'disability in relation to trial' (its proposed term for 'unfit to plead');
* medical and social inquiry reports;
* remands to hospital;
* the decision of the court;
* hospital orders (including a proposal for 'interim' hospital orders);
* guardianship orders;
* psychiatric probation orders;
* provisions for juveniles and young adults;
* the 'special verdict', where it proposed to call this 'not guilty on evidence of mental disorder' in place of the existing 'not guilty by reason of insanity' and, in discussing the old McNaughtan Rules, raised the issue of separating the 'burden-of-proof' and the 'disposal' issues (the present requirement to establish 'intent' as a prerequisite for guilt combines these - see Chapter 23);
* the concept of 'diminished responsibility', which it hoped would become redundant with the end of capital punishment and if its recommendation was accepted for an end to the mandatory life sentence for murder, so that the judge could suit sentence and disposal to circumstances; and, finally,
* issues of co-operation between the various professions involved.

In the course of all this, the committee expressed its disappointment that its interim report's recommendations had not been implemented and it urged therefore that revenue funding should be available to maintain its proposed regional secure units as well as capital to set them up.

Much of a report like this has no effect unless it is subsequently incorporated into an Act of Parliament, although the influence of a committee of this weight was bound to produce some changes and some of its recommendations did not need to wait for new legislation. Those to do with RSUs were one. A number of others would obviously generate differing degrees of enthusiasm or resistance and so would influence the shape of emerging practice or eventual legislation. But whilst the analyses and discussions of many key topics have been described as 'seminal' and were certainly 'informed and informative', not all the resulting proposals and recommendations received the same degree of unanimity or approval. Some of these call for comment in the context of the evolving history of Broadmoor.

First, the committee decided to speak of Mental 'Disorder', not Abnormality as in their title. They recognized that 'abnormality' referred to extremes of a beneficial as well as a hindering kind and, to avoid this, chose 'disorder' as indicating a condition that needed remedying. This also reflected the overall term used in the 1959 Act. So far: uncontentious. However, the Butler Committee thought it 'not their business to become involved in the ... controversies about the concept of mental disorder' and accepted the established framework of the legal, penal, health and community systems. This naturally met with no objection from the aforesaid 'established systems'. However, it rendered irrelevant a significant part of the British Psychological Society's evidence which had specifically addressed the problems of revising the definition of mental disorder to include psychological as well as medical concepts.

Informed by the kinds of developments described earlier in Chapters 12 and 13, the evidence from the British Psychological Society had emphasized the relevance of distorted thinking, extremes of emotional reaction, impulsivity and other temperamental factors upon an individual's behaviour, with invariably distressing and sometimes harmful consequences. The psychological evidence argued for these aspects of human activity to be regarded as just as relevant to concepts of 'mental disorder', the impairment of responsibility and the need for remedial action as the more familiar, longer accepted aspects of mental illness, injury or disease. Ironically, many of the diagnostic indicators of a mental disorder, except where actual injury, infection or physical degeneration is demonstrable (a minority of cases), consist precisely of these thinking and emotional abnormalities but attested differently. The quantification and new perspectives brought to the subject by psychologists which extends it to other behaviours should enhance the evidential process and certainly raises the question of how these other behaviours should be regarded in law.

The climate at the time of the Butler Committee was clearly not ready for such change, although the very fact that discussions were aroused in the debate over 'mental disorder' are testimony to the awareness of the problems that awaited future legislation. One prominent psychiatrist member of the 'Butler' Committee, during a 'comfort break' in the oral session accorded to the British Psychological Society which had submitted written evidence, remarked to me that 'of course, you're right, but twenty years too soon'. It is not surprising, therefore, that the committee decided to define mental disorder only in terms of its four component disorders and to shelve the problem of defining the first of these, 'mental illness', altogether. (The late Sir Frederick Lawton, then Mr Justice Lawton, has more recently said that mental disorder would be better not defined in terms an expert witness would have to attest because it is essentially a lay term which should be understood according to ordinary English usage.)

Having acknowledged as understandable the disinclination of the Butler Committee to become embroiled in discussions of the meaning of mental disorder, and particularly of mental illness, it was something of a contradiction of this decision for it to go on to indulge in just such a discussion of the associated topic of 'psychopathic disorder'. Presumably, since this is specifically defined in the 1959 Act, although excluded from the parallel Scottish legislation, and had given rise to difficulties and arguments over its interpretation and implementation, the committee felt it constituted a different problem from that of mental illness. Whatever the reason, the committee gave considerable coverage to psychopathy and provided a useful review of the condition and controversies over it and its treatment.

The committee reported the views it had had put to it that it was not really a medical condition in the way other mental disorders were (despite the alternative views on that, too) and that it could not be said to be invariably treated medically, if at all. Instead the treatment was to be found in a 'psycho-social' approach when it might more often be said to be feasible. However, and probably because the committee had refrained from examining the concept of mental disorder itself, it felt that a disorder only amenable to this basically educational or retraining sort of treatment should lead to this being done in prison and not in hospital. It recommended, therefore, that training units for psychopaths should be created in the prison system. By the time the 1959 Act was reviewed and amended by the 1983 Mental Health Act, Parliament must have been rather more convinced by the arguments put forward by the British Psychological Society (and indeed, by then, by other organizations too) that 'psychopathic disorder' should remain within the Act (although, once again, not in Scotland), for remain it did. However, this is for a later chapter (see Part III and especially Chapters 22 and 23). For the present it is at least to be welcomed that the proposal where the prisons were concerned did lead to the creation of more units and programmes there for the treatment of various kinds of personality disorder (the wider category in which psychopathic disorder was included) and especially where sex offending was concerned. (Note that these terms are not interchangeable: not all psychopaths are sex offenders; not all sex offenders are psychopaths.)

Meanwhile, psychopathic disorder continued to be on the special hospitals' agenda and, from a psychologist's point of view, this is appropriate. Treatments of a retraining or educational kind do not fit a fixed-term sentence and it is not usually possible to say when such treatment will be successfully completed. A court order of indefinite duration is therefore necessary. Of course, the Committee's proposal for reviewable sentences would accommodate such treatment requirements but this recommendation was not favourably received and was not enacted in the subsequent 1983 Act. There was reluctance to commit someone to a longer term of deprived liberty in a hospital context than would have occurred under a prison sentence for the same crime. Only for an offence attracting a life sentence, therefore, would treatment of an indefinite duration be possible.

This gives rise to other problems: one practical, in that it is rarely possible to effect a discharge when the treatment time is ripe, given the long process that has to be negotiated for this to happen; and the other ethical, in that it is questionable whether a therapist should embark on a treatment programme requiring someone to change, effectively, their way of life, when there is no guarantee at the end that discharge will be granted. Happily, or unhappily, according to your point of view, the eventual 1983 Act overcame this problem by requiring discharge of mentally disordered patients unless reason could be given to hold them further, instead of the 1959 Act's principle of holding someone unless reason could be given to discharge them. A hornet's nest of conflicting practical, social and moral principles was to arise.

Another idea of the Butler Committee was also absent from the subsequent 1983 Act, namely for a category of 'severe mental illness' to be created to cater for the 'special verdict', the 'not guilty by reason of insanity' finding (or 'not guilty on evidence of mental disorder' as the Committee wanted it). This was the successor to the old McNaughtan Rules provision for those found insane at time of trial or at the time of the offence. This category had been dwindling under the 1959 Act's changed nomenclature, and presumably was not thought a significant enough problem, within the more flexible provisions of the Act, to be worth continuing. Legislators are, in any case, reluctant to enact conditions dependent upon an adjective like 'severe' which bears as many interpretations as there are likely to be witnesses to attest it. The 1959 Act already had the two categories of mental subnormality differentiated by the term 'severe' but these were more concretely affirmable by both their levels of self-sustaining competence and measurable IQ.

Another Butler proposal not subsequently enacted was the extension of the Aarvold principles to all special hospital patients. Possibly by 1982, the year of the Mental Health Amendment Bill, when exceptionally a great deal of evidence was taken from professional bodies in oral session during the committee stage of the Bill, the workings and difficulties of the 'Aarvolding' procedure had become apparent and enough other precautionary safeguards were thought to be available. At any rate, the Aarvold procedure disappeared altogether with the 1983 Act.

Butler recommendations which were to appear in the 1983 Act, however, included enabling magistrates' courts to commit to a higher court with a view to making a 'restriction order', i.e.: the order restricting subsequent authority for discharge to the Home Secretary (although this authority was to be extended also to MHRTs - Mental Health Review Tribunals - when chaired by a

QC). Butler envisaged these orders being confined to cases where serious harm seemed likely and this, too, was enacted. The recommended hospital remands were also enacted, of two kinds: for assessment (one month) or treatment (three months, renewable), to enable the need for treatment and feasibility of carrying it out to be assessed. Alternatively, if the remand chance were missed, at the later stage of sentencing an interim hospital order could be made to achieve the same ends.

Reactions to the 'Butler' Committee's Report

The general climate created by the publication and resultant discussion of, first, the Aarvold and Glancy Reports and, later, the Butler Report was of public approval and reassurance. Something was being done and 'heavyweights', in the public's mind, had been involved in doing it.

RSUs and the 'Aarvolding' procedure were the principal immediate outcomes of all this committee activity, although the further recommendations of the Butler Committee were to be slowly gestating and generating either support or opposition during the period up to the introduction of the next Mental Health Act. Whilst the Butler Report was a 'seminal' document, attracting commendation for its analyses of a great many weighty and relevant issues, it did not receive the same degree of commendation for all its proposals. The reviews at the time, appearing in a diversity of both professional journals and popular 'pressure group' type publications, demonstrate this. A long letter appeared in the *Bulletin* of the Royal College of Psychiatrists from Dr Robert Reeves, by now departed from Broadmoor but speaking from his experience there, deploring what he saw as the retrograde consequences of creating RSUs. He foresaw, correctly, that they would become dumping grounds for the difficult patients that the local services would not want and could not adequately supervise in their open conditions. This, of course, might be argued to have been one of their purposes, in order to lighten the load on the special hospitals, except that they would then become so filled with patients from elsewhere they would have insufficient room for the discharged special hospital patients they were also intended to accept. They were intended to be short stay facilities but how could this be ensured? In any case, he said, how could a small unit of a score or two patients provide the breadth of treatment and educational, occupational and recreational activity that a large special hospital campus provided (a point developed in Chapters 7, 8 and 9 of this present history). This could only happen with the agreement and collaboration of the larger psychiatric campus on which most of these RSUs were sited, which would undermine the very concept of a 'medium secure' facility.

All in all, therefore, Aarvold, Glancy and Butler had provided the much needed immediate measures to reassure parliamentary, press and public disquiet and some much needed analyses and discussion points for future legislation. Unfortunately, however, the RSU solution turned out to have provided only partial relief but a great deal of controversy and local 'NIMBY-ism'.

THE 'CIVIL LIBERTIES AND HUMAN RIGHTS' LOBBY

The 1970s were the era of 'flower power' and 'let-it-all-hang-out'. Sexual freedom and equality grew out of the now widespread availability of 'the pill', women's rights were championed and 'bra's were burned'. During this era the social work and psychology departments at Broadmoor were growing and SHRU was active with a number of research projects and their associated researchers. Many of these were women who, together with the librarians and expanding secretarial and clerical staff, constituted a significant presence on the male side of the hospital for the first time in its history. With the long flowing hair and skirts of the time, this gave rise to considerable ribaldry and criticism from the more traditional sectors of the staff. Men, too, were appearing at work in sweaters and open-necked shirts and also often sported long hair and beards. Nursing staff still wore uniforms, however, although there had been a change from the stiff, button-up collars and navy blue serge of the centenary photographs and the uniforms were now a softer, mid-blue, worsted trouser and jacket with collar and tie. Quite a change. The DHSS was reputed to have obtained the services of Hardy Amies in their design.

The first member of the nursing staff to appear in one of the new uniforms was a well-known Broadmoor character of a relaxed, easygoing and debonair manner who wore the new peaked cap at a jaunty angle and immediately attracted greetings in a Yankee accent accompanied by an American salute, such was the change in the character of the uniform and its resemblance to that of the US Air Force. The Female Wing staff, too, had now abandoned their starched aprons and caps and wore the now familiar nursing staff cotton dresses, different colours denoting the different grades. Even so, the contrast between the nursing and other staff gave rise to quite serious complaints that discipline and morale would be undermined and patients with problems over restraining their sexual impulses would not be helped by the flagrant display of sexuality inherent in the changing times and fashions. Psychologists were derided as the 'long-hair and jeans brigade' despite the fact that we had taken a deliberate decision never to wear jeans at work. When it was pointed out that one psychologist, very active and well accepted in a number of new ward treatment programmes, had long hair, a beard and open necked calico shirt (but no jeans) the response was simply: 'Oh, well, we know Kevin, he's our psychologist. It's the others!' Of course, it did not help that 1975 and 1976 were the years of the long hot summers when one came to work as coolly dressed as possible.

The social climate of the 1970s also had its influence on the patient population. Beards and long hair were the uniform of the younger generation of male patients, too, whilst sweeping calico dresses alternated with miniskirts with the women patients. A revolutionary cult was created amongst a group of these younger male patients who produced their own protest newspaper and strove for self-determination: in other words, they argued for greater patient autonomy within the hospital and more say on decisions about their treatment. This was the trend at the time in a number of other treatment settings, albeit informal or voluntary ones, such as the Henderson Hospital in Surrey, with which some exchange visiting was taking place in the 1970s. The idea was treated with a mixture of disdain, dismissal (mostly) or good-humoured tolerance (sometimes) by the staff which, of course, only increased patient antagonism because even the tolerance was seen as patronizing. Some of the RMOs, who had responsibility for the younger psychopathic patients, took all this in their stride as part of the pattern of youthful protest to be worked through in the course of resolving adolescent conflicts. The group loyalty of some of these, however, went to extreme lengths and involved at least one rooftop protest and several other similar attempts and even the killing of one patient. One of the ringleaders of the young revolutionary movement took responsibility for this, on the basis that the deceased man had a right to take his own life and to obtain assistance if he needed it, but there was always a strong belief on the part of many staff that another patient had been the real culprit. The young man who claimed responsibility later admitted he had taken only moral responsibility as leader of the group and had not been the actual one to have done the killing.

This was the atmosphere of the times in which the legislative and administrative discussions of the Aarvold, Glancy and Butler Committees were taking place. Parallel with these, however, the civil rights movement was showing itself in increased activity on the part of the charities and pressure groups which spoke for patients and disadvantaged groups in general. Revolution was in the air. Charities which people had hardly heard of, with complicated names and initials, were adopting higher profiles and brisker titles. In the psychiatric field the National Associations for Mental Health and for Mental Handicap became 'MIND' and 'MENCAP'. MIND appointed a particularly able and articulate lawyer, Larry Gostin, as its legal officer. He effectively led the MIND campaign for revision of the 1959 Mental Health Act in the direction of a greater voice for psychiatric patients in their own treatment and many credit him, in large measure, for the legislation we now have in the 1983 Act. This, of course, was in parallel with a similar movement on the part of NHS patients generally who were pressing for more information and consultation in their own care.

There is little doubt, especially looking back, that this was a much needed initiative which has been responsible for the greater openness about people's lives, jobs, health and treatment generally. But it brings problems, especially in areas of confidentiality and of the degree of freedom that should be afforded to people whose mental state reduces their capacity for rational thought, or whose offending has led society to decree they must forfeit some of their civil rights for a time. All three of these criteria - confidentiality, mental disorder and offending - are relevant to the special hospitals' patients and it was not surprising, therefore, that the writings and pronouncements of MIND, through Larry Gostin, were unpopular in Broadmoor. It didn't help that Gostin, an American, unfortunately had one of those rasping accents that, in a Perry Mason film, makes people glad when they get their come uppance.

Many in Broadmoor often wished he would. This was a pity, and unfair. Gostin had an agenda and it was a necessary one in the light of the shortcomings that had emerged in the use of the 1959 Act. In spite of the revolutionary changes in the Act by comparison with the situation that preceded it, there were further changes needed. Unfortunately, what resulted has still not solved all the problems and further adjustments look to be needed. Nevertheless, as will be discussed in Appendix A, there are provisions in the 1983 Act, which Gostin was so influential in bringing about, that could still be used, or used differently, to bring about the results that nowadays seem necessary. Gostin was right in much of the change he wanted to see in the 1959 Act.

Nevertheless, Gostin's advocacy was set in the climate of the 1970s illustrated at the start of this section. It was a time of protest against the established views of the post-war generation. It was also a time when the threat of war was receding and technology had brought great advances to the enjoyment of the material world: in travel, communications and particularly in going about one's daily life. People now expected to enjoy rights to all these changes and advances and that science and technology would ensure their personal safety while doing so. This must therefore extend to disadvantaged groups such as those who were seen to be suffering unnecessary exclusion, and therefore loss of liberty, because of their mental disorders. Unfortunately, more freedom for detained patients threatened the freedom and safety of the rest of the world; while more scope and security for people in the brave new materially perfect world threatened the self-determination and integrity of those detained for breaking society's rules.

Patients and prisoners strove for recognition of their individuality and their right to a future whilst the public at large now expected success in controlling danger to be total. This atmosphere determined not only the shape of the coming revision to the mental health legislation but, more immediately, the demands upon the services of the country's secure institutions and the character and direction these took.

SUMMARY

The doubled 'throughput' of patients resulting from the 1959 Act and other associated legislation had resulted in overcrowding, transfer bottlenecks and, inevitably in due course, discharge failures. When several of these resulted in high-profile killings and an inevitable press outcry, the government set up the equally inevitable inquiries.

The immediate short term inquiry of the 'Aarvold' Committee instituted a categorization for patients presenting particular difficulty in assessing their condition, and hence future dischargeability. Their recommendation that such patients should be recognized early and labelled as such provided an immediate additional safeguard but a further obstacle for a patient to negotiate before achieving discharge.

The longer term inquiry was that of the Committee on Mentally Abnormal Offenders chaired by Lord Butler, with a much wider remit to examine the whole field of the law pertaining to this group. Its 300 page report three years later was regarded at the time, and confirmed since, as a seminal document on the problem, providing much of the material for the next revision of the Mental Health Act. It included crucial discussions of dangerousness, psychopathic disorder and the problems of discharge and aftercare, before going on to examine the legal problems of 'disability in relation to the trial' (unfitness to plead), diminished responsibility and the 'special verdict' (the old 'guilty-but-insane verdict). It examined variations on remands for assessment and treatment, and reviewable sentences, the place of probation and other reports, and the problems of juveniles. Crucially, to the extent of quickly issuing an interim report, it recommended the setting up of the regional secure units which were slow to materialize but are an accepted feature of services to this day.

These events were happening at a time of great social change. Civil rights, self-determination and personal freedoms were the watchwords. Charities were taking on new 'image' names. MIND, MENCAP and NACRO were amongst these and fulfilled their images with a new vigour and outspokenness. They campaigned on the plight and rights of patients and prisoners in parallel with other civil rights with which, of course, they inevitably clashed. They had their counterparts within hospitals and prisons including, of course, Broadmoor where increasing numbers of bearded young patients tended to protest their rights from cyclostyled pamphlets and even the occasional rooftop escapade. The eloquent legal spokesman for MIND put all this into cogent argument which, together with the prestigious 'Butler' Report, no doubt shaped the eventual amendment of the Mental Health Act.

CHAPTER 16

THE PRESSURE FOR ACTION AND ANSWERS

Aarvold, Butler, Glancy and Gostin had reviewed, reported, pronounced and pressured at a time when Broadmoor was not only struggling with innovative legislation and a doubled caseload but was also generating new ideas, clinical procedures and research from the activities of both its newer and older professions. The newer ones were now more consolidated and self-confident. They were small in number, however, and their activities were usually seen as peripheral in comparison with the essential daily tasks of maintaining security, and providing nursing care and a means of occupying over eight hundred patients.

Nevertheless, it was the advances in assessment, medication and the psychological therapies, linked with more carefully co-ordinated ward and workshop practices, that had to be deployed to greater effect if patients were to be understood and helped to change more quickly and effectively. Student nurses were taught about these advances in the improved education centre described in Chapter 14 and arrived on the wards with wider knowledge than their predecessors. Even so, too many left for posts elsewhere after training and for the rest there was nothing so disheartening as to be told: "Now you've finished with the School, you can learn how it's really done" - the age old defensive riposte familiar in every workplace. Encouragement arose from the activity of the new professions on the wards. Nursing staff would have been involved anyway, but were increasingly taking part because of the necessity for their presence in all ward activities for security reasons. In any case, the Home Office and DHSS ministers and officials were now aware of the contribution of what was soon to become known as the 'clinical team' and would look at any report recommending a discharge or transfer to see what information and opinion there was from disciplines other than that of the consultant originator, the RMO. Whether this was out of recognition of what these others could contribute or merely to 'cover their backs' in the event of a mishap one 'could not possibly comment' but the effect was that a range of professional opinion was quoted in any recommendation submitted to headquarters.

TREATMENT DEVELOPMENTS

Gradually, then, staff of all disciplines became more aware of what their colleagues were doing and could contribute collectively to the newer and broader treatments that were being developed. Ward staff became more familiar with the rationale of new treatments as psychiatrists, psychotherapists, speech therapist and psychologists all ran their various programmes for both individuals and groups all round the hospital. Principles that were strange at the time of that venture with the patient in the Female Wing who would not leave her room without becoming violent, became more familiar and more often practised. The growing practice of treatment in groups, using the potent influence of fellow group members on each other, not only required nursing staff participation but enabled larger numbers of patients to experience these new forms of treatment. Later on a staff support group was started by Dr Murray Cox and met each week in a lunch hour to study and discuss the events of the past week's therapy groups, enabling everyone of all disciplines to learn from each other's experiences.

317

Initially, of course, there were arguments over the best approach to adopt. Murray Cox ran groups of a mainly non-directive kind where problems and their origins and consequences were explored. Interpretations of the often obscure reasons why someone did things in a particular way, especially if violence was involved, might be offered, or prompted with an oblique question, or might be left for the patient to work out. Similarly with the possible consequences of doing something differently. Some psychotherapists were less directive, some more. There are many styles and fashions in psychotherapy and at that time there was opportunity to use them all, provided, of course, that security was not jeopardized.

Psychologists tended to be more explicit and goal-directed in their treatment approach, stemming from the work emerging in that era and described in Chapter 13. The 'Attribution Theory' and *Gestalt* approaches, as has been said, were explored by Kevin Howells. Skinner's approach was initially followed by David Crawford. When 'Social Skills' arrived, they and others following on saw the obvious relevance of this to the problems of patients who had almost exclusively, and by definition, used aggression to solve their problems. Initially, however, and as described in Chapter 13, a development of basic interactional skills had been found necessary and was explored with a group of socially withdrawn and anxious patients. Expansion into 'Anger Control' and further methods of what has now become known as the 'cognitive-behavioural approach' were seen as obviously related to the problems of patients who acted out their aggression, and these followed later but, because of the obvious need for remedying the social skills of the many gauche young men in the 'adolescent' unit, who were inhibited, withdrawn, uncommunicative and unable to mix at social events, the social skills approach actually began with these.

All these behavioural methods explicitly set out to identify both precipitating situations and desired outcomes and involved imagining or actually practising the effects of alternative behaviours and strategies, usually through 'role play'. Having identified a desired outcome, this would be practised through a range of possible scenarios to try to generalize the new strategy and so that it would become automatic, or second nature, when dealing with everyday situations in the outside world. The principle was similar to that of learning any other skill, such as a hobby or sport, where instructions and the guide book are necessary but not sufficient without the opportunity to practise.

Nevertheless, this is not to decry the traditional psychotherapies. For very troubled people with mental conflicts or for badly damaged personalities with highly traumatic early life experiences it will invariably be a long and painful process, requiring sensitivity and patience, to explore these conflicts or experiences with the therapist so that they are recognized, accepted and, one hopes, resolved. After that some positive solution may be sought and acted upon. Broadmoor at that time had a number of specialist staff who could apply current knowledge and practice and develop them for wider use. I have vivid memories of discussions with Murray Cox about his hopes and ideas. We had both enjoyed YHA fell-walking holidays in the Lake District in our student days and our two families met up there on one holiday during our Broadmoor careers. There was an 'Outward Bound' school there and this stimulated our thoughts about some similar corporate activity where people's mental needs were concerned. We even coined a name for it: the 'Inward Bound' school.

Murray Cox had always been intrigued with the psychodynamic implications of Shakespearian plots and later became involved in exploring these with the Royal Shakespeare and other theatrical companies to the end that they might the better understand the

319

nature of the characters they were portraying and the stories they were unfolding. This developed to the extent of even bringing companies of actors to Broadmoor to present Shakespeare's plays to the patients (see Appendix B). I don't know whether any of them ever used the pillars on the stage in the way Koko did in *The Mikado*; or what interpretation they might have made of it if they had! (Unfortunately, we shall never know: the Shakespearian tragedies were performed 'in the round' on the floor of Broadmoor's central hall and the stage with its two pillars was used to seat some of the audience.)

A great deal has by now been practised and published in the psychological treatment field, which has continued to expand, and it is important for what is intended to be an historical, not a scientific, account to restrict the jargon to what is necessary to illustrate historical developments. Nevertheless, the subject cannot be left without describing a feature of treatments in secure settings that does not occur elsewhere. It has important consequences, for both the treatment itself and the arrangement of placements for mentally disordered offenders subsequently, and it is this. When using a social skills or a similar behavioural treatment programme, what is practised in the artificial environment of the hospital must be transferred to the normal world outside. The patient must become accustomed to using new behaviours in the natural setting where they will be required, not the artificial setting of the hospital. This is all the more important when the previous behaviours, for which the new ones are being substituted, have always been the natural responses in the old surroundings. Those surroundings will naturally prompt the old behaviours again because that is where all the familiar cues and pressures are present.

The problem of transferring new behaviours is easier with an 'informal' (voluntary) patient in an open setting. The therapist there can accompany the patient into the world outside or can set an agenda for the patient to practise on his or her own in the period between treatments. In this way the patient can overcome the problem of transferring the new behaviours to familiar old settings. However, this is not possible with special hospitals patients who do not leave the hospital until their discharge or transfer takes place (except, perhaps, occasionally for a shopping or recreational outing under supervision). This is one reason why so many special hospitals patients cannot complete their treatment in that setting. It must continue in the setting to which they next move. If that setting is another institutional one, say an RSU or a ward in a conventional psychiatric unit, and unless there is a facility for treatment to continue under supervision on outside visits, then the programme will need to continue yet further in a supervised community placement.

This is what is meant by 'continuity of care' and it needs careful co-ordination. The problem may not occur with all special hospitals patients, depending on their disorder and the treatment it requires, although a period of supervised living back in a normal environment is almost always necessary after a long spell in the artificial and restricted environment of a special hospital. This enables new behavioural strategies to be maintained; helps to ensure that any medication is taken as prescribed; and provides the means to spot any signs of relapse or other potentially dangerous development.

This may seem to contradict a theme in earlier chapters where the value of the Broadmoor environment in treatment was emphasized. The purpose there, however, was to point out that the environment was not the negative influence that a prison environment so often is. Organized as a total community it did and still does provide support, stimulation and diversity. It is now supplemented, eclipsed even, by the plethora of specific treatments available but it is still a component of treatment. There is still a big transition to be made to the outside world, however and, paradoxically, this can now be even more difficult when the residential community is managed and run, as it is, in both a comprehensive and self-contained way. There are more and different pressures to be coped with outside. The transition requires a bigger behavioural 'leap'.

The milieu and the psychiatric treatments of the day were all that were available in the time of Partridge's account of Broadmoor, for reasons that have been described: that was the extent of the knowledge and the resources. With the advances across a wide front in the era between the 1959 and 1983 Mental Health Acts, however, it became possible to supplement the existing knowledge and treatments with procedures and practices that could be directed at the specific problems of change and adaptation that were the accompaniments, or even sometimes the causes, of a patient's disorder and transgressions in the first place. This was the start of the 'individual treatment plan' familiar today.

EXPANDING RESEARCH ACTIVITY: THE FIRST DISCHARGE FOLLOW-UP STUDY

The steady expansion of staff in the clinical disciplines and the spread of treatment activity of a psychological kind to augment and complement the similarly growing range of pharmacological treatments called for a similar expansion in research activity to monitor the effects of the new procedures being applied. The reports of the Aarvold, Butler and Glancy Committees and the challenges presented by Gostin, MIND and the civil rights movement essentially called for the verification and validation of the procedures being carried out at Broadmoor. Some of this could be substantiated through reference to the scientific literature of the day, detailing the development of new procedures, but their application to the specific problems and clinical conditions found within Broadmoor called for specific study of their relevance, usage and efficacy in that setting. Research was required, therefore, to meet the criticisms of these official and pressure group reports. Finally, there were yet further new assessment procedures being developed, which also needed validation, such as those of the specialisms of psychophysiology and neuropsychology. The 1970s were seeing the birth of a new era. SHRU, for instance, was now in its stride and spawning a great many research projects, drawing in researchers from elsewhere, particularly the Institute of Psychiatry in London.

A crucial forerunner to the new spate of experimental work, however, was a specifically Broadmoor based one, in direct response to the events that prompted the Aarvold, Glancy and Butler reports. Cambridge University's Institute of Criminology offered periodic 'Cropwood Fellowships' for 'busy people' in the criminological professions to take time away to study or complete a project. Dr McGrath had earlier been awarded such a fellowship to complete his maternal filicides project. He therefore urged me to apply for one of these awards to undertake an analysis of the data I had accumulated on discharge assessments.

The old 'punched cards' had been started in 1960 for assembling social, clinical, criminological and psychological data on newly arriving and departing patients (Chapter 12). By the end of 1965, with six years of data stored, no more new patients' data were entered but data on those already in the card system and subsequently discharged or transferred had been added when they left Broadmoor and were reassessed. Under growing pressure to provide clinical services the data, after yielding some initial demographics, had been set aside and awaited further time and opportunity to be analysed (still awaited and there are still data unanalysed!).

By the mid-70s it was high time to see how those who had by now been discharged for some years had fared and, more significantly, how their success or failure related to their treatment response and the effects of their stay in Broadmoor. Variables such as the age at which they arrived, their offence, diagnosis, Mental Health Act category, how long they stayed and so on, all needed investigation. Could any pointers be derived that might improve future decisions on discharge readiness? The Cropwood application was accepted and I spent the winter months of 1975-76 in the congenial surroundings of Cambridge wrestling with the data.

At that time, also, the Butler Committee published its final report which demanded immediate digestion and commentary. Part of the time in Cambridge had to be spent doing this. Summaries were prepared for circulation with the Broadmoor *Staff Newsheet* as well as a review article for the *Bulletin* of the British Psychological Society. Others were doing the same for their own professional bodies and were also in demand for public discussion. It was a time of great debate. The Cropwood project suffered somewhat as a consequence and its full results and implications were not completed and reported until later, but enough of the basic outcomes of discharge and their relationships with patient profiles were obtained to indicate the overall levels of success and failure and the characteristics associated with each of these outcomes.

The period in Cambridge had therefore been highly profitable and the aims of the Cropwood facility fulfilled, although not entirely as initially planned. It was, however, a great help to have been able to detach oneself from the day to day work at Broadmoor long enough to complete the large 'number crunching' job, statistically analysing the follow up data and compiling tables, graphs and histograms to illustrate how the discharged patients had fared.

Some annotating was done there and then but a full write-up was only done later. Nevertheless, enough material was available for some informal reporting amongst colleagues within Broadmoor and to professional groups elsewhere.

The fuller aspects were only published gradually. One of these was as a chapter in the first of a series: *Current Research in Forensic Psychiatry and Psychology* edited by Gunn and Farrington, but not published until 1982, some six years after the spell in Cambridge. This still only described the gross outcome results and some of the characteristics of those who succeeded as against those who failed in their post-discharge careers, but did describe some of the psychological characteristics of each. A discussion of the specifically predictive indices which were later derived with the help of Roger Tarling at the Home Office research unit, and where Penny Spinks was later responsible for much of the data assembly and drafting, was published still later in *Prediction in Criminology*, edited by Farrington and Tarling, in 1985. Because of the publication of these two aspects of the work, the full collection of data, which had been intended for the SHRU monograph series, was regarded as ineligible, being considered too much a repetition of already published material. This was a pity as it contained the full data analysis, a great deal more than had been reported elsewhere, which was one of the objects of setting up the SHRU series. Stencilled copies, therefore, were made for the staff library and individual inquirers (this was before the days of desktop computer publishing).

David Farrington, psychologist at the Institute of Criminology, had been the adviser for the Cropwood project and David Thomas, a lawyer there, had been struggling with some data analysis of his own, using the new SPSS program (statistical package for the social sciences) on the University's mainframe computer. With data fed in by Hollerith punched cards, questions could be asked by means of a menu of statistical programmes, yielding such bread-and-butter print-outs as tabulations, correlations and 'tests of the significance of differences between means' (i.e.: how much meaning one can attach to differences between the averages of such things as ages, lengths of stay and scores on the various clinical and personality measures). All this can now be very simply done on desktop or even laptop computers. In 1975 it needed the university's mainframe computer but with David Thomas a chapter or two ahead of me in the SPSS manual I was helped quite quickly to grasp from him what was required. I would feed data and statistical questions into the computer on my way back to my lodgings each night and pick up the results in the morning, to analyse and direct me to the next set of statistical questions to be asked.

Since this was the first ever follow-up study of discharged Broadmoor patients and the results nicely complement the facts and figures on the patient population of Chapters 3 and 4, illustrating their careers and characteristics, it seems relevant to the history of Broadmoor to include their essence here.

TABLE 16.1 STUDY OF DISCHARGED MALE PATIENTS

Number discharged	128
During the period	1960 to 1965
Followed up for	5 years
By means of	Hospital Records, SHRU Records The Mental Health Register
Average age - on admission	34.07 years
- on discharge	41.54 years
Average length of stay	7.48 years
With previous convictions	77 (60%)
With previous hospital admissions	63 (49%)
With previous Broadmoor admissions	13 (11%)

TABLE 16.2   OFFENCES FOR WHICH ADMITTED TO
BROADMOOR

Homicide	62 (48%)
Other Offences against Persons	33 (26%)
Property Offences - damage	6 (5%)
- acquisitive	23 (18%)
Sexual	4 (3%)

(but this may be concealed within the more serious offences of murder, attempted murder, manslaughter, WWI and GBH)

Victims - family or other known person	76 (59%)
of which - wife, partner, cohabitee	32 (25%)
- casual acquaintance or stranger	20 (16%)

The study was confined to the male patients as the female patients were a much smaller group and had not yielded, during the period 1960-65 when the original data frame was set up, a large enough body of data for meaningful results to be obtainable. Even the male discharge sample only amounted to 128, the greatest number of patients leaving hospital doing so by other routes such as transfer to a local psychiatric hospital (see Chapter 4). There was also no attempt to relate the data to the specific treatments patients had received. This would have greatly complicated and lengthened the study and would have been largely meaningless as most patients had received many treatments but at varying times, in varying order and for varying durations. The inclusion of this kind of information awaits the luxury of a more sophisticated study in the future.

The results of the study are, therefore, a reflection of the overall effect of being in Broadmoor, not of any specific treatment. It was, however, at that time, the first attempt at a follow-up study of Broadmoor discharges, although there had been one at Rampton some years earlier by Tong and Mackay. Whilst all the information from their time in Broadmoor was provided from the psychology department's records, the all-important follow-up information was provided by SHRU, through Elizabeth Parker who was in charge of the case register.

TABLE 16.3 DIAGNOSES OF THE 'CROPWOOD' SAMPLE

Schizophrenic type	33 (26%)
Affective Disorders	41 (32%)
Psychopathic or similar	54 (42%)
Organic	14 (11%)
Subnormal	5 (4%)
Total*	147

(* exceeds the sample total of 128 because of several dual or multiple diagnoses, especially with subnormality which would not, on its own, have been eligible for Broadmoor at that time).

The study was a retrospective 'paper' one, i.e.: was carried out using data collected earlier and without needing to contact patients in person. The data were then compared with the later data on success or failure of subsequent discharge obtained from official records. Not only did this obviate the need to contact former patients but the data was 'blind', i.e.: no patient was personally identified, his data being the object of the inquiry not his personal identity. All were identified by a number only.

A comparison with the demographic information displayed in the figures and graphs of Chapter 4 shows that the constitution of this discharged group differs from both the incoming and the resident populations of the hospital. Of course, similarity would not be expected. Discharge is a highly selective process, depending on such considerations as: the type and severity of the original offence and mental disorder; how the latter resolves with treatment; the patient's response to social and occupational activities; the view of the original offence taken by Home Office ministers; and the home, family and work circumstances to which the patient will be returning. Some patients respond and leave more quickly, others more slowly. In addition, however, this discharged group was only a quarter of all those who left the hospital in that period. (See Figures 4 and 5, Chapter 4.) Half of those who left were transferred to other psychiatric hospitals; they were considered first to need further treatment and rehabilitation or were elderly chronic patients who no longer needed secure care. The remaining quarter who left comprised those who went back to prison, to their country of origin, to another special hospital, or who died in Broadmoor.

TABLE 16.4 OUTCOME FOR THE 'CROPWOOD' SAMPLE

	Yes	No
Subsequent psychiatric admissions \	24	102
\		
}	both 36	89 neither
/		
Subsequent Broadmoor readmissions /	24	102
Subsequent court appearances	50	76
Subsequent imprisonment	29	97
Remained in the community for all 5 years	64	61
Committed further offences against the person	13	112

(No homicides in the 5 year follow-up period but 2 later)
[Discrepancies indicate missing information]

The outcome of the 'Cropwood' Study can probably best be summarized by quoting the report that was carried in the Broadmoor *Staff Newsheet* of April 1976, which details and comments on the tables as follows:

I. THE SAMPLE AND HOW THEY FARED

One hundred and twenty-eight men were discharged in the 6 years 1960-65. These were a quarter of all who left hospital during the period. There were 62 who had originally been admitted following a homicide. Seven and a half years was the average length of time spent by this group in Broadmoor. Exactly half the sample (64) remained in the community for the whole of the follow-up period. Fifty had subsequent court appearances, 24 had further psychiatric admissions, 24 (but not the same ones) were subsequently readmitted to Broadmoor. Most of the convictions were trivial (petty thefts and driving away a motor vehicle) involving only fines or probation, though 29 were serious enough to result in imprisonment. Only 13 were subsequently involved in personal violence in the follow-up period (though this increases to 17 if assaults which took place after the 5 year follow-up, and which we know about, are taken into account). None of the group was involved in a homicide during the follow-up, but two were later (though both had already offended in other ways during the follow-up period and one committed his homicide against a fellow inmate where he was imprisoned).

II. GENERAL FACTORS ASSOCIATED WITH SUCCESS AND FAILURE

(a) *Predictive*

As expected from studies elsewhere, a record of previous convictions proved to be the best predictor of future offences; likewise a history of previous psychiatric attention is the best predictor of future psychiatric readmissions. Readmission to Broadmoor is not surprisingly associated with *both* sorts of past record. Many other features of a patient's record, clinical condition and personality are also significantly associated with success or failure of discharge but none is such a good predictor as past record. Nevertheless they help to fill in the picture of what sort of patient succeeds and what sort fails and, therefore, what possible explanations there may be.

(b) *Reoffending* is most frequent amongst those whose past and current offences are assaults and property offences; who are younger; who are classified and diagnosed psychopathic; whose victims are strangers or casual acquaintances and who are admitted under a fixed sentence (Section 72 then).

(c) *Success* is highest amongst those without previous offences; whose current offence is homicide; who are older; diagnosed as some kind of affective disorder; whose victims are well known (normally wife or other family) and are admitted under an indeterminate sentence (hospital order then).

III. PSYCHOLOGICAL CHARACTERISTICS

(a) *Readmissions* tended to show on their discharge assessment rather more signs of disturbance of a psychotic, hostile kind.

(b) *Further imprisonment.* Those who subsequently serve a prison sentence for a further offence emerge clearly as more psychopathic and impulsive.

(c) *Violence.* Those few who were involved in further

personal violence showed a wider range of disturbance, including anxiety as well as impulsiveness and other psychopathic traits.

(d) *Success*. Conversely those who succeeded showed less disturbance and more social conformity and control. More surprisingly, however, they also showed more signs of some uncertainty and hesitancy when tackling practical tasks.

IV. A POSSIBLE PREDICTION INDEX

The best predictor has once again been shown to be past behaviour (for both law-breaking and psychiatric), and most of the other social criteria significantly associated with outcome lost significance when the statistical influence of previous history was discounted. Nevertheless, some of the psychological measures, whose associations with outcome were less dramatically significant, often retained their associations independently of past history. For example, when 'previously convicted' and 'previously conviction free' groups were examined psychologically meaningful associations remained. This promises hope for deriving an improved prediction index by incrementing 'past record' with some apparently independent psychological measures.

It might seem obvious that some of the findings on patient characteristics, detailed above, would be associated with their subsequent failure to remain trouble free on discharge and that, knowing this, they should not have been discharged. It should be pointed out, however, that many of the findings would not have been available when making a discharge decision. A few would have been referred for psychological assessment in connection with their possible discharge but most were not and were only assessed for purposes of this research when their discharge was decided and about to take place. These data were from the early days of the 1959 Act and the object was, independently, to discover whether there were indicators from a psychological appraisal that could add to the decision-making process.

The derivation of prediction indices did feature in the further work on the Cropwood study, published in the Farrington and Tarling book on prediction in criminology and included in the full set of tables and graphics made available in the cyclostyled version produced by Penny Spinks and myself for the hospital library. This point, perhaps rather technical for a historical account, is emphasized particularly to refute the criticism, raised by some colleagues who should have known better, that the results of the study were quickly out of date because of the changes in the constitution of the patient population and of discharge and transfer practices. Of course these were always changing. The essence of the Cropwood study, however, was to see what *relationships* would emerge between the various offender and diagnostic categories on the one hand, and the more recently gathered information on psychological characteristics on the other, and then to relate all of these to the various kinds of discharge success or failure. If features emerged that typified some kinds of success or failure then these could be expected to hold good for future generations of patients, although the numbers in any particular offender or diagnostic category would almost certainly vary over the years. In other words, gross results would vary but the features that typified each group should not. Naturally this work was subsequently applied to clinical appraisals and thereafter influenced the psychological reporting of patients who were being considered for discharge.

It is worth picking out here, therefore, a feature of the more successful patients and, in contrast, some features of those who subsequently reoffended, particularly those few who did so violently, all of which relate to some of the results of the early research described in Chapter 12.

Amongst the more successful ones were those who, all those years earlier, appeared defensive on the original forms of personality assessment. This was Megargee's and Blackburn's 'over-controlled' group - repressive and socially conforming - but whose offences were disproportionately in the murder and manslaughter category. However, this is the group that arouses the greatest misgivings where discharge is concerned and which, therefore, tends to spend longest in hospital; unnecessarily so, apparently.

It is the impulsive, psychopathic but generally less serious offender that more often and more rapidly reoffends. Where further serious offending is concerned, this happens later, if at all. If the 'Megargee-Blackburn' over-controlled type kills again, this tends to happen a long time afterwards (cf: the two killings which happened in the 'Cropwood' sample but after the five year follow-up period had expired). It seems that this group does not need to stay longer in secure care - shorter if anything - but needs another form of therapy elsewhere and then closer monitoring thereafter. This other form of therapy might well include psychotherapy directed at self-realization and awareness of the need to deal with stress and problems openly and without repression, suppression, denial and avoidance. This is not easy.

Even then, however, the job is not complete, for some new strategies for dealing with stress and provocation will need to be learned and incorporated into the patient's repertoire of means of coping with life and its frustrations. This will be more of the 'assertiveness training' type akin to the social skills approach which was first applied in Broadmoor by Howells, Crawford and others in the psychology department with another but more anxious and inarticulate group. The 'over-controlled' are not all lacking in basic social skills - far from it: many are often described in the files of newly admitted patients as 'models of good citizens, ideal husbands and fathers and pillars of the local community'. Broadmoor case-notes are replete with newspaper cuttings of their trials which marvel at this apparent paradox. This is a different kind of group in need of a different kind of assertiveness training from those who present a picture of inarticulate ineptness and who require to learn a more basic self-expression and confidence before learning assertiveness. Once again the need for careful individual prescription of treatment is emphasized: 'assertiveness training' is not a blanket treatment and 'social skills' covers a widely varying area of activity and attention.

By contrast and where the subsequent violent reoffenders in the Cropwood study are concerned, the opposite tendency emerged: features of both impulsive extraversion and of anxiety and tension. This is characteristic of one of the other two variants Blackburn identified in the 'under-controlled' category often referred to as the 'secondary psychopath'. Together with the primary psychopath, whose features appear more typically in the 'reconvictions' category generally (not necessarily assaultive) this is the group that needs, amongst other things, 'anger control' therapy. Here the problem of acted-out aggression needs to be confronted and then ways learned and practised to deal with frustration and provocation with alternative non-aggressive strategies which deal with these in socially acceptable ways. For the high-anxiety variant of this group there would almost certainly be a need to include some relaxation training to enable the anxiety to be coped with and, no doubt, some more traditional psychotherapy to understand the causes and susceptibilities which prompt the antisocial reactions needing to be changed.

This exemplifies the complex interaction of therapeutic needs which this problem and type of patient presents, understandably rejected as a medical problem. It illustrates the issue of assessing treatability in the context of categorizing and placing psychopaths; for this is the cluster of characteristics to have emerged from the various studies described here and defines one sub-group of psychopathic or personality disorder.

Of course, a key element is 'motivation for change': this last group is notoriously resistant to any suggestion that change is needed. Indefinite renewal of a hospital order is one means of motivation but is a negative one and likely to increase the antagonism of the patient. It needs to be combined, therefore, with the prospect of both a successful and a personally satisfying outcome. This is where group treatment is valuable. Home truths from other group members carry more weight than those of a therapist. A treatment plan is needed which convinces the patient that a changed future life strategy will lead to keeping out of trouble whilst not 'losing face' with one's peer group. A later follow-up study comes at this problem from a different direction and will be described in the next chapter.

The 'Cropwood' study has been described in some detail because it broke new ground for Broadmoor. It also further illustrates the characteristics of the male patients within Broadmoor and reveals some interesting associations with the earlier findings from the admission assessments of the 60s. Opportunity arose from this to illustrate some treatment needs, as well as complexities and difficulties. Much further work followed, enlarging the picture but, in the present context, the Cropwood study will suffice as illustration and we should return to briefer outlines in illustration of what characterized the final years of the 1959 Act.

SUMMARY

The changing socio-political climate of the 1970s, with the government inquiries and reports described in the previous chapter, made it imperative to do two things. The first was to expand and refine treatment methods, focusing them more closely upon patients' specific offending behaviours rather than only generally upon diagnostic conditions or occupational rehabilitation. The second was to examine the now increasing amounts of clinical and research data for answers to the key questions about safe discharge.

This chapter first describes the expansion in group psychotherapy, and the common variations of this method, as well as the development of psychological treatments which took place at this time. Jargon terms abound here but some fairly clear differences have been important to explain. A common feature was, however, that treatment was conducted in small groups of 4 to 8 people, which both increased the numbers who could be offered these treatments and tapped into the potentially powerful force of peer-group pressure.

An important point to emphasize has been the need to carry over what is learned and practised in the relatively 'sterile' world of the institution to the 'normal' world outside, where pressures and influences are more frequent and varied. This is why treatment can so rarely be completed in any one setting, especially a highly secure one. 'Continuity of care' requires progression into the real world so that new life strategies can be revised and tested against those real world pressures and hazards.

The chapter concludes with details of the first discharge follow-up study conducted at Broadmoor in order to demonstrate both the relatively high level of success and the therapeutic needs of the patients under the new 'individual treatment plans' which were becoming the accepted way of delivering care and treatment.

Marked differences emerged between offender categories and between diagnostic groupings in their degree of success after discharge and, more particularly, the kind of failure that occurred. It was not the group characterized by the most heinous crimes that fared worst: the homicide group, for instance, was the most successful. Nor was there uniformity in the psychopathic group. Whilst the so-called 'primary psychopath' was more involved with further and mostly petty crime, the 'secondary psychopath' (with added neurotic features) was more likely to be involved in something violent.

Whilst these findings were identifying gross levels of success and failure in relation to original offence and mental disorder, they were also identifying the specific characteristics of smaller groups of patients within, and independently of, their diagnostic categories. Diagnosis and offence category are important but are insufficient for purposes of initial placement, for determining treatment and for predicting outcome. This situation is developed in the next chapter and its wider implications discussed in Part III.

CHAPTER 17

MORE CLINICAL INNOVATIONS

INCREASING PROFESSIONAL DEMANDS

One of the venues where the Cropwood study was reported was the British Psychological Society's annual conference which, in 1977, was at the University of Exeter. The society was just forming a new 'Criminological and Legal Division' to focus the work and needs of not only those in the Prisons Service but also of those who worked with antisocial problems in the NHS, such as the special hospitals and the emerging RSUs. Few of these would be involved in actual court work, so 'forensic' would have been an erroneous title, as it would have been for those academic psychologists who taught and researched in the field of legal issues generally, not necessarily to do with presenting evidence in court. Hence the adoption of the cumbersome title: the handier name of 'Forensic Division' was rejected as too narrow, although it has been adopted since, for simplicity and because 'forensic' has tended to take on a wider meaning.

Just as Dr McGrath had been elected the first chairman of the forensic section of the Royal College of Psychiatrists (which was much more truly 'forensic') when it was formed at the beginning of the seventies, I was elected chairman of this new BPS Division. Broadmoor seems to have that effect. Such work involves a great deal of time at meetings and to digest and draft papers of all kinds. This takes up evenings and weekends to the extent that it is a well-known marriage disrupter. That mine stayed intact was entirely due the good fortune of a happy and supportive family who tolerated the absences and incursions. Whilst most of the work involved one's spare time, nevertheless, when events occurred during the week, Dr McGrath once again encouraged participation as both redounding to the benefit and good name of the hospital and being Broadmoor's contribution to 'the war effort', i.e.: to national duties and to developing scientific and professional knowledge. This liberal view has now sadly gone. Cost effectiveness and accountability have taken precedence, to the detriment of public life generally.

In 1977 it was just as well Dr McGrath took the view he did, for chairing the BPS's new division of criminological and legal psychology brought in its wake *ex-officio* membership of the BPS's Council; Professional Affairs Board; Joint Standing Committee with the Royal College of Psychiatrists; Membership Committee; and the working party on a proposed College of Applied Psychology (which never materialized). I list these, not out of self-importance, but to emphasize the pressures upon one's time the longer one stays in a specialist post and is in demand for an accredited input on professional matters.

PUBLICITY AND THE PUBLIC PROFILE

Additionally, and as a result of presenting the Cropwood study results at the BPS Annual Conference, there was also press attention. Gradually learning to cope with this consequence of working in a high-profile public sector setting and having to respond to media queries with short sound bites, coincided with the BPS restructuring its public profile, developing its press committee and, shortly afterwards, appointing a specialist press officer. The

Cropwood research publicity experience helped me to learn to bridge the gap between the complex jargon of scientific papers and the media's need for brief digests. I was therefore recruited to the BPS press committee as someone who had been dropped into the deep end and learned to cope with press inquiries. An input on my area of experience was needed and I might also help to convince and coach reluctant others of the need to be 'media-friendly'.

Communicating with the press was not, however, among Dr McGrath's favoured practices and all such contact had to be discussed and cleared with him beforehand and notified to DHSS headquarters. It did not take long, however, to learn what was wanted and how to communicate brief digests of what we had discovered and was newsworthy whilst still remaining within the bounds of hospital and DHSS confidentiality. There must not be any mention of individual patients' clinical particulars nor any criticism implied of hospital or DHSS practice. This actually presented no great problem. One carries out what is currently accepted practice until something different is indicated from new developments. Even then, changes must be tried and tested. This is what our work was about. Findings from research projects were first and foremost telling us more about our patients, their characteristics and their needs. Criticism would not arise because this information would not previously have been available. Suggestions for change would be just that: suggestions; not criticisms. They would need to be confirmed through monitored practice in comparison with already established procedures.

This is how scientific and clinical advance is achieved: slowly and with careful checks. Reporting these results at a scientific or professional gathering exposed them to critical scrutiny, and the discussion of their significance and implications, from a wider audience of people qualified to do so. This is why time away at a conference is periodically necessary for people involved in scientific and clinical work. As well as keeping themselves up to date they should be prepared to submit their own work to criticism and should also be available to criticize the work of others. Subsequent publication provides further accreditation because it is subject to the scrutiny and approval of appropriately qualified referees and also reaches a wider and, again, potentially critical audience which may respond with confirmatory or contradictory research findings or raise alternative explanations for what one has found.

Much of what was being discovered in the 1970s at Broadmoor was new to both the public and the official mind. It needed to be publicized if changed concepts and practices were to attract public, and especially official, support. The DHSS, of course, was conversant with this situation. If assured that patient and hospital security and confidentiality were not being jeopardized, it backed publication of clinical and research advances, took on board the findings where its own responsibilities were concerned, and coped with the resultant publicity.

It was not surprising, in the light of all this widespread professional involvement, that completing the analysis and reporting of the Cropwood data, not to mention any further research endeavours, was delayed. Fortunately, there was now an active and better staffed psychology department, together with other research minded medical and social work staff and an increasingly wide range of projects and people associated with SHRU (the Special Hospitals Research Unit). A history of clinical developments must give a flavour of these and the present chapter establishes the chronology.

SEX OFFENDER WORK

Another paper presented at that 1977 BPS annual conference

symposium was by David Crawford on his treatment innovations with Broadmoor sex offenders, the beginnings of which were introduced towards the end of Chapter 13. Until then, the initial NHS treatment developments for these problems had been largely experimental and directed mainly at sexual incapacity or deviance rather than offending. Research reports were mostly of the single method type, e.g.: of the efficacy of aversive conditioning of unwanted habits; or of the positive conditioning of acceptable alternative behaviours. The first of these, usually involving developing a revulsion for the unwanted practices by means of, say, electric shocks associated with pictures or verbal descriptions of these, had been giving rise to widespread criticism, both scientifically of the methodology and ethically of the procedure involved. Despite the apparent justification of such procedures in the case of people whose activities had resulted in the injury or death of their victim, nevertheless, because these were compulsorily detained patients, there were both professional and public misgivings.

David Crawford's conference reporting and subsequent journal publication of his investigations and treatment programmes for sex offenders, therefore, gave rise to considerable interest because, as indicated in Chapter 13, it combined a number of different therapeutic strategies in one programme. Not only did it combine 'aversive' and 'rewarding' elements in the conditioning part of the programme but it also extended the overall treatment of a sex offender patient to the inclusion of social skills training; desensitization for, in effect, a heterosexual phobia; and, finally, basic sex education.

This is where the combination of research with ongoing clinical investigation and treatment proved vital. Extensive knowledge of a patient often revealed that sexual offending had occurred in a context of either or all of several other problems. As well as ignorance of the basic 'facts of life' there was often also what amounted to a 'fear' of approaching and attempting to form a relationship with a young woman, associated with a lack of skill at handling social relationships generally. With the onset of sexual maturity and the obvious need to channel sexual activity into some meaningful relationship, such a young man found himself not only unable to carry through the approaches and encounters that would normally facilitate this but also petrified of trying to do so and ignorant of what was involved in the event of succeeding. In his ignorant ineptness, but driven by his natural appetites and accentuated by the often lonely condition brought about by his ineptitude, he would either 'cop-out' of an attempt to form an adult relationship and seek the less threatening friendship of a child, or would make an attempt at an adult relationship and 'botch' it. Either way, successive attempts could lead to some disastrous turn of events when his approaches would be misconstrued, or his efforts turn to violent desperation, or his frustration result in anger. His 'target' might then be the victim of his resulting violence or, on his victim imagining that was his intention, she might react with panic, which caused him to panic too, again resulting in violence. Scenarios vary, but this kind tended to emerge in various forms, sequences and outcomes.

Hence David Crawford's development of the multifaceted treatment programme referred to in Chapter 13. Included might be the reduction of abnormal sexual arousal, or arousal to abnormal situations such as those involving children or violence, using an aversive conditioning approach. The conditioning schedule, however, would comprise images of both the abnormal practices, which would be accompanied by the aversive shock, until the patient switched to the next image of contrasting acceptable practices where arousal was appropriate and was rewarded by relief from the aversive shock. Following or sometimes preceding this, however, there might be a desensitising programme for the difficult images of mature and desirable femininity so that the patient was enabled to learn to become relaxed instead of fearful and panicked by such images. This might then be further followed by a social skills programme to work through the repertoire of socially competent behaviours and emotional experiences involved in enabling a relationship to be developed. Finally, David Crawford and his colleagues devised an educational programme to inform these patients about sex and adult relationships about which their personality, clinical state and, probably, social and family background too, had left them in ignorance.

Within this model, or 'paradigm', it might well turn out that an aversive treatment element was not actually necessary. More crucial was the sex information and social skills training, together with the strategies for countering incapacitating anxiety. The patient might actually prefer normal sexual activity with a consenting adult partner but have been driven to use an under age partner or to have resorted to violence through lack of knowledge or competence. Enabling a normal form of activity was the need, not removing an abnormal one. Sometimes RMOs, and even the patient himself, found difficulty in believing this was the answer to what had often been catastrophic offences and that some more direct action to extinguish the prohibited behaviour was essential. An aversive programme might therefore be included on a 'belt-and-braces' basis, as it were. This did, at least, afford the opportunity to obtain measurements of the patient's associated physiological responses, which thereby provided an overall assessment of treatment response. (See below.)

Of course, there are sex offenders motivated differently. The above is a common and often unappreciated scenario, so is worth emphasizing first. Others, unfortunately, occur where violence is used in a sexual setting because it has become the preferred or only means of obtaining arousal. More commonly, however, sexual violence is used, not for gratification but as a form of domination and humiliation deriving, say, from early life experiences of abuse from others or of neglect during the crucial period of adolescent development. Sexual activity is seen only as physical relief, a mechanical pleasure or, worse, a form of vengeance. These distinctions were able to be made as a result of the groundwork of clinical and personality assessment developed by the psychology department over the years but with the added discriminations afforded by the repertory grid type of approach used by Howells (Chapter 13) and now with the added advantage of the laboratory assessments of types and degrees of sexual arousal.

From the earlier attempts at psychological treatments, especially of the social skills kind described in previous chapters, there developed, therefore, this more comprehensive psychological approach which tended to characterize the psychology department's strategy from then on. It also spilled over into the work of other disciplines. The social work department, which by now had enough staff to be able to expand its activities from solely compiling social and family histories and liaising with families and outside bodies, was able to integrate the vital information thereby derived into treatment applications of its own. A nation-wide trend for the psychiatric nursing profession to adopt a wider treatment approach was also increasingly noticeable and psychological methods were incorporated into their training and clinical activities. Treatment effectiveness was therefore greatly enhanced, delivered on a much wider front.

This wider front also included male homosexual patients and the patients of the female wing. Because some of the men described above might have included homosexual exploits amongst their past activities there needed to be an assessment of whether they were actually homosexual or were, again, using this avenue of expression, as with children or adolescents, because of heterosexual phobia. Where a homosexual orientation was established or claimed, there was no pressure used to change this unless the patient wished to do so. If it was a 'phobic' alternative to heterosexual activity, this would be explained but, again, no coercion used to change things. After all, as explained to visitors who were aware, in those sensitive days, of the emergence of equal rights for all sexual orientations and who tended to jump to the conclusion that we were running programmes to establish heterosexuality in all our patients, it was of no consequence to us where someone obtained their sexual satisfaction, so long as it was with a consenting adult, not a child, and done without harm. Our main job was to help those to change who had imposed their sexuality on an unwilling person and done so with resulting damage or death.

MIXED SEX THERAPY

Lest it should be thought this was entirely a problem of the male patients, there was equivalent work developed for the women patients. Of course there are women who have similar heterosexual fears or phobias as the men; who lack social skills in relating to other people; whose sexual knowledge is sparse; and who may lead miserable lives as a result. They do not usually commit indictable sexual offences as a result - rape and indecent assault are male offences in the main, although there are now debates even on this. Their offences will have been different, but still violent for them to be in Broadmoor at all. These offences may have been unconnected with their sexual problems or they may have been the female equivalent of the inept young man's 'botched' attempt at a sexual liaison. The promiscuity of some young women may sometimes come into this category, even occasionally prostitution. More often, however, there is a less obviously connected equivalent, such as arson or other damage of the property or home of a partner who is seen as rejecting her, or even the abduction of a child in an attempt to gain the acceptance of a partner. She may have lacked the knowledge, skill or confidence to maintain the relationship normally, or have had an inept or punitively possessive partner who had driven her to an antisocial or unlawful extreme in her attempt to maintain the relationship.

Women patients requiring a therapeutic programme to control and reduce anxiety and tension, develop social skills and improve sexual knowledge did not, of course, have the added requirement of physiological assessment and treatment of their sexual arousal. They were not, therefore, at that time or for that purpose, any part of the laboratory developments described in this chapter. They did, in parallel with the men, however, figure in the psychotherapy developments at this time in Broadmoor's history.

The psychotherapists and speech therapist particularly developed these groups and it was not long before the question of mixed therapy groups arose. This seems an obvious requirement now but was surprisingly long in coming at Broadmoor. All kinds of objection were raised, both ethically and where staff involvement was concerned. However, integration of staff was gradually happening at this time, too. The first move was to put some male staff in the most disturbed ward of the Female Wing, in Lancaster House, because of the growing number of incidents involving violence from some quite strong, heavily built women patients. The male nurses introduced, however, would always be part of a mixed team of nurses and never alone with a woman patient. The next move was to put some female ward sisters on the shifts in Essex House, the male parole house, where they were thought to add an important element to the work of rehabilitating men for discharge to the mixed world outside. From there it was only a matter of time before mixed staff complements were appearing all over the hospital.

There is no doubt that this was a welcome and long overdue move, generating an atmosphere of normality in keeping with the outside world. Of course there were mishaps, with relationships getting closer and more emotional at times than was desirable. These were outweighed by the advantages, however. Many patients were helped to regain confidence in their everyday attitudes and dealings with the opposite sex as a result and some were also helped more specifically with relationship difficulties. It was also quite touching at times to see how staunchly supportive, even 'chivalrous', many of the men patients became towards female staff on their ward. Now, it may well have become accepted and no longer a novelty; then, it was a distinct advance.

Mixed therapy groups also arose, therefore, at this time. This was particularly important for those patients of both sexes whose problems were principally to do with relating to the opposite sex, in which case the stage at which joining a mixed group occurred would need to be carefully assessed. Usually a patient would begin group therapy in a single sex group until thought ready to benefit from a mixed group. The misuse of this facility for 'chatting up' or obtaining association with the opposite sex scarcely arose because the problem for this group of both men and women patients was the lack of confidence and ability to carry through such activity. There was certainly insufficient opportunity for men and women patients generally to meet socially such that many would seize any opportunity to do so. Their problems were different, however, and needed handling differently. The mixed sex social skills groups were essentially, and initially, for those socially anxious, uncertain and damaged individuals of both sexes who needed to gain or restore confidence in their ability to meet with the rest of the human race.

Anger control groups came later.

DEVELOPMENT OF THE 'PSKYLAB'

Monitoring of patients' responses to personal and social situations that were significant for them, either pleasurable or aversive, was no longer done by psychometric methods alone, even by the 'repertory grid', rating scale or other interview based kind such as a psychological history (which would include compiling a list of significant life events that might have been rewarding or traumatic and, therefore, helped to establish long lasting changes in behaviour).

The small laboratory cubicles in the psychology department had by now become a centre of increasing activity for monitoring these emotional responses physiologically. One wag gave them the name 'Pskylab' following a 'Skylab' put into orbit around the Earth at about that time. Psychophysiological monitoring equipment was certainly now much more sophisticated and had a 'mission control' look about it. It enabled small and, to the outward eye, unobservable changes to be electronically measured for such physiological activities as heart and breathing rates, blood pressure and the electrical conductivity of the skin (the 'galvanic skin response' resulting from small changes in sweat gland activity). As we all know from such phrases as 'my heart was in my mouth'; 'I broke out in a cold sweat'; 'my hair stood on end'; or 'it took my breath away', emotional situations are accompanied by physiological reactions. They are measurable electronically when they are not always apparent to the eye. Even the person exhibiting them is not always aware of them, as with the deadpan manner of the poker player whose reactions can, nevertheless, be physiologically detected.

The equipment to do this is known as a 'polygraph' which simply means something that is displaying several things graphically. In fact it is picking up changes in electrical resistance with the 'galvanic skin response' (or GSR); or in pressure with pulse and respiration. Such measures are the basis of the 'Lie Detector' which is actually just one application of a 'psychophysiological' polygraph. Arguments over the validity and reliability of lie detecting are, therefore, not necessarily relevant to other uses of the same equipment. The measurement of physiological changes has many uses, either for the function itself, as when recording, say, pulse rate and blood pressure for medical purposes; or as measures of change when some external event takes place to which the person reacts; or as measures of comparison when different stimuli are presented to which one person might react differently from another. These measurements have acceptable 'reliability', i.e.: they can be consistently repeated and shown to give virtually the same results under the same conditions, but it is their 'validity' which is often difficult to establish, i.e.: the meaning of the levels and changes being measured. In other words, pulse, blood pressure, breathing and GSR do go up and down 'reliably', or consistently, in association with changes in emotional experience but they are also sensitive to other influences and the variations may not be 'validly' related to the circumstances or experiences to which one is attributing them, such as lying. Of crucial importance is the constancy of the conditions under which measurements are made - a basic requirement of any scientific procedure - but even then the meaning of the results need great care in the design and carrying-out of the investigatory procedure.

The 'Pskylab', the little laboratory in two cubicles of the psychology department, described in Chapter 12 for the measurement of perceptual and physiological phenomena and accommodating what Dr McGrath called the 'demented pianola', was therefore developed for this new psychophysiological monitoring. Better than this, however, a much improved polygraph was acquired as a result of a parallel research project mounted in the mid-1970s. Dr John Hinton, a research psychologist at Southampton University where I had taught the undergraduate abnormal psychology course for a while at Professor Gordon Trasler's invitation and where Ron Blackburn had gained his PhD, was available. He had just completed a psychophysiological research programme relevant to our own proposed next phase of research.

John Hinton was appointed to the SHRU staff to carry out a polygraph-based programme of measurement of physiological reactivity in Broadmoor patients. The stimulus material was in the form of slides which were assembled from various sources or else specially created to display a range of both neutral (for control) and potentially traumatic stimuli. The latter comprised a wide range of situations relevant to aspects of the similarly wide range of Broadmoor patients' offences. A biochemical element to the research was added when David Woodman's help was enlisted from the Windsor laboratory, whilst Mike O'Neill joined as a research assistant. The work grew into a considerable project, with numerous co-workers recruited to develop supplementary aspects at various times. Importantly, John Hinton developed a set of rating scales for use by the ward nursing staff to provide comparative data to set against what was coming out of the lab. He also added what was then a quite novel measurement aspect, namely the variation in dilation of the pupil of the eye - another variable sensitive to emotional arousal. This 'pupilometry' became possible through the advances in measurement technology being achieved at that time. An interesting stream of results ensued, adding to the already large bibliography on the physiological correlates of stress and, more specifically, differences between diagnostic groups. In particular, some psychopathic sub-groups were differentiated. This is another specialised subject which is difficult to summarize adequately in the present context but was a significant event in Broadmoor's life, important to put on record.

THE 'PSKYLAB' AND ASSESSMENT OF SEXUAL PHYSIOLOGY

The 'polygraph' was widely used, and still is, for the measurement of physiological changes associated with sexual arousal. Clearly changes in pulse and breathing rates, and in blood pressure and GSR, are likely to accompany this. More specific in men, however, is penile erection. It was obviously necessary to confront this sensitive subject and try to measure such a basic physiological re-action in the case of sex offenders and relate the measured changes to particular sexual situations, normal and deviant. It would also be relevant to discover if penile changes accompanied the portrayal of details associated with other violent crimes. Sexual motives or components are often attributed to other forms of violence and would therefore constitute a relevant subject for investigation. Then it would be relevant to try to establish patterns of response which might be valid indicators of changes as a result of treatment. This might then provide indicators of reduced dangerousness relevant in the consideration of readiness for discharge.

There is obviously a succession of questions and problems for assessment here: a tall order, but clearly relevant to the problems of Broadmoor patients and the role and responsibility of the staff if discharge is to be recommended with any confidence. How used it to be done? Clinical skill, experience and intuition? Can this be improved upon? Can objective criteria be obtained with which to supplement clinical opinion? With all the imponderables that need their validity establishing, how soon will answers result? A large research sample is essential for the wide range of sexual activity involved and the similarly wide range of offences occurring among Broadmoor's patients.

The polygraph, then, was now to be used as a 'penile plethysmograph', or PPG, as it is commonly called. The 'plethysmograph' is better known as the cuff wound round one's arm to measure blood pressure through a mercury gauge. A small syringe pump inflates the cuff - something familiar to everyone who has had this done at the GP's surgery or in hospital. It is now often done with an electronic device instead and the equipment in the Pskylab used just such an electronic procedure. Instead of a large cuff around the arm there is a small rubber ring around the penis. This needs no inflation as there is no pulse to be listened for. The ring simply acts as a strain gauge sensitive to changes in penile diameter.

David Crawford made use of the Pskylab for monitoring, through this range of psychophysiological activity, the responses of patients he was treating for sexual problems and sexual offences. The 'PPG' was of specific relevance. John Hinton also added the feature of sexual arousal monitoring to his programme of psychophysiological research and, separately from his research samples, provided some assessments for clinical purposes as well, at the request of RMOs. Liz Bonham carried out a research project on arson as part of her clinical psychologist training requirement at Surrey University. All of these people needed a good range of stimulus material, not readily available 'off the shelf'. It was also known that the movement element of film material or videotape provided a more effective arousal stimulus than the static quality of a slide.

There arose, therefore, the difficult and sensitive problem of either obtaining or making what was required. In fact both avenues were used. Through an arrangement with the DPP's Office (Director of Public Prosecutions) a number of confiscated pornographic films were borrowed. Despite a thorough search through this material (quickly found by all of us to become both a boring and thoroughly unpleasant task; those who get their kicks from this kind of thing were certainly confirmed in our minds as sad and inadequate people!) we rated only a small amount suitable for our purposes. One of the main problems was of lack of standardization of participants and backgrounds: different films portrayed different people with different characteristics; relevant scenes, or more particularly shots, varied in length. This, of course, worked against the construction of standardized contexts and lengths of time for the stimulus presentation. Nevertheless, programmes were compiled and did prove to have some effectiveness, especially as the main object was not to obtain comparisons between individuals but to obtain comparisons within any one individual's range of reactions through the series presented to him, either clinically relevant or neutral (country scenes would be used for the latter). Comparative responses tend to be more meaningful than absolute ones and the main object was to discover whether a patient reacted more strongly to one situation than another and to assess the nature and content of these.

Inevitably this programme of clinical assessment and research gave rise to criticisms. It was not going to be possible to keep the work secret, nor was there any reason to do so. These were legitimate enterprises if the hospital's proper duty to its patients and to the public was to be fulfilled. There was a duty to return a patient to the normal world as soon as s/he was fit to do so and a duty to the public to ensure that there was minimal danger in so doing. Nevertheless, there was the inevitable public criticism raised in some quarters 'that patients were being subjected to, or allowed to indulge in, viewing of pornographic material' and that this must therefore be to their detriment; it would 'salaciously excite people already depraved in this respect.' There seemed to be an image of patients collectively enjoying pornographic films in the comfort of a TV lounge when, in fact, they were alone in a cubicle, linked up to a machine with electrodes attached to various parts of their anatomy, viewing short sequences of detached activity under staff supervision. This would be followed, moreover, in many cases, with a treatment programme designed to extinguish their 'depraved' responses and substitute normal ones.

Of further relevance was the opposite criticism that these people might be suffering insult and indignity; that the process was inhumane. This, indeed, was a possibility that had been envisaged and raised concern. Great care was taken to explain to a patient at every stage, therefore, what was going to be done, and why, and to obtain their signed consent to it. No doubt this could be said to have been obtained under duress, to the extent that all patients were in Broadmoor 'under duress', i.e.: not by their own choosing. At the stage in their careers when these research and treatment programmes were being carried out, however, all those who took part knew full well 'what the score was': that they were in Broadmoor because they had transgressed the law in a way and in a mental state for which they needed help to change. Not only were they agreeable to the procedures but most were eager to do whatever they needed to do to achieve a return to normality and the outside world. Despite this, and to re-emphasize, their knowledge was ensured at each stage and their consent gained to what was to be done. They could opt out at any point.

Probably public awareness and potential criticism was increased as a result of this work having been preceded by a programme that had been run for the treatment of sex offenders by the SHRU director at the time, Dr Gavin Tennent, and one of the Broadmoor consultants (RMOs), Dr Kyp Loucas. This had used methods being developed and clinically evaluated during that era involving both libido reducing drugs (e.g.: Benperidol and Cyproterone Acetate) and hormonal implants to reduce sex drive. These were assessed, compared and reported in a series of papers including the SHRU monographs. They were essentially a chemical form of castration, reducing both sexual ability and desire. They have their place, both for some patients totally and for others initially. At the time their long term effects were not known but certainly they seemed effective in the short term and enabled other strategies to follow. There were side-effects, some of them feminizing: men tending to develop breasts.

Like the comprehensive programmes being developed by David Crawford and later others, however, these procedures needed to be supplemented by other treatments to deal with the various social and emotional facets of sexuality that often underlie sexual dysfunction, as discussed earlier in this chapter. Often these facets may be the main reason for the offending and merely removing the ability to perform the sex act itself does not remove the need for love and affection and the mutual comfort and support through life which is the aim and aspiration of most of the human race. The motivation to associate with other people, especially a partner, in a loving relationship, is not removed by castration. Castration certainly removes the ability to inseminate and properly to copulate. It does not remove the need to love and be loved, to be near a loved one and share their joys and sorrows and to show that love through a bodily embrace. If the need is still strong, which it usually will be despite castration, and the sufferer is lonely, still craving the warmth and comfort of human contact, he will still strive to maintain a relationship that provides these essentials and, if inadequate or damaged in this department of his life, will still be prone to make a 'botch' of the process. He could still struggle in his inadequate ineptitude to obtain that all important physical closeness that confirms to him that a relationship exists. He could again be accused of a sexual attack even though technically incapable of actual rape.

So castration, too, would need to be part of a larger, more comprehensive restorative programme to enable a fulfilling normal emotionality to be achieved in relationships. In which case, it should be a reversible chemical castration and not a permanent physical one, so that a fully and mutually satisfying relationship can be the aspiration at the end of treatment.

Castration seems to be a recurring topic in public debates and invariably arises on TV chat shows whenever a fresh sex offence hits the headlines. It is still assumed by audiences to be the only proper answer to the problem of sex offending. They howl their appreciation of compères or panellists who urge castration upon sex offenders, failing to acknowledge the emotional aspects of the human sexual relationship and that sexuality comprises more than the sex act alone. The surprising thing is that so many of those audiences howling for castration are women who, on another chat show, in another context, are bewailing the inability of men to appreciate that sex is a tender, caring, emotional relationship as much as a physical event. Perhaps, in the frustration and anger of the moment, they feel that if a man is unable to appreciate and participate in the emotional element of a relationship then at least he should be prevented from imposing a callous and loveless physical assault upon them.

The confiscated pornographic material borrowed from the DPP's office was not in use for long. As already described, it was unsatisfactory aesthetically and methodologically and, although its use was defended, it was preferable not to have to use it. Gradually a more comprehensive, methodologically objective and ethically acceptable collection of material was assembled, both of a visual and auditory nature. David Crawford had spent a year visiting and working at Atascadero, in California, where Kevin Howells had worked earlier. This is an American near-equivalent to Broadmoor where Richard Laws had been pioneering innovative assessment and therapy for sex offenders. With his co-operation a British equivalent was drawn up in video format on David Crawford's return. It portrayed interactions of a normal affectionate sexual kind, an aggressively sexual kind and an aggressively non-sexual kind using the same participants for each and for the same standardized length of time. An independent sex therapy clinic collaborated in the preparation of what was required. This, therefore, allowed a more standardized comparison to be made of patients' reactions. Norms accrued from its repeated use, together with the other lab assessments, and joined with the rest of the growing bank of specially developed and researched methods of appraisal, description, categorization and explanation that were proving relevant for the problems of the Broadmoor population of patients.

EEG, NEUROPHYSIOLOGY AND NEUROPSYCHOLOGY

Partridge describes the advent of the electroencephalograph, or 'EEG' as it is always known, and speaks optimistically of its capacity to identify brain damage of various kinds, especially epilepsy. It is sometimes confused with ECT, through similarity of its abbreviation no doubt, and because electric currents are involved with both. However, the two are quite different. ECT, as described in Chapter 8, involves giving an electric shock to the brain to bring about a kind of fit and is a form of treatment. The EEG monitors the electrical rhythms of the cerebral cortex through miniature electrodes, causes no sensation and produces no 'fit', and is an assessment method, not a treatment. Different neural rhythms are found to occur in the cerebral cortex and to be characteristic of different activities and of the contrasting states of sleep and wakefulness, as well as varying in different people. Damage to parts of the cortex can show in the form of variations, or disruptions, of these rhythms and specific patterns have been observed to characterize the cortical rhythms of many epileptics. The procedure has, therefore, been of long-standing assistance in helping to identify the form, degree and location of some kinds of brain damage and of epilepsy.

Like any other method in psychiatry, psychology and their neurological counterparts, however, EEG identification is not 100% accurate. Abnormalities do not always appear in the EEG when one might expect them whilst, conversely, they sometimes appear with no apparent basis. Nevertheless, there is a sufficiently high degree of concordance to make the procedure and its expensive equipment a worthwhile investment for any large department of psychiatry. Furthermore, there are changes in the rhythms which occur under changing external circumstances that make it a worthwhile and relevant part of many assessment programmes to include these. Sleep and wakefulness have already been mentioned, so that medication-induced sleep may be one of these. Otherwise the standard ones are 'hyperventilating' (overbreathing), and a flashing 'strobe' light, both of which can induce fits in those prone to them. The accompanying changes in rhythms can therefore be observed.

Occasionally, in the special circumstances of Broadmoor patients, other situations would need EEG investigation, such as the effect of alcohol. A number of patients were on record as having committed their offences when large amounts of alcohol had been consumed. This is not a defence in law under the Mental Health Act but where the alcohol had been thought to have aggravated a psychiatric condition to the point of precipitating a catastrophic reaction the underlying mental disorder would be considered the reason for admission under the Act. It would subsequently then be relevant to assess the effect of the interaction of the mental disorder and excessive alcohol ingestion. Hence an EEG would occasionally be carried out whilst the patient consumed a succession of measured amounts of alcohol.

The obvious and growing need for EEG assessments in the Broadmoor context made it desirable to have the equipment available on site, rather than having to send selected patients elsewhere for this to be done. In this 'inter-acts' period, therefore, the equipment was obtained and installed in the medical centre. Instead of recruiting an EEG recordist, however, it was decided to send a senior staff nurse away to be trained to do the job. This would also provide the necessary escort for patients while undergoing EEG assessment. Jim Clarke, already a 'doubly trained' nurse (i.e.: with SRN as well as RMN qualifications), was the first member of staff chosen for the job, until he eventually became the first male nurse in the Female Wing, in Lancaster House, when mixed staffing of wards was introduced, as described earlier in this chapter. Bill Ferguson then followed him in the EEG recordist role, to be followed in turn by Neil Rattray.

During this period standard EEG assessments were obtained and provided for all incoming patients; others by referral when required. The evaluations required a report from a neuropsychiatrist and could not be provided by the EEG recordist, Jim Clarke or those who followed him, although all these people inevitably became very conversant with the varying patterns of EEG rhythms and could give an immediate impression of the findings if required. George Fenton, consultant at the Middlesex Hospital, provided the necessary reports. This was combined with use of the data in his larger research programme. When he, an Ulsterman, later moved to the post of Professor of Psychiatry in Belfast, the EEG reporting was continued by Peter Fenwick, but the two of them continued collaborative research which incorporated data obtained from Broadmoor. The research psychologist in their team, Rick Howard, spending increasing time at Broadmoor, eventually took over the EEG recordist role himself, thereby freeing a nursing post (patients always came over from the wards under escort anyway). His involvement eventually led to his own PhD on aspects of the Broadmoor work.

Some specific applications of EEG monitoring were developed. Changes in rhythms or wave forms resulting from carrying out a button-pressing task in response to an auditory signal was one. The EEG 'expectancy wave' arising from anticipating a required response is referred to as the 'contingent negative variation' and 'varies' amongst different people. The interest was in variations that might be specific to particular clinical groups as work in this area had shown differences in some of these, particularly some psychopathic sub-groups. These might then provide insights into their brain functioning or at least a means of differentiating them for diagnostic and prognostic purposes. The findings of different workers in different countries are not all in agreement but, as they have not all worked with the same populations (offender, mentally disordered, psychopathic, etc.), defined in the same way, under the same conditions or carrying out the same tasks, it is not easy to evaluate the reasons for the differences and whether they are significant or artefacts. As usual, research tends to raise as many questions as it resolves. Refinements of the tasks giving rise to the EEG responses will no doubt continue to reveal more interesting results.

Towards the end of this 'inter-acts' period, however, Rick Howard obtained some interesting results from studying the anticipatory EEG responses to a discriminatory task where a button had to be pressed in response to one signal but not pressed in response to another. His real life analogy was of traffic lights where one initiates action in response to the 'green' but inhibits it in response to the 'red'. Inhibiting action is, of course, a typical known difficulty of psychopaths and Rick Howard was excited to discover that, whereas most patients showed the expected differences in their EEG 'expectancy waves' under the contrasting conditions, some psychopaths did not: they tended to show the same kind of EEG wave response for both the 'stop' and 'go' situations. Were their brains failing to make the necessary distinction? And was a similar mechanism responsible for their failure to inhibit their actions in other life situations?

At the same time interesting related findings were emerging from some work on anticipatory perception and memory undertaken by Paul Devonshire and Carol Sellars in the psychology department. Errors on the part of some patients were not random and variable but tended to follow a pattern. Nor was the tendency an artefact of age or ability - it appeared also in groups of schoolchildren who were given the same tasks. Those showing the anomalous responses seemed to have some features in common with Howard's psychopaths. Devonshire, Sellars and Howard reported their findings at yet another annual conference of the BPS.

Intriguing results were occurring across a wide spectrum of activity and there were more people working at the problems than hitherto. Their principal responsibilities lay with the day-to-day clinical work of investigating the continual throughput of patients and carrying out treatment programmes, however and, as the succeeding chapters will describe, clinical teams were now being created. The menu of activities and demands was growing. The opportunity for research was limited and still seen as a luxury but the procedures on which reports were based were at least reflecting the advances in research based knowledge. Recommendations for discharge and transfer, and outcomes of MHRTs (Mental Health

Review Tribunals) had a growing range of findings and predictions available. The results should be showing in discharge success and a speed up in the movement of patients generally. That was if growing knowledge was paralleled with increasingly effective treatment which, as described earlier, did seem to be happening. Were there suitable places for special hospital patients to go when their treatment response warranted it? And would they be accepted?

SUMMARY

Familiarity with the workings of the 1959 Act, combined with increased national and international reporting of clinical and research progress, brought with it a greater pressure for staff to be involved in the organizational and training developments of their professions. More demands; less time.

As well as the discharge follow-up study reported in the previous chapter, progress was being made with new treatment methods. Research trials of these underlined the importance of combining more than one approach to a patient's problem, which in turn demonstrated that there was seldom merely one but usually several, linked and interacting problems needing attention, especially in the case of sex offenders. The hardly surprising trend of failure in generating and maintaining relationships also eventually brought mixed-sex group therapy. All this activity, and Broadmoor's high public profile, aroused the inevitable media attention and broke the tradition of media reticence.

Innovative treatments brought new assessment needs and were helped by the creation of another research project, this time of a 'psychophysiological' kind (as the laboratory technology now existed for measuring the sweating, breathing, pulse, penile and similar physiological reactions to emotional arousal). The stimulus material for these measurements was lacking and the initial use, on loan, of confiscated pornographic material proved unsatisfactory as it was not constant over the variety of situations needing to be assessed. An arrangement with a sexual therapy clinic, however, enabled a satisfactory set of assessment videotapes to be made.

A SHRU project in collaboration with one of the consultants at this time was assessing the use of 'libido' (sexual arousal) reducing drug treatments - a kind of temporary castration. This has enabled the point to be made that, once again, this needs to be combined with other treatments to deal with the emotional as well as physical, aspects of sexuality, a rather obvious factor overlooked by those who call for castration as the answer for sex offenders.

All this, of course, also gave rise to public criticism both that patients were being allowed to enjoy undesirable activities and that they might be having unacceptable procedures inflicted upon them. This chapter explains and defends what actually went on.

Finally, the contribution of the EEG is discussed. Broadmoor obtained its own equipment and trained its own nurse-recordist, so enabling routine assessments to be obtained for all new and referred patients. Advances in this technology were yielding greater clinical and research data. It was also used not merely as a measure of abnormal activity in the cerebral cortex but now as a measure of the changing cortical rhythms arising when carrying out various tasks. Interesting results were obtained, discriminating some sub-groups of psychopathic patients.

Questions are raised as to the consequences of these advances for the transfer, continuing care and subsequent acceptance of offender patients.

CHAPTER 18

THE VIEW FROM OUTSIDE

AS SEEN BY SUSANNE DELL

The research carried out by Susanne Dell, as part of SHRU, suggested 'yes': there were suitable places for patients to go but 'no': they were not being accepted. Her work was set up to investigate just this problem, for the experience of the special hospitals' RMOs (the consultant psychiatrists who, as responsible for the care and treatment of patients, were also responsible for recommending their eventual discharge or transfer) was that their patients were not being accepted by the rest of the NHS when they should have been; RMO recommendations were repeatedly being made and repeatedly refused.

Dell's research covered all the special hospitals and found some marked differences between the mentally ill offenders of Broadmoor and Park Lane Hospitals and the mentally handicapped 'civil' patients of Rampton and Moss Side Hospitals. The latter are not strictly the subject of this history but it is interesting nevertheless to note what Dell found in their respect, which highlights the difficulties of transferring Broadmoor and Park Lane patients.

The movement of consultant psychiatrists between posts understandably left many patients awaiting discharge or transfer. Fresh consultants needed time to get to know their patients and could not be expected immediately to accept the evaluation of a former consultant in such a serious matter with potentially dangerous outcomes. Similarly, there were differences in outlook between consultants, some being more ready to recommend transfer of their patients elsewhere than others. So far, nothing unusual or unexpected.

Dell then gave figures for the length of time patients had been waiting for transfer in the years 1976-79. In that time those who had been waiting for only a year or less dropped from 71% to 40% whilst those waiting for over three years rose from 3% to 22% (over seven fold). There were proportionate rises for those in between.

Susanne Dell selected for specific study a group of 161 patients, being all the patients approved for transfer by the DHSS on RMO recommendations in 1976. Ten per cent of the original admissions from which these were drawn were identified as not having needed to be in a special hospital in the first place. They were there, however, because no local hospital could be found to take them. If they had not been sent to a special hospital they would have ended up, even more inappropriately, in prison.

Where Dell's sample of 161 was concerned there was greater difficulty in transferring the subnormal and severely subnormal (as they were then called) because of lack of available places. Residential places for these patients were already reflecting the trend towards community rather than residential care. Whilst their facilities were improving, for those remaining (in terms of space, conditions and quality of care generally) there were far fewer of these places available. So patients who had completed what treatment they could in a special hospital context and were ready to move elsewhere, could rarely and only with great difficulty have places found for them. This is despite the fact that a greater proportion of these, by comparison with the mentally ill, were 'civil' patients, i.e.: had not been committed as a result of a criminal conviction.

For both types of patient, the convicted mentally ill and the 'civil' mentally 'subnormal' or 'handicapped', the same trend remained, however. The latter's more pronounced problems highlighted the problems for the former. Greater success was achieved in transferring all types of patient when the approach was made direct by the special hospital RMO. The potential receiving hospital's RMO would then visit to see the patient and discuss the matter, probably also bringing one or more members of his/her clinical team. Less success resulted from the more proper channel of an application through the DHSS who would then contact the hospital in the patient's catchment area themselves. This is not surprising, perhaps, but shows what Dell found throughout, that resistance was frequently not clinically defensible but arose from fear of the offender and the special hospital image. The occasion of a visit would afford the opportunity to demonstrate a patient's improved appearance and behaviour following treatment and emphasize that the original problems had now been resolved. In the end patients were successfully moved independently of the gravity of their original offences and their clinical histories. The slow movers were those where the consultant and/or clinical team had not visited; were without families to keep contact with them; and had spent a longer time in a special hospital.

Dell's work adds to the picture of the special hospital patient, Broadmoor included, and illustrates some of the problems of public *and professional* awareness and acceptance and, conversely, preconceptions and resistance, which Broadmoor encounters. Dell published her study in the SHRU monograph series, in a paper in the *British Journal of Psychiatry*, and in a chapter in the selfsame book edited by Gunn and Farrington which carried the initial report of my follow-up study of men discharged from Broadmoor. She had already completed projects for SHRU and continued to work on special hospital problems, in collaboration later with Graham Robertson. She typifies the period of growing research activity in conjunction with teaching hospitals and universities.

AS SEEN BY MARGARET NORRIS

Another view of the problems faced by patients leaving Broadmoor, this time in the community after discharge or transfer had been achieved, is afforded by a further follow-up study, this time by Margaret Norris.

One of the meetings and seminars at which the first follow-up study was reported, described in Chapter 16, was attended by Margaret Norris, a social psychologist at the University of Surrey who had studied the careers and characteristics of people discharged from various kinds of in-patient treatment for antisocial problems. It was opportune that she had just completed a project and was looking to start a new one. The Cropwood study suggested just such a possibility to her and her research proposal was accepted for funding by the DHSS. Her plan was to carry out a further follow-up of departed patients from Broadmoor, to include both the discharged and the transferred patients. This study would not replicate the Cropwood work but would take it forward by looking at the integration of patients into the community.

Whereas the Cropwood work was concerned, basically, to look at psychometric associations with post-discharge careers, Norris was concerned to look at patients' reported experiences and attitudes to their discharge and transfer. The discharged patients received the additional assessment of their individual adjustment which, of course, in contrast with the Cropwood study, would mean actually contacting them in person. This involved an interview but one which incorporated an objective measurement of integration, namely one using the repertory grid technique described in Chapter 13 for assessing treatment needs and responses. This method is, in effect, a structured interview, adaptable for many purposes according to the 'elements and constructs' that are included. (To recap: the people or circumstances are the 'elements' and the former patient's feelings or attitudes about them are the 'constructs'. These may be supplied either by the interviewer or the subject or may be a mixture of both.) It was therefore eminently suitable for the job and had, moreover, been used by Margaret Norris in previous studies where she had found the concept of 'self-esteem', as measured by the discrepancy between the 'actual' and 'ideal' self concepts, to be particularly important in reflecting the extent to which patients had successfully adjusted to new environments.

For a study that was to approach and interview former patients in person, great care had to be taken to ensure that they were agreeable. Similar care had to be taken, moreover, that their compliance or refusal was not known to their community supervisors in order that the study could not be said to have influenced the supervising relationship. Yet the supervisors also had to be agreeable to their charges being approached. A complex system of sealed letters and means of replying was set up.

The results of the Norris study were both interesting in themselves and different in many ways from the Cropwood study, which was not surprising as the two were differently designed and directed at different objectives. The Cropwood study certainly looked at overall success and failure rates but was concerned more to relate these to the criminological, psychiatric, psychological and social characteristics of the sample. The Norris study looked primarily at the results of the discharge provisions, their successes and their difficulties, and then looked at the attitudes and feelings of the discharged patients towards their circumstances and their needs. Some interesting findings resulted here, too, which are relevant to the story of Broadmoor and specifically, at this point, to discharge issues.

Fewer patients were discharged, per annum, in the period 1974 to 1981 comprising Norris's study, than in the period of the earlier study. The large accumulation of chronic and elderly patients had by then been transferred. Park Lane (now combined with Moss Side to comprise Ashworth Hospital, the 'Broadmoor of the North'), was open and taking patients from the northern half of the country as well as a good many of the overcrowded numbers from Broadmoor itself. Some RSUs were opening and taking patients who might otherwise have come to Broadmoor. Above all, this period was seeing the departure of many who had been admitted under the 1959 Act's provisions, whereas the Cropwood study's sample had mostly arrived before that, under the pre-war legislation. Different philosophies and practices had evolved.

The success rate of the Norris patients was slightly superior to the Cropwood sample - which is no doubt as it should have been with the benefit of time, experience and advancing knowledge: the Cropwood readmissions peaked in the first two years after discharge; the Norris ones not until the third year. In particular, the younger, psychopathic group did better. One 'political' point emerged which had already given rise to censure from the European Commission for Human Rights. The provision to recall patients under medical and social supervision who were showing signs of relapse could occur without any right of appeal. This situation was remedied in the 1983 Act. A smaller proportion left for the first time, many having already been discharged, returned and been discharged again. This was again an advance, emphasizing the nature of a hospital in contrast with a prison, enabling recovery to be tested and then reassessed and reinforced, if necessary. But it really needed some kind of appeal or review procedure to avoid charges of arbitrariness or abuse of the practice. The recalls, however, also emphasized the lack of any formal, organized rehabilitation, in an NHS hospital or anywhere else. This was only available to those who were transferred to such hospitals and therefore became their responsibility, not Broadmoor's.

There was a difference of perception of responsibility on the part of supervising doctors and social workers. Some felt their charges were not in need of medical supervision and only provided this because it was a condition of discharge. There was 'hostility and anxiety' on the part of some receiving doctors and nurses even though the study showed the ex-patients were no more troublesome than other groups. Some supervisors did not realize referral to the Home Office would bring them assistance; there was frustration over 'bureaucratic interference' and often it was also not realized that ending supervision was up to them. The later 1983 Act brought mandatory supervision for patients discharged from most compulsory sections but even then, problems were not entirely eliminated. There was a lack of awareness of what psychopaths needed: there were fewer psychopaths in rehabilitation programmes or sheltered workshops although they themselves said they would have welcomed this. Nevertheless, the psychopathic group had a better work record, despite more changes of job and accommodation: they stayed longer in their first job. The repertory grid results of the former psychopaths showed more associations with activity, proactivity and social activity than the former schizophrenics. This is not, after all, so unexpected and is, of course, relative: the former schizophrenics would still tend to show some chronic disability; the psychopaths would be more active *per se*, despite any residual antisocial trends.

Most post-discharge offences were similar to or less serious than original offences but the level of reoffending was, in any case, slight. Supervisors expected restriction orders to be important and to affect post-discharge careers but they seemed not to. Nor had they affected the discharge itself. Supervision was more important to success than restriction. Refusal of medication was associated more often with restriction orders. There was a lack of evidence for any benefit from longer stays in Broadmoor, the self-esteem scores from the Grid being better in those discharged earlier from NHS hospitals and poorer in the middle-aged groups who had stayed longer. The shorter stay patients also scored well on the integration measures, even though their rule-breaking scores were higher. In fact Norris found length of stay to be unrelated to any other measure, in contrast with the earlier Cropwood study, which suggested that patients did not need to stay so long in secure care.

This highlighted the 'tariff' principle that seemed to underlie a great deal of the thinking where the gravity of offence was concerned and which belies the principle that people who are so mentally disordered that they cannot be held responsible for their actions should not be punished for them. The tariff principle seems to be openly accepted today but was denied in the 1959 Act's time. It seems that the tendency for discharge recommendations to remain 'pending' in the 1970s until the lapse of what would have been the normal sentence for such an offence, is no longer necessary. The explicit recognition of the tariff principle is an abnegation of the old McNaughtan principles and their replacement by the ostensibly more enlightened and flexible mental disorder concept, which operates after conviction and not instead of it. This has paradoxically opened the way for changing times and changing administrations to put more punitively minded constructions upon the procedures.

There were some disconcerting findings with the non-whites in the sample. Whilst former schizophrenics received more post-discharge support and attention than their younger, psychopathic fellow patients, the non-white schizophrenics were the exception to this. Whilst it may be thought this might have been an age-related phenomenon, the non-whites being younger, the cynics will say it was a colour one. In any case, all groups should have received support, none should have been left without what would have helped ensure both their reintegration and public safety. Non-whites received more police attention and made more court appearances, again like the younger, white psychopaths, not like their schizophrenic counterparts. Yet the non-white group generally behaved more acceptably and were better integrated than their white counterparts.

On the 'repertory grid' assessments, associations were found with all groups for recall, relapse and recidivism. A lack of association between grid 'adjustment' indicators and various kinds of supervision and training was interpreted as a result of the lack of positive rehabilitation programmes available. A significantly disproportionate number of drinkers were associated with post-discharge offences, especially the more serious ones. They tended to be the younger, psychopathic ex-patients with a criminal history and, as above, with poorer quality aftercare. Leaving off medication was not associated with more incidents, however. Often they stopped when they should not have done or when they were seldom seen and supervised, so it would not seem that medication was no longer thought necessary; it seems instead to have been irrelevant, or at least a factor of much lesser importance in the overall discharge process.

Some hints at what might have been of greater importance emerged from further analyses of Norris's findings, including the 'grid' results. There was some evidence that supervisor rapport facilitated rehabilitation and none that it hindered it. Where disclosure of a patient's past was concerned (in which the supervisor would frequently have been involved) some discrimination exercised about this was associated with the best levels of self-esteem: either complete disclosure or none at all worked against self-esteem. This is important in that self-esteem was not high in those former patients in employment yet employment was strongly associated with successful integration, so any bolstering of self-esteem would be helpful. Another aspect of support was where the ex-patient lived. Hostels were the most often used form of accommodation yet these were associated with a greater likelihood of being involved in incidents. Even though living with relatives was associated with poorer 'grid' integration scores there was less likelihood of involvement in incidents in these circumstances. The family helps, it seems, even though the former patient may not like it and families may not be all that sympathetic! One problem with supervisors was that they too often changed. Families don't. Social work is a very fluid profession.

All in all many patients in Norris's sample did well, despite difficulties, and their careers after Broadmoor were better than before. Non-white patients did better, despite disconcerting the helping services and the police. Homicides caused the most anxiety but were the least likely to reoffend or be readmitted (in keeping with my own Cropwood study). The younger, assaultive, psychopathic and drinking ex-patients were the most troublesome. Norris criticizes 'labelling': the name sticks. She thinks it better simply not to use the Mental Health Act disorder category until much later in a patient's career. The community is scared of homicides and of psychopaths but these tend to be two different groups, not the same, and at the discharge stage neither of these 'labels' should be relevant if treatment has achieved the change necessary for discharge or transfer to have been recommended. Where there is an unusual combination of offender and disorder features, these are the ones that should receive special attention (again concordant with the Cropwood study's results).

Transfers to other hospitals, as a stepping stone to the

community, reveal that 10% had left hospital after 3 months; 22% after 6 months; 50% after 1 year and 80% after 2 years. NHS doctors thought these were long stays when 'civil' and non-sectioned patient stays were normally measured in weeks. For the special hospitals such periods are brief! Yet a long stay in Norris's sample was not associated with better outcome, rather the reverse.

Like the Cropwood study, more space has been given to Norris's work than to some others in this history of Broadmoor. There were, of course, numerous other important research developments in the 'inter-acts' period. Analyses of what happens when patients leave hospital, however, are rare, yet are crucial in indicating what is important and relevant about a patient's condition, treatment and aftercare. They are the 'acid test'. So there is no apology for selecting these works as illustrative of Broadmoor's progress and achievements. As with other research, however, this dip into Norris's findings can only give a flavour. Some results defy interpretation, others bear alternative explanations whilst yet others seem perverse. This only emphasizes the need for replication and for careful design, both in data gathering and analysis. Statistics don't lie, despite the jibe to this effect that unpalatable results attract. It is the understanding of them that may err - the conclusions people draw and the interpretations they make - and what will minimize this is an independent monitoring of research proposals and peer review of the results submitted for publication. Puzzling results may need presenting tentatively. Replication may be essential. But research is not a dispensable luxury. It is a basic necessity. It saves mistakes, misery and expense in the long run.

Again Margaret Norris published her full results, both in her report to the DHSS and in a book published by Gower in 1984: *Integration of Special Hospital Patients into the Community*. She put forward a proposal for a further study to replicate and extend the work and to include the other special hospitals, but this was not successful. It should have been, especially in the light of the scepticism expressed towards the initial work and what has been said about verifying unpalatable results. Susanne Dell's findings were critical, too, but the criticism was of the outside world, the world that should have been accepting special hospitals' patients but wasn't. Norris's work suggested there might be things about the special hospitals themselves, their formulations, treatments, decisions and disposals of their patients, that might need re-thinking. Maybe she just didn't express herself in the right way, or didn't discriminate sufficiently between the firmer and the more tentative findings. Maybe the importance she attached to alcohol abuse was given too much emphasis although, goodness knows, it emerged repeatedly from the analyses as a critical factor. Whatever it was, the work did not get the credit it deserved and, therefore, the further funding to carry it forward.

And perhaps further research is not the crucial issue? Do we really give enough attention to the research already undertaken, studying its findings and teasing out their meaning? The pressure to publish and enhance one's CV seems to override the more mundane task of scrutinizing what has already been done. Incorporating research results into the melting pot of clinical practice is the test of whether they are relevant. But it takes time for research to trickle through in this way. Practitioners need to be convinced and this is not surprising when wrong decisions can have fatal consequences.

Fortunately, as we shall see in the next chapter, clinical teams were on the way, pooling the information of different disciplines and supplying arguments to the DHSS and the MHRTs which would gradually improve the decision-making process. Fortunately, too, the 1983 Act was to raise aftercare to an official, mandatorily required level of importance. Unfortunately though, this has proved difficult to implement as the new Mental Health Act Commission found; it has been somewhat hit-or-miss because of its heavy demands upon supervisor contact and, hence, budgets.

Eventually, however, there must be further follow up studies of discharged patients in the community to see if new criteria and new procedures are working any better and what really are the most important factors.

SUMMARY

Complex and detailed research findings are difficult to condense for a chapter like this and even more difficult, therefore, to summarize. They have been selected for inclusion in this history, where many other researches have not or have merely been given passing mention, because they deal with how patients achieved (or failed to achieve) discharge or transfer and how they fared afterwards. This, above all, reveals how successful their stay in hospital has been and what helps to sustain or mar this success afterwards.

Susanne Dell described the difficulty and resistance met in trying to move special hospital patients to another treatment and rehabilitation setting, instead of directly into the community, in order to continue the treatment process and introduce the patient to situations more approximating the outside world. The difficulty was the same with civil patients as with offenders: the special hospital was the frightening element. The RMO was more successful when a personal visit was made with other clinical team members than when a request was simply made through the official DHSS channels, not surprisingly, but at the cost of precious staff time. At least this enabled reassurance that the patient had progressed and was not an ogre.

378

Margaret Norris researched the careers and attitudes of discharged patients by actually meeting and interviewing them (through a complex system of protected confidentiality for both them and their social worker supervisors). This work both supplemented and complemented the study described in Chapter 16 and was with a sample admitted almost wholly after the inception of the 1959 Act where the Cropwood study's patients had mostly arrived originally in the time of the pre-war legislation. Different discharge procedures and constraints also applied. Nevertheless, many of the same features emerged.

Crucial, however, in the Norris work, was the outcome of interviewing patients (where greater objectivity was achieved by use of the 'repertory grid' as an interview tool, illustrating a different application of it from that of Chapter 13 where it was introduced). Amongst a rich collection of findings, some obvious, some obscure, some reassuring but many disconcerting, the overall level of success was good, and encouragingly superior to the earlier 'Cropwood' group. A safer life was led by most. The former psychopaths did rather better than the former schizophrenics, despite receiving less aftercare supervision (which they would nevertheless have liked to have received). Self-esteem, as might be expected, but only now reliably measured by use of the repertory grid method, was of crucial importance. It was related to work success where, again, former psychopaths did rather better than others. Success was also better when a former patient had family contact and supervision, albeit often disliking it, rather than living in a hostel with social worker supervision, albeit appreciating it.

Length of stay in Broadmoor, in contrast with the Cropwood study, seemed unconnected with any aspect of success or failure, further undermining the 'tariff' concept in the case of people whose mental condition is supposed to have rendered this irrelevant. The role of medication seemed equivocal, many neglecting to take it without apparent adverse effect. Alcohol actually loomed larger in the failure rate than any of the more sophisticated factors, leading Norris to make recommendations which were much criticized; yet another case of 'shooting the messenger'? An application to carry out a more penetrating study encompassing all the special hospitals was turned down, some thought in consequence. Nevertheless, this form of monitoring of special hospital work must continue. It is the clearest way of demonstrating to government and public alike that the best and proper use is being made of expenditure and resources.

CHAPTER 19

MANAGEMENT UNDER SCRUTINY

CLINICAL TEAMS

The clinical team is now the accepted way of managing patient care. It was a necessity born of the increasing diversity of professions working in the clinical field and of the increasing specialization of the professional groups already there, including those within medicine and nursing themselves.

A team, however, implies collaboration, a sharing of information and responsibilities. In the hospital world, before teams, and particularly as described in Chapter 10 where Broadmoor was concerned, information and responsibility were the prerogative of the medical profession and, effectively, of the consultant psychiatrist, specified in the Mental Health Act as the RMO or responsible medical officer. He or she would gather information predominantly from his or her own examinations, or those of the registrars or house officers, possibly amplified by some specialist opinion from a visiting consultant, from x-rays, or from blood or other samples, all of which would give rise to a supplementary report for the case notes. Nursing notes were entered directly into the consecutive case note pages. The consultant would discuss all or any of these on ward rounds. Discussion with a specialist or the lab, if required, would be done by phone. So it would have been up to the consultant, the RMO, to inform him or herself for the decisions that needed to be made. The resulting treatment action would be the consultant's responsibility anyway, again specified in the Mental Health Act, whether carried out by him or herself or through registrars, other junior medical staff, nursing staff or non-medical specialists.

In 1959 there were only two consultants at Broadmoor and not enough other professional specialists to make more than a doubles team or a coxless pair. Those few who were there took their remit from the consultant, as with senior registrars or the social worker, or submitted the information they obtained to the consultant in the case of the nursing staff and the clinical psychologist.

By the middle of the 1970s, however, as well as Dr McGrath himself, there were now some six or seven further RMOs. This became enough effectively to allot a different consultant as RMO to each house. Still this did not lead explicitly to clinical teams, however, and it was a visit from the hospital advisory service (HAS), whose critical reports carried weight with district and regional health authorities (RHAs), that finally triggered the introduction of clinical teams. In the case of the special hospitals, the DHSS itself, of course, was the hospital management and was anxious to ensure its own hospitals set the example to the rest of the NHS and did not lag behind.

Where the nursing input to the team was concerned, each house had its own DN/DS (departmental nurse or sister, later nursing officer or NO) and each ward its own charge nurses or ward sisters, by now three, to cover the shift system under reduced working hours. Team coverage and representation was therefore no problem.

Where the occupations staff were concerned, following a number of key retirements, there was a considerable restructuring. First Mick Ball and then, after his sad death, Barry Goswell, as COO, headed a group of SOOs and OOs which gradually allowed representation in each clinical team.

Unfortunately, neither the social work, patients' education nor clinical psychology departments had sufficient numbers to allot someone to each team and had to do so on a one-to-two-teams basis. This made adequate availability difficult and was a constant source of irritation to the teams and their RMOs. There was pressure for the trainee clinical psychologists to be team members and even the psychological 'technicians', as they were called. These were psychology graduates but not clinically trained. A few were increasingly employed to learn to carry out routine assessment tasks and assist on treatment programmes when it became difficult to recruit to the basic and senior grade clinical psychologist posts. Rather than leave these posts vacant and risk losing them from the overall establishment, they were temporarily filled with graduates, who were plentiful and eager to gain experience towards being accepted on a postgraduate course. Because they stayed only a year or two, the post could be periodically readvertised in an attempt to recruit a qualified clinical psychologist. The profession was understaffed generally, unable to supply sufficient people for the country-wide demand, and closed institutions were becoming increasingly unpopular places to work. This was because of the greater attraction of the trend for organization of services within a District Health Authority (DHA) which could then offer a wide range of work with all age groups and specialisms.

Where the smaller professional specialisms were concerned, Broadmoor was fortunate to have attracted a group of people dedicated to this corner of clinical work but they were still not enough to provide someone for each team. The pressure to allocate trainees or new graduates to teams, without supervision from qualified practitioners, had to be constantly resisted. They could not be held legally responsible anyway.

Clinical psychology trainees were in any case only intermittently available as their training required them to cover spells in a variety of settings before they could sit their diploma or master's examinations. Training was increasingly organized on a regional basis and Broadmoor participated at different times in both the Oxford RHA in-service training scheme and the Surrey University postgraduate course. It also accepted trainees country-wide who wanted to spend one of their training options in special hospitals work and people were commonly attached from the Maudsley and Wessex courses as well as occasionally from elsewhere. This helped placate the hospital secretary, John Roberts by that time, after Eric Cooper's departure, who was sceptical of the outlay on a probationer post when the holder was elsewhere for much of his or her three years training. There was fortunately almost always someone else in place of Broadmoor's trainee, for whom some other authority was paying!

The reputation of the department was enhanced by this training exchange system and, even though many probationers were critical of the very different environment they found at Broadmoor, they were invariably fascinated by the problems posed. This has without doubt led to a substantial sprinkling of clinical psychologists throughout the NHS who have an understanding of the special hospitals' system and its problems. Many of these have gratifyingly since gone on to positions of seniority and influence elsewhere, whilst others, equally gratifyingly, have remained or arrived from elsewhere to give Broadmoor the benefit of their experience.

The problem of being unable to provide a person from every professional group to each clinical team persisted throughout the 'inter-acts' period and continued to be a cause for vexation. Inevitably clinical teams wanted to see themselves as an administrative unit, with team members accountable to the team rather than their own professional group. This might work where each profession supplies team members of a similar grade, as with medical consultants. Each team, for instance, comprised an RMO, a 'junior' medical member (who might also, incidentally, be covering another team), a nursing officer, charge nurse and staff nurses. These were professions which had all grades represented in each clinical team.

Occupations officers, social workers, and clinical psychologists, however, were organized on a 'pyramid' structure, with one chief, consultant or principal at the head and a series of increasingly less senior grades beneath. With the education department of four teachers they also had too few for one-per-team. Not only would a team have to tolerate, perhaps, a less senior representative of one particular profession in their team but that person would not necessarily be able always to offer the specialist expertise required or, if they could, they would be needed to offer it to other teams as well. It was a matter for the head of each discipline to find someone who could supply the range of experience or expertise for each team and this would not necessarily always come from the same person when they were not all of the topmost grades or of a similar range of experience or specialist interest.

Management of clinical services, therefore, had to remain with the head of the discipline concerned and not with the clinical team. In the case of clinical psychology, one qualified person was allotted to a pair of teams with a trainee or technician, who was also having to cover several teams, available as back up. The essential advantage of the team arrangement, however, was that someone was available to attend the team meetings; contribute information and participate in the discussions; note the priorities requiring attention; advise on suitability and availability for that attention; arrange for someone to provide this; advise on the likely timetable; and discuss the outcome with the rest of the team.

Inevitably the creation of a team arrangement raises the question of who is to be the team leader. This was not a problem for the psychiatric profession which simply pointed to the Mental

385

Health Act's designation of the consultant psychiatrist as 'responsible medical officer' who decided on the treatment and when it was completed. This would seem to be a conclusive argument, despite the parallel but separate responsibilities accorded to the social work profession in both the 1959 and 1983 Acts (particularly where compulsory admission to hospital was concerned). It became difficult to accept, however, when a particular RMO did not fully consult with the team, ignored advice, or otherwise failed to enjoy the team's confidence or convince them about his or her decisions.

A particular problem arose when a course of treatment or training was decided upon that was to be carried out by a non-medical member of the team. That person was legally responsible for what was done. The RMO, however, remained responsible for the overall care and treatment of the patient although, in this situation, would not be competent to judge when the treatment had been completed. Ideally the clinical team would review the progress of each patient regularly and be advised of the timing of any phase of treatment. They could also see the patient for themselves and reach their own decision, although patients, particularly at special hospitals, are notorious for maintaining they are making better progress than they actually are. In technical matters it would be difficult and inappropriate for an RMO to make an independent decision where use of technical material or laboratory equipment was involved, such as that described in Chapter 17.

A variation of this problem would arise when a change of treatment was effected. Autocratic RMOs have been known to do this when another team member was still carrying out an as yet uncompleted course of treatment or had reached a particularly sensitive phase of a programme which it could be harmful and, therefore, unethical to interrupt. This even extended to occasions when a patient was transferred to another house or even another hospital in the middle of someone else's treatment programme, leaving critical clinical issues unresolved or the patient in a state of conflict. Some treatments can be stopped or transferred to another location at any time, such as medication, relaxation training or an educational programme. Others can't, such as a programme for extinguishing one focus of sexual arousal (say children) and replacing it with another (a mature consenting adult): sexual arousal cannot ethically be left undirected, without any source of attraction.

The RMO who made decisions independently of the team might charitably be thought to be following a habit from the days when this was the custom and there was little alternative. As time went on, fortunately, teams worked out practices for themselves and generally avoided head-on clashes but, whereas elsewhere in the NHS it gradually became less unusual to find clinical teams in specialist areas or units led by professional members outside medicine, the 'sectioned' and usually 'restricted' nature of special hospitals' patients has continued to mean the RMO remains the team leader[1]. Whilst some might feel relief that they did not have to bear sole responsibility for potentially life-threatening decisions and would have welcomed the chance to share this burden with the rest of the team, this seemed not to be the view of the Broadmoor consultants at that time. Perhaps it was seen as a sign of weakness (in my view it is the opposite) or maybe an abrogation of professional responsibility. Ironically, I remember seeking the views of my colleagues at our own departmental meeting on one occasion, only to be told by one colleague that this was my

---

1.   Since drafting this a government white paper has appeared which proposes changing 'responsible medical officer' to 'clinical supervisor' for the purpose of widening the range of professions fulfilling the role. It remains to be seen, at the time of writing, whether this is enacted in subsequent legislation.

responsibility and this was the reason I was paid a higher salary than he was!

THE BREAK-UP OF THE OLD UNITARY HOSPITAL

One of the consequences of clinical teams, or perhaps of the expansion in numbers of consultants who then each had responsibility for a house (a building of three wards, it should be remembered), was the break up of the old format of a unitary hospital. Partridge describes an institution which, for all its shortcomings, enjoyed a corporate spirit. The medical superintendent was in charge, not only of the administration but of clinical responsibility for the entire patient population. As both the 1959 Act and Dr McGrath himself entered their final years, the expansion of consultants and the move to clinical teams meant that each team area, each house (or wing in the case of the female side), achieved clinical autonomy. This meant that each team wanted to provide its own complete service, receiving patients from the admission unit, treating them comprehensively from start to finish and then discharging or transferring them.

The notion therefore faded of a unitary hospital providing a series of progressive environments through which patients moved. Certainly some facilities remained: an admission unit; a maximum security sector; an 'adolescent' ward. Norfolk and Monmouth (later Somerset) Houses (formerly Blocks 1 and 6) subsumed these among other functions, served by consultants who also had responsibilities elsewhere. But the 'big blocks' of Kent, Dorset, Gloucester and Cornwall Houses all tended, under their respective RMOs, to become mini-hospitals independent of each other and no longer inevitably feeding their patients on to, ultimately, Essex House, the parole house.

Each of these former 'front blocks' now set up their own rooms with parole-type facilities and privileges and their clinical teams, understandably, wanted to complete their work by seeing their patients go out of the gate, either to the community or another hospital. No doubt this represented an advance and certainly it was beneficial for each house to have its clinical team which could give closer attention to its residents' needs than the former, sparser staff could ever have done. But the divisions also broke up the sense of community that had characterized the old hospital. There had always been the 'block concerts' and inter-block competitions of various kinds but these were insufficient to outweigh the sense of separation and independence that arose from each team aiming to provide the majority of its clinical services within its own house and staff capabilities.

The chaplain's office, which had always co-ordinated recreational events, had given way to an 'activities department' headed by a nursing officer with supporting staff. Outside working parties had dwindled from some half dozen in 1959 to just one by the start of the 80s but, instead, there were many more internal events of a hobby, recreational and sporting kind, again devolved to house level. Flowers and vegetables at the annual show gradually dwindled as gardens fell out of favour in the face of competition from the growth of educational and recreational hobbies and the fatal grip of television. Music, painting, drawing and writing took the place of garden produce at the Annual Show and, together with the increasing numbers of handicraft exhibits, provided the competition pieces and exhibits instead. Outings and visits by small groups from all the new team areas became a regular feature of hospital life, carefully selected and supervised by staff familiar with them. All these gave some continuity to the community pattern but somehow on a more 'disconnected' scale. The growing autonomy of the houses and their clinical teams tended to break up the unity of earlier years and created the impression of a number of disparate units and activities.

Once again it seemed that a 'knight's move' had occurred: two steps forward and one sideways. Important clinical advances had been achieved within a medical model, facilitated by pharmacological advances and as intended by the 1959 Act, just as it was emerging that this was not the whole story. Developments and changes were also needed at a personal, familial and social level to enable a patient to meet and deal with everyday eventualities in an often new and fundamentally different way from that which had led to the catastrophic damage in their former lives. After dealing with the confusion of psychosis which might either have been a cause, an element in the cause, or an effect, there was an urgent need to acquire new strategies for dealing with the demands of their lives. These needed, therefore, as well as medicine, the means and the help to recognize what was required, work out a new way of life for themselves and then perfect it so as to be discharged without hazard to those they had formerly endangered. This requires hard work on the part of both patient and therapist. It is not achieved simply by sitting in groups chewing over problems, although this plays a part. As has been said already in this history, it also needs intensive practice, in the manner of an athlete or musician.

Just as all this was becoming clearer, however, the larger community of the hospital that could have incorporated such a paradigm or philosophy within its traditional scope was becoming divided into a collection of clinical clones, each containing treatment within itself and using the hospital's wider potential simply as 'time off'. The expansion of medical and nursing knowledge and resources was the knight's leap forward. The fragmentation of the hospital, its division into autonomous units and its ambivalence towards the growth of psychosocial concepts and methods of service delivery, were the sideways jump. To straighten out the crooked leap there needed to be a comprehensive strategy that combined modern medicine with social, psychological, educational and occupational approaches to the changing of life-styles. Services for these latter aspects of therapy had no sooner been brought into existence than they were subordinated within an expansion of medically oriented thinking. To give them expression required a degree of assertiveness and protest that inevitably led to conflict instead of the collaboration that should have marked their arrival and the advancing interest of the patients. The growth of the hospital concept had been achieved at the expense of the former Broadmoor community. Could the development of competence be delivered together with the treatment of disorder which was the hallmark of the former environment, albeit primitively expressed? At the time of the change-over to the 1983 Act the answer seemed to be 'no', or at least only partially 'yes', judging by Dell's and Norris's findings from their studies described in the previous chapter; and judging, too, by the difficulties that have ensued with the movement into a wider use of community care for people, many of whom are not yet ready for it and which does not provide the comprehensive treatment package needed.

MANAGEMENT TEAMS AND COMMITTEES

The team concept was not confined to clinical areas. It was incorporated, rightly, into the overall hospital management structure itself. A hospital management team was created, comprising the physician superintendent, the chief nursing officer (CNO) and the hospital secretary (later known as the hospital administrator). At the time these were Pat McGrath, Jim Clarke and

John Roberts. Jim had progressed from his appointments as the first EEG recordist, and then the first male nurse in the Female Wing, to succeed Tom Smith who, in turn, had succeeded Tom Sands. By now the nursing officer structure had meant the disappearance of a separate matron in the Female Wing and no successor followed Mary Osborne on her retirement. SNOs became responsible for groups of houses, male and female alike, with NOs in each house and several CNs (charge nurses) or WSs (ward sisters) on a shift basis for each ward. Offsetting the break up of the hospital into mini-hospitals, the Female Wing became a closer part of the overall establishment, with a man, Derek Crosweller, as its first SNO.

The hospital management team (HMT) was essentially a compact management unit for dealing with immediate everyday internal and external issues of an administrative nature. It could not adequately respond to the more long term policy matters concerning the rationale of the hospital or accommodate the information and views of the rest of the hospital on these matters. To this end there was the medical advisory committee (MAC) which comprised all the RMOs (consultants) and a representative of the 'junior' medical staff (commonly a senior registrar). To pass on information to and draw in views from the other disciplines there was created a heads of departments committee (HoD) chaired by Dr McGrath and including the other HMT members together with the heads of social work, occupations, education and psychology, the chaplain and librarian, a representative of the MAC and, as secretary, the senior executive officer (SEO) who headed the medical office.

The MAC clearly co-ordinated medical policy for the hospital and discussed matters of organization of the team areas, more than which it is difficult to say for one who was not a member of it. Actually there was a point at which my inclusion was mooted but I declined, being of the view that all professional groups needed the opportunity to discuss matters of importance to themselves by themselves. Whether the invitation was a compliment or a strategy to suppress my periodic protests and opposition, I was never quite sure!

Instead, first a clinical advisory committee (CAC) and then a professional advisory committee (PAC) was formed to try to give coherent voice to the views and information of the other professions in the hospital. The CAC included not only the non-medical professions but also nursing and an SNO was appointed to it. The idea was to provide an equivalent group to the MAC. However, it was pointed out that the nursing profession had its own forum through the CNO's meetings with his SNOs. The PAC therefore replaced the CAC to represent the non-medical and the non-nursing professions. This group usefully discussed the matters of concern arising from the HoD meetings and generated issues of its own concern. However, it was pointed out, quite logically, that if it were equivalent to the MAC then it should send only one representative to each HoD meeting, like the MAC. (This was before the HMT was additionally formed. When that happened, and a more formalized structure related to it through the HoD meeting, the PAC was wound up.) The professional groups it represented, with medical and nursing representations as well, were all represented at HoD, the justification for this being that the PAC members each headed a different discipline within the hospital. The MAC and the CNO's meetings each represented only the one professional discipline, of course.

The HoD meeting, therefore, was the essential policy-making committee for the hospital as it included all disciplines. Initially, before the creation of the HMT, it was very much an earpiece and mouthpiece for Dr McGrath who, as physician superintendent, made it clear that he saw its function as a channel of information between himself and the rest of us, so that he knew what was going on in the hospital and could tell us what we needed to know about his and the DHSS's planning and policies. He was always courteously concerned to know our views, which he clearly valued, but also made clear that responsibility for decisions was his own alone, whether or not he had our support. If something went wrong it was his head on the block, not ours. On the other hand, if things went right, he would be the first to give credit where it was due.

Dr McGrath always stressed the importance of being kept 'in the picture' on any matters that might rebound on him as head of the hospital. He respected professional independence and could accept differences of opinion but was understandably embarrassed if the first inkling he had of anything came to him by way of a question from HQ as to what was going on. He would come on the 'phone, sometimes in sorrow, sometimes in anger, complaining of the difficult position it put him in. Most of the time we were all only too happy to comply and let him carry the responsibility! Occasionally, however, something which had seemed too trivial to bother him with would re-emerge in another context with unexpected consequences. Perhaps we had been asked from DHSS headquarters for a psychological definition of, say, a psychopath. It could then perhaps have been applied to a particular patient being considered at HQ for discharge and interpreted in a way that contradicted an RMO's report. Misunderstandings would arise, awkward questions would be asked and the angry 'phone call would follow.

After the creation of the HMT and clinical teams, and the short life of the CAC and PAC, the proceedings of the HoD's meeting became more democratic, with consensus more often sought although, even then, votes and majority decisions did not occur; the responsibilities of the HMT and RMOs were still paramount. Contentious issues were taken away for consideration by HMT from which they would re-emerge later, resolved we knew not how but usually cautiously.

THE DHSS 'OFFICE COMMITTEE'

However, by this time the role of the DHSS was emerging more prominently. Previously this had been simply the superintendent's line of communication with headquarters but now it became more an avenue of discussion and negotiation, HQ clearly being concerned to know what the whole hospital thought rather than just the 'old man'. 'HQ', of course, meant a branch at DHSS which dealt with special hospitals matters within a division that dealt with mental health. The immediate administrator was the assistant secretary who headed the special hospitals branch, whilst the under secretary who headed the mental health division chaired the six-monthly meetings of what was first called SHOC (the special hospitals office committee) and then, simply, OC, the office committee.

The six-monthly meetings involved a look at any aspect of the hospital that needed it or had figured in some report or recommendation; together with a meeting with the local branch of the prison officers association (the nursing staff's union; see below), and another with the HoD committee. For this each head of discipline had to prepare a report, submitted to SHOC in advance, which could then be discussed at the meeting. From the tone of the questions and the reactions to the discussion, HQ, or SHOC, were clearly concerned to know what everyone thought and paid careful attention to all points of view. One would like to think they had been impressed with the cogency of what had been submitted to them and, indeed, they gave every impression of this. They also repeatedly countered attempts by the RMOs to crowd out an issue by encouraging views from others, apparently

395

expecting alternative views to be forthcoming, but often finding that people were reluctant to develop contentious issues in the open forum of the SHOC meeting.

Mental health division was, of course, the origin of any changes in policy that governments effected and was the initiator of lesser administrative changes that inevitably occurred from time to time. In this they had access to national advice from all the professions represented in the special hospitals, having their own appointees for the principal ones such as medicine, nursing and social work and advisers on others. May Davidson, at Oxford, was for many years the psychological adviser.

There was no such equivalent to SHOC at the Home Office, Broadmoor being the administrative responsibility of the Department of Health. A Home Office division, however, had responsibility for decisions on admitting and discharging patients, other than the 'unrestricted' ones, and so close liaison was maintained by the hospital with them and between them and the DHSS special hospitals branch.

After the change of government in 1979 it gradually became clear that a major change of policy was taking place, apparently giving heads of disciplines a wider range of control over matters within their field of responsibility. This was generally welcomed throughout the service. Unfortunately it turned out to look very much like a back door method of cutting down on staff and, therefore, expenditure. Where hitherto we had been supported from the hospital's finance, personnel and supplies sections for our budgets, recruitment and equipment, merely putting in applications for the necessary action or expenditure (supported with analyses and arguments, of course), now we were expected to manage the budgets and the processing for ourselves. Working to our own budget, albeit set by the hospital finance officer, was reasonable. It allowed us to choose to use, for instance, less expensive forms of travel and accommodation and so make the budget go further for more purposes. Previously one tended to claim the standard rate, regardless, because the claim was being met from an overall hospital budget managed from the finance office. We could also weigh up between ourselves the pros and cons of several equipment needs within the budget allocation, instead of just putting in a bid for each one in turn and not knowing if and when each would be forthcoming.

The extra control, however, was to be set against the extra office work in managing the budget (and supplies, equipment and personnel). This might have been acceptable if we had been given extra staff for the extra work and to make up for the incursions into clinical time. However, this was not to be; it would merely have spent on the roundabouts what had been saved on the swings. The change was increasingly seen as a cynical ploy to save administrative costs, not to give us more control over our own affairs. Protests that the work resulted in further incursions into clinical time only brought the response that we must scrutinize our schedules and become more efficient. Because, by this time, as mentioned in Chapter 17, professional prominence had meant that demands were escalating for inputs to all manner of professional activities and, as well as the ones away from Broadmoor, there were also the escalating and unavoidable mail and 'phone calls coming into our office, this suggestion struck very hard. The result was a rather bitter comment in one of my semi-annual reports to the office committee that: 'it seemed we were having to spend more and more of our time doing things outside our professional competence, for which we were not trained and which we had not chosen, at the expense of the things within our competence, for which we were trained and which we had chosen.' It wasn't that I minded management and administration, I even fancied I made a good job of it, but it had to be done without any extra help and at

397

the expense of the service to patients. Since this couldn't be allowed to happen and kept on coming anyway, it just meant working more hours at Broadmoor and doing even more work at home.

The ultimate result of this state of affairs would be (and was beginning to be seen by the time the 1983 Act arrived) that services such as clinical psychology would come from independent providers whose cost would be the greater because it would include the cost of administrative, equipment and training back-up incurred by the independent company in running itself. I preferred that the money should go to the in-house service and be managed from within an adequately staffed and backed up organization. Outside contractors don't feel part of the organization and the organization doesn't see them as such, which they need to be if they are to be effective.

By and large, however, visits from the HQ office committee were welcomed. It was always an opportunity to make our progress and needs known and one felt there was a sympathetic reception to ideas, in contrast with the wariness with which one's suggestions were met within the hospital by this time (which was in contrast, again, with the more open minded reception of the early years of the 1959 Act). No doubt our critics would say that this was due to being fed up with the badgering we gave them. Compared with the authority accorded to the medical profession and the numerical superiority of the nursing staff, however, the rest of us had to survive on our powers of persuasion and on driving home the relevance of what we did. Whilst we ourselves might have seen this as paramount, the assumptions of the traditional medical and nursing approaches meant that the information and services requested from us were seen as subsidiary and supplementary, not central and complementary. We were clearly now growing too big for our boots in wanting a greater say in clinical decisions and management.

THE PRISON OFFICERS' ASSOCIATION (POA)

Despite Broadmoor being often regarded as a prison and its patients called 'prisoners', surprise is often expressed that the staff union is the POA. By the time someone has reached the point of finding this out perhaps they have already realized that Broadmoor is a hospital. Anyway, the tradition derives from the time Broadmoor, although always a hospital (or 'asylum'), was administered from the Home Office and its staff were aligned with the rest of the Home Office's establishments. The staff had, therefore, always been represented by the POA in its negotiations over salary and conditions and, despite the change of management with the creation of the NHS and then the Mental Health Act, had never seen any necessity to change what was an advantageous arrangement.

A history should dispassionately recount events but invariably, unavoidably and permissibly includes evaluations, and hence opinions, on what it describes. This is acceptable - indeed it would otherwise be very dull - so long as the facts and the opinions are clearly distinguished from each other. This is not easy, and what one person sees as facts will often tend to be seen by others as opinions, or at least coloured by opinion. In arriving at the topic of the POA it is almost impossible to satisfy everyone's idea of what is fact and what is opinion. Yet the subject must be covered as it bears so strongly on Broadmoor's way of life. At the same time, just as I was not acquainted at first hand with what was discussed at the MAC, or HMT, or at the DHSS, I had no first-hand acquaintance with the deliberations between the hospital management and the local POA. I did, of course, receive plentiful accounts of what each side thought, simply because they were widely discussed throughout the hospital and because their outcomes were relevant to how I and my colleagues were going to be able to fulfil our duties. It was important, therefore, for those of us who worked there but were members of neither the POA nor management to be able to react to their discussions and to express opinions on anything that affected our work.

The POA's main concerns were, of course, appropriately the welfare of their members: salary and the special hospitals' 'lead' payment, in line with national increases, cost of living, etc, and working conditions. All these were, of course, inseparable from considerations of security. Even accepting Dr McGrath's principle that the best security was a thoroughgoing knowledge of one's patients, there were procedures to be followed with regards to movement of patients from A to B; the degree, duration and time of day of patient mingling and access to recreation, their rooms, ward facilities and so on; parole procedures; visiting other wards; the list is endless. This was a high security hospital caring for patients who had done violent harm to be there in the first place, many of whom were liable to do something harmful again. There had to be procedures for anticipating and preventing violence within the hospital and dealing with it if it occurred.

All this was the proper concern of the POA and it did not make the hospital a prison to be so concerned although, if security was not discussed in tandem with treatment, there was always the danger that the difference would be imperceptible, as many patients clearly felt. Life could certainly not be compared with the rest of the NHS's psychiatric hospitals or units. In fact, the rest of the NHS was able to be different largely because the special hospitals existed to cater for those who could not be treated elsewhere. Usually, the independence from both prisons and traditional psychiatric hospitals could be judged by the comments of visitors:

those from the prisons commented that it was more a hospital than a prison; those from hospitals said it was more a prison than a hospital.

After the second world war changes had rapidly taken place: forming the NHS; transferring responsibility for Broadmoor from the Home Office to the Ministry of Health; the 1959 Mental Health Act, etc. The staff with everyday responsibility for the secure care of patients were faced with many changes which required guidance and rulings as to what the new procedures were to be. Previously the senior nursing staff - the 'principal attendants' formerly and then the 'departmental nurses' - had had the responsibility for determining the day-to-day procedures. There was effectively no one else, given the many duties of the sole consultant psychiatrist - the medical superintendent. After 1959, however, the rationale was changed and the responsibilities reallocated, except that there were only, at first, three consultant psychiatrists where there had been some ten DNs (allowing for each block, male and female, and a night superintendent). DNs were perplexed because the decisions they previously made still needed making but were liable to be overruled when the few available consultants got around to being aware of what needed deciding. Furthermore, there were no new sets of rules or guidelines, apart from the Act itself. Were they to do as they had always done or something different and, if different, then what? Of course, they tended to do as they had always done, until told differently.

Being overruled, however, and not just occasionally, caused loss of morale, frustration, friction and was a threat to status and authority. There was an understandable groundswell of requests for guidelines as to how the new legislation was to be operated. Unfortunately, these were not forthcoming. Dr McGrath's response was that the senior nursing staff should 'use their clinical judgement' according to circumstances. He always maintained that this would afford the staff the freedom and autonomy that their status warranted. Unfortunately, this was to overlook the long line of communication in nursing management and the threat to professional status posed by countermanding the clinical decisions of nursing line managers. Doubt, uncertainty and eroded morale were the result. Dr McGrath would have done better to recall his military background and the military parallels he had drawn with the hospital staffing structure. A new 'drill book' was needed. Operating the 1959 Mental Health Act was radically different from what went before.

A new Act of Parliament with a new patient philosophy, a recently arrived physician superintendent, new consultants who took responsibility for matters previously the domain of the nursing officers; all these were upheaval enough. Whether they were sufficient to account for the subsequent suspicion and militancy of the POA is difficult to say. Probably not. The POA would probably maintain it was their duty to be suspicious and militant. However, there is little doubt that the changes of the 1959 Act fuelled the situation.

At a factual level, the POA was frequently in conflict with the management, i.e.: Dr McGrath and the HMT, locally, and the office committee at headquarters. Its periodic industrial action when some incident occurred was usually of the work-to-rule kind, mainly consisting of banning the essential overtime by which the various activities such as education, occupations, recreation and visiting were maintained. Patients would spend more time locked in their wards as a result.

At an opinion level, it would seem that these problems and disputes, although ostensibly relating to working conditions, were really the result of the POA seeing the balance of their role as more concerned with hospital security and public safety and only delivering treatment once a secure framework had been established.

This, of course, was to see 'treatment' as only the delivery of medicines and ECT and not the wider 'adaptation to life' that was to amplify the treatment ethic in the following decades. And yet, prior to the 1959 Act, the old asylum philosophy had been essentially that of a slow change of life-style with only some occasional assistance from medicine. The 'knight's move' to a medical philosophy must surely be held accountable for some of the POA reaction: medicine was now to achieve security, where previously security was achieved through change of life-style within a system of imposed control. Dr McGrath's view (as mentioned already), was that good security resulted from good knowledge of one's patients and that this knowledge comes from therapeutic interaction with them, not merely from observing them on the ward and about the hospital. Put this way, probably neither side would disagree. However, it is disappointing to recall the comments over the years that too many ward staff remained remote from patients, neglecting to use the long hours on the wards to interact with patients and thereby help them to achieve the change of outlook and behaviour that would help their progress towards discharge.

Disputes certainly affected the well-being and working lives of all staff. Conflict and argument tended to recur repeatedly throughout this 'inter-acts' period, especially when working conditions changed or an escape or other incident occurred. These invariably gave rise to an inquiry, of varying levels of prominence and publicity ranging from an HQ committee to a full-blown public inquiry, such as the time when Broadmoor's security was included in the remit of a government committee under Lord Mountbatten.

There is no doubt that a large staff such as that of the special hospitals needs a staff association that can represent their concerns and disputes over employment. So few were the other professions in 1959 that the POA was the only association represented on the local Whitley Committee for negotiating staff salaries and working conditions. It was customary then for each NHS Whitley committee to comprise only one staff association. As time went on, however, more staff of different disciplines, and hence different unions, came to work at the special hospitals and this gave rise to difficulties where representation was concerned. Still the nursing staff were by far the largest group and it would have been ridiculous to try to have a number of other representatives in the face of this disproportion. In any case they were represented through other Whitley committees at a national level. There was never any question of including the BMA for the medical staff on the local Whitley, for instance. Psychologists' conditions were negotiated on a Whitley council also representing biochemists and biophysicists in the NHS. The union in this case was first the AScW, which became the ASTMS and was later incorporated into the MST union.

A problem with staff employment is that there will often be one body that sets and monitors standards and another that negotiates working hours and conditions. With doctors the Royal Colleges and the GMC constitute the former and the BMA the latter. With psychologists the former is the BPsS and the latter, for the NHS, the MST. For the nursing profession the same body fulfils both functions, i.e.: the Royal College of Nursing (RCN) although there were in those days other unions that could also represent nurses together with other NHS staff, such as COHSE (Confederation of Health Service Employees) and NUPE (National Union of Public Employees), nowadays UNISON. The special hospitals nursing staff were unique in being represented by the POA and towards the end of this 'inter-acts' period there gradually emerged a tendency for some staff to prefer to belong to the RCN although this, too, created conflict.

At one point towards the end of the 1959 Act's lifetime there arose a dispute concerning the presence of female staff on male wards and the movement of women about the male side of the hospital generally. Two social workers, one male, one female, had been visiting a male parole patient during the evening. The patient had been studying for a social sciences degree. This visit would nowadays, in the NHS generally, be encouraged as a rehabilitative initiative but was not an accepted, or more importantly negotiated, practice in Broadmoor at that time. Whether the visits had been properly notified to the house nursing staff I do not now recall, and probably there was disagreement over the precise purpose of the visits. The patient was, in any case, a former psychopath over whom there was disagreement as to whether he had 'matured' and genuinely changed: he had been prominent in the earlier 'revolutionary' period described at the end of Chapter 15 and aroused sharp divisions in staff opinion. This social worker initiative would have been appropriate encouragement for his changed way of life but aroused misgivings with many nursing staff concerned with the wider issues of hospital security routines and schedules.

It took a long time to establish that monitoring and reinforcing a treatment schedule might entail 'shop time' staff attending an evening function and this often seemed to arouse curiosity, even resentment, in those working 'shift time'. Leaving late in the evening would often attract comment from the gate staff such as 'time owing?' and conversely a late arrival would be met with 'time in lieu?' As with most things in an institutional regime, it usually avoided trouble later to advise in advance that something out of the ordinary was planned. If one assumed this was acceptable, rather than asking if it was, it was generally accepted and even championed later as an innovative idea to the credit of the ward staff.

Anyway, the evening visits by the two social workers were unfortunately not seen in this way and resulted in draconian measures from the POA. All women were banned from the male side of the hospital. As women secretarial staff working with the RMOs had to go through the male side corridors and cross the terrace to the portacabin accommodation of the medical staff, this action entailed their having to be escorted on this route. Then there was a problem with student nurses (some of whom would be women) and their tutors (one of whom was a woman) visiting male wards as part of their training. An exception had to be made, therefore, but not until much negotiating had taken place. Women social workers, teachers, psychologists and researchers, of whom there were a good many by now, were also excluded from working on the male side of the hospital, it being said that they should work on the female wards and men work the male wards. This was impossible as the psychology department, for one, actually had a majority of women at that time and could not have maintained a service to the male wards of the hospital with men only. In any case treatment dealing with relationship problems needed to mix patients and staff of both sexes. This dispute dragged on and was the cause of many of the professional staff deciding to join a civil service union, IPCS (Institute of Professional Civil Servants), which could deal with problems in government department settings. Even then, the situation was only slowly resolved and normal practices resumed.

Disputes and staff action are an inevitable if regrettable fact of life in any large organization, and especially so in those days. Change is a painful business within a long-standing traditional establishment, especially with the growth of various additional and smaller staff disciplines. The safety of staff and visitors has always been a proper concern of the POA, and now other unions at Broadmoor. Their sometimes excessive reaction to the changes that occurred in the 'inter-acts' era reflects both the pain of adapting to the kinds of change that the 1959 Act introduced and the probability that a staff association rooted in the prisons will always tend to see matters in terms of retribution: paying debts to victims and to society, rather than in terms of repairing damaged minds and impaired responsibility. It is a pity that catering for the latter is seen as incompatible with the former rather than seeing both as integral parts of each other.

THE ETHICS AND RESEARCH COMMITTEES

As the 1959 Act wore on there were increasingly introduced, throughout the NHS, committees for monitoring ethical standards of clinical practice and the conduct of research, especially where medication was involved, or an intrusive procedure such as surgery or an injection.

Ethical concerns would, in any case, be covered through the professional standards of many of the disciplines working in a hospital, especially medicine, but local monitoring was increasingly realized to be a matter of additional importance. Eventually the 1983 Act introduced a Mental Health Act Commission, which included the monitoring of proper clinical practices amongst its watch-dog functions. However, that did not remove the obligation for individual hospitals to set up ethics and research committees which could monitor these matters round-the-clock in a way that the Commission could not possibly do in the course of its brief and intermittent visits. As a daily routine there would be obligations to inform patients of their rights, what was to happen to them, what treatment they were to receive and what effects this might have, both with regards to their treatment and especially in connection with any research programme in which they might be asked to participate, to which their consent was required. At a special hospital the frequent use of side rooms, for patients who were going through a phase of behaviour dangerous to themselves or others, also needed careful monitoring and recording. Until the 1983 Act introduced a means of formalizing this scrutiny and requiring documentation which established that it had been observed it became increasingly pressing to have local provisions to do the job. The Mental Health Review Tribunals were only concerned with whether a patient was properly detained under the provisions of the legislation and whether they might be said to have recovered from their mental disorder to the extent that they should now be discharged. The Tribunals did not have a remit to scrutinize the standards of detention and treatment, or the ethical implications of research programmes.

As the 1959 legislation began to look inadequate and green and white papers appeared heralding the eventual amending legislation of 1983, therefore, both an ethical and a research committee were formed. The former was a management initiative and introduced someone from outside the hospital, Donald Harris, a lawyer from Oxford, to chair it. The latter was the initiative of Dr David Tidmarsh who took on the role of research co-ordinator at the local level when the SHRU had somewhat changed its emphasis and was run from the Institute of Psychiatry in London by the Professor of Forensic Psychiatry, Dr John Gunn.

Both committees were not without their irritations to some of us, which is, of course, likely to be seen as 'paranoid'! It was irritating where the research committee was concerned, because a large proportion of research had always been initiated by, or under the umbrella of, the psychology department which had always been scrupulous in observing ethical research principles as well as sound research methodology, psychologists having undergone specific training in such methodology and ethical principles being incorporated in their code of practice. Moreover, it seemed unwarranted to scrutinize projects which often only involved searching case records and not direct patient participation, and so made no demands upon patients or other staff. Speed was often vital in getting a project under way when students had a limited time-span to undertake work during their course, so delays could threaten the viability of the work and discourage students contemplating a project in the first place. As students often contributed something that had long been an outstanding need and which resident staff had not had time or opportunity to do, any delay was very frustrating. Nevertheless, the principle of peer group vetting and support is a sound one and had to be incorporated into Broadmoor's way of life.

Where the ethics committee was concerned, topics in addition to the ethical aspects of research were important, particularly aspects of clinical practice, although at the start it seemed to be only research issues which were thought to present ethical problems. Before the 1983 Act's creation of a Mental Health Act Commission to scrutinize proper compulsory detention under the Act, consent to treatment, and complaints, the introduction of an ethics committee was the first safeguard for patients other than appeals to the managers and the DHSS, which were somewhat remote avenues of appeal to most patients' perceptions. The proper explanation to a patient of why he or she was in Broadmoor, what being there would entail and what appeal or recompense there was for anything to which he or she objected, was all somewhat vague. A set of booklets was eventually prepared which explained, for newly arriving patients and their relatives, what the hospital was all about and what services were available to assess, treat, educate and occupy them while they were there. Methods of appeal and likely discharge or transfer options were also set out.

By the end of the 'inter-acts' period the ethics committee had begun to tackle all these issues but it will be up to the next volume of Broadmoor history to chart how well it has succeeded and what further effect has been achieved through the 1983 Act. It has only been with this later legislation, for instance, that a complaints procedure has been finally and fully drawn up and put into practice. The ethics committee was well aware of the problems and resistance it faced, especially of getting reliable information on how clinical teams functioned, carried out their assessments of patient needs and monitored their treatment programmes. Individual care plans had not been formalized by the end of the 'inter-acts' period although regular team meetings had generally begun to tackle the need to regularly review and record the progress of all patients in their care and the case notes, of course, carried records of assessments and treatments given. Consent issues, however, were very variable and difficult to verify. The 1983 Act was to remedy and formalize all these, but not without difficulty and argument for some time to come. Use of seclusion and any incidents of violent altercations that might have given rise to seclusion being used were also within the ethics committee's remit and a seclusion policy was later to be drawn up, including requirements for justification, review and termination of each use. The ethics committee made a much overdue start on the problems involved.

SUMMARY

This chapter has covered a wide range of management changes largely brought about by the increased diversity of staff and the complexities of clinical role, interaction and responsibilities caused by this in the context of the very different nature of the 1959 legislation compared with what went before.

The increase in number of RMOs, which coincided with the creation of clinical teams, can now be seen as the most probable cause of the fragmentation of the hospital. Each team wanted to 'do its own thing' and see its patients through from start to finish in contrast with the old hospital's use of the different blocks, now houses, for different types of patient and treatment regime. Of course, the more effective treatments of the new era contributed to the feasibility of this. Only the most disturbed and the youngest groups were now separately contained. At the same time not all the professional groups were numerous enough to be able to supply a person to every team, nor did they comprise people of equal seniority or experience. Some ingenuity had to be exercised to avoid partially qualified people being exploited whilst trying to provide cover for every team.

The team principle extended to management, with the greater number and diversity of clinical teams and professional disciplines needing to be included within the policies and day-to-day functioning of the hospital. This naturally led to some upheaval and reorientation as the physician superintendent's solitary management position at the top of the whole structure became inadequate and inappropriate for the new spread of teams and professions. The role and relationship of the hospital managers, the DHSS, has also had to be described, therefore, together with the relationship of the Home Office sections dealing with special hospital matters.

Crucial within this complex equation was the staff association monitoring the conditions of the overwhelmingly most numerous staff, the nurses, which remained the POA from the pre-war days of the institution's Home Office parenthood. Their concern for their members and their perceived public duty turned so largely upon the safety of both of these that conflict inevitably marked the progress of the new Act. Fashioning a system that located security more largely in the clinical knowledge and progress of patients was slow to come about, with many hiccups, and looks unlikely ever to do so.

The complexity of service delivery within a much more 'individually-aware' society and era, as well as legislation, meant that committees were also created to monitor ethical issues and research activity, although ethical concerns were almost solely confined to research to begin with: it took some time for the penny to drop that day-to-day clinical practice might also need ethical scrutiny - strange when the next Act was imminent, with its much greater focus on patients' rights. Even when the 1983 Act did come, there was much resistance and protest against what was seen as interference from the MHAC into clinical independence.

CHAPTER 20

THE END OF AN ERA

AN UNCERTAIN INTERREGNUM

Dr McGrath reached the age of 65 and retired in 1981. 1983, however, was the date of the new Mental Health Act, replacing the 1959 Act which has been the backdrop for this continuation of Broadmoor's history. Two years of uncertainty accommodating to a new leadership was compounded, therefore, by the uncertainty of the impending legislative changes, and all of this in the context of the changes and developments already taking place in the world of psychiatry and which have been the themes of the immediately preceding chapters.

Once again, as with Dr Hopwood, the end of a long 'reign' was marked with an escape which was out of the ordinary, not because of resultant murders, although a murder was to follow a year later in Holland, but because the escape was one of the few which were successful and was of a patient who had occupied an enigmatic position within the hospital, with a psychopathic classification that illustrated all the arguments and disagreements that has bedevilled that classification over the period of the 1959 Act and since. This case can now be mentioned because, firstly, the escape is public knowledge and, secondly, a book was subsequently published by the patient (Alan Reeve) giving an account of his early life and his experiences in Broadmoor.

Although the Straffen escape halted the steady progress of the Hopwood era and further progress awaited the arrival of Dr

413

McGrath and the 1959 legislative changes, the Reeve escape did not have the same effect. The pressure for change from all directions - the various professions and the pressure groups - had a momentum, and took place in a social climate, that was now unstoppable. In any case, Alan Reeve escaped to Holland and his discovery and subsequent killing of a policeman there occurred a year later and was dealt with under Dutch law. Its repercussions were not felt in England until several years into the new Act.

The 1983 Act was the result of the 1982 Mental Health Amendment Bill to which all professions, as well as the various charities and pressure groups, were vigorously directing their views and interests. All this was a prescription for further uncertainty in the life of the special hospitals, for professional working groups were set up ahead of the 1982 Bill to prepare evidence for it. These continued in existence during the parliamentary committee stage in order to respond to the issues and arguments arising over the discussion of the Bill. During the committee stage, delegations from a number of professions and charities were invited to discuss their recommendations with MPs.

DR EDGAR UDWIN AS PHYSICIAN SUPERINTENDENT

Perhaps unsurprisingly, the superintendentship after Dr Patrick McGrath's retirement passed to Dr Edgar Udwin, the first consultant to have been appointed following the 1959 Act and, with Dr Brian O'Connell having moved elsewhere long since, the most long-standing one. This was just reward for his patience and zeal over those many years, although he had always been a somewhat contentious figure in the thinking and outlook of the hospital's policies. Nevertheless he had grasped the nettle of the psychopathic patients, even though his ideas of what to do with them had not always commanded agreement. Alan Reeve had been his patient and Reeve's book makes numerous references to the interchanges between them. Despite Reeve's scorn for the hospital, which he consistently refers to as a prison, its staff as 'screws' and the patients as 'cons', he describes a relationship with Udwin which developed a degree of mutual respect.

Alan Reeve's escape occurred in the August of 1981 after Dr McGrath's retirement in the June. Nevertheless, it was not a protest against the new superintendent, Dr Udwin, but a protest against the repeated refusal of successive tribunal and Aarvold Committee reviews to agree the recommendations by Udwin for his discharge. In this Udwin was supported by most of his clinical team, although there were strident voices around the hospital against Reeve's discharge.

The psychological input to this was mine as I had extensively assessed Alan Reeve at intervals since his arrival in Broadmoor as a teenager at the end of 1964. The details, of course, must remain confidential and are in any case irrelevant to the issue here, which is that of the procedures with regards to psychopathic disorder. Whilst Reeve's history (and as he tells this the antecedents are striking) illustrates the variations, complexities and contentiousness of the disorder, it also demonstrates the difference between the legal classification and the clinical condition. There are discrepancies between the clinical features of psychopathy and the story and description Alan Reeve gives of himself, yet little doubt that he had developed a mental state and way of life that, whatever name it is given, was best dealt with as a mental disorder under the Act. The question of whether he was appropriately treated in Broadmoor, according to his own account of events there, is another matter, and requires comment which will feature in the next chapter.

There is little doubt that the personality problems, which resulted from a compounding of his background, his personality and his life experiences, needed help to enable Alan Reeve to achieve the ability to function appropriately in the normal world. He would probably say that he changed in Broadmoor as a result of his own dogged efforts and that of the friends he made. Edgar Udwin would equally probably say that he enabled and encouraged Alan to make the necessary changes in his outlook and way of life through his combination of attention, care, concern and challenge.

The situation ultimately assessed by Udwin and his team at the point discharge was recommended is often described as one of a psychopath having 'matured' or 'grown out of' his condition, which is another way of saying that the various traits and tendencies had changed, were under control or he had learned to recognize and cope with them. He himself describes how he reassessed and restructured them. He obtained his 'O' levels and a degree while in Broadmoor. This is not to say that he had become a conforming or conventional character and his steadfast adherence to a communist, revolutionary philosophy aroused the antagonism of many staff. In his book he attributes his failure to achieve discharge to this steadfast resolve not to abandon his political beliefs. Of course, once a negative result from the tribunal and/or the Aarvold Committee had occurred there would almost inevitably be a similar refusal from the DHSS and Home Office. They were unlikely to endorse an RMO's recommendations in the face of a negative MHRT or Aarvold outcome.

Alan Reeve understandably criticizes these procedures as the workings of 'malign state control'. In the context of the run-up to a new Act, it is interesting to note that, although the emphasis of the 1983 Act has been described in this history as changing from, in effect, requiring 'good reason to discharge' to requiring 'good reason to detain', the sections concerning the MHRT procedures have nevertheless still left the patient to establish 'discharge-worthiness' rather than the MHRT to establish 'detainability'. This has not been rectified until recently when a statutory instrument (No. 3712 of 2001) precipitated by European human rights legislation and a successful appeal by a patient, has brought the MHRT process into line with the rest of the Act. Instead of an MHRT being required to be *satisfied* that a patient *is not suffering* from a disorder (putting the onus on the patient to establish 'wellness') it is now required *not to be satisfied* that a patient is *suffering* ... etc. (this text's emphasis).

In any case it is doubtful if Reeve would be detainable under the new Act's re-working of the psychopathic disorder concept with its emphasis on treatability. The clinical team's view had been that this was resolved (it cannot be 'caught' again like an infection or 'relapsed into' like mental illness). It is difficult to see how an MHRT could be other than *not satisfied* that he was *suffering* from a psychopathic disorder and even if he failed to *satisfy* them of the more stringent criteria that he was *not suffering* from the disorder there would remain the problem of establishing the treatability criterion. The clinical team did not believe there was anything remaining to treat. Any remaining problems were not of mental disorder.

Although some would no doubt point to the subsequent murder in Holland as justification for their view that he was not suitable for discharge, retaining someone in Broadmoor must be justified essentially on their mental disorder. The evidence for this, by 1981, was not forthcoming, whilst he had long since completed any 'tariff' interpretation of a sentence for murder, especially one committed as a very immature teenager. The further murder of a patient in Broadmoor is denied by him in his book and this tallies with the opinion of many staff close to the incident at that time. His ultimate escape, after numerous discharge recommendations had been turned down, far from arguing the error of the recommendation, seems rather to corroborate the desperation of a man with much of his life still ahead of him, to achieve the freedom he was denied through any other avenue. I had wondered what act of desperation would follow his final failure to achieve discharge, thinking that suicide was a possibility (and he refers to such a solution at several points in his book), so his escape was not a surprise.

These issues are for the next book on Broadmoor's history to discuss, when a long view will be possible of the changes in the 1983 Act's provisions, but it is an interesting and relevant situation to describe in this 'end-of-the-Act' era when discussions of the new Act were taking place and when Alan Reeve's escape happened.

This, as might be expected, was not the only contentious case at the time. It is in the nature of a special hospital for these to occur continuously. What was unusual, or new, was that, with the creation of clinical teams and the awareness of the DHSS and Home Office that 'multidisciplinary opinions' should be sought, there was a greater potential for disagreements to appear than previously, when the sole arbiter of clinical decision-making had been the consultant (RMO) and the ultimate arbiter of hospital policy had been the physician superintendent.

The clinical team phenomenon and the issues ventilated for the 1982 Amendment Bill gave rise to a great deal of internal debate over the form that management and decision-making should take in the future. The arrival of the computer as a desktop facility and the amenability of much clinical data to computer processing led to suggestions that this new facility should be used to enhance the team's decision-making process. Dr Udwin, however, even before his appointment as superintendent, had always been sceptical of any impersonal procedure that might detract from or outweigh the personal element of clinical decision-making, despite the best endeavours of many of the rest of us to assure him that such modern aids could always be subordinated to personal clinical opinions if that was the policy that was favoured.

WHAT SORT OF HOSPITAL MANAGEMENT?

With the implementation of clinical teams, the retirement of Dr McGrath and the prospect of a new Mental Health Act, the subject of how the various service organizations were to be run and managed in the future was a foremost topic. Dr McGrath had always sensed that the days of medical management were passing, just as medical superintendents had been fading from the scene for a number of years, and he frequently expressed his misgivings over what he foresaw as the arrival of the lay administrator. In this he had the virtually unanimous support of his HMT and HoD (heads of departments) meetings. Although they might have had misgivings over the succession to Dr McGrath there was virtual unanimity over the need for hospitals to be run by clinicians, who understood what they were about, rather than lay managers who would not but would be bringing concepts of industrial and commercial management to a system considered unsuited to them.

Interestingly, this history is being compiled well after the end of the 'inter-acts' period when lay management has been the norm for most of the post-1983 Act period. It is probably too soon (and outside the self-imposed framework of this history anyway) to assess the relative merits of the alternative management systems. However, it is impossible not to remark that the period of the 1983 Act, so far, has been punctuated with scandals and inquiries over the running of the mental health care system generally and the special hospitals in particular. Of course, there have been other issues than management that impinge on these but it is interesting that the book which covers the period of the Special Hospitals Service Authority's responsibility for their management (Kaye and Franey, 1998, *Managing High Security Care*) describes the agonies of the change and the struggles experienced by the new lay management, especially in relation to the POA. This is in some contrast with the chapters by the clinical contributors to the book which set out the problems and progress in their areas of concern with less reference to problems of staff relationships.

With the prospect of a change of leadership in 1981 and in the context of all the representations to Parliament on the new legislation, therefore, it was natural for the several professional groups comprising HoD, the hospital's internal management forum, to make known their concerns and recommendations on future management to the DHSS. Since the medical staff were already the holders of the clinical management reins, the hospital secretary was a civil servant and the CNO was a member of the HMT anyway, this HoD concern was essentially expressed by the rest, i.e.: the heads of the occupational staff, social work, psychology, education, the chaplain and the librarian, who became known as the 'gang of six' (a topical reference at the time, following the emergence of the new Social Democratic Party and its 'gang of four' founders). Spurred on by the members of the several professional groups they represented on HoD, various discussion papers were drafted and circulated and the opinions of the group were forwarded to the office committee (OC) at the DHSS where the imminent leadership succession was assumed to be under consideration.

The thrust of the argument was broadly that the existing HoD procedure was the preferred management system, with a chairman, or director, from a clinical background either appointed as before or chosen from within the HoD. A sympathetic response resulted, with assurances that changes were under way with the prospect of a new Act, but in the meantime the existing procedure was to continue. No doubt the office committee had in mind that Dr Udwin would himself be reaching retirement age in a couple of years, by which time the new Act would be in force and the matter could be reviewed again in the light of any changes it might introduce. In fact, on Dr Udwin's retirement, the same structure continued, of a triumvirate HMT, with the much younger Dr John Hamilton as medical director, and it was to be a few more years before the Special Hospitals Service Authority was created, chaired by an overall manager and with a separate manager at each individual hospital. In some cases this local manager was a clinician (initially the medical director at Rampton and the nursing director at Park Lane) and in others a lay manager.

THE 1982 MENTAL HEALTH ACT AMENDMENT BILL

A foundation for new legislation was provided by the 'Butler' Committee on Mentally Abnormal Offenders which had reported in 1975, some years previously. It had not only been responsible for the concept, now at last being put into effect, of smaller, regional, medium security units (RSUs) but had provided cogent reviews and recommendations on, amongst other things, the concepts of dangerousness, of the 'special verdict' (guilty but insane) and of psychopathic disorder (see Chapter 15).

The Royal College of Psychiatrists was largely content with the radical advances brought in by the 1959 Act but proposed some improvements, especially the creation of regional forensic psychiatrists heading teams based on the new RSUs. The non-medical clinical professions were, not surprisingly however, keen to establish greater autonomy of responsibility. The British Psychological Society, for instance, drew upon its earlier evidence to the Butler Committee to argue that there was now a wider range of professions involved in the delivery of care and treatment within a largely 'health' context but which were independent of medicine. The problems of the responsibility for treatments, outlined in the previous chapter, were discussed. There was even a suggestion, following its unsurprising failure to persuade the Butler Committee of the desirability of uniting Home and Health, as in Scotland, to avoid the difficulties over the administrative divisions where secure care was concerned and adopt a quite different alternative of a separate service: a kind of 'National Social Care Service' to parallel the NHS on the one hand and the criminal justice system on the other, these being already uncomfortable bedfellows in the provision of secure care for mentally disordered offenders. Unsurprisingly, this did not find support either. It would only have created yet another service with barriers to negotiate where joint or crossover use of staff was concerned. The Amendment Bill only served to continue to emphasize the problems and strivings of providing an ever increasingly wide range of services within the constraints of a medically determined and directed NHS on the one hand and a penally orientated CJS on the other.

The principal pressure for change, however, came from the various civil rights groups which found a focus in the main mental health charity 'MIND' - the National Association for Mental Health. As discussed in Chapter 15, they had for some years been vociferous in their criticisms of the special hospitals. This derived mainly from the lengthy incarceration that characterized the committal of most of the patients in them. As has been said already, this resulted from discharge depending upon a positive recommendation being made, which was often difficult to sustain and, of course, put the reputations of both RMOs and ministers (and their civil servant advisers) on the line. People were naturally reluctant to make recommendations which might go wrong and so tended to play safe.

MIND was also indignant on behalf of those they deemed to have done little to merit a long hospitalization period, citing cases where no 'crime' had been committed. These actually tended to be cases where either a violent past history existed or where, in the case of someone who had not come through a court, there had been considerable violence or irresponsible, hazardous behaviour when, say, in another hospital or on a previous conviction. Caution was exercised on these grounds, therefore, rather than the immediate 'index' offence, which seemed appropriate for a care context in contrast with a criminal justice one. Clinical assessments could have revealed continuing morbid preoccupations, delusions or hallucinations turning upon a violent theme such that no responsible clinician could contemplate discharge until they had been resolved, treated and were in remission. This might well not be apparent from the bare details of current offence or method of committal, which were what determined MIND's criticisms.

As was mentioned earlier in Chapter 15, the spokesman for MIND was its energetic and loquacious legal director, Larry Gostin, who was to be seen and heard widely at meetings and conferences during the period up to the new Act, expressing his concerns and propounding solutions. MIND was very influential in the 1982 Mental Health Amendment Bill and the Act which resulted reflected this in altering the emphasis of compulsion in care, as has been said several times already, from one where incarceration continued unless an end was recommended to one of expiring after an interval of time unless essential reason was given for it to continue.

The results of this are outside the time span of this book but are nevertheless now familiar, with government under pressure again to amend the mental health legislation. So it is worth remarking that the 1983 Act, so heavily influenced by MIND, and despite introducing much needed changes, need not have resulted in the difficulties that arose had it not been paralleled by quite independent but draconian closures of residential psychiatric hospitals in favour of the 'community care' concept.

It is interesting to observe that, when new ideas and procedures are introduced, it is always assumed they should replace, rather than augment, the existing ones. The more sensible strategy would be to run them together until they are compared and tested. Maybe they will be incompatible but this was not the case with residential and community forms of care. The cynical amongst us observed that community care, as an alternative rather than an additional facility, must have been supported because of a supposed financial saving, although this disappears if the level and frequency of carer contact is maintained that is necessary to spot and avoid trouble.

Of course, the old Victorian institutions were notoriously out-of-date and steeped in Dickensian images of neglect. This was not because they were old and Victorian but because the internal organization and the care systems inside them were antiquated. This was reason enough to modernize, replan and restaff them but no reason to close them. It is bizarre that what were considered in-humane for psychiatric patients are now modernized and re-furbished as desirable blocks of expensive character flats with delightful grounds and views. That is if the site has not already been sold for redevelopment and the buildings demolished and lost for-ever. Why couldn't the money spent on expensive alternative facilities have been spent instead on modernization for psychiatric patients? As it is, the potential for creating up-to-date residential care facilities out of existing ones has been lost. With it has gone a crucial part of the knowledge and skill in observing and caring for mentally disordered people which derived from everyday contact in a residential setting. Instead, psychiatric patients must face a hostile world, for which they are not ready, with inadequate contact and support from those who understand them. They then live hand-to-mouth existences in isolated bedsits or community houses. They could have been enjoying the support and facilities of a specially constructed campus, from which they could make periodic forays into the world outside when they were ready and felt able to do so. A King's Fund group reported along these lines (the 'Lost Souls' Report) in the 1970s.

There is an apparent loss of perception of what were the common features and progress of psychiatric disorders; and an insufficient number of clinicians in the community to provide the close and frequent observation that is enabled by a residential setting. Psychosis commonly remits and recurs and its sufferers are notoriously capable of concealing their disorder. Certainly patients in Broadmoor previously spent too long being vetted as free from mental disorder before being discharged and Chapter 18 describing the findings of Dell and Norris bears this out. After 1983, however, the pendulum seems to have swung too far the other way: too many psychiatric patients seem not to have been vetted for long enough within a series of intermediate settings before being allowed again to be at large unsupervised. It is not, of course, easy to establish whether insidious mental disorder or the behaviours that give rise to this classification still linger, even for the most skilled and experienced of clinical observers. But it would help to have a system that provides a gradual, phased return to independence and closer support and observation by skilled staff. In the end a balance has to be struck between too much and too little restriction of liberty. The 1983 Act's changes were another knight's move: one step forward and two sideways, whilst their implementation has seen haphazard progress in all directions and none: forward, back, sideways and standing still.

REPORTS, POLICIES, SEMINARS, VISITORS, NEWS-LETTERS AND BLEEPS

The run-up to the 1983 Act was not surprisingly, therefore, characterized by a marked increase in the production of reports and policies. Annual reports for Broadmoor were revived and, having produced my only previous ones in 1959 and 1960, the next was not until 1980. Policy documents abounded. Again clinical services were put under considerable strain while extra attention was given to compiling these. The creation of the ethics committee and the visit of a Health Advisory Service team late in the 1970s stimulated reviews of violent incidents; the use of seclusion; information for newly arrived patients and for visitors; and a complaints system. A great many new meetings and seminars began to take place.

The hospital had always entertained parties of visitors which took place weekly on a Tuesday. Such was the demand that these had to be restricted to relevant professional groups such as staff from RSUs and other psychiatric hospitals, magistrates, social workers, prison and probation officers and student groups from the various professions involved. More could not be accommodated without what Dr McGrath regarded as unwarranted intrusion upon patient life. 'This is their home' he always said, 'and they should not be treated like goldfish in a bowl'. Nevertheless, there were always groups of VIPs from abroad to be accommodated, usually in small groups of only two or three (the 'Tuesday' visiting parties were of groups of twenty) ranging from politicians to academics, invariably concerned with the creation of comparable facilities in their own country.

Other meetings were constituted that did not impinge upon patient privacy. A monthly seminar series had been created by Dr Gavin Tennent and was revived by Dr David Tidmarsh, with visiting specialists giving talks on their area of work. These took place in a conference room in the consultants' administrative building. Periodic psychiatric seminars were arranged in the staff education centre in conjunction with the Institute of Psychiatry's psychiatric registrar training. Similar seminars took place for other disciplines. Annual conferences were arranged for consultant psychiatrists from all over the country at a residential conference centre in Windsor Park. These became associated with the Royal College of Psychiatrists' Forensic Section. All these activities were both for general information and for policy making purposes and to enable the mental health world to get to grips with the problems of secure care and of dangerousness in psychiatric patients. There was the additional objective of improving NHS colleagues' understanding of special hospital patients in order to promote acceptance of them when they were considered suitable for transfer; so the assessment of the necessity for secure hospitalization and the converse - suitability for discharge or transfer to non-secure care - figured largely among the topics. All this was more particularly relevant with the Mental Health Amendment Bill in the offing, and then being processed through parliament, after which there was its implementation and discussion of its implications and usage.

On the information scene, there had been a hospital news sheet implemented in the 1970s. This was produced by the chaplain who was always appealing for contributions. It mainly consisted of the programme of events for the coming month but even this was a useful advance. As time went on it grew and was used to circulate synopses, back in 1975, of the 'Butler' Report and later of the new legislation when it emerged. A full analysis of the 1983 Act, with tabulated comparisons of the new and the old sections, appeal and second opinion procedures, was painstakingly compiled, in a special brochure, by two tutors from the staff education centre: Trevor Walt and Chris Sharpe. It provided a clear and comprehensive reference manual which was widely drawn upon for use in other establishments.

Communications about the hospital were greatly improved with the coming of 'bleeps'. Before the arrival of mobile 'phones all that these would do was signal that the holder was wanted, whereupon they had to find the nearest 'phone and call the hospital switchboard. They were then told who wanted them and this meant a further call to that person. This amounted to quite a palaver and was particularly irritating in a meeting or case conference: first the bleep itself and then two 'phone calls. The subject of the bleep was usually urged to go to another room to make the return call but would often not do so, using the 'phone, in the room in which everyone was trying to get on with the case conference or meeting, so interrupting the entire proceedings. It seemed to be a status symbol establishing the importance of whoever was being bleeped. Looking back, it only foreshadowed the arrival of the mobile 'phone. Somehow I managed to avoid having one, never asking for one and never being told I should have one, although surprise was often expressed that I 'wasn't on a bleep'.

DISCUSSING WITH PATIENTS THEIR FORMER OFFENCES

Whilst this description of Broadmoor's history has traced many changes and developments in comparison with Partridge's account, one feature he emphasizes has not yet been remarked upon. Within a system comprising a continuum or spectrum of care and treatment which extends into subsequent treatment settings and ultimately the community, it clearly becomes necessary to both talk about and face the consequences of a patient's violent behaviour. Yet Partridge makes a strong point of arrival in Broadmoor being seen as putting one's past life behind one. This principle has continued. However, Partridge includes with this the principle of avoiding mention of past crimes, including the one that brought the patient to Broadmoor. One wonders whether Partridge, as an outsider visiting the hospital, got this one quite right. Maybe staff in the hospital generally didn't talk about a patient's admission offence (known as the 'index offence') and this certainly still tends to be so. But I suspect that Dr Hopwood, as the hospital's only consultant psychiatrist, and the one concerned with a patient's discharge recommendation, did talk to patients about their original offence.

Of course, if the offence was seen as unconnected with the mental disorder (in those days 'insanity') and the purpose of the hospital solely to treat the 'insanity', then the offence might be irrelevant. However, there was never any doubt in 1959 and thereafter that the mental disorder and the offence were seen as either definitely or probably connected and in most patients' cases the connection was obvious, to the extent, say, that the patient had held delusional beliefs about his or her victim that had directly prefaced the crime. It is highly likely, and Partridge gives no indication otherwise, that in Dr Hopwood's time and earlier, mental condition and the admission offence would have been seen as similarly connected. It has been the form of this connection that has preoccupied people since 1959. 'Which was the chicken and which was the egg?' How much was due to the illness, how much to the underlying personality and how much to the background situation. Simply because a court had decided the defendant could not be held responsible for his or her offence did not mean that the Broadmoor staff could not distinguish a connection between them.

So in the post-1959 era it was certainly accepted that the original offence had to be faced and discussed. Indeed, it would invariably be expected to figure in the treatment at some point, although possibly not initially. Psychological treatment would invariably entail discussion of offences when linking them with the obvious need for a patient to come to terms with and change his or her urge to respond violently to threats, provocation, insults, etc. With a psychiatric assessment, too, offence and illness would both be discussed and, where there was no obvious link, the effort to understand both would invariably lead to prolonged and repeated investigations. I recall several puzzling cases where, even after many years in Broadmoor, neither patient nor psychiatrist had achieved an understanding of the reason for the offence. These had led to repeated referrals for further psychological reassessments to probe into the question. Nor were they cases of independence of offence and illness: it had often been the bizarre nature of the offence and the perpetrator's lack of explanation for it that had led to being in Broadmoor in the first place. No other clear indication of 'insanity' (pre-1959 and many patients from this era persisted in residence into the 1959 Act's time) had been apparent to the court and no other motivation than insanity could be attributed.

So a change to be noted from Partridge's time (if, as I have said, it really was a change) is that it was no longer taboo to talk of a patient's offence. Such discussion was of the essence of a patient's stay in Broadmoor and it was expected by both patients and staff, although confined to the more formal and confidential assessment and therapy sessions. In the course of life about the hospital, patients' offences would be unknown to other patients unless the patient him or herself, or media publicity, had made it known. Some confessed it as a kind of expiation of their feelings of shame and guilt, though few bragged about it; the Broadmoor atmosphere was not one of status being accorded to someone according to the enormity of their crimes, as is often the case in prison settings. Nor were sexual offenders, conversely, ostracized, as can happen in prison, where they often have to be isolated from other prisoners for their own safety. So many patients had done horrific things to their victims that judgements were shunned. Sometimes offences became known inadvertently, or through a breaking of the rule of confidentiality in group therapy, and even the occasional deliberate leak could happen. But any leak through staff indiscretion would be in disregard of hospital policy. Much later a complaints procedure was introduced, after much difficulty and several ineffectual drafts, but this did not exist in the time of the 1959 Act.

SUBSTANCE ABUSE OR MISUSE

We also cannot end this historical narrative without specific, rather than merely passing, comment on a topic which has risen to high prominence in the final decades of the 20th century. It has scarcely received a mention in this history, except to note that alcohol emerged as one of the most significant factors in Margaret Norris's study of patients' post-discharge adjustment, giving rise to both strong and strongly criticized recommendations from her as to its status in discharge arrangements and aftercare. It has also been noted as a critical factor in many of the crimes of those in Megargee's and Blackburn's 'over-controlled' personality category. However, with the increasing incidence and clinical prominence of alcohol and drug addiction latterly it may seem odd that it has not received more specific comment.

Of course, questions about abuse of alcohol, and later other drugs, would invariably figure in the initial appraisals and case conferences and, if established as a significant component of the patient's clinical state and problems, would also feature in treatment programmes and the subsequent periodic reappraisals. Alcohol and other drug abuse do not feature except as such an adjunct, however, simply because they are not regarded as psychiatric disorders. This is appropriate. Nevertheless, where they occur, they are very much indications of some problem which in all probability is a component of or has aggravated the psychiatric condition and will have played a part in the offence.

Drug abuse had not reached the widespread scale in the 'interacts' period that it has since so, although it was always questioned, it was not a high profile problem. One of the reasons for this was, of course, that patients tended to arrive in Broadmoor many months after the date of their offences. A period on remand for psychiatric and social reports after appearance in the magistrates' court, often a lengthy trial and then delays for appeals, further investigations and deliberations as to where they were to go, accounted for this delay. They would, therefore, usually have worked through the withdrawal period of alcohol or other drug dependence by the time they arrived.

Investigations of the significance of alcoholism to the crime sometimes figured in EEG assessments, with the rather bizarre procedure of the patient being required to consume measured quantities of alcohol at standard intervals during the assessment. The object was to observe whether abnormal EEG patterns resulted which might contribute to the explanation of the offence.

As time went on and the treatment regimes expanded, of course, substance misuse would figure in individual and group treatment sessions, with strategies being rehearsed for their elimination or control. Practical consequences could not be pursued inside Broadmoor, of course, and this would have been another reason for treatment needing to be continued in community based settings. By and large, substance abuse was a factor not well dealt with in Broadmoor, partly because of these difficulties in effecting a practical treatment programme but also, it has to be said, because it was not usually considered to be of foremost importance in the treatment of the mental disorder or the associated offence. Just as alcohol addiction was not categorized as a mental disorder, it was not a factor that could be brought into a 'disability defence' in court. Alcohol problems were, of course, identified and often recognized as important within the patient's disorder but not usually considered to be something that could be done much about except to impose an alcohol ban on discharge where it had been a feature in the original offence. This actually could be very effective and one might say, therefore, that it did actually receive the priority it warranted, even if at the discharge rather than the diagnosis and treatment stage. Patients were regularly recalled from a conditional discharge because they had resumed drinking, thereby putting a partner or family member at risk. The liability to such recall was well known among patients, therefore acting as a powerful incentive to refrain from excessive drinking when they, in their turn, came to be discharged.

Alcohol was often implicated in the crimes of the 'over-controlled' group defined by Megargee in the USA and similarly revealed at Broadmoor by Blackburn. This group's excessive social conformity and inhibitory controls were postulated to have suppressed any hostile feelings aroused by life crises. Only excessive provocation would overcome these controls and this was thought to have accounted for the excessive aggression which had led to the disproportionate incidence of homicide in this group. Cumulative provocation would be most likely in the context of a long-standing relationship and it was a close relative, commonly a spouse or partner, who was usually the victim. Hostility would accumulate only in highly repressed, or 'over-controlled', people as it would be discharged at lesser levels of provocation in normal individuals, often through indirect or displaced activities (kicking a football, or the cat; jogging; working out; thumping the piano). Alcohol, as a disinhibiting drug, was proposed as a factor reducing the patient's normally excessive controls to the point where the accumulated hostility levels would more readily 'discharge' into overt aggression and, moreover, could do so in the absence of further provocation. This was held to account for the sometimes lack of any obvious immediately precipitating cause. This all sounded very plausible at the time but Blackburn, in his 1993 book, *The Psychology of Criminal Conduct*, now warns of its probable oversimplicity in the light of more recent work on the differential effects of alcohol.

Whether or not the alcohol problem was realistically addressed in those days, it would, by the 1980s and Edgar Udwin's superintendentship, be given close attention, together with other substance abuse, not only in diagnostic formulations but also in the psychiatric and psychological therapies that characterized Broadmoor's individual and group treatments at that time. It would be regarded at least as a symptom of other problems which were in need of assessment and treatment. Alcohol and both hard and soft drugs will surely add another facet to the next report of Broadmoor's history.

CLINICAL HISTORIES OF SEXUAL ABUSE

This is another topic figuring prominently in public awareness these days but which has received scant mention in this history. Once again it is something that has only emerged as of widespread significance much more recently.

The sexual drives and orientation of Broadmoor patients were, of course, always carefully assessed in the medical histories compiled on admission and accorded major significance in the formulations of the aetiology (causation) of patient's conditions. The expression of sexual impulses and the choice, form and extent of patients' relationships with their partners were of key importance. Sex, money and religion, in that order, were reckoned to have been the primary motivators in the lives of Broadmoor patients. Dr Edgar Udwin had always gone so far as to maintain that there was not a single patient's psychiatric condition that did not feature a sexual problem. This was only too obvious in a large number of cases and many that at first seemed to be of different origin were revealed later to contain a critical sexual element. Suspiciousness, jealousy, resentments, rivalries and mutual adjustment problems do not necessarily include sexual abuse, however, and the actual incidence of sexual abuse within families, especially of children, did not have the prominence that it has today, unless it comprised the actual 'index' offence for which the patient had been committed to Broadmoor (incest, rape, buggery). Even then and as has been said before, such features might be concealed within an indictment or conviction for a greater offence, e.g.: murder or attempted murder.

Many patients' offences did feature some overt sexual motive, of course. Apart from rape, indecent assault and other specific sexual offences, the killing of a spouse or other partner would be an obvious and frequent one. An abusive prior relationship, or sexual interference or damage to the victim before or after death, would establish this. Other lesser problems within the relationship would count as implicitly sexual, whether or not overtly expressed and whether or not violent, although overt sexual damage to a victim, related or unrelated, occurred only too often. Sexual motivation of a different and less overt kind would also be noted in the case of some offences of arson or other damage to property, such as that to the patient's own home. Commonly a woman's expression of anger towards a partner will take the form of such indirect damage rather than an overt sexual assault. Men's aggression tends to be more direct. Damage to the home of a parent in the case of, say, a teenager or even an older unmarried person, may also sometimes be the act of someone struggling with problems of an actual or imagined sexual relationship kind.

The family and sexual histories investigated and reported by the social work department would often be extremely complicated, with many changes of partner or temporary relationships. These were difficult to describe in reports and at case conferences so that they would often be illustrated with charts or diagrams to show the complex interrelationships of the household and the often numerous half-siblings. Within this situation incest was a frequent feature, of course, but actual abuse was not reported as frequently as one might now have expected.

The work of the Psychology Department also included assessment of sexual orientation and problems and has been described in the development of a number of new treatment programmes. Sexual difficulties and offending were directly addressed in research programmes, including incestual relationships. It was also well known that the backgrounds of many offenders featured their own abuse by parents or other relatives. Nevertheless, again, allegations of outright abuse, rather than merely an implicitly consensual relationship, did not seem to occur as often as one might now expect. Present day knowledge of this phenomenon would now suggest that many more of these scenarios must have included abuse.

What might be the reason for this under-reporting? Sexual abuse must have been as common a feature then as it turns out now to be. Clinical histories were extensive and comprehensive. It seems surprising that the phenomenon did not feature more often. Did patients feel they could or should not report these events? Has it only recently become acceptable to do so? This seems to be one possible reason. Blackburn reports child abuse as only becoming an explicitly acknowledged social problem during the 1960s and wife abuse even later.

THE END OF PATIENT LABOUR

Earlier in this continuing history, and in Partridge's account, patients were described as working in many settings about the hospital. Not only were there formal workshops and handicrafts centres but a great deal of work of use to the daily running of the hospital was also carried out by patients. By the time of the 1959 Act, farm work by patients had ended and the farm had been let to an independent farmer. Work continued, however, on the grounds inside the walls, tending the kitchen garden, whilst some half dozen working parties, of five or six patients each, and a staff man in charge of each, looked after the grounds outside the walls all around the estate, including the staff playing field and some gardens (notably that of the physician superintendent). As said at the end of Chapter 8 and intermittently throughout this history, much of the internal work was of economic importance to the hospital. The workshops included the making of staff uniforms and patients' clothing, the cleansing and remaking of soiled bedding, various furniture and soft-furnishing requirements around the hospital, printing and bookbinding, a hospital laundry and sewing room and a tinsmith's shop. Patients also worked in the hospital stores and kitchens.

With the end of the 1970s and certainly in the 1980s, however, all these activities had been reduced to only work of a recreational and occupational therapy nature. The shoemaking, tailoring and upholstery workshops, sewing room and laundry, were all closed or converted to solely recreational work. Outside parties were reduced to one. Patient labour in the kitchens and stores came to an end. Printing requirements went to outside contract, as did uniforms and laundry. Clothing and footwear were bought to patients' requirements, as indeed were books and audio-visual equipment, from outside suppliers. Orders could be placed with mail order companies, provided patients had sufficient credit in their account, to which the patients' cash office (lay staff administering the patients' ledgers) credited benefit payments and any gifts from families.

Much of all this constituted considerable advance, using advancing technology and marketing and, in principle, suiting activities to the individual clinical needs of patients. In other ways, however, it was once again a knight's move - one step forward and two sideways. The previous system had used patient labour in activities of the hospital that were part of its basic economy. Countless patients commented on the feeling of usefulness that this conferred upon them: they felt of value in contributing to the running of the place where they lived. They also learned about quality standards, production schedules, working to instructions and collaborating with fellow workers: all aspects of normal life which many had never experienced or never managed to cope with successfully in the past. Dr Edgar Udwin, whose particular responsibility and interest all this was, always dismissed this element of work activity and felt that it was more important to get a larger proportion of the patient population activated in some way than being concerned about the actual form of the activity. This exemplifies the medical approach to a disease-illness concept, rehabilitating people with lost abilities, rather than also recognizing the need for many patients to acquire skills and habits that they never had. This does not only, or even principally, mean job skills but, as described earlier and discussed again later in Part III, it means developing essential life-coping skills such as the self-regulation of daily work schedules, in relation to leisure activity, and relationships with peers and with authority. These are often lacking in people with mental health and personality problems. Their lives have come to grief largely through never having managed to develop the self-help capabilities and interpersonal awareness that underpin successful adaptation to life. A full range of occupational and recreational opportunities where a valued contribution is made, rather than merely passing the time, helps to promote both effectiveness and self-esteem.

The argument was brought to an end and the matter of contributing to the hospital's economy was resolved finally by two factors. The first was increasing disquiet over trade practices and possible allegations that work was being done 'on the cheap'. The second was the complaint by patients' rights groups that patients were being exploited: patients undergoing treatment (but what is treatment?) should not be employed in doing the day-to-day work of the hospital. Patients, of course, received their benefit entitlements and those attending the hospital's various occupational units an increment on top of this. The total did not, however, amount to the standard rate for equivalent work outside. This was a pity. A valuable treatment resource was lost. Somehow it should have been possible to devise a way of enabling it to continue whilst overcoming the objections. Care would, of course, be needed to ensure that patients were not exploited as 'skivvies' but treatment plans and, now, the Mental Health Act Commission's visits, should be able to ensure that. The 'closed shop' issue should have been resolvable too. Somehow, however, there did not seem to be any real conviction that the matter was important, which is once again to emphasize how far the social learning element had yet to go in its struggle with medical assumptions about mental disorder.

SUMMARY

The 1959 Mental Health Act was replaced a few years after the retirement of another charismatic superintendent just as the pre-war legislation had been. As Dr Hopwood's benign reforms were spoilt by a tragic escape, so Dr McGrath's liberalizing influence was marked at the end by another dramatic escape, the only successful one during his superintendency and one which, a year later, was also to culminate in a death. The legislation was about to change again and there was doubt as to what form of managership it would bring. Dr Edgar Udwin, whose own retirement was only two years off, took the helm for the two year run-up to the next Act, so enabling a further re-think if necessary. The escaper later published a book on his life experiences which thereby circumvents the rule of silence on individual patients and enables the problems of psychopathic disorder to be illustrated through his situation.

What sort of legislative changes would be made; what sort of management of the system would result; what would be done about the more enigmatic forms of mental disorder in the new Act? Some of the answers are tabulated and discussed later, in Appendix A, but the questions were what dogged the period after Dr McGrath's retirement and during Dr Udwin's short term of office. Staff were absorbed in the debate and in making their points to government through their professional bodies, as were those of the many pressure groups. The chapter reviews some of the pressures and conflicts that marked this period. It was a time of increased information generally: reports, policy papers, seminars, newsletters were all on the increase, facilitated by the information technology revolution.

Winding up the era of the 1959 Act also prompted mention of several topics not so far mentioned in the sequential unfolding of events. Partridge, for instance, makes a point of patients being encouraged to put the enormity of their mentally disordered deeds behind them. In the era of the 1959 Act, however, it became an accepted necessity to deal with the original motivation in order to understand and resolve it.

Substance abuse was another topic needing more attention than the mandatory monitoring of drinking habits that had hitherto marked conditional discharge. Augmented by the increasing incidence of drugs other than merely alcohol, it was accorded more importance than alcohol alone seems to have been but still it was not the high-profile issue that it has become since, possibly because abuse is not, of course, classified in terms of a mental disorder. Nevertheless, it has increasingly become recognized as a significant aggravator of whatever mental disorder might already exist and an accompaniment to many personality problems.

Sexual abuse, too, seems to have occupied a lower profile in patients' case histories than one might have expected, now that it is recognized as a much more common occurrence than was once thought. A prominent feature in the committal of crimes, it received only occasional comment in patients' own histories.

Finally, patients were no longer working in the hospital's various service areas and workshops. The occupations centre became much more recreational (shoemaking and repair, uniform tailoring, furniture and bedding renovation, together with labour in the kitchens and stores, were all stopped). The reason was both clashes with union agreements over remuneration and allegations of exploitation. As a result a useful introduction to the discipline of work, to instruction, to collaboration, to time scheduling and, above all, the reward of seeing an economic or marketed end-product, were all lost. The knight's move of medicalization had side-stepped a useful social therapy from the pre-war era.

PART II ENDPIECE

And so an era ended. Another Act replaced the one that revolutionized the care of mental disorder in 1959. Procedures had changed. The patient population had changed, too. New categories of staff had been introduced and existing staff groups both grew and were reorganized, often more than once as in the case of the nursing profession. Treatment had been revolutionized, both with more effective medications and the introduction of many new therapies. Research had begun in earnest. The hospital was interacting with the rest of the NHS and psychiatric services in a way that had not happened previously. It was also interacting with the outside world through reports and submissions to government and through participation in the bodies of the various professional disciplines to which the Broadmoor staff belonged. Informal interaction was on the increase through more open visiting, the formation of a League of Friends and responses to the demands of press, radio and television.

Part III of this history will summarize and discuss what was learned about mentally disordered patients in these three decades and what the implications were for the systems which manage them and for the legal processes which put them in Broadmoor.

PART III

WHAT IT MEANS

CHAPTER 21

PATIENTS AND PRACTICES REAPPRAISED

REAPPRAISAL OF THE TASK

With the implementation of a new Mental Health Act in 1983, the period of Broadmoor's history covered in this book comes to an end. Compiling it so many years later it may seem odd that the story is not continued. There are, however, several compelling reasons to stop in 1983. Firstly, the changes following the 1959 Act are quite enough to fill one book. Secondly, as said already, I have not had the experience of working at Broadmoor with the 1983 Act which would be needed to continue its history or that of its sister special hospitals in the form and from the viewpoint I have adopted. Thirdly, the history has effectively now been continued by others.

The 1983 legislation has been followed with a succession of new management regimes and the story of the first principal one of these has been properly told by the people who have worked with it (*Managing High Security Psychiatric Care* edited by Kaye and Franey and published by Jessica Kingsley in 1998). Although their account does not use Partridge's format, which I have tried to follow, particularly in the early chapters, and it approaches the subject from the standpoint of the management issues that the 1983 Act and the end of the medical superintendent era posed, it does present a collection of chapters by authors from several disciplines, so illustrating the range of problems, procedures, practices and opportunities faced by the special hospitals within the framework of the 1983 Act. It provides, therefore, a further continuation of the special hospitals' story and this established the third good reason for the present account to go no further. One day it will be interesting to have a longer view of how the 1983 Act has worked out, along the lines Partridge used, but until a further Act replaces it or the dust of the current changes has settled, we shall have to be patient.

Although the period covered is therefore much shorter than Partridge's history it is nevertheless packed with a great deal of change and development, which it has been this book's job to describe. Scientific, technical, and hence social, changes have accelerated as the 20th century has progressed. Kaye's and Franey's book describes the problems of assimilating further change and covers a yet more foreshortened period in the history of the special hospitals.

I experienced the first three years of the 1983 Act at Broadmoor and then its next four years from the perspective of a Mental Health Act Commissioner, visiting psychiatric hospitals where patients were compulsorily detained and monitoring the Act's workings. This included the special hospitals of Moss Side and Park Lane (later to be combined into one administration as Ashworth Hospital) as well as a number of RSUs.

Appendix A of this book therefore describes the changes in the 1983 legislation, which provides a basis from which to see what were considered to be the shortcomings of the 1959 Act and how they were thought to be best remedied. When another author takes a longer view from a future standpoint some answers may be forthcoming to the many questions raised today that, in turn, see shortcomings in the 1983 Act. Will the present phase of the special hospitals' history be their last? Their end has been repeatedly urged, yet they continue, and look likely to do so until some alternative can be found which effectively provides both the treatment and the security that their patients and the public need and, just as important, which is accepted by local authorities as their responsibility. The special hospitals' critics seem to overlook this.

Ralph Partridge's coverage of the much longer period, from its building and opening in 1863 up to the retirement of Dr Hopwood in 1952, was marked at the end by the history-shaping escape of John Straffen. Coincidentally, thirty years later another charismatic superintendent was to retire and another high-profile escape took place, to which the previous chapter has referred. Broadmoor's history, however, is not defined by escapes and superintendentships but by legislation. It is this which sets the conditions and definitions for sending someone to Broadmoor, thus determining the constitution of the patient population, and when and to where they will move on. The currency of the first postwar legislation on mental health happens to coincide closely with Dr McGrath's superintendency. Dr James's short spell in the post after Dr Hopwood's retirement, luckily for this history, took place before the 1959 Act, when the pharmacological revolution was in its infancy, and before the arrival of the new therapies and their attendant ideas. The ensuing significant events and changes conveniently took place, therefore, almost entirely within Dr McGrath's period in office.

REAPPRAISAL OF THE PATIENTS

Chapters 3 and 4 in Part I of this book described how the 1959 Act, in the space of only its first decade, considerably changed the patient mix. The former groups were still there but some dwindled, or assumed a lesser profile, such as those who, formerly, had been admitted when capital punishment was the sentence for murder and when their crime had been so bizarre, or had given rise to such perplexity, that the court had concurred with the medical evidence and opted for an 'insanity' verdict; or a death sentence had been respited on subsequent Home Secretary's review. With the abolition of capital punishment in 1965 the impetus to be extra sure in such cases was removed and they could be reviewed at leisure in prison, being transferred to hospital if need be.

Amongst the newly defined groups, on the other hand, growing numbers of 'mentally disordered' people, as the new terminology defined them, were arriving in special hospitals who would not have met the former 'McNaughtan rules' criteria for insanity. These were people who had come before the courts, having committed violent acts, or who had been violent in other psychiatric hospitals, and who were often more obviously 'mentally disordered' (i.e.: displaying more acute psychotic symptoms) than many of those previously admitted from the courts under the 'McNaughtan madness' criteria. These latter would have met the criteria more often through the inexplicable destructiveness of their crime, or the utter bizarreness of both it and their accompanying behaviour, rather than their currently displayed mental state at the time of trial. Counsels, judges and juries were persuaded that 'they must be mad'. After 1959 they only had to be convinced from the medical evidence that a 'mental disorder' existed and that the severity of the violence of the offence warranted a secure rather than an ordinary psychiatric hospital.

The inclusion of 'psychopathic disorder' in the 1959 Act meant that this category of patient was now admitted explicitly from courts, the community and other hospitals instead of having to be first convicted, sent to prison and then transferred under some other 'insanity' diagnosis. Their conditions of detention, appeal and discharge were then different. This resulted in both an increase in this category of patient and their presence under different conditions. As a younger group they also brought down the average

age of patients on admission.

The first result of these changes in the patient population was a great increase in numbers admitted which, particularly at first when there were new and different statutory procedures to be complied with, greatly increased the consultant (RMO) workload and responsibilities. It also brought overcrowding and pressure on bed space, work opportunities and staff vigilance. Consultant and other specialist staff increases to cope with this were only gradual. Pressure on the ward and workshop staff (nursing and occupations officers) increased, again from both patient numbers and the different clinical and offender characteristics which they presented and which had to be met with more diverse clinical and nursing strategies.

Clinical practices changed and more psychiatrists, social workers and psychologists raised the patient profile and required new information and skills on the part, again, of the ward and workshop staff. The changing profile of the patient population increased the range of practices employed, especially taking account of the new concepts and terminologies introduced by the new professions. New medicines arrived thick and fast, together with new therapies. Research was initiated and gradually presented new challenges as well as much information of immediate practical use, such as the over-control concept and then construct theory, which opened the way to the social skills and cognitive therapies.

REAPPRAISAL OF PRACTICES

The organization of patient diagnosis and treatment had always hitherto been on the basis of an initial case conference, chaired by the physician superintendent in his auspicious office, large enough to double as a conference room, and attended by the hospital's various 'officers', each of whom (except where the nursing staff were concerned) was virtually the sole representative of their discipline.

Patients were then moved on through the hospital, starting at a 'block' (later 'house') providing the level of care intensity relevant to the severity of their disorder and progressing through successive 'blocks' until they reached the parole 'block'. This was the usual avenue for discharge, or for a quiet and peaceful existence if discharge was not going to happen for them (as would often be the case for notorious offenders or those with recalcitrant personality disorders that defied treatment and confident prognosis).

This system made use of the entire hospital in a graded way and was particularly suited to there being only one or two psychiatrists of consultant grade to set the initial diagnosis and assess the patient's state at the finish. In between, reviewing the patient's progress was very much the responsibility of the 'principal attendants' (later 'departmental nurses') heading each 'block', since they and their ward staff were the people in constant touch with patients, medical attention only being available from the small number of psychiatrists of mainly senior registrar level.

The 1959 Mental Health Act established a much more medical approach to what were no longer 'mental hospitals' (formerly 'asylums') functioning within a form of social rather than medical legislation, but were now 'psychiatric hospitals'. The changes required a greater medical input whilst advancing knowledge was also bringing new professional specialisms, an expanding range of diagnostic and therapeutic practices and an explosion in the development of medicines for the control and alleviation of mental disorders.

Numbers of consultant psychiatrists increased (designated responsible medical officers, or RMOs, in the new legislation), matched by their attendant senior registrars, together with other professional staff: social workers, clinical psychologists, teachers, psychotherapists, librarians, research workers, etc. The legislation was parallelled by similar developments in other countries who were all seeking their own way of dealing with the problem of the small group of psychiatric patients everywhere whose behaviour needed secure supervision and who could not be treated in the new 'open-door' hospitals being introduced throughout the psychiatric hospital system. Broadmoor became a focus for visitors world-wide. The many changing governments of different hues during the 60s and 70s, faced with the radical 1959 legislation and their direct responsibility for the 'special hospitals', sent their ministers and officials on numerous visits to this high profile establishment for which they found themselves having direct responsibility and which were now becoming embarrassingly overcrowded.

Committees, working parties, and inquiry panels also visited. Mental Health Review Tribunals (MHRTs), the creation of the 1959 Act, were held virtually every week in order to deal with the numbers of appeals deriving from a wholly 'detained' patient population. Visiting parties of related professional groups from elsewhere in the legal, penal and health care systems became a further weekly feature. The staff understandably came to feel under constant review themselves - or 'spied upon' as many put it - despite the praise that every visiting group invariably heaped upon them. Finally, when the virtual doubling of the admission rate and the spreading of discharge responsibility amongst the new cohort of consultants brought the inevitable, albeit small, percentage of discharge failures (but a few of which resulted in fatalities) major government action was initiated in the form of the Aarvold and Butler review bodies. The first of these introduced the ('Aarvold') procedure for tightening up a patient's security and discharge classification, whilst the latter provided a seminal and encyclopaedic report that was the basis for the next, 1983, Mental Health Act.

Research programmes began to yield more extensive and refined knowledge of patients' conditions and problems and were reported on prestigious occasions like the hospital centenary and the formation of the Royal College of Psychiatrists, as well as the regular conferences of the different clinical disciplines. Advancing technology, such as the arrival of video recording and the computer, facilitated both research and new treatment practices, which were happening anyway as a result of the increased numbers and range of professional groups in the hospital. An EEG service (electroencephalograph) was initiated and later expanded, through SHRU (the special hospitals research unit) which provided a further, neurophysiological, refinement to both clinical reports and research. Links were developed with several London teaching hospitals.

The changing times and advancing knowledge, together with gross hospital overcrowding and the pressure on beds in already old buildings, led to the decision to rebuild and modernize the hospital. Originally this was to have been in its entirety but later, because of costs, it was reduced to only a partial rebuild. A new special hospital (a 'Broadmoor of the North') was in any case built to relieve pressure and provide a more easily reached facility for the relatives of the many patients from the other end of the country, obviating a long and stressful journey to keep in touch. Everyone became involved in the planning for both these projects, through a special 'rebuild team'. Many nursing staff transferred to the new Park Lane Hospital, providing a nucleus of experience when it opened and its first medical director spent the year previous to its opening gaining experience at Broadmoor. The new special hospital and the rebuilding of Broadmoor provided the opportunity to redesign aspects that were considered unsatisfactory in the old buildings.

Overcrowding should have been avoided by the transfer, to other psychiatric hospitals around the country, of patients who had completed sufficient of their treatment to no longer need care in maximum security. To these should have been added the many older patients who also no longer needed secure care and who should have been moved long before had there only been the facility to do so. Certainly this happened, and initially went well but, unfortunately, the 'open door' revolution (forerunner of the community care philosophy) soon meant that local psychiatric facilities (and by now psychiatric units in general hospitals as well as the transformed former mental hospitals) increasingly became reluctant to accept what they saw as people who would jeopardize their new 'open' developments. In fact and in contrast, those Broadmoor patients who were accepted for transfer tended to complain that they were put in restricted and limiting conditions by comparison with the freedom they had enjoyed in Broadmoor. They were usually put with the more chronic and deteriorated patients who needed greater security and supervision, as the transferred Broadmoor patients were also erroneously thought to need - a very frustrating experience for people who were actually in a much more rehabilitated state and ready for a more diverse and challenging regime.

The Aarvold and Butler Committees had highlighted a situation where there was clearly the need for a more rigorous and explicit recommendation system for discharges, together with more valid and reliable indices on which to base the recommendations. Clinical teams were not yet operative in Broadmoor, nor the individual patient care plan. The expansion of clinical services was clearly moving this way, however. The setting up of research data bases, first by the psychology department and then by SHRU, led to the first discharge follow-up study at Broadmoor (one had been carried out some years previously by Tong and Mackay at Rampton), followed by another later which specifically contacted patients and obtained adjustment indices from their interviews and assessments. The earlier one had merely looked at the relationships between post-discharge success or failure and the information gathered about patients while in hospital. There was also a telling study by Dell confirming the difficulties in obtaining places for patients who were ready for transfer.

Despite their different designs and objectives all the studies confirmed a number of findings. By and large all the discharged patient groups did well, certainly by comparison with both other patient and offender populations. Reoffending was on a low scale and less serious than the original admission offences, or the pattern of their previous history. This was despite very variable levels of support from all agencies which the results showed was, nevertheless, much needed and welcomed when it happened. The group which did best was, surprising to the outside world but not to those at Broadmoor who had treated and studied them, those originally admitted for murder. Most of these had killed only once, later in life and without a previous criminal or psychiatric history, the victim usually being a spouse, partner or other well-known person. Their violence was specific and they were not a danger to the public as a whole.

It would be heartening to report both that these studies had been repeated and expanded and that their findings had passed into routine casework but, by the time of the 1983 Act, there was little indication that this had happened. Indices derived from the psychological findings were incorporated into discharge assessment reports of that department and it was encouraging that clinical teams paid attention to recommendations drawing upon them. Nevertheless it was disappointing that no resulting plan or policy was forthcoming from either local management, or the Department of Health or the Home Office, to capitalize on this work and make any systematic use of it. The costs of such work had actually been small when it is considered that much of it grew out of use of routinely gathered clinical information, so the costs of repeating and expanding it would not be great, whereas the costs saved in terms of treatment time and length of stay would be far greater and, therefore, well worthwhile. It is to be hoped that the continuation of the SHRU case register work, even after SHRU itself has now been wound up in favour of another research co-ordinating arrangement, will provide the basis and impetus for further work of the follow-up kind and that, like most research, in time the implications will have impact.

One source of resistance, one cannot help feeling, is a hostility towards something that might reduce the length of stay of patients (even though this would reduce costs), especially of those who originally have offended the most seriously. This seems to stem from a public and political conviction that offender-patients should serve some notional tariff sentence equivalent to 'normal' offenders coming through the criminal justice system who are considered responsible for their actions. This is despite their original committal as people whose mental state has been seen as in need of treatment, not punishment.

In fact, as has been explained at several points in this history, any fully effective treatment programme properly requires continuity through a succession of more open treatment environments culminating in the community at large. Someone whose original mentally disordered behaviour has been responsible for, or associated with, the death of their victim, could reasonably be expected to submit to licensing and supervision conditions, just as would a person paroled from prison. The 1983 Act, as will be seen, has introduced mandatory post-discharge supervision for several of the longer-stay categories within the new Act, both in civil and court cases, which should be adaptable for a quasi-parole purpose. Since this post-discharge supervision is of indefinite duration, until its ending is authorized, it can hardly be construed as a 'let-off' or 'soft option', and this concept should be irrelevant, anyway, for those whose mental disorder is regarded as impairing their responsibility for their actions.

But it seems there is still a considerable investment on the part of parliament and the judiciary, and hence public opinion generally, in 'paying the penalty', whatever the perpetrator's mental condition - a state of affairs where our Victorian forebears might be able to teach us something. The McNaughtan rules absolved the perpetrator of responsibility for actions undertaken during or as a result of 'insanity'. The ensuing court verdict was an acquittal from the crime but a committal to a safe place for public safety and the care of the patient.

The 1959 Act broadened the 'insanity' category to all mental disorders but convicted the perpetrator for the offence and only then ordered a committal for treatment. Of course, the contentious issue of the inclusion of 'psychopaths' in the new Act (whom the Victorians dismissed as 'moral imbeciles', although they still tended to put them in institutions rather than prison) has clouded the issue and tended to tarnish the thinking in respect of their more obviously disordered counterparts, the 'insane' or psychotic group. Increasing knowledge has tended to complicate rather than clarify, raising more issues where previously there had seemed to be just a straightforward few.

REAPPRAISAL OF THE CLINICAL SYSTEM

While the changes in patient mix, and therefore clinical requirements, were taking place, accompanied by expansion of both numbers and kinds of professional groups in the hospital, the organization of the system for delivery of services was changing and brought changes, this time, in concept and rationale.

The increase in medical staff at consultant, 'responsible medical officer', level meant that each RMO needed his own area of responsibility (there were no women RMOs during this period). The hospital buildings lent themselves to an RMO in charge of each ward block, or 'house', comprising three wards and roughly 100 patients. There were variations and exceptions, of course, but this was the principle and it was both rational and appropriate. However, it had a number of consequences for change of clinical approach. Although clinical teams were only to become explicit some time later, it effectively created these and broke up the hospital into a number of separate units. This ended the system of patients progressing through a number of different environments, although some of this persisted because of the need to provide different levels of security, with their different staffing levels and clinical requirements, but insofar as these could be provided within a three ward house, they were. Exceptions were special units for new admissions, the very disturbed, and for the younger male patients, while Essex, the parole house, as well as comprising the rehabilitation base from where many patients were discharged, continued to act as a comfortable sanctuary for those unlikely ever to leave. As well as this break-up and the spreading of clinical responsibility among several consultants, however, this development consolidated the 'medicalization' of the hospital.

In so doing, as has been said, the post-war NHS Acts and the 1959 Mental Health Act between them medicalized what had previously been a predominantly social emergency system and effected a 'knight's move': it progressed patient care with the use of the rapidly expanding field of psychiatric care and advances in medication, yet it left behind what had been a rather exhausted and, indeed, discredited social approach to mental disorder just when a fresh set of socio-educational criteria and strategies were coming on stream. The disciplines of psychotherapy, social work and, particularly, clinical psychology were not only bringing the methods of traditional psychoanalysis into briefer, more practical effectiveness but, more significantly, developing a new range of behavioural psychotherapies. From the early behaviour therapy itself, deriving from classical learning theory and the various conditioning approaches to treatment, this progressed to the applications of social learning theory with such procedures as social skills training and then cognitive behaviour therapy. All these analysed aspects of inappropriate or maladaptive current behaviour from the point of view of the various personal and emotional goals it satisfied and how these were to be extinguished or substituted with preferable goals or routes to them (in the case of Broadmoor patients, non-offending ones). Training routines would then be devised to eliminate the unwanted behaviours and enable the new ones to become as automatic as the old ones.

This brief and somewhat perfunctory description of the wide range of derivatives and applications to have sprung from the psychological methods of the 'interacts' period may seem trite but its purpose here is merely to indicate that the system is in a different scientific and methodological domain from the medical developments of the same era (the subject receives more attention in the next chapter). It provided in some cases an essential additional strategy needing to follow the effects of medication, in others an altogether alternative one. It focused on the process rather than the structure or, to use a modern computer analogy, the software rather than the hardware.

REAPPRAISAL OF THE RESOURCES AND THEIR USE

To carry out the *practices* reviewed above; within the *system* reviewed above; to accomplish the *task* recapitulated above; for the benefit of the *patients* reviewed above: resources are needed. These are the buildings, equipment, facilities and, above all, staff. All of these have been described in the various chapters of this history and here it is the changes, developments and advances that need to be summarized.

The buildings were erected over a century earlier and their still effective security has always been considered appropriate for their continuing purpose. It is the purpose which is argued. Given that this large campus exists and will continue to exist until an alternative is devised, the rebuilding that has taken place in the period of the 1959 Act has had the aim of both consolidating security and of accommodating modern practices. Security has always been primarily a matter of the perimeter wall so that as much freedom of movement as possible can take place within it.

I have described it as a secure 'community' because of this and of the size of the area within the walls. This term is worth emphasizing in the light of the 'community care' concept which has predominated in much of the 'interacts' period, especially the later part. The old mental hospitals, housed in the Victorian asylums, have been first opened up, their doors unlocked, admission made voluntary where possible, and then have been closed, demolished, and their sites sold. Whilst they were out-of-date, however, their awfulness was less a matter of their architecture, which could always have been adapted and modernized, and more a matter of the way they were run. They had become dumping grounds within a system that gave their inmates little chance of leaving yet provided them with but primitive care in an even more primitive environment. Yet, as said in the previous chapter, their

457

abandonment and closure has been a case of 'throwing out the baby with the bath water'. How else can one regard their reopening, in several desirable parts of the country, as blocks of prestigious, private flats, suitably renovated, providing luxury period homes?

When community care has been seen to have been too often premature and insufficiently staffed to provide the necessary support and protection, it is galling to see so many of the Victorian asylums demolished and their sites sold and redeveloped, when they could have provided the village communities that many discharged psychiatric patients need. Open to the outside world but modernized to contain flats, hostels, shops, entertainments, and with therapy clinics and support services on site, how much more effective as well as staff and cost efficient they could have been. Some work opportunities could have been located on site, just as recreation and entertainments could have been provided there, but residents could equally have been able to go out to work, recreation or entertainment, just as anyone else does who lives in a block of flats. Visiting would have been simple and residents easy to locate, instead of having the worry of wondering where they were and what problems they were suffering.

This may seem to have wandered off the subject and be riding some personal hobby horse. The purpose of this apparent deviation, however, is to emphasize that Broadmoor, one of the Victorian asylums still operational, nevertheless constitutes a community within which as many as possible of the facilities described above have been made available for the therapy, occupation and recreation of those compelled to be there. Of course residence is not optional but, given the constraints, it provides as much of a community as security allows. The chapters on the environment as a therapeutic community and on the various recreational provisions of Broadmoor describe this community in some detail, developing what Partridge has already described. Chapter 14 describes the planning and start of the programme to rebuild a large part of the hospital and make it a more effective treatment community. This has been happening when the prevailing opinion instead favours the development of small local secure units, as proposed by the 'Butler' Committee. These are, of course, immensely important but, again, should not be seen as necessarily invalidating and replacing what went before, but complementing them, as 'Butler' envisaged.

RSUs have eventually and gradually been set up around the country and place the responsibility at local level where it belongs. Locally, however, there will not be enough mentally disordered offenders to justify more than a small unit. Although some cater for larger areas of the country and have a capacity of a hundred beds or more, most only serve small areas and hold a dozen or so. They facilitate better contact with families, home visits and local activities, even employment, but until their residents can be assessed as safe for such activities, the unit is a small world in which to confine someone if their treatment is to be fully effective in the way that a community provides. No workshops, sports teams and other group recreational activities are feasible unless the facilities of the psychiatric hospital campus where they are generally located are open to them, which they generally are not; RSU residents are too much feared and shunned in the locality.

RSUs have so far tended to take the less severe, lower security patients who have not reached special hospital severity or are being rehabilitated after leaving special hospitals. Already, as the Mental Health Act Commission has found and wrestled with, there have been backlogs of special hospitals patients, whose progress no longer warrants high security, waiting to be transferred to a local facility. Dell's research, referred to in Chapter 18, has highlighted the resistance to transfers: in short, they are not wanted. Even allocating the cost of their care to the local authority from where they originate has not solved the problem. Many local authorities prefer to pay for these patients to continue their treatment in the private secure units which have sprung up around the country. Not only is responsibility not accepted where it belongs, and as the various pressure groups would want it, but a new kind of special hospital is providing an increase in capacity for a system which its critics want to see done away with altogether. The problems are at risk of being repeated all over again.

REAPPRAISAL OF THE STAFF

The 'Big Issue' to many of their critics where continuing to use a large institution like a special hospital is concerned, however, is not what care, treatment, work, education, recreation and other facilities are available but what sort of staff run the place. What is their attitude and behaviour towards those over whom they have power and what management policies and powers exist to ensure that the establishment runs as it should?

Being only too well aware of these criticisms and misgivings about special hospitals, especially in the light of the scandals and revelations that punctuate their progress and have been particularly prevalent since the new, 1983, Act took over, I pointed out early in this history that few staff who were not present on the wards day in and day out would know for certain what went on. If anything happened that shouldn't have, it would be out of sight of anyone who might blow the whistle. This may strike many people as strange: surely one should know what is going on in such a small community? Well, of course, there might be a general sense of harshening attitudes but this does not mean that specific instances can be substantiated. One may discern attitudes through conversations but it is quite another matter proving some malpractice. Staff will not break ranks. They could not survive within the system if they did. Over the years it was fairly clear if the general atmosphere was deteriorating and sometimes there were misgivings that vindictiveness was growing. But this is very different from being able to prove that some specific abuse had occurred. It must be witnessed. Hearsay is worthless. As I have said, nothing would happen in my presence that could be taken amiss.

When one considers the level of violence that seems to be habitual in all parts of the world, which we read and hear of and see on our screens daily, there seems little doubt that those in power abuse those who are not, in all places and circumstances, and it is just a question of how much, how often. The best that it seems one can hope and work for is that it is not excessive, that it is monitored and under control. Although Alan Reeve alluded to violence from Broadmoor staff in the same terms as elsewhere, it is interesting that he is relatively unspecific and remarks that it never happened to him (to whom, of all people, one might expect that it had). He even speaks well of a number of staff by name and in this his opinion of them coincides with my own.

Another perspective on staff attitudes to patients is provided by two further sources. There were many patients who volunteered that coming to Broadmoor had given them the jolt that they needed, some even praising the effects of having started their stay in Block 6, later Monmouth House, where they were confined to a bare room for some weeks. Their comments would include reference to their treatment being strict but fair and that their previous record was not held against them: they were reckoned to be starting their lives afresh. Peter Thompson, another former patient who has written about his Broadmoor experience and who founded and runs the Matthew Trust, has said that without the help of Broadmoor nurses and psychiatrists he would never have got better and is forever grateful to the staff who give their lives and time to helping people with mental health problems. He regarded Broadmoor as his 'university and home' and was proud to be 'an old Broadmoor man'.

The second source was Mrs Paton, the sole social worker at Broadmoor in 1959. Every Christmas she received quite the largest number of cards and letters of anybody I know, and a copious flow of letters and postcards throughout the year in between. Large numbers of former patients kept in touch, telling of the ups and downs of their lives, enclosing family snapshots and speaking of the gratitude they felt for the experience of Broadmoor to which they attributed being able to start their lives afresh and make a go of them. These examples don't seem to tally with a brutal environment.

Another aspect of attitudes attributed to the staff derives from their uniforms. These were not remarkable in the immediate post-war years because uniforms were accepted as part of institutional life everywhere; at the 'county mental hospitals' just as much as at the special hospitals. Uniforms were a way of life in the Victorian, Edwardian, inter-wars and immediate post-war periods. Informality of dress is a very recent development. So special hospitals' staff uniforms were not so very different from any other; perhaps a little more stiff and starchy but not much, whilst the women staff's uniforms looked like nurses anywhere. But as time wore on the difference became more noticeable. Uniforms everywhere else were being made more informal or abandoned altogether.

Broadmoor and the other special hospitals resisted this trend. Pundits will offer a variety of motivations for this; and they did. The argument offered at the time, however, which is difficult entirely to refute, was that staff needed to be immediately identifiable in any emergency. In a fracas, staff needed to know whom they were helping and whom they were trying to restrain. In an emergency, like a fire, they needed to know whom to follow as the person who had the keys to the outside. For a long time, therefore, uniforms persisted.

On the Female Wing there was less protest. The women staff were nurses, just as much as the men, but they looked more like the traditional image of a nurse, so were presumably more acceptable for this. On the male side, and despite the introduction in the 1960s of a mid-blue worsted with traditional modern jacket, in place of the former navy blue serge button-to-the-collar tunic, staff still affronted visitors and many patients as too authoritarian. The peaked hat didn't help, even though it was only worn outdoors and the Hardy Amies design looked like the US Air Force in comparison with the former strict British military appearance. Too many staff favoured the fashion of re-angling the peak to the near-vertical of the guardsman but at least this forewarned patients and non-uniformed staff of the attitude they were likely to encounter. Of course, on the wards, many staff discarded their jackets and some wore white coats on more medically orientated duties, which conveyed a clinical appearance. Some patients preferred staff to be uniformed - it helped to promote confidence, they said - but still protests continued.

Eventually uniforms did begin to disappear. It started with the chief nursing officer and his deputies, the SNOs. With their scrambled egg hat and sleeve insignia they had always looked rather like Ruritanian generals anyway. Unfortunately, they adopted instead suits of a style that somehow managed to get them the nickname of 'the Mafia' when they trooped into the staff restaurant for lunch. Specialist staff, such as tutors, however, took to 'civvies' and gradually the uniform tradition began to erode.

Later, when working with the Mental Health Act Commission introduced in the 1983 Act, commissioners would visit numerous hospitals all over the country and, since these visits were only annual and even the special hospitals quarterly, it was unlikely one would get to know many of the staff. It was therefore sometimes disconcerting when entering wards not to know who were staff and who were patients. Dress had become so informal as often to be scruffy. Staff, moreover, would not necessarily be in their offices but, appropriately of course, among their patients around the ward. One developed the habit of avoiding any tactless assumptions and simply asked to have the person in charge pointed out. This was probably to the patients' benefit as they were then addressed normally and not condescendingly. Some of them might have 'twigged' this one and presented themselves as staff, of course, to obtain confidential information but I never heard of this happening.

The continuing history of the special hospitals, recounted in Kaye's and Franey's book, gives an extensive account of the problems of agreeing the philosophies and practices of patient care with the POA, the staff association representing the majority of the nursing staff. As was the case during the period of the 1959 Act, the POA's first concern has always been security, on which they would no doubt have the support of the majority of the public. Dr McGrath, and no doubt any later management system, would not disagree but would differ on how this co-exists with the duty of care and treatment. I have quoted Dr McGrath's adage that the best security is the knowledge of one's patient and this in turn is best afforded by interacting with patients in their treatments.

This, of course, assumes that treatment entails such interaction and too many staff in the 'interacts' period seemed still to see treatment as merely supervising the handing out of pills or, at the most, of accompanying patients to see the specialist staff who carried out the more formal treatments, instead of using such contacts to achieve closer understanding. It was difficult to break through this attitude and for individual staff to adopt a more proactive attitude to patient care. But in this it didn't seem that they were so much opposed to such treatment initiatives as reluctant to 'break ranks' - it just 'wasn't done' and until it was done they weren't going to be the first to do it. Those who did take an initiative were referred to as 'having got the nursing on them'. On the other hand, supportive relationships would invariably spring up between a patient and a particular member of staff. Inquiries would invariably reveal which nursing staff member one should approach if one needed to contact and get the confidence of a patient in order to carry out an assessment or start some treatment. This was accepted. It was, in fact, a way of life in Broadmoor. It was, however, somehow seen as different from 'treating patients'.

As typified by the 'normal distribution' - the 'bell-shaped curve' - characteristic of most human qualities, a quarter of the world seems to occupy the 'fierce' personality extreme; another quarter the opposite 'tolerant' extreme; and the remaining half in the middle, are normal, decent people for whom it takes a great deal - a fire, earthquake, bomb or rail disaster - before they will stand up and be counted. Broadmoor was like every other situation in life in this respect. The trouble is that the minority quarter at the 'fierce' extreme tend to dominate the scene and quell the rest. This often seemed to be the problem during the McGrath era and has apparently also been the problem for the management system which followed the 1983 Act, described by Kaye and Franey.

The building of Park Lane Hospital (later amalgamated with Moss Side Hospital into Ashworth Hospital) presented a chance to start afresh, with a new remit and new staff who would be trained from scratch. Certainly the ones that went there from Broadmoor were amongst the best and would have met the grudging approval of even Alan Reeve. However, it wasn't to be. What happened? It doesn't seem to have worked out. Perhaps they needed a new staff union to go with a new hospital. But would pride, apprehension and uncertainty have driven it the same way as its predecessors?

Dr McGrath was a firm but fair superintendent, as

understanding of his staff as he was of his patients, coming down hard on any professional inefficiency or misbehaviour and liked and respected as a result. Even so, he periodically encountered industrial action from the POA which he found difficult to resolve. Kaye and Franey seem to have found no difference. Would it be any different in a smaller unit? The same problems don't seem to have arisen in the RSUs. Is this because their smallness makes it more difficult to be abusive without it becoming obvious? Or is it perhaps that a different union operates with a different philosophy? Size and staffing may well prove to be the crucial factors in the survival or extinction of the special hospitals.

SUMMARY

Introducing this reappraisal section of Broadmoor's history, the task has been to trace the development of Broadmoor after the 1959 Mental Health Act. This radically changed the way psychiatric patients were defined and detained. Partridge's original history had covered the period from its inception up to 1952 and little changed after this until the 1959 Act. Kaye and Franey's book (see particularly Appendix B) follows on for the period of the 1983 Act, albeit from a rather different perspective.

Reappraising the patients, these were differently defined in the 1959 Act. No longer did someone have to be 'insane' under the McNaughtan criteria but the new fourfold criteria of 'Mental Disorder' allowed a wider range of people to be detained for care and treatment. This happened after conviction so that patients were no longer acquitted of their crimes as they were under the previous 'guilty-but-insane' procedure. The new Act also introduced the category of 'psychopathic disorder' which brought yet another group of patients into the picture. Patients could also be transferred between Broadmoor and conventional psychiatric hospitals. The results were a rapid doubling of the admission rate.

Practices also changed. The new Act introduced many more statutory procedures, gave responsibility for patient care to the responsible medical officers (RMOs) and created a new appeal procedure via the Mental Health Review Tribunals (MHRTs). A medical ethic replaced the mainly social one of previous legislation and further medical staff were recruited. Other clinical disciplines also arrived and clinical procedures and treatments expanded.

The hospital's long established pattern of functioning as a unitary whole, with patients moving through as they improved, and being discharged from one of the parole houses, gradually changed to one of a series of mini-hospitals, each run by its clinical team, receiving patients from the new admission unit and discharging them directly. Research began, the special hospitals research unit (SHRU) was formed and new clinical procedures as well as information sprang from this, greatly expanding the assessment and treatment repertoire.

The almost inevitable result of the doubling of patient throughput and the dispersal of clinical authority to a larger number of RMOs was that a small number of discharged patients made headlines by reoffending, a few dramatically. Transfer to other hospitals, initially a helpful avenue for those recovering, or the more chronic elderly patients, became much more difficult to achieve as the countrywide tendency for psychiatric hospitals to open their doors led to greater reluctance to receive what were seen as potentially dangerous patients. The special hospitals 'silted up'. Local authorities were urged to accept patients from their catchment area who had completed their special hospital treatment. Government committees inquired into the problems. Regional secure units (RSUs) were recommended but were slow to materialize. Tightened up procedures were introduced to prevent future mishaps. Still local authorities were reluctant to take their patients back. Research studies addressing post-discharge outcome confirmed that the majority of patients did well and serious re-offending was minimal. Sadly, these researches have not been repeated and their findings do not seem to have provided the necessary reassurance.

Fortunately, therapies were expanding promisingly on the back of research and the initiatives of a number of dedicated therapists. These, too, spawned their own criteria for the change and ultimately greater safety of their patient recipients. The crucial importance of 'continuity of care' was thereby underlined, again demanding a system linking secure, semi-secure and open environments in a continuous sequence.

Unfortunately, research, assessment and treatment developments only emphasized the drawbacks of the 'knight's move' of the 1959 legislation, medicalizing a problem that was only partly medical and where the principal advances were not medical but psychological, i.e.: in the 'process', or software, of human activity rather than in its 'structure', or hardware.

The final resource reappraised has been the staff, recognizing their enigmatic position as providers of both care and security. In the context of changing treatment methods and philosophies the opportunity to return to the more socio-educational forms of treatment of Partridge's history re-emerged, just when legislation had medicalized the concept; treatment was seen mainly as 'dishing out pills'. Nevertheless, the nursing staff's reservoir of knowledge of patients was enormous and needed to be capitalized upon if significant treatment progress was to be achieved. Allegations of abuse occasionally arose and this history has tried not to duck the issue but, as in any large organization or community, these were difficult to assess. Incidents in out-of-the-way corners were unlikely to be observed by anyone other than the staff in the immediate vicinity. Sensitivity to the hospital atmosphere, together with the comments of patients themselves, suggested that the conduct of people in the community of Broadmoor was no different from that of people in any other community.

CHAPTER 22

PRINCIPLES AND SYSTEMS REAPPRAISED

At the beginning of this history a number of questions were raised and the ensuing chapters have inevitably raised others. Would the developments marking the progress of the 1959 Act establish the definition and limits of mental disorder and its several sub-categories? Are these conditions diseases, illnesses, injuries or personality defects and, if so, are they acquired or inherited, or are they to be attributed instead to environmental circumstances? Are they the cause or the result of the violence? What conclusions can be drawn about treatment: is it the appropriate strategy or is it an abrogation of civic responsibility? If treatment is to continue to be the rationale for mentally and personality disordered people who behave dangerously or break the law, what kind of treatment is it to be and where and how is it to be provided?

PROFESSIONAL SOURCES

Answers to some of these questions have emerged as the book has gone on. It would have made for a strained and artificial narrative if the consequences and questions had not been addressed at the point they arose. This chapter, however, must attempt to gather together the issues and the answers that have emerged in the time of the 1959 Act and look at the implications for the principles under which the system operates. In doing so it should be said that the professional literature is replete with evidence and commentaries of a more comprehensive kind than can be accommodated here. As a history, this account has intentionally avoided the frequent punctuation with references that would mark a scientific, medical or legal publication, although a few have been included where they seemed essential and helpful. A bibliography lists these and some further ones of relevance.

Places where the several professions publish their views and findings might helpfully be mentioned at this point, however. Each medical specialty has its own journal but the Royal Colleges and the Associations of other professions also publish their findings and views on particular issues in special papers and reports. These may be obtained from their offices, addresses for which may be found in directories at public libraries. Where provision of secure care is concerned, the Royal College of Psychiatrists, the British Association of Social Workers and the British Psychological Society, amongst others, have all addressed the issue through special reports, obtainable from their headquarters offices.

The latter's report, *Psychology and Antisocial Behaviour* (BPS, Leicester, 1993) is particularly familiar to me, since I was its editor, and contains what I would naturally regard as fundamental analyses and recommendations for the problems addressed in this book. Unfortunately, these still seem to be regarded in some quarters as a novel, peripheral, or somewhat irrelevant viewpoint.

Then there are the government's own publications on the issues, as well as the legislation itself, to be found at The Stationery Office. The authoritative and comprehensive book in this field, however, containing far more than could be accommodated in any special report (for those who want more or are sceptical of my standpoint) is Ronald Blackburn's *The Psychology of Criminal Conduct* (Wiley, 1993).

MENTAL DISORDER, PERSONALITY AND ENVIRON-MENT: CAUSE OR EFFECT?

So we come to the first of the essential questions raised at the start of this book and the one to have occupied the minds of legislators and clinicians when Broadmoor was built, and of philosophers and the church long before that.

The course of Broadmoor's work following the 1959 Act and the developments and discoveries of the growing range of professions described in this history strongly suggest that both personal and environmental factors are involved in the offences of most patients. Rarely can it be said that it is wholly the mental disorder that is responsible for violent, dangerous behaviour.

This is irritating for those looking for unitary causes. The media always like to ask: 'What is the cause; who is to blame?' But as soon as one tries to explain the number of apparently interacting factors that are responsible, you can see eyes glazing over: it doesn't have impact. 'Are you trying to excuse these people?' is the common follow-up question. 'No, you asked about causes. Explanations are not excuses. Explanations are essential for knowing what best to do for public and personal safety as well as trying to ensure the offender doesn't do it again. They are also essential to our job of treating the disordered offender.' 'Well, perhaps it really boils down to their just being 'bad'?' 'That's not an explanation, it's a description: of course their actions were bad but we need to know why if we are to prevent it happening again.' 'Well, perhaps we should just lock them all up and never let them out?' 'OK, but that's up to Parliament and no major party in modern times has proposed it. The civil rights lobby would quite properly point out that it would deprive a large number of people of their liberty because of the small number who might be dangerous again. Anyway, at current rates of admission it would

472

need a new Broadmoor building every five years to hold the accumulation of mentally disordered offenders. Would the electorate approve the expenditure?' 'Well, perhaps we should just bring back capital punishment and get rid of them all?' 'Ah, but when capital punishment was abolished it only applied to murder and fewer than a quarter of the special hospitals' patients have murdered. Those who injure or sexually molest don't usually murder as well. What about the rest?' And so on!

To get back to causes: not only is mental disorder apparently not the only cause of the violence bringing someone to Broadmoor but 'mental disorder' as a category is itself not a unitary factor. It is a legislative term which encompasses a range of conditions with a multitude of causes. The 1959 Act specified four mental disorder categories: mental illness, mental subnormality, severe subnormality and psychopathic disorder. These may be subdivided again (although the Act does not, of course, do so) into: mental illness of injurious, infectious or degenerative origin? Subnormality of congenital or traumatic origin? Psychopathic disorder of congenital or acquired origin?

Then, after determining origins, the further question arises of the aggravating or ameliorating influences of environment, especially upbringing.

Finally, and quite apart from the question of the cause of the mental disorder, there arises the question of why any of thèse precipitating causes should give rise to violent rather than non-violent behaviours. Every time a discharged mentally disordered person commits some headline-making offence there is a quite understandable and appropriate concern to allay public fears by pointing out that only a very small proportion of mentally disordered behaviour is dangerous and amongst these the danger is more often to the self than to others. Most mental disorders are distressing rather than dangerous, involving perceptions and preoccupations which impair rational and efficient thinking, and they manifest themselves in terms of confusion and withdrawal or harmless mutterings and gestures. The small proportion that are expressed in terms of harm to others are the exception, not the rule. No wonder the eyes of journalists glaze over!

This is not to duck out of the problem but to understand the fuller picture and to address the question of causes, not blame. What the work at Broadmoor strongly confirmed during the currency of the 1959 Act and this history has tried to set out in the results of both assessment and treatment, is that psychosis, especially involving paranoid delusions, whether or not it is to be regarded as an illness, seems to derive its expression from problems and preoccupations of personality and circumstances. These might sometimes seem to constitute the disorder itself, escalating the distortions of thinking and emotional reaction to bizarre, out-of-control levels of provocation. In other cases they would seem to have accounted for the form the subsequent psychosis took, the onset of psychotic disorder reflecting the problems preoccupying the individual. So the delusions, for example, would turn upon the person or situation at the centre of the patient's concerns, prolonged and unresolved aggravation from that source mounting up to a catastrophically violent climax.

Whether this scenario constitutes a mental illness or an extreme development of a personality problem might seem a quibble and even to amount to the same thing to those who see psychotic disorder not as an illness, 'visited upon the person from outside' but as a reaction to unresolved interpersonal problems. Such a construction is increasingly used by psychologists these days. But to those who do still construe all or most psychoses as illnesses, the distinction must be acknowledged, even though it hardly matters here. Either way, the work at Broadmoor, and throughout the psychiatric services during this period, points to violent mental disorder deriving its dangerous expression from pre-existing personality and situational factors rather than some independent quality or component of an illness or disease. Assessing a disorder therefore requires parallel assessments of the underlying personality and its problems, and how these are acquired or develop, as well as the signs and symptoms of mental disorder. In this way the form taken by that disorder and how it is expressed will be better understood and more appropriate actions taken to remedy matters.

THE ROLE OF LEARNING

If pre-existing personality and the environmental situations which help or hinder it are so important, and affect or even constitute any subsequent mental disorder, how may these be changed?

Changing the environment will be the more easily understood, although not always easily achieved. It is nevertheless an increasingly and appropriately targeted component of treatment programmes nowadays, especially as treatment progresses towards the community stage where the environment becomes an element that can be realistically and tangibly tackled. Leaving it with this brief mention (although it recurs regularly throughout this history) is not to belittle its significance but merely to indicate its more readily understood nature as a factor to be changed, requiring less explanation here, and that it is less accessible as a therapeutic strategy at the secure hospital stage of the treatment continuum. Changing the personality is not so easily understood, or achieved, and requires more explanation in this history.

Once one has 'grown up' the formative learning period is passed; one cannot go back and grow up again. During the early period of trying to explain at Dr McGrath's case conferences how one might treat patients through use of learning strategies (what he enjoyed marginalizing as 'operant conditioning') he used to comment: 'If you are telling us the results of your assessments of personality indicate permanent characteristics, inherited or acquired in early life, how can you then talk of changing them, through operant conditioning or anything else?' At the time, I never managed to answer this adequately but, of course, later I would argue that personality did not, indeed, change, for the very reasons to which he referred. The behavioural strategies a person used were what changed. The assessment of personality characteristics might explain and predict tendencies to use some kinds of strategy in preference to others whilst the environmental background would point to how these might have been selected in the first place and then reinforced. Assessing the underlying personality could both help explain the kinds of strategies that had developed and, in the mentally disordered patient, how they had become distorted and inappropriately used. They could also help indicate what options there were for promoting a change of strategies. It has to be said that some psychologists regard behaviour as defining personality and therefore equate the two. Changing the behavioural strategies *would* then change the personality. Actually, in this context it hardly matters what we call it (except for theoretical purposes and the development of the science). The end result is the same in this case and so is the methodology. We are merely using a different name for the phenomenon we are changing: behaviour or personality.

Learning, then, is the process that the personality undergoes in relation to its environment to develop behavioural strategies that enable it to cope with that environment. Different personalities use different behavioural strategies, or the same strategies in different ways on different occasions. Different environments require different strategies for dealing with them. The job is to distinguish all of these and then to devise methods for changing strategies that don't work or get the person into trouble; or changing personal situations; or more probably both.

Reminders of the kinds of cases described in Part II (especially Chapters 13 and 17) will probably help to illustrate here.

Take first the case of an otherwise normal young man emerging from adolescence and needing to feel an affinity with adults of his own age and eventually a close intimate relationship with a young woman. He is, however, exceptionally shy. He has an over-protective mother who resists relinquishing him to another woman, chiding him for neglecting her, and is then derided by his father who despises his lack of 'get-up-and-go'; he has been punished by both in childhood for wetting his bed and later on for masturbating.

A 'prescription' or 'menu' for adolescence problems therefore exists. In learning terms his shyness has stopped him learning how to initiate and react to social situations. The fear and anxiety experienced from being punished for activities that are now associated with his emerging sexual feelings inhibit him further. He expects resistance to his wishes for a girl friend from his mother and to be denigrated by his father. Normal physiology nevertheless drives him to attempt to associate with a young woman but he is unsuccessful, lacking the skills to bring this about. He manages to get to a disco, cajoled by friends and (after numerous cop-outs) eventually persuades a young woman to be accompanied home. In his ineptness, he fumbles a sexual advance which is repulsed. On this occasion no violence ensues but he is now reinforced (i.e.: has learned again) that women can be rejecting, as his mother has been. After a succession of unsuccessful attempts, he eventually funks the disco but lingers in the area. He intercepts a young woman on the way home and attempts a groping embrace which is rejected. He runs away. Next time, more embittered, he forces sex upon a woman, and injures her in the struggle. He is identified, prosecuted, convicted and categorized as suffering from psychopathic disorder, so is sent to Broadmoor.

Treatments that are essentially learning based are needed. These must make up for lack of learning at the appropriate time or may have to undo and replace inappropriately learned behaviours. Probably the first treatment task would be to tackle the shyness, social withdrawal and inhibitedness by means of the step by step kind of social skills programme described in Chapter 13. This would include facility at initiating conversations. Concurrently he needs relaxation training to learn composure in stressful situations. He also needs a sex education programme. Group therapy with others with similar difficulties will also help promote sharing of common problems and social learning. After leaving Broadmoor he will need to continue the programme of expanding social competence within the more realistic environment outside, probably through an open ward of a local psychiatric facility and then day centre attendance.

Another and quite different example would be the man who has attacked a supervisor at work. He is deluded that harm was intended towards him. He is a quiet and cautious person and has had a succession of bad work experiences, being criticized for slow work and lack of co-operation with others. In becoming accustomed to criticism, he has learned (in fact falsely) that he is disliked. He is being criticized by his wife for numerous personal failings. He notices people in a pub from his workplace who keep looking at him. He cannot think why this should be and decides they have been told by his supervisor that his work is bad and that he is to be sacked. (The actual reason is that they are aware of the supervisor's criticism of him and are sympathetic.) Other events then come to assume malevolent significance in his by now negative mind set (i.e.: learned attitude) albeit trivial, e.g.: a rebuff from a friend, a misunderstanding from a supermarket check-out, a near miss from a car coming out of a side turning. To 'validate' his negative interpretations because he cannot accept any personal fault or that events might be chance happenings, he builds up a repertoire of false beliefs (i.e.: mislearns).

His supervisor asks him to do some overtime for an urgent job which involves them both being together alone late at work. He construes this as the occasion when the supervisor intends finding an excuse, when there are no witnesses, to sack him for bad work. He accuses the supervisor of this and the argument gets out of control. He attacks and injures the supervisor with a heavy spanner. Prosecuted, his delusional ideas emerge and he is committed under the Mental Health Act to Broadmoor.

Diagnosed paranoid schizophrenic he is medicated and stabilizes, although still maintaining delusional beliefs. He is persuaded to join a psychotherapy group, however, where people air their problems and discuss their beliefs about the motives of others. Several members acknowledge that their attitudes have been mistaken and the group is encouraged to role-play alternative strategies for dealing with frustrating and threatening situations. Still unconvinced, he nevertheless agrees to take part 'for the others'. With the aid of video feedback group members are enabled to see how their manner and attitudes can be misinterpreted and how different approaches engender different responses. He is encouraged to try some alternative strategies himself which the other group members applaud as more appropriate and acceptable and he can see this for himself in the video feedback. Learning a wider range of possible responses for a variety of social encounters convinces him that a different way of seeing and dealing with situations could be of advantage to him. Although never quite acknowledging that his original beliefs were entirely misplaced he nevertheless finds the new way of dealing with social interactions both more successful and more gratifying. He feels happier and less stressed. He will need to continue group therapy, possibly also medication, and to have professional support and supervision, first in an open ward of a local psychiatric facility and then through attending a community day centre.

DISTINGUISHING PSYCHOLOGICAL FROM PSYCHIATRIC TREATMENTS

Psychiatric treatment is publicly well understood when set within a medical 'hardware' context. Medicines set right the malfunctioning bodily systems. Surgery repairs them or removes intrusions. Set within a 'software' context, when it is the processes which are seen as pathological, it is less easily understood. When one then comes to psychological treatment within a similar 'paradigm' or model but where the processes are not pathological but are inappropriate, inefficient, unadaptive or simply lacking, so that treatment is a matter of effecting change, the matter is even less familiar and even more difficult to grasp. Because so much of the development and advances in the work at Broadmoor after the 1959 Act were in this domain, however, it has not surprisingly loomed large in the present history, and needs to be understood.

Changing behaviour: acquiring new modes of behaviour for dealing with needs or problems that previously were dealt with in a way that led to failure and, in the case of special hospitals' patients, violence, essentially depends upon principles of learning. This may merely entail acquiring new patterns of responding to life situations, in which case it may be likened to childhood learning, making good something that should have happened in childhood but didn't. More often, however, it will involve first 'unlearning' or eliminating a behaviour pattern already inappropriately learned, and which has had violence as a consequence somewhere in the behaviour chain, in order to replace it with another that is appropriate, effective and non-violent. This is more than 'eliminating bad habits' as it involves the replacement of one behaviour with another. Athletes know all about this when correcting technique, golfers or tennis players when trying to perfect their swing or serve, artists or musicians when striving for the perfect interpretation.

Once it is established that psychology uses the principles of learning, it all seems much clearer. We all know about learning. Or do we? The subject is frequently misunderstood. Most people's concept of learning is of the formal instruction they associate with school where, even with flexible modern methods, this is to miss the much more pervasive phenomenon of learning as a continuous activity of daily life where everyday experiences determine the extent and quality, not only of our knowledge and skills, but of the much more complex emotions, attitudes and ambitions of life. Repertoires and routines are established as a result of success following some endeavours and failure following others, thereby consolidating some and extinguishing others.

Without established routines, as anyone knows who is struggling with a new procedure or situation, life becomes very much more difficult and tiring. Depending on the importance of the objective for which one strives, and the positive emotions associated with success, failure of one strategy will either be followed by seeking another, which will in turn become a routine if it succeeds, or abandonment in favour of another objective. According to the objectives any one person selects or is presented with in life, and the values, feelings and motives associated with them, so certain behaviour patterns will become reinforced, entrenched and pervasive, whilst others will be rejected or never even considered. This is not to imply any particular psychological model in this learning process, of which there are many, but merely to differentiate the psychological approach from the more familiar medical one.

The pervasive patterns of behaviour learned in response to the requirements or pressures of someone's environment will vary, therefore, according to their perceptions, abilities, temperament, motivational and emotional needs, attitudes and so on, i.e.: 'personality', together with the nature of the environment they have inhabited and which has shaped them. Where antisocial and aggressive forms of behaviour predominate, which constantly get the person into trouble or which they or their immediate community or society more widely prohibit, then there are strategies for undoing this learning and relearning an alternative. But, as this history has tried to explain, it requires both acceptance and motivation, help and hard work. This holds both for the behaviour of antisocial but otherwise rational people and for the irrational and often bizarre behaviour of those in the psychotic category. With the latter it may not be possible until a medical strategy has first been used to restore some normality of physiological functioning to the brain and nervous system involved. This might, actually, be all that is required. However, it is more likely that medication's suppression of neurological overactivity (extraneous 'noise') or restimulation of inactive neural pathways will still leave new or changed behaviours needing to be acquired.

This analysis seems all the more likely, from the studies and experiences described in this history, when one considers that patients' pre-psychotic lives will often have been characterized by inefficient or inappropriate strategies, or even a failure to have acquired any strategies at all for coping with some of life's contingencies, so that those lives have gone awry. It may even be that psychotic states are the result of confusion arising from dealing with life circumstances with inappropriate strategies, and some psychological opinion favours this, as was said earlier. But again, whether these are illnesses or extremes of personality reaction, the combination of a medical approach to the physical condition and a psychological approach to the coexisting personal, personality and situational condition seems to be what works best.

Where medical alleviation of the psychotic confusion or impaired neurological functioning reduces overactivity or rejuvenates inactivity and is regarded as completing treatment, problems occur. Even supervised gradual transfer to the real world can be followed by relapse. Worse, failure to cope, due to not having established a different and more appropriate repertoire of behaviours for dealing with life, may equally lead to further unlawful conduct.

The other misconception surrounding 'learning', as well as its simplistic restriction to formal aspects of schooling, is that it is a process which only involves passive acceptance of instruction, although interactive learning systems by computer are gradually demolishing this image. Nevertheless, the misconception has tended to be maintained by the traditional image of 'talk therapies'. Again it is worth recapping an earlier chapter where this practice, although helpful, especially in engendering confidence and the ability to talk about one's problems, was described as only part of the process of learning. The example of learning a skill such as a sport or playing a musical instrument was used to illustrate that, as well as 'book knowledge' - being taught the principles - one invariably has to undergo hard practice to ingrain a technique or procedure so that it becomes fluent and automatic. This is especially so where behaviour has to be changed. 'Old habits die hard' and it is not easy to undo them so that new ones can be substituted. The field now known as 'cognitive behavioural therapy' is not an easy option.

Nor is it one that can be imposed as many medical procedures can. Where medicine is concerned, consent has become a crucial issue in recent years and, for those who do not consent there are safeguards and second opinions required, especially with the introduction of the 1983 legislation. With psychological therapies, however, most of which cannot be imposed, consent and co-operation are a prerequisite. This poses a problem for legislators. How can a court set a 'sentence' which is dependent upon the consent of the convicted person? As Appendix A will describe, this has given rise to various provisions for remanding for the assessment of 'treatability' which, in some cases, will mean the agreement of the recipient to undergoing, in effect, a voluntary procedure. Of course, as with probation, where treatment is sometimes a condition, it can be made clear that non-acceptance will entail the alternative of imprisonment. This imposes a degree of coercion which is often held to be antithetical to the concept of treatment but, then, so is a hospital order anyway: the court imposes this. The ethics of the law allows action on behalf of the community in imposing penalties. But this also offers opportunity for reform and rehabilitation. That is society's counterbalancing responsibility. It is, however, one that is often overlooked these days. The power to penalize and restrict the liberty of an offender is too often seen as the end of the matter.

PROFESSIONAL ETHICS

This, of course, broaches the subject of professional ethics, which had scarcely emerged as a significant issue in the time of the 1959 Act. *Who is the Client?* (Monahan, 1980), questioning whether psychologists in criminal justice settings were serving the needs of the offender or the state, became a clarion call only as the era was ending. Previously, it had always been assumed that conviction in a court of law brought forfeiture of rights. What rights? How many? Which ones? Surely there were basic rights which were inalienable? These needed spelling out and by the end of the 1959 Act the questions were being more urgently asked.

Previously, health care professionals in secure hospitals (those in prisons seemed to have no problems - their primary concern was that prisoners were fit to be punished) seemed to assume that, as the law had deprived their patients of their freedom, it was up to them to use their professional knowledge and skills to the best of their ability to restore mental health to the point that their patients could resume both their lives and their freedoms. '*Who is the client?*' was irrelevant. Both patient and state stood to gain from their professional attention. If they failed to fulfil these duties then that might be a matter for professional investigation but was not necessarily one for ethical concern.

It is worth holding on to this principle in examining the situation subsequently. The added factor became the awareness that the detained person might not want to change and to require him or her to do so through some treatment or correctional programme, in order to be returned to the free world outside, amounted to coercion and was therefore unethical. Note the change of terminology in the question: 'Who is the *client*?' The detained patient was no longer an object to be treated willy-nilly but an active participant to be consulted.

The debate continues and looks unresolvable. It certainly attracts protagonists on all sides who make it clear that it is a political issue. Can there be a non-political, factual, scientific answer? At present the resolution remains the pragmatic one that, although numerous inalienable human rights must be respected and are now more clearly defined and recognized, harming other people is not one of these rights. To require someone to change such behaviour before allowing them to rejoin a free society, and to offer them the means of doing so, fulfils a professional duty at one and the same time to both the individual and the state and is therefore ethical. Political arguments may change this insofar as governments may change laws but, where professionals offer the means to change unlawful behaviour (and won't behaviour which harms others always be unlawful?), they cannot be said to be functioning unethically. Because of their situation, however, and the forfeited rights of their patients, they will need to be continually subject to ethical scrutiny and answerable for their practices.

THE PROBLEMS OF NORMAL VARIATION

To return from the ethics to the explanations of treatment, and having claimed a clear distinction between the 'content' or 'process' approach of psychology and the 'system' or 'structure' approach of medicine, it has to be said that psychiatry also uses a 'process' approach as well as a structural one.

However, the medical approach of psychiatry to processes is again different from the psychological. It views them as either healthy or diseased; functioning or malfunctioning. That is not a criticism. The job of medicine is to deal with illness, disease and deterioration. Psychiatry is a medical specialization so it takes a similar view.

A psychological view of 'processes', by contrast, is to see them from the standpoint of a normal phenomenon but with variations which may have abnormal consequences. In this, the concept of 'abnormal' is not of a sick or diseased process but of a rare, exceptional or extreme variation from what is usual or common. The psychologist's role has not been to identify malfunction but to ascertain what are normal variations of function and their consequences, whether the variation is towards the excessive or the deficient. Psychologists then offer strategies for overcoming problems arising from these, enabling change, modification, enhancement or amelioration to happen. (For completeness and accuracy, this role has now extended to identifying, not only extreme variations, but any behavioural characteristic or combination of these that gives rise to someone wanting to enhance or reduce their effects. It has also expanded to include the psychological components of physical disability or illness.)

Two examples from contrasting psychological fields, one of reasoning ability and the other of emotional responsiveness, illustrate the essence of the different approach to 'process' used in psychology. Both of these psychological phenomena vary widely in the human species and variations within the common or 'normal' range are associated with 'normal' characteristics such as competence and warmth of feeling. Excess or deficiency of either may be associated with difficulties in dealing with life. Insufficient ability or capacity to learn may prevent someone from earning a living or even, in extreme cases, from managing their lives without help from others. Excessive or inadequate emotional responsiveness may lead to disruption of the ability to cope with those same daily lives through the interference of fears, worries and depression or, conversely, failure to appreciate the feelings and needs of others, to respond socially and hence to failing to maintain relationships.

Similar scenarios can be constructed for other personal qualities comprising the personality mix. Impulsivity and its converse - excessive inhibition, repression and control of impulses - have emerged as particularly relevant in special hospital patients. Sociability and its converse, shyness or withdrawal, have also proved to be important. All these key psychological characteristics, and many others that have been put under scrutiny by psychologists at the special hospitals, are personal qualities of human response which, like our height and weight, vary widely about a general average, or statistical 'mean'.

Unlike an illness, disease or injury, therefore, which we either have or don't have, so that we are either sick or well, the difficulties attaching to variations of ability, emotion and temperament vary widely in their effect, either singly or in combination. We may be mildly inconvenienced, or sometimes extremely distressed, as can happen to all of us, without it halting our daily activities; or we may be among the statistical few who are rendered incapable by 'neurotic' levels of emotional reaction.

The fact that we all experience some disability or distress at times no doubt accounts for the saying 'pull yourself together' so often directed at sufferers. But in extreme cases the sufferer cannot do this without help. While most of us welcome help, even when we are only under the normal pressures of life, for people at the abnormal extremes of personality dimensions, which often render them incapable of coping with events, it becomes a necessity. Their excess or lack of some psychological quality, or more likely combination of several, render them incompetent with certain daily routines; or with certain relationships; or liable to disruptive emotional reactions when trying to do so; or to using solutions which are unacceptable or break the law, in some cases violently.

Yet despite recognizing our own distress when under the normal pressures of life, we commonly fail to accept their incapacitating effects on others less well equipped to cope. We accept that some people lack an ability for figures, or languages, or ball games, or are tone deaf and can't sing, but we are reluctant to accept that similar variations in human ability and temperament make some people crumple in the face of stresses with which most of the rest of us manage to cope. We tend to condemn rather than understand. The story of the judge is well known who chides: 'We all experience these problems but most of us manage to deal with them.' Of course we do! Most of us have adequate personal resources or a supportive environment.

It is therefore not easy to draw cut-offs between what is normal and should be treated judgementally and what is abnormal and needs help. Being ill or well is a clear distinction (more or less, given the in-between states of going down with an illness and recovering from it) but being short of or overwhelmed by an excess of some psychological quality is different: it can happen to slight or to extreme degrees. It is this which makes for the problem of recognizing when a situation needs the intervention of some helping agency or, in the case of unlawful behaviour, when it may be so severe as to impair the capacity to act responsibly and to call for a wider range of options than merely judicial punishment.

As well as the difficulty in adapting this 'continuous variation' of human characteristics to the medical concept of 'ill or healthy' and the court process of 'guilty or not guilty' there is the further problem that variations of some psychological characteristics are not recognized by the people displaying or 'suffering' from them. They therefore fail to see why they have done what they have done and that they need help to change. Again, people with a poor ability in some respect, or with a tendency to catastrophic emotional reactions, may well feel embarrassed or affronted to have their characteristics revealed and disputed in court. People with impulse control problems (typical of psychopathic disorder) tend to deny this is a problem. Those holding paranoid delusional beliefs will usually deny they have a problem at all - this *is* their problem!

WHAT SORT OF CARE AND TREATMENT SYSTEM FOLLOWS?

If personality interacting with environment is the basis for potential violence (whether or not this is severe or bizarre enough to be construed as illness or there is mental illness in addition); if these are complex and not unitary entities; if a learning (or unlearning and relearning) approach is fundamental to lasting change, whatever medical strategy may also be required; and if the concepts of abnormality that arise from this are of a gradually and widely varying kind rather than the more distinct categorizations of being ill or well; what sort of health, social or other care system is required to deal with the problems and restore normality?

One consequence for an appropriate care system is that the 'knight's move' must be straightened out. Whilst capitalizing on the forward leap of improved medical strategies since 1959, the sideways step of abandoning socio-educational strategies, or relegating them to a subsidiary position, must be retraced and taken forward by means of the opportunities now afforded by psychology. This is the basic science that not only informs applied psychological practices, of which clinical and forensic psychology are the relevant branches in the present context, but also constitutes the essential basic science upon which much of modern psychiatry and the practices of, for instance, social work and the probation service depend. What might be the practical consequences of making the 'crooked knight go straight'?

For a start, and before they are all gone, those that remain of the former residential psychiatric hospitals must be saved, modernized and developed as the sort of communities envisaged in the previous chapter's section on reappraisal of resources. These would provide the necessary follow-on from the special hospitals and the RSUs, to be followed in turn by the community psychiatric facilities we already have today, but developed into a total health and social care service which can provide help to change both the 'hardware' and 'software' elements of human distress and aberration.

Whilst someone's 'processes' (normal or extreme, healthy or pathological) are leading them to behave dangerously then they will need to be helped towards change within a secure setting which affords public protection. When they have achieved sufficient change for high security to be unnecessary they can move into a less secure setting to take their programme of change a step further, subjecting it to the test of progressively more realistic situations until they are able to cope with a normal environment without hazard to others.

At each step, however, this new ability to cope, or cope differently, will need reinforcement, support and supervision. It is not merely a question of a community psychiatric nurse visiting periodically to check medication is being taken and symptoms continue to be in remission; nor of a social worker visiting to see that family or other social support remains in place; nor of both these satisfying themselves that patients are looking after themselves. It needs these people to know how 'processes' change, which ones are being changed in any particular case and what to do to ensure the patient takes the next step safely.

This degree of help and supervision is both more extensive and intensive than that available in residential care already. So far, the community care concept seems to have been based on the assumption that this is a service that needs less supervisor contact. The tasks to be accomplished in the open community for continuing the change process, however, are just as demanding as those begun in the secure community. Added to the existing community services, they will make more extensive demands than at present. It is the reduced risk of dangerous behaviour that brings about the move from secure residential care to a more moderately secure setting and eventually to the open community, not the degree of help and support required for effecting therapeutic change.

The care and treatment system must therefore reflect these essential needs. A different concept of care must be introduced. Staff will need different or additional training and deployment or new forms of care staff will need to be constituted and trained. The use of community facilities in continuing care will need to be differently conceptualized and operated to provide the expansion and continuity of treatment programmes begun earlier elsewhere. This means that day centres must provide not merely occupational programmes, group therapy and social rehabilitation (do they even do all this now?) but must be able to create the situations for continuing a behavioural retraining programme. All this has to happen in a context of secure supervision in order to carry conviction with the public that safety is being ensured. Care in the community is a much more complex and staff-intensive concept than has hitherto been envisaged. It will no doubt be rejected on cost grounds, which is to neglect the much greater cost of inaction and the consequent failures. Already there have been too many of these, which have sullied the community care concept.

VICTIMS

Any discussion of what should be done with offenders always brings a cry of 'what about the victims?' and 'victims don't get the consideration you give to the criminals'. If the question is not anticipated and answered it will be held against this history as a shortcoming which weakens its conclusions.

Quite apart from the question of whether 'state of mind' impairs responsibility for actions, and that the law of the land requires secure care to be provided for those who break the law while their state of mind is disturbed, the themes running through this history should have made clear by now that it is the victims (both individuals and society at large) just as much as the perpetrators that lie at the heart of Broadmoor's work. Investigating, remedying and researching into the lives and situations of those who inflict violence upon others, and trying to return them to society no longer harmful, is vital to protecting their former victims and others who might suffer from them in the future. It also provides important information for the understanding and prevention of future violent crimes. The findings of special hospitals' work feeds into the health, social and penal services more generally so that potential offenders are identified earlier and preventative strategies are improved. An example is the 'over-controlled' personality who is not found in other psychiatric settings - no mental disorder is apparent until established (or sometimes inferred for lack of another explanation) from the bizarre nature of the crime, usually a violent murder. Sometimes presenting as schizophrenic and sometimes depressed, the underlying problem is often rather one of a rigid underlying personality which cannot perceive and adapt to encroaching stresses and disasters if and when these become extreme. In these circumstances it may be appropriate to say that the mental disorder is the effect, not the cause, of the offence, although the cause will have been a personality problem often construed as a mental disorder.

Another example is of the shy, withdrawn, almost 'socially crippled' young men who comprise the majority of sexual offenders (instead of the 'slavering, sexual beast' beloved of the tabloids) and who have been described at several points in this history. These, furthermore, indicate our need to expand the concept of 'psychopathic disorder'. They comprise more than merely the 'psycho' beloved of novelists and playwrights.

Both these examples, and others described in this history, will repay greater awareness where future potential victims are concerned, as will the importance of the interplay between their problems, their circumstances and the attitudes and behaviour of their partners and families. This is not to imply that the 'victim is at fault' - a common misinterpretation in our blame obsessed society. It does emphasize, however, that interpersonal behaviour does not occur in a vacuum. Just as it 'takes two to make a quarrel', it takes two (or more) to create the situation in which one becomes a victim. Explanations, not blame, demand that the interaction is understood and once it is, the principles will provide a better understanding of a wider range of distress and suffering.

More widely and indirectly, educational services will benefit too. Families and environments that feature violence will be better understood and the understanding can then be built into government policies: educational, social, health and penal. 'Pie-in-the-sky'? Not at all. Only by constantly searching out knowledge about offenders and then making it known will victims be helped and violence reduced. The Suzy Lamplugh Trust learned this when it embarked on its programmes for enabling people in the workplace, and particularly those in isolated, vulnerable situations, to deal with violence when confronted by it.

This is not to say that enough is done for victims. This is really another question but since Broadmoor's work has always attracted the kinds of aspersions and criticisms anticipated here, and this history will probably be no exception, it is worth trying to deal with them in advance. The implication of the question is that one's time could be better spent caring for victims directly. Certainly victims need more attention than they have tended to receive in the past and, happily, this is gradually happening. Victim counsellors and support groups are relatively recent innovations but are on the increase. Yet, had those of us who have worked in settings like Broadmoor spent our time instead providing palliative victim care, we would have accomplished very little before finding that we needed to know a great deal more about the people who had inflicted the harm and the situations in which it happened.

Caring for victims is more than replacing what they have lost and giving moral support. Understanding their attackers and the interactions that led to them being victims is part of the recovery process. Victimology is a science in its own right these days, which many who make the complaint probably do not realize. More is increasingly being done for victims and there are even some initiatives that are based upon bringing victims and attackers together (not necessarily the victims' own attackers or the attackers' own victims but groups of each who can together achieve understanding of benefit to both). This is not universally approved, nor does it remove the need for people to work with both victims and offenders separately and understand more about them. It will not help victims, however, either at present or in the future, to ignore offenders or cease to pay any attention to them once they are under lock and key. In fact, one of the arguments against capital punishment, although I have never heard it used, is that it destroys one of the most relevant sources of knowledge by which we shall better understand how to prevent future murders.

DECISION MAKING

During the period of the 1959 Act the co-ordination of clinical information advanced significantly. From the early restriction to the opinions of the only consultant psychiatrist (the medical superintendent), a few senior registrars, a chaplain and the chief male nurse or matron with their ward staff, there were in 1959 also a further consultant, a social worker and a clinical psychologist. By 1983, in contrast, there were some seven or eight clinical teams, each with an input of information from all these disciplines, together with a member of the occupations staff, education department and, where relevant or required, the psychotherapists, speech therapist, librarians and research staff. (Where the 1983 Act required a second opinion outside doctor to consult with a member of the resident staff about compulsorily imposed treatment, any of these might be called upon if they knew the patient well.)

The gathering and reporting of information, conclusions and recommendations was always the responsibility of the consultant, to whom the 1959 Act had referred, therefore, as the responsible medical officer (RMO). Gradually, as teams came into existence, explicitly in the end, the officials at the Department of Health and the Home Office, responsible for vetting and acting upon the recommendations from the RMOs, would ensure they had as complete a picture as possible on which to act by insisting that they were supplied with the opinions of all the members of the team who had been involved in the patient's care and assessment. This required sight of any reports on file, but not all disciplines make reports: nursing staff make entries into the case-notes; others make no reports or only if specifically asked.

The tradition is to make verbal comments informally on ward rounds, at case conferences, at face-to-face meetings in offices, or over the phone. The RMO's secretary only makes notes and produces a report where a case conference is held. Those at the DHSS or Home Office needing to distil this information would have difficulty gathering and weighing it all unless relying on the report submitted by the RMO. Whilst this should have done the necessary distilling of the proffered opinions, of course, and would have attached copies of reports of any of the team who had made them, there would always be a risk of issues being missed or misrepresented in the process, thereby repeating one of the errors of the former system for which teams had been the intended solution. How were the DHSS and Home Office to ensure they received the views of all those who had had dealings with the patient? It would be a time-consuming process to require all of these to make written reports; it would be a cumbersome process to extract all the case-note entries. By the end of the 'interacts' period and the arrival of the new, 1983, Act it had to suffice that the RMO made a synopsis of opinions received and meetings held, incomplete and selective though this might be, and attached any separate reports he had received. In the future it must surely be a challenge to make use of the growth of computerization to produce more comprehensive coverage of the available evaluations.

Then there is the question of quantifying all this information. Whilst some disciplines work on measurable procedures, the practice is not widespread. There is potential for greater use of, say, rating scales and checklists by more staff disciplines whose work, information and opinions might well be summarized in this way. Medical staff have tended to resist such procedures as contrary to established clinical practice and likely to introduce oversimplifications of their findings and opinions. There is, however, no reason why narrative opinions cannot be added and, indeed, some verbal comment and conclusion added to bald figures is essential.

A promising procedure that has emerged since the era of this history is 'Risk Assessment'. Symposia devoted to finding common ground for the interactions of the clinical professions with, say, lawyers, have developed this concept. 'Decision Trees' (see figure), which proceed through a series of dichotomized alternatives, requiring a 'value' to be put on each and then a probability of it happening or being achieved, have been among the procedures promoted at these symposia. They would seem to have something to offer for the way clinical teams work: each step could be agreed collectively by the team, values and probabilities being estimated from the several opinions and a final decision presented clearly for action and outside consumption, such as that of the DHSS, the Home Office and the staff of a potential receiving hospital.

DECISION TREE

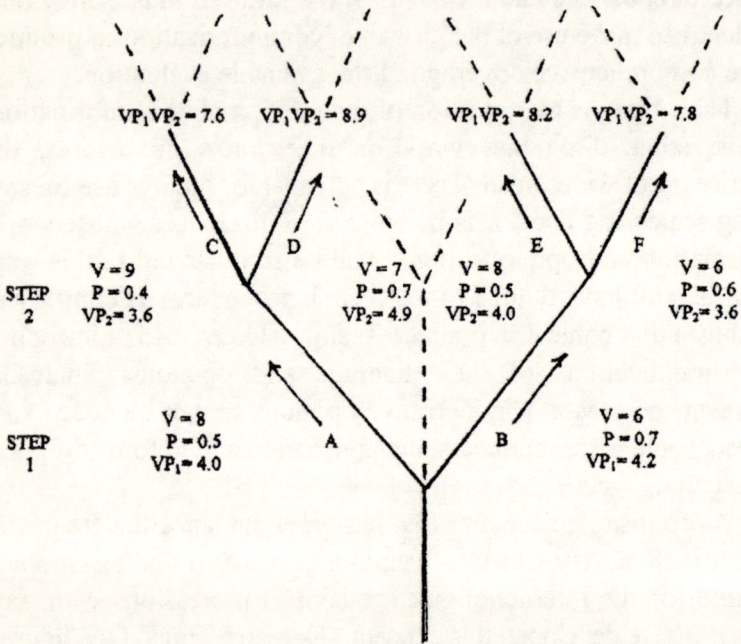

$VP_1 VP_2 = 7.6$ $VP_1 VP_2 = 8.9$ $VP_1 VP_2 = 8.2$ $VP_1 VP_2 = 7.8$

C   D   E   F

STEP 2	$V = 9$ $P = 0.4$ $VP_2 = 3.6$	$V = 7$ $P = 0.7$ $VP_2 = 4.9$	$V = 8$ $P = 0.5$ $VP_2 = 4.0$	$V = 6$ $P = 0.6$ $VP_2 = 3.6$

STEP 1 $V = 8$ $P = 0.5$ $VP_1 = 4.0$ A   B $V = 6$ $P = 0.7$ $VP_1 = 4.2$

V = Value attributed to chosen course of action (arbitrary scale of 1 to 10).
P = Probability of choice proving successful (statistically 0 to 1, i.e.: from no chance to 100% certain).
VP = Product of V & P.
$VP_1 VP_2 ... VP_n$ = sum or product of VPs for each choice.
E & F may well be the same options as C & D but have different values and probabilities through being on another choice route.

This example illustrates how the preferred choice at Step 1 would have been 'B' but, with step 2 incrementing this, 'A' followed by 'D' would then be better (and subsequent steps might change the picture again).

Choices in the example above have been intentionally limited to two at each step but there could, of course, be more. This would complicate the calculations and therefore make the use of a Decision Tree even more relevant and necessary.

If the outcomes of the method are sometimes surprising, and decision trees are like that, then, of course, the team has the means of checking back and revising the values and probabilities they have estimated. A mere team discussion does not have this potential. Some people dominate; others are reticent. If disagreement occurs then backtracking often leads to more confusion and arbitrary decisions. With a 'decision tree', or similar procedure, everyone is expected to make an input and no one feels excluded. When they are finally satisfied with the values and probabilities they are assessing then they have the assurance that the best decision possible has been reached. A basis has also been set for reassessment in the light of the outcome which provides, in turn, an objective basis for research.

Procedures of this kind, and more of them will inevitably arise, have the added advantage of being 'research amenable'. If a team member cannot accept such a collective and objective form of decision-making then he or she still has the option of making a separate verbal report and recommendation, which is what I always used to point out to those RMOs who felt that verbal reports were richer and fuller than statistics. Interestingly, in the Cropwood study of discharged male patients, the conclusions of the psychological report produced some significant correlations with outcome where the component assessments on which they had been based had not always done so. Encouragingly, therefore, there seemed to have been some element of successful synthesis in the evaluation of the findings presented in the report. Even so, this is not necessarily support for the superiority of clinical opinions. Had it been available and accepted practice in those days, conclusions might have been reached more simply and effectively through use of a decision tree, or data matrix, with the added advantage of it being in a form amenable to more precise statistical analysis and subsequent research inquiry.

Whatever decision-making system emerges in the future - and there must be one to objectify the *ad hoc* procedures which operated in the 'interacts' era - it must comply with the requirements of statistical validity and reliability; i.e.: 'is it relevant and does it work?' In other words: 'does it relate to what it is intended to relate and does it do so consistently?'

These would seem to me to be some of the lessons and implications arising from the developments which took place at Broadmoor in the period between the 1959 and 1983 Mental Health Acts. The final chapter in Part III of this history must go on to attempt a reappraisal of the legal background and framework in which all this happens and with which this history began.

SUMMARY

This chapter has looked at the conclusions to which Broadmoor's history points us where the nature of mental disorder is concerned and its role, if any, in violent acts: cause, effect or irrelevant. Inevitably this also leads on to what may best be done to remedy the various mental disorders and, in Broadmoor's context, how we should regard criminality and deal with that too. In passing, the sources of professional services and viewpoints are identified.

Inevitably, and not surprisingly, the conclusions are that mental disorder may lead to or result from criminal actions or it may be unconnected. This is only to be expected when one considers that 'mental disorder', under the Act, comprises four sub-categories and that each of these may arise from any of a number of origins and be variously affected by environmental experiences.

This may seem unhelpful. The positive point to emerge, however, is that the interaction of personal and environmental factors determines behaviour when people are mentally ill, just as it does when they are well. The result may be so bizarre as to compel a mental illness conclusion and some construe all mental illness this way but even independently defined mental illness reflects the personality-environment interaction. Psychopathic disorder, categorized as a mental disorder but not a mental illness, fits the personality-environment explanation and, this being so, learning becomes the process to be understood as bringing about change. Medicines may help the process but seldom accomplish it alone. The chapter therefore recaps and develops the learning theme, the effect of incentives in the previous and the new environment, and the problems and ethical issues involved if applying the principle within sentencing.

This also recaps and extends the discussion of categorization within a 'personality' concept where variation is continuous, in contrast with the 'present/absent' dichotomy of physical disease. Irrationality, distress, incompetence, failure: all become relative terms, with different meanings and consequences for different people and difficult to incorporate within a rule system. Cut-offs are difficult to make and prone to be arbitrary. The consequences for a care system will be fluid, requiring continuity through different environments and different levels of security, and with differing degrees and kinds of contact and supervision.

Victims are obviously part of the equation within the perceptions of the offender so the common criticism that offender treatment neglects victims is refuted. Better understanding of offenders complements direct help to victims.

Finally, there is discussion of decision-making processes. Clinical opinion is measurable only by reference to outcome. We trust those who have been right before. Continuously distributed ('spectrum-type') variables require a different form of measurement and attention needs to be paid to the ways of quantifying these actuarial-type opinions of the clinical team or of individuals supplying reports for the courts. 'Decision trees' are one possible method exemplified.

CHAPTER 23

REAPPRAISAL OF THE LAW: IMPLICATIONS FOR THE KIND OF LEGAL PROCESS NEEDED

STATE OF MIND

And so we come back to where this history started: how does the law provide for people who offend when their state of mind is impaired? Does it do it well enough? What have we learned that might suggest ways it could do it better?

'State of mind' will have to do here as the best available shorthand to be going on with and which encompasses the psychological functions reviewed in the previous chapter. 'Mind' is not a clinical or psychological entity, amenable to investigation; it is an abstract concept. However, it is one which incorporates the many psychological functions which, in conjunction with the environment, determine behaviour and are amenable to definition and investigation.

'State of mind' is also the most convenient term to use in a legal context as encompassing both the pre-1959 concept of 'insanity' and the post-1959 one of 'mental disorder'. The 'mind' occurs widely in legal thinking: 'being of sound mind' is necessary to make a will, whilst *mens rea* describes the element of intent assumed to underlie all people's actions unless evidence is brought and accepted in rebuttal. The law does not work on ideal principles but on the concept of the 'common man' (and now 'woman', of

503

course) with all his or her faults and prejudices but also what is assumed to be his or her common sense and understanding. The pre-1959 concept of insanity, being a legal and not a medical or psychological concept, by contrast would have been founded upon a 'common man or woman' whose state of mind was unsound and therefore not to be relied upon as capable of using common sense.

The 1959 Mental Health Act's concept of mental disorder (Section 4) understandably, therefore, defined all its four categories in terms of some kind of 'state of mind'. ('Environmental situations' may be set aside for the moment, being 'mind-impairing factors' only when in combination with one of the defined mental conditions and not on their own. They are irrelevant to 'state of mind' as it applies in law to 'insanity' pre-1959 and 'mental disorder' post-1959.)

The 1959 Act defines mental disorder in terms of these four sub-categories and then defines (or describes more fully) three of these: subnormality, severe subnormality and psychopathic disorder; it does not define mental illness. It essentially defines the first two in terms of degrees of *'arrested or incomplete development of mind which render the sufferer incapable of living an independent life or of avoiding exploitation.'* It defines the third of these in terms of *'persistent disorder or disability of mind which results in abnormally aggressive or seriously irresponsible conduct.'* The omission of a definition for mental illness and the use of 'mind' in all the rest leaves the interpretation of these terms to the court and whatever expert evidence is called.

This is helpful and no doubt intentional in view of the abstract nature of 'mind' and the flexibility it thereby allows to its interpretation and application. It is unhelpful, however, in the legal arguments that are liable to arise as to its meaning and whether a defendant can be held to fall within the definition. Nevertheless, it is difficult to envisage any legal definition of 'mind' or 'mental' which could go further without resulting in even more arguments as to meaning. The 1959 Act has been relatively free of protracted arguments in court over mental disorder in the way that insanity and the McNaughtan Rules were not. It is broad enough to be all-encompassing for most contingencies and to be accepted on all sides. Exceptions were the high profile cases where heinous or repeated crimes led courts and public alike to press for what they saw as the greatest punishment and to shun what they saw as a 'let-off', even though a secure hospital stay was likely to be as long or longer than a prison sentence and with a greater likelihood of a safe release in the event of its ending.

INADEQUACIES OF THE PRESENT LAW

How, then, did this radical 1959 legislation fare? Of course, it was a great advance on what it replaced. It benefited many who needed its provisions to commit them to care and treatment but who would not have met the criteria of the previous legislation. It also allowed many who had unnecessarily mouldered their lives away in institutions to move into alternative forms of care in the community. Some of its provisions, however, did not adequately provide for the interactions of mental disorder and antisocial behaviour which brought their sufferers to Broadmoor in the 'interacts' period.

One of these concerned the problem of unlawful acts arising in conjunction with neurotic or personality disorders not regarded as amounting to either mental illness or psychopathic disorder within the Act's four categories of 'mental disorder'. The most prominent examples would be various kinds of molester, abductor and sex offender, especially who target children, although many addicts and 'drop-outs' also show features of neurotic and personality disorder requiring care and treatment. These attract little sympathy, are often thought to be malingerers or 'milking the system' but are difficult to distinguish from those with other disorders; if, indeed, such a distinction can ever be made. It is arguable from the results of work world-wide during this period of Broadmoor's history whether a mental disorder definition should not more appropriately apply to such people and that a remedial strategy would not always be preferable, more appropriate and cost effective than a sterile period of detention in prison alone. This must, of course, include some form of secure care, at least initially, for those whose condition constitutes a personal or public danger. The overriding need for imprisonment also arises from the attitude of the 'common man and woman'. Irrespective of effectiveness, the '3-Ps': punishment, public protection and prevention (i.e.: deterrence) take priority, where public opinion is concerned, over the more positive values of the '3-Rs': reform, rehabilitation and reparation.

The second aspect of law that does not match the requirements of mentally disordered people, as their characteristics and needs have emerged at Broadmoor during this period, arises from the 'continuous distribution' of personality traits and characteristics which makes it difficult to set boundaries between the 'normal and 'abnormal' and the 'ill' and the 'well' ('sane' and 'insane' under the pre-1959 nomenclature). The result is an inevitable arbitrariness in whether a particular defendant ends up in the 'mentally disordered' category, and hence in psychiatric care, or not, thereby presenting problems for the prisons. In a way this is a variation of the previous problem of whether a person's condition is to be considered a mental disorder or not: classification is often a matter of degree or severity. In the case of subnormality (as it was then termed), severe subnormality, psychopathic disorder and even some instances of mental illness, it rarely depended entirely upon factors independent of the offence the court was considering as, strictly speaking, all evidence should. This is because 'behaviour' lies at the heart of the diagnostic process (independent 'signs and symptoms' are often elusive and insufficient alone to establish mental disorder independently of aspects of overt behaviour) and it would, of course, be aspects of behaviour that the court considers with regards to the offence for which the defendant stands trial.

The Broadmoor work similarly illustrates the artificiality of another dichotomy which fascinates the public - and hence the media - and bedevils the thinking of the court: that between the 'mad' and the 'bad'. Many behaviours arising from mental or personality disorders may have 'bad' consequences without the perpetrators being 'bad people'. There are varying degrees of badness in the outcomes of people's behaviours which may arise from varying degrees of mental or personality problems and difficulties. They will therefore tend to emerge in a similarly arbitrary way as a result of the present court requirement to find the defendant either 'guilty' or 'not guilty'. This would be less important if the subsequent sentence, or 'disposal' procedure, were to be more flexibly oriented around a constructive goal of solving the precipitating problem (the 3-Rs) rather than whether or not to impose a punishment.

THE CASE FOR CHANGE

These problems essentially turn upon the long-standing assumptions of the criminal justice system that the 'common man or woman', possessing the free will to choose between right and wrong, is to be held responsible for his or her actions and punished if he or she chooses to contravene the law. Unfortunately, whether or not 'free will' continues to be a tenable concept, and it is not feasible or appropriate within a history such as this to digress into that argument 'responsibility' is certainly impaired or distorted in many people who come before the courts. The law has recognized this in its provisions for the insane, pre-1959 and the mentally disordered since.

What the experience of the working of the 1959 Act suggests is that there is a larger group of people outside the provisions of the Mental Health Act who also lack the ability fully to exercise responsibility. They are in need of attention to their impaired or disordered mental state and to undergo an appropriate remedial programme. To condemn or condone is irrelevant. Whether the outcome of their state of mind, therefore, is harm to other people or merely harm to themselves through impairment of their own effectiveness as human beings, judgements of a condemnatory kind do not form part of the process of understanding and remedying the situation. Whatever the outcome of their impaired or distorted thinking or emotionality, the need is for these impaired functions to be restored to normality. In this way, and if successful, not only will more satisfactory and satisfying lives be possible but, where harm to others has been a consequence, further criminality will be avoided or reduced.

The 3-Rs of reform, rehabilitation and reparation receive scant attention today, or are derided as 'soft options'. The punishment principle persists vigorously in the face of evidence that punishment fails to effect positive and lasting change and only engenders further hostility and an urge to 'get even'. This seems strange when we only have to envisage our own reactions to being punished and to consider the reactions of persecuted minorities the world over. It is not 'society', or their peers, moreover, that offenders see as punishing them, or in some way 'making-the-scores-even' between them, which might have an element of logic to it, but some impersonal agency: the court or the state. This is even more likely to happen when their motivation has been their disordered reasoning, distorted emotions, uncontrolled impulses or experiences of neglect, deprivation, pain and humiliation. Their perceptions of justice, however, will often be sharpened by what they see as unfair or discriminating, so that not only do they feel strongly about their own treatment but they will accept the principle of making reparation to victims if this is set within a programme that addresses their own problems as well. 'Hard work' is accepted in this context.

If the criminal justice system were able to effect the 3-Rs, constructive strategies, rather than punishment, the destructive component of the 3-Ps, it would address more appropriately and effectively the phenomena of confusion and disarray that typify so many of those categorized as mentally disordered as well as many others that shade into them but who are categorized as 'normal' in our dichotomized system of attributing guilt. Then it would not matter that so much of the evidence of mental disorder derives from actions essentially part and parcel of those for which the defendant is on trial.

Scottish law has moved closer to a system that caters for these phenomena in introducing the process of 'diversion'. This involves recognizing the needs of some offenders whose situation can be remedied by 'diversion' into some other system of dealing with their problems, such as psychiatric treatment. It has had limited use so far but may well prove to be a principle that is seen to have wider relevance and application, with wider 'diversionary' strategies being drawn from a wider range of professional standpoints. In England and Wales, of course, there has long been the principle of probation but this is traditionally seen as a 'let-off' and unlikely to be to the public liking for more serious offences, even though these might sometimes be even more strongly indicative of a need for help than for castigation.

The principle of 'continuous distribution' of character strengths and weaknesses, of human potential and need, and of the phenomena we see as constituting mental illness and the other mental disorders, and which between them establish whether someone may be regarded as 'responsible' in law, require a similar 'continuously distributed' range of responses from a court of law.

It has sometimes been suggested that this might be facilitated by the separation of the concept of *mens rea* from the process of establishing guilt. 'Guilt' does not merely mean responsibility but culpability, or blameworthiness, a state of mind, and hence should not be confused with the question of 'agency', i.e.: 'did the defendant commit the act for which s/he is on trial or not'. Blameworthiness is properly a matter for the sentence, or the action to be taken to achieve the 3-Rs as well as the 3-Ps. If that part of the trial concerned, therefore, with establishing 'agency', or the facts (*actus reus*) were to be detached from issues of intent, or guilt (*mens rea*) then intent could properly be considered only if the facts were proved, when motivation would then be relevant to considering what sentence the court should pass. This is not a radically new idea. The 'Butler' Committee describe the careful consideration which they gave to it before they, somewhat reluctantly one feels, abandoned it. It would, in any case, have needed legislation above and beyond the new Mental Health Act to change a *process* of the law, rather than just its application.

All this would require a greater range of options than currently available if the preventative-deterrent and public protection objectives of the 3-Ps were to be augmented with the 3-Rs. Such a transposition of the 'guilty mind' concept, it is argued, is not the equivalent of introducing 'strict liability', as applied to many summary offences and as alleged of these kinds of proposition by critics. 'Agency' is strict when it is detached from notions of motive, to which it should be irrelevant (but see below), but liability is far from 'strict' if *mens rea*, the 'guilty mind' issue, is removed from its inappropriate position as a determinant of criminal agency and put where it belongs as a relevant, and indeed crucial, factor in determining outcome ('sentencing', or whatever expanded concept replaces it).

PROBLEMS IN ACHIEVING CHANGE

Whether it is possible to effect these sorts of change, of course, only the legislators can determine. But without an indication of the difficulties, and indeed illogicalities and injustices, in the existing system from those who work with the results, no one will realize that change is necessary. And without describing the nature of the difficulties and suggesting what might resolve them, legislators would not know what they were required to resolve.

From the standpoint of someone who has worked with mentally disordered offenders for many years it does not look difficult to bring about the required change. The procedure in court might even be simplified if evidence of motives were disentangled from the process of proving whether the crime had actually taken place and, if so, who had done it. Of course, its proponents will say, motive for a crime like murder, as in all the best whodunits, is important in a court's decision whether it was likely that the defendant committed the crime. This makes the point precisely. Here, motive would be treated as a fact to be assessed in establishing *actus reus*, the likelihood that the defendant was the perpetrator of the crime. It would not at that point influence the assessment of degree of guilt, *mens rea*, or 'culpability'. Judgements as to the nature and culpability of motive would then be considered in the next part of the court process, namely deciding on the appropriate outcome in the light of the 3-Rs as well as the 3-Ps. This might require further evidence, or the reconsideration of evidence from a new standpoint which would previously have been presented at an earlier stage of the trial.

In other words, motive should not confuse the consideration of facts. It has become a fact in itself and is not yet part of ascribing culpability. Later it would be considered for its motivational implications, not its factual status, when it would become a factor in the decision on sentencing. It would then no longer merely have the status of a plea in mitigation but would be a required element within the trial process and, most importantly, would itself have requirements in the form of a more widely developed range of disposals than we have at present.

It may be thought that fines, imprisonment, hospital orders, probation (with various conditions), conditional discharge and community service already comprise a fair range of disposals. Certainly the potential is there, which makes the change altogether more achievable. There is, however, a tendency to see these options in a limited and limiting way under the present system of determining and dealing with guilt. The latter three options above: probation, conditional discharge and community service, would not be thought appropriate for some of the more heinous offences. They might become appropriate, however, if, firstly, the 'guilty mind', or culpability, or responsibility concept were given its main emphasis at the sentencing stage of the trial and, secondly, a wider range of '3-R' options were available within the spectrum of hospital orders, probation, conditional discharge and community service orders.

Some of the provisions within the 'continuum of care' concept between the high security hospital at one extreme, through the medium security unit to the community care facilities at the other extreme, would be one part of such an expanded concept. These would, however, need to be comprehensively implemented as envisaged in the previous chapter. There would probably also need to be a new disposal provision created in order to afford offenders the means of fulfilling the 3-Rs. The 'reparation-restitution' principle requires both work and remedial opportunities to be available. Community centres would need to include a wider range of work, treatment and other activity provisions than is generally found at present although, for those of lower security risk, existing neighbourhood facilities might be adequate. Counselling, advice and therapy for individuals and in groups must all be included. This will inevitably be scorned by those of a punitive outlook and care must indeed be taken to ensure that all these facilities and services err towards neither the 'soft option' nor the 'penal colony', which could happen without proper planning and supervision. The 3-Rs are not punishment but could degenerate into this. Conversely, they could be misinterpreted or misused in the other direction and community centres could degenerate into a sinecure, a place for merely passing the time.

Change is essential, however, if the law is not to become out of date as clinical practices become out of date. If the law lags behind, inconsistencies will multiply, justice will not be done and the social equilibrium, which it is the law's function to preserve, will be at risk. Interprofessional collaboration and learning exchange has increasingly characterized professional activities at the end of the 20th century, however, so it is greatly to be hoped that it can achieve the kinds of advance that now seem to be indicated.

Professional bodies are conservative, of course. It is their function to protect the public and their members by preserving what has worked in the past. Change, and the consequent upheaval, is not introduced until absolutely necessary. During the deliberations of the 'Butler' Committee on mentally abnormal offenders, for instance, where the remit included examining whether changes were needed in the law, the British Psychological Society's delegates received a surprised comment from one of the committee during the oral session to discuss their evidence: 'But this would entail a change in the law!' The BPS delegates were speechless. The committee, of course, construed their remit, which included 'possible changes in the law', to mean the legal provisions for mentally abnormal offenders, not the legal process itself! Interestingly, however, as mentioned above, they did 'dare to tread' in this direction in their final report, supporting a two-stage trial process when 'unfitness-to-plead' was at issue.

A likely consequence of these arguments and proposals is that people will protest that the elimination of boundaries between the 'mad' and the 'bad', the 'ill' and the 'well' (and 'sanity-insanity' still creeps in at the edges via the Criminal Procedures [Insanity] Act), will mean that we will not know where to draw the line between those we may punish and may not punish. Just so. I hope the sterility, indeed harmfulness, of the punishment ethic has been established. A more positive reparative-restitutional approach to retribution needs to be devised.

Where practicalities are concerned, it is likely that the great majority of offenders for whom no motivation other than that of the 'common man or woman' is assumed, will continue to pass through the legal process as before. It is likely to take a long time before all 'common men and women' are seen as motivated by complex interactions of their personalities and backgrounds so that explanations for their crimes other than wickedness, fear, hatred or greed are sought. All of these, like 'badness', are insufficient explanations in themselves without tracing what prompts them and what, therefore, needs changing.

The devising of a wider range of 'sentences' for the mentally disordered, and then the neurotic and personality disordered, will gradually demonstrate that these form the basis of more effective procedures for a great many other offenders too; and that will lead

514

to a reconstruing of criminal motivation generally.

Alternatively, it may not. The capacity of the human species to accomplish its own evolution by means of the technology its intelligence has developed may fail when faced with the exigencies of the modern world, such as the dire consequences of overcrowding and a dying environment. This will accentuate its tribal survival instincts, which have never died out. They have served the species well for 99% of its existence and it is probably expecting too much that adaptation or mutation will produce the change now required for the non-tribal collaboration-requiring conditions which the species has now evolved for itself. Engulfed in internecine strife, as animals are observed to do in experiments on overcrowding, justice will return to the age of the savage, which is what we are now beginning to see.

If a civilized solution is achieved, however, the need for public protection and prevention-deterrence will remain, so secure containment will remain a feature of the mid-21st century. Punishment, however, as required by the public need for vengeance, should be sufficiently provided by this loss of liberty and by the 'reparation-restitution' concept which imposes an obligatory response upon the offender in repairing the damage done (or some of it, since no reparation is possible for a life taken). This will often be a painful process, requiring self-sacrifice, but it is a positive one rather than the negative one that is punishment.

If these are insufficient to satisfy the vindictive feelings of the 'common man and woman' then perhaps we should rather be addressing the question of how to help the said 'common man and woman' deal with these negative and sterile feelings. In this respect the law should surely be looking to moral principles and ethical standards rather than some common denominator of public opinion? After all, we elect our governments for their knowledge and judgement and expect them to act on our behalf more judiciously and wisely than we could ourselves. Interestingly, at the end of the 20th century, Parliament has repeatedly rejected a return to capital and corporal punishment when the 'common man and woman' would clearly wish to have brought them both back.

CONCLUDING POLEMIC

Two phenomena from psychological principles and the work done at Broadmoor during the period of this history argue for changes in the law.

The first stems from the inappropriateness, arbitrariness and potential error in drawing distinctions between the medico-legal concepts of mental disorder and those of other categories of psychological dysfunction and distress.

The second stems from the difficulty and confusion in drawing distinctions between degrees of disorder, dysfunction and distress which vary continuously across a spectrum and which, therefore, make it irrelevant and misleading trying to draw distinctions between normality and abnormality.

Lawyers may say that such a distinction is not being drawn but, instead, a distinction between excessive and insufficient disability which might or might not, therefore, have impaired the defendant's capacity to act in a normally responsible manner. This only moves the argument into another set of semantics and what might seem a clear distinction is always likely to appear unclear after a skilful counsel has dissected it. Better, therefore, to be done with such potential hazards and stick to the *actus reus*, leaving the *mens rea* to be assessed in the context of the most appropriate form of sentence to satisfy the protective and preventative elements of the 3-Ps, together with the 3-Rs.

Changes will be difficult to achieve satisfactorily and will clearly clash with long-standing attitudes and assumptions, which will give rise to resistance and hostility and make change even more difficult to achieve. One of the members of the 'Butler' Committee remarked during a comfort break in our oral session: 'You are quite right, of course, but twenty years before your time'. Twenty five further years have now passed. Is the law, and the 'common man and woman', any more ready to consider the 'psychological facts of life'?

One of the phenomena of personality research that repeatedly emerges from studies of all kinds, from whatever the school of thought, is the permanence and stability of a major personality dimension with 'radicalism' at one extremity and 'conservatism' at the other. Like 'introversion vs. extraversion' and 'emotional over-arousal v. under-arousal', it keeps appearing. As with other 'continuously distributed' characteristics, it is only at the extremities that the traits appear in pronounced form, the large majority of people in the middle of the distribution showing greater flexibility, or variation, on the occasions and in the frequency with which either trait appears. Nevertheless, like the characteristics of the Broadmoor staff, the majority of whom do their job with uncomplaining fairness, firmness and friendliness, but where the minority at one extreme can exercise a disproportionately harsh influence, there is always a group of the population with an extremely strong 'small-c' conservative tendency who will call for ever firmer rules, harsher sentences and severer punishments.

I was invited, not long ago, to participate in a TV late-night discussion on what should be done with sex offenders. The invited contributors were sprinkled among the audience. It turned out I was to be one of only two who would be explaining the cause of the problem and the purpose of treatment. The majority of the audience howled for punitive confinement and castration and, to my consternation, was urged to do so ever more vehemently by the presenters and studio staff.

The Butler Committee member who foresaw twenty years as necessary for change may have been unduly 'conservative' in his estimate. It looks like taking some time yet for the majority in the middle of the 'radical-conservative' spectrum to decide that a more constructive solution is required for mentally, emotionally and personality disordered offenders, let alone for offenders generally.

I responded to a press inquiry, some years ago, with the opinion that a secure hospital would do a better job of making a sex offender safe than prison, and was labelled a 'mad doctor' as a result by a tabloid newspaper. I am glad to say that my rebuttal letter was published prominently. Subsequent events have made my point. Sex offenders have been released at expiry of sentence only to offend again or be shunned by any and every community where they proposed to live. It would have been better had they been treated for their disorder for as long as necessary in a secure hospital and then only released under surveillance through the kind of continuing programme I have described. Broadmoor has patients who include such behaviour in their offences, for whom a court made a hospital order rather than a prison sentence, many of whom have led anonymous and successful lives since discharge. Others have failed to make sufficient progress and have had to stay there. In this way, the greatest opportunity has been possible for the greatest number with the minimum risk.

Whilst this history seems to me to argue for changes in the law and in court procedure to achieve more just and effective outcomes for offenders and public alike, Part III of this history has summarized a great many other issues as well. The professions in the NHS which deliver health care to the mentally disordered include many as well as psychologists who know that it is in changing behaviour that the future of the service lies, not merely in giving a medicine that suppresses or regenerates activity, or disentangles distorted thinking.

Efforts still need to be channelled into constructive outcomes. It is easier and less time consuming just to dispense medicine, and less threatening to professional egos, especially as delivering the appropriate psychological treatment might not work on everyone, at first, or all the time: remember the truism that you cannot go back to childhood and grow up again. But if we don't do things right we won't find out how to do things better.

In an era of cost cutting it is, of course, also difficult to persuade managers and accountants to do things differently, especially if new programmes require new staffing and new units in which to carry them out. The arguments must also address the potential savings of doing the job properly in the first place.

A history should perhaps not become involved in polemics. But if this present history does not examine the arguments, or attempt to draw conclusions about the evolving system it describes, it would surely be selling its subject short. These reappraisal chapters of Broadmoor's history could not finish without emphasizing the need for a wider examination of the system within which its patients find themselves.

When the costs are all reckoned up: police time; remand and investigation; the court process; prosecution and defence teams; social reports; secure residential care and treatment; local authority social services; halfway houses and hostels; community support and sheltered care facilities; pension and benefit payments; then all the structures to provide these and the places which train the people who work in them; and, last but not least, the wasted lives of those involved; isn't it better to do the job properly to save the time and expense of doing things wrongly and having to do them all over again?

SUMMARY

This final reappraisal chapter looks at the law, not only concerning the criminally insane (or mentally disordered offenders now, which is itself an advance) but more widely bearing upon the court process itself. How should the court deal with concepts of responsibility, normality, the 'reasonableness' of the ordinary man and woman and, more pertinently, absence or distortion of these qualities affecting culpability? What has the history of Broadmoor during the post-war era to tell us about all this, with the radical changes in legislation, clinical knowledge and social outlook which have taken place in that time?

Criminal insanity replaced criminal lunacy and mental disorder replaced both, with its four sub-categories defined so as to allow responsibility to be not so much regarded as impaired or removed but to be sidelined. Instead of a verdict that acquitted the insane and imposed secure asylum care, the offender was convicted and then a 'disposal' (sentence?) was ordered that provided the necessary care and treatment. The acquittal on grounds of not being responsible was effectively abolished but, to compensate as it were, a wider range of mental disability was allowable, enabling a mentally disordered person to receive care and treatment instead of punishment. So far, so good. Nevertheless, it was a conviction, no longer an acquittal, and the matter of responsibility and normality was thereby shelved.

This left unresolved the problem of where to draw the line where an offender's 'state of mind' was concerned. The line was drawn more tolerantly to include any mental disorder (a term which Lord Justice Lawton held to be one which the court, not an expert witness, should determine, unlike its four sub-categories). Mental disorder could include any mental illness (even the neurotic ones where, unlike psychosis, reason is still intact but emotionality distorts behaviour) and the new, contentious, sub-category of psychopathic disorder where not only is emotion affected, but also the control of volition. However, not only did this prove a contentious classification and was not allowed the full range of outcomes that could occur with the other mental disorder categories, but it was not taken to its logical conclusion of applying to other volitional disorders, such as those leading to sexual offences. Whilst allowing the line to be drawn more tolerantly as to category, however, the problem of drawing the line with regards to degree of disorder was left unresolved (probably not surprisingly: creditable headway had been made with regards to categorization; degree had to be left to another day).

The developments described in this history have emphasized that not only is 'state of mind' liable to a wider range of dis-ordering processes than 'insanity' (i.e.: the reason disabling mental disorders), but it is an elusive concept to pin down in regard to degree of disability. Once reason ('cognition') is extended to in-clude some features of the second aspect of human mental activity: emotionality ('affect'), and then the third aspect 'connation' (or drive), then the question of degree becomes paramount. Reason is conceivably something that might be regardable as 'present or absent' (although cognitive abilities are, in fact, continuously distributed just as others are). When affect and connation are added it becomes even more difficult to avoid the problem of where to draw lines. 'Reasonable' behaviour, the attribute of the 'common man or woman', is reckoned to be subject to 'free will' but free will (setting aside whether this is a tenable concept) is itself expressed to a variable degree which we now know to be influenced not only by reason but also by emotion and impulse, and their offspring, attitude.

The human capacities determining the variable degree of responsibility and control over personal conduct, therefore, would seem to require a similarly variable degree of court response. This is achieved for those considered mentally disordered through the wider variety of conditions that can be admitted under the 1959 (and now the 1983) Acts. For the remainder, however, the job is unfinished until it is recognized that, whatever the enormity (or triviality) of the indictment and the supposed commensurate sentence, punishment is not the solution to the precipitating problem. Certainly public and personal safety require that dangerous actions must be expected to recur and therefore require their perpetrators to be contained safely until... well, until when? Justice concepts require a tariff to be met. Tariffs, however, look only at the severity of offences, not the conditions that give rise to them. Until we have a system that also (or instead) looks as causes, we shall have offenders embittered by their plight and lack of attention to it, and then being unable to avoid re-offending when they should have been helped not to. This won't help victims either.

This final chapter draws from Broadmoor's considerable (and to many, surprising) success in coping with the radical changes of the 1959 legislation, lessons for wider application. It extrapolates from Broadmoor's experience the kinds of systems in less secure establishments and in the community that would address the problems of care, resolution, and even cure, for a wide range of antisocial conduct that might or might not meet criteria of 'mental disorder'. The label loses meaning when dealing with a sliding scale. The requirement is to establish causes and devise remedies whilst not neglecting public and personal safety.

Whilst psychologists are not legislators it is their responsibility, as it is for any other profession, to draw attention to discoveries and developments from their work which have legislative implications. Shortcomings revealed and changes that could remedy matters must be communicated to those who can effect change. History informs, teaches, and points the way to change.

APPENDIX A

ANOTHER NEW ACT

The history of Broadmoor and its development following the Mental Health Act of 1959 would be incomplete without a look at the legislation which succeeded it, i.e.: the Mental Health Act of 1983. This should give some indication of what was considered to need changing. We can then see how far Broadmoor's developments were reflected in that Act and whether there are still changes that need making.

As this history did not begin with a tabulation of the provisions of the 1959 Act, it seems worth using one now for the new Act and, more importantly for setting out the changes from the old one. Acts of Parliament are lengthy and turgid documents, and tables seem the best way of bringing out the salient features.

Table A.1 summarizes the main changes under the heading of Definitions, Admission Provisions, Consent to Treatment, MHRT Appeals and the MHAC.

Table A.2 selects the main provisions in daily use, especially in a security setting like Broadmoor. These tables are based on material used in the British Psychological Society's report, mentioned in an earlier chapter: *Psychology and Antisocial Behaviour*, which were also used as appendices in another BPS publication, the *Professional Psychology Handbook* (1995, BPS Books, Leicester) where I supplied the chapter on the 1983 Act. I am therefore grateful to the BPS for permission to reproduce these here as well as drawing on some parts of the text of the latter. First, however, and because it was not described in this way at the start of the book, a synopsis of the 1959 principles, and comparison with their 1983 successors, will be useful.

The purpose of both the 1959 and 1983 Mental Health Acts was to provide for the rights of 'mentally disordered' people, as defined, to receive or refuse treatment for their disorder; for the general public to be protected from the possible damage or injury resulting from their behaviour; and for members of the professions concerned to carry out their duties in this context.

The 1959 Act was the first amending legislation following the 1939-45 war and made sweeping changes in comparison with pre-war thinking and procedures. The Royal Commission of 1954-57 (the 'Percy' Commission) was the influence in this and its recommendations were set in the context of the introduction of the National Health Service Act in 1946.

The 1959 Act was reckoned to have been a major piece of liberalizing legislation for the mentally disordered and changed radically the definitions and procedures that went before. 'Mental hospitals' no longer provided a haven of refuge ('asylum') primarily as a social expedient for the protection of society, with treatment secondary for effecting some possible relief but more often merely reducing the patient's troublesomeness. 'Mental patients' were now to be treated like physical patients: entering or leaving hospital on medical authority and accepting or rejecting treatment of their own free will.

The 1959 Act also introduced safeguards for patients' civil liberties, for the way patients were to be detained (and their detention renewed if necessary) and how they could appeal against their detention to a Mental Health Review Tribunal.

The 1959 Act, however, despite its radical and emancipating swing over to a medical philosophy from a socially based one, found itself clashing with the burgeoning civil rights lobby of the 1970s (described in Chapter 15). Numerous rights had been recognized in the 1959 Act, such as the introduction of the 'informal patient' (voluntary admission), the requirement to justify continued detention and the Mental Health Review Tribunal as an independent body to which a patient could appeal.

Even so, the position for patients committed through the courts, especially with 'restriction orders' attached, was one where detention was likely to drag on unless a concerted effort was made on all sides to bring about discharge. The 1983 Act required clearer and more specific justification for many of the detention and treatment procedures to be carried out; increased opportunities for appeal; strengthened the appeals procedure; and created a Mental Health Act Commission to keep an eye on it all.

It also, crucially, became easier to discharge patients under civil sections, although not court orders, from district psychiatric hospitals and units. In fact, perhaps too easy: one of the problems that has emerged with the 1983 Act, in contrast with the 1959 one, is difficulty in some instances in admitting and then keeping in hospital some patients who need to be there but whose presenting symptoms fluctuate so that they can sometimes conceal these for the duration of a short psychiatric examination. The status of records and the testimony of staff and relatives had so often been seen as routine, superficial or even antagonistic to the patient's best interests, under the old legislation, that they tended with the new Act to be viewed sceptically when they advised against the discharge of a patient from secure care. Preservation of rights and freedoms has demanded a more cogent marshalling of arguments if someone is now to have a Mental Health Act section renewed to detain them compulsorily for a longer time.

Freedoms, rights and responsibilities, therefore, are largely what the 1983 revision of the 'mould-breaking' 1959 Act are all about. It therefore revises and reformulates definitions to many of the procedures, such as those for detaining someone in hospital compulsorily and for the professional opinions which should be involved in this; for the imposition of treatment against people's wishes or when they are not capable of deciding for themselves; and for the second opinion consultation process which applies for some treatments at any time and for others when patients refuse them or are incapable of making their own decision.

The Mental Health Act of 1983, by comparison with 1959, contained many amended or tightened up definitions and procedures, resulting in more explicit safeguards for the protection of both individual patients and public safety. In creating the Mental Health Act Commission (MHAC), the 1983 Act restored a provision that had existed in earlier legislation. The 'Board of Control', which had replaced the 'Commissioners in Lunacy' in 1930, disappeared with the 1959 Act, leaving no independent body with a statutory duty to monitor the rights of detained patients and their standards of care. Following the reports of several inquiries into alleged incidents and 'scandals' at mental illness and handicap hospitals, there had been a widely felt need to restore this watchdog function.

An important new role of this watchdog body, the MHAC, as well as checking that all the required procedures had been fulfilled (by inspecting the relevant documentation), responding to patients' complaints and checking on the state of accommodation and the use of seclusion, was to ensure that patients had either consented to their treatment or, if not, that independent second opinions had been obtained. (The treatments coming into this category were specified.) More than that, such second opinions upon what treatment the consultant psychiatrist (the RMO) proposed to give had to take into account the opinions of two further members of the clinical team on the matter, one a nurse and the other neither a doctor nor a nurse.

This innovation clearly recognized the growth of multidisciplinary teams and the alternative strategies than other team members might be able to suggest when a patient refused ECT or a course of medication (these being the treatments specified in the Act as requiring consent from the patient or, failing that, a second opinion). Another doctor on the same team or in the same hospital was ruled out for providing this independent opinion but a nurse on the ward was allowable and an obvious further person to consult. Another professional with first hand knowledge of the patient proved not always so easy to find. A social worker was the most frequent choice: many would have been involved in recommending the patient's admission in the first place. A member of the workshop staff at a special hospital (occupational therapists elsewhere, and later at the special hospitals, too) was also relevant and usually available. But psychologists, being relatively scarce, were not always so readily available and would ideally need to be if some psychological treatment was the most likely alternative to ECT or medication, and especially if it were a case of treatment for a psychopathic personality disorder. This development needs mentioning as both a direct result of the representations made by the many professions which put evidence to Parliament when the Act was at its committee stage and which would also follow from the developments described in this history.

Another innovation in the 1983 Act which went some way towards meeting one of the outcomes of the 'interacts' experience at Broadmoor, namely the need for continuity of care, was the requirement in Section 117 for aftercare to be provided for patients discharged from the longer 'civil' section (3) and the sections in Part III for patients committed through criminal proceedings or under sentence (37, 47 or 48).

It took some time and much prodding from the MHAC to get this going properly, with documented procedures (the care continued until a decision to end it, which needed recording). One of the difficulties in achieving this, but one of its intended strengths, was the requirement for the District Health Authority (DHA) to liaise with the Local Authority Social Services (LASS) in its provision. It entailed a member of one or the other acting as the patient contact: usually a community psychiatric nurse or a social worker. This in turn meant that a representative of LASS needed to be present at case conferences in the psychiatric hospital or unit.

It is this section that has particular importance where a 'continuum of care' is concerned. It should not be seen merely as a period during which the supervisor has to ensure that medication continues to be taken. If new behavioural strategies have been developed then this is the crucial period when their resilience under pressure of former life situations is consolidated. Support from the various day care centres in the community will usually be important in this. A compulsive gambler or drinker, someone formerly with a phobia or a sexual problem, or someone who is simply trying to use a different approach to their relationships, cannot be said to have completed treatment until their new strategies have successfully survived in real life environments where the pressures exist that precipitated the problems in the first place.

There are also, in the new Act, treatments where consent AND a second opinion are required; it is not sufficient that the patient requests the treatment. These were envisaged to be the 'irreversible' treatments such as brain surgery but the requirement has also been extended to include hormone implants for the control or suppression of sexual drive. They have proved to be sufficient 'high-profile' for the SOAD (second opinion approved doctor) usually to be a member of the MHAC itself and for a nurse and lawyer member of the MHAC to accompany him or her. For instance, someone from another country might well be attending a private clinic in Britain for the operation. These are circumstances where consultation with a psychologist member of the clinical team might particularly be required as questions of alternative treatment would almost certainly be of a psychological nature.

The ensuing tabulations, as said at the start of this appendix, therefore summarize (Table A.1) the main changes or innovations in the 1983 Act, under five headings, and then (Table A.2) the sections where they occur, within a list of those sections most likely to involve or affect patients at Broadmoor.

TABLE A.1

SOME IMPORTANT CHANGES IN THE 1983 ACT BY COMPARISON WITH 1959

DEFINITIONS

1. Mental 'Subnormality' and 'Severe Subnormality' become 'Impairment' and 'Severe Impairment' and include a 'conduct' element.
2. Psychopathic Disorder's age limits are removed, but the requirement added that they may only be admitted to hospital if treatable. Sexual deviancy, and drug and alcohol dependence on their own, are excluded.

ADMISSION TO HOSPITAL

1. Application and consultation conditions strengthened.
2. Admission 'for assessment' introduced.
3. Renewals, reviews, checks and appeals strengthened.
4. Nearest relative definition clarified and extended to include co-habitee.
5. 'Treatability' introduced (see definition 2 above)
6. Holding powers introduced for nurses.
7. Remands to hospital and interim hospital orders introduced for offenders.
8. Further facilitation of transfer of prisoners.

CONSENT TO TREATMENT

1. Codified with regard to those requiring consent AND a second opinion (mainly psychosurgery), and those requiring consent OR a second opinion (ECT and medication).
2. Exclusions specified for 1st 3 months (not ECT) and 'urgent' treatment (i.e.: to save life; prevent violence, serious deterioration or suffering).
3. Second opinion procedure specified, including consultation with other staff who are clinically involved in the patient's treatment.

APPEALS TO MENTAL HEALTH REVIEW TRIBUNALS

1. In general, opportunities for appeal increased, in some cases earlier.
2. Powers introduced to delay discharge following successful appeal (to allow appropriate planning to be undertaken).
3. Automatic reviews for long-stay patients who fail to appeal on their own behalf.
4. Legal Aid introduced.
5. 'Restricted' patients brought within MHRT powers when tribunal chaired by a judge (previously this authority 'restricted' to the Home Secretary)

MENTAL HEALTH ACT COMMISSION INTRODUCED

1. Watch-dog body with powers to visit and report on detained patients and their conditions (visiting psychiatric hospitals annually, special hospitals more frequently).
2. Responsibilities: to appoint and review 'second opinion' doctors; to check on statutory documentation, complaints, appeals, seclusion and policies (e.g.: aftercare requirements); to draw up and keep under review a Code of Practice.

TABLE A.2

THE MAIN PROVISIONS OF THE MENTAL HEALTH ACT 1983

Section	*Description*	*Duration, Implications, Etc*
PART I: APPLICATION OF THE ACT		
1	Definitions	Mental Disorder, Mental Impairment, Severe Mental Impairment. Mental Impairment and Psychopathic Disorder defined but not Mental Illness
PART II: COMPULSORY ADMISSION TO HOSPITAL AND GUARDIANSHIP		
2	Admission for Assessment	28 days, convertible but not renewable
3	Admission for Treatment	6 months, renewable for 6 months then at 12 monthly intervals, indefinitely
4	Emergency Admission	72 hours, convertible but not renewable
5	Emergency detention of patient already in hospital	
5(2)	... by a doctor	72 hours, not renewable
5(4)	... by a nurse	6 hours, not renewable
7	Application for Guardianship	Powers and circumstances defined, for LASS or person accepted by them
17	Leave of absence from hospital	during which 'detained' conditions continue to apply; often used as 'trial discharge'
20	Duration of authority	Procedures for renewal of sections, etc.

PART III: PATIENTS CONCERNED IN CRIMINAL PROCEEDINGS OR UNDER SENTENCE

35	Remand for Assessment ('Reports')	28 days, renewable by court twice, up to 12 weeks in all
36	Remand for Treatment	28 days - ditto -
37*	Court Order for Hospital Admission or Guardianship	6 months, renewable for 6 months, then at 12 monthly intervals indefinitely
38	Interim Hospital Order	up to 12 weeks, renewable in 28 day steps up to 6 months total
41	Power of higher court to restrict discharge	applied with s.37 for specified or indefinite time where there is risk of further serious harm
47*	Transfer to Hospital of sentenced prisoner	6 months, renewable as for s.37
48	Transfer to Hospital of other (e.g. remanded) prisoners	Not specified, but would end with trial
49	Restriction on discharge (for risk of serious harm)	Can be applied to s.47 & some s.48s as s.41 may be applied to s.37 above

PART IV: CONSENT TO TREATMENT

57	Treatment requiring consent AND a second opinion	Effectively surgical and hormonal treatments
58	Treatment requiring consent OR a second opinion	Effectively ECT at any time and medicines after 3 months

59	Plans of treatment	Applying to treatments under ss. 57 or 58
60	Withdrawal of consent	when ss. 57 or 58 will be required
61	Review of treatment	Reports variously required, e.g. when renewing ss.3, 37 and 47 orders
62	Urgent treatment	Conditions overruling lack of consent, i.e.: to save life; prevent deterioration; alleviate suffering; or prevent violence or danger to self or others.

PART V: MENTAL HEALTH REVIEW TRIBUNALS

66	s.2	Entitled to appeal within 14 days
	ss.3, 37, 47, 48	Entitled to appeal within 1st 6 months then 2nd 6 months, then annually (but see s.70 following)
68	Various duties of Managers	Including referral to MHRT of patient after 3 years who has not appealed on own behalf
70	ss.41 and 49	Restrictions rule out appeal at the end of the first 6 months

PART VI: REMOVAL AND RETURN OF PATIENTS WITHIN UNITED KINGDOM

PART VII: MANAGEMENT OF PROPERTY AND AFFAIRS OF PATIENTS

PART VIII: MISCELLANEOUS FUNCTIONS OF LOCAL AUTHORITY AND SECRETARY OF STATE

114	Appointment of Approved Social Workers	Requirements of LASS to appoint approved social workers (i.e.: appropriately trained and qualified)
115	Powers of Entry and Inspection	By approved social workers, with an authenticated document if required
117	Aftercare for patients Discharged under ss. 3, 37, 47 or 48	Planning and liaison between health and local authority required
118	Code of Practice	Required from Secretary of State, in effect from the Mental Health Act Commission. Unacceptability of first two drafts led to delay; parliament accepted third draft, Nov 1989
120	Protection of Detained Patients	Sets out requirements for patients to be visited, interviewed, and their complaints investigated
121	Mental Health Act Commission	Constitution and functions

PART IX: OFFENCES, i.e.: in the operation of the Act

PART X: MISCELLANEOUS AND SUPPLEMENTARY

131   Informal admission of patients

132)
) Duties of managers
133)

134	Correspondence of Patients and duties of MHAC in respect of mail	When special hospital patients' mail may be withheld and to whom they may correspond without inspection
135	Warrant to search for and remove patients	Powers of police, accompanied by approved social worker and doctor, to enter premises
136	Mentally disordered persons found in public places	Powers of police to take a person to a place of safety for examination
139	Protection for acts done in pursuance of this Act	Provides protection for staff, e.g.: to restrain patients 'in good faith' without necessarily incurring risk of prosecution

* Note: that before these sections (37 and 47) can be applied for psychopathic disorder or mental impairment (but not severe mental impairment) it must be established that the condition is treatable ('likely to be alleviated or deterioration prevented.')

SUMMARY

Whilst this appendix largely comprises tabulations of comparisons between the 1959 and 1983 Acts, preceded by tabulations of definitions, it has also summarized the principal changes between the two Acts and, in so doing, described the essence of the 1959 Act which so differed from the pre-war legislation which it replaced.

Frequent reference has been made throughout this history of the change from 'criminal insanity', established by the McNaughtan Rules, to 'mental disorder' and its four sub-categories. These are defined and located. Mental patients were to be treated like physical ones and could enter hospital voluntarily ('informal patients'). If admitted compulsorily, this involved several NHS personnel, no longer only a magistrate, and renewal and appeals procedures were instated (the MHRTs). Offenders sent by the courts to hospital were treated similarly but could have their discharge restricted to the Home Secretary's authority. It became possible to move patients between local and special (secure) hospitals as necessary.

The 1983 Act preserved the essential structure of its predecessor but increased the safeguards for patients, increasing the frequency with which appeals to a MHRT could be made, creating the MHAC as a watchdog body and requiring a more complex system of scrutiny for imposing treatment against a patient's wishes (through the SOAD system and its mandatory consultation process for some controversial treatments and where a patient refused treatment which the RMO considered essential). Mandatory aftercare was also instituted for patients discharged from a compulsory section. These changes reflected the perceived weaknesses of the 1959 Act. Remands to hospital and interim hospital orders were instituted for the assessment and treatment of offenders. The tables set out these conditions and their location within the 1959 and 1983 Acts, although the Acts themselves and the various official commentaries must be seen for full details.

APPENDIX B

RECENT PUBLICATIONS AND
FURTHER READING

Compiling a history some time after the relevant period has ended inevitably raises the question of changes that have since occurred. The reader familiar with the subject will be irritated at the omissions whilst the newcomer will be in the dark as to how far the account falls short of the here-and-now. This account of Broadmoor's history between the Mental Health Acts of 1959 and 1983 cannot finish, therefore, without some indication of what other information exists, both about other events and developments at the time and about what happened next. Mention has been made of several books and papers which supply some of this information and these are listed in the bibliography. However, discussion of these will have been limited to the subject of the chapter in which they occur. It will be helpful to look at them again, and indeed others, for any further light they may throw on the way this history developed.

For this purpose the references are divided into two groups: the first, of publications about Broadmoor and the second of other relevant publications. Each of these are then again divided into two groups: the first relates to those in existence at the time of this history and which might be expected to throw further light on matters described here; and the second relates to those which have been published since 1983 and which take the subject onwards. Note that the publication date does not necessarily coincide with the period with which it deals.

BROADMOOR PUBLICATIONS BEFORE AND DURING THE PERIOD OF THE 1959 ACT
(Arranged in chronological order)
* Publications by former patients

Child Murder & Insanity, by J. S. Hopwood, *J.Ment.Sc,* 73, 300, 95-108, 1927. (A scientific paper).

*Inside Broadmoor, by John Edward Allen; W.H. Allen, London, 1952.

Broadmoor, by Ralph Partridge; Chatto & Windus, London, 1953.

The Trial of J.T. Straffen, edited by L. Fairfield & E.P. Fullbrook; William Hodge & Co Ltd., London, Edinburgh & Glasgow, 1954.

Morbid Jealousy & Murder; A Psychiatric Study of Morbidly Jealous Murderers at Broadmoor, by Ronald Rae Mowat; Tavistock Publications, London, 1966.

*Bound for Broadmoor, by Peter Thompson; Hodder & Stoughton, London, 1972.

*Back From Broadmoor, by Peter Thompson; Mowbrays, London, 1974.

Obsessive Poisoner, The Strange Story of Graham Young, by Winifred Young (his sister); Robert Hale, London, 1973.

The St Albans Poisoner; the Life & Times of Graham Young, by Anthony Holden, Hodder & Stoughton, London, 1974.

(As regards these last two books, see also the paper by Bowden, 1996, below).

The Late Richard Dadd, by Patricia Allderidge; The Tate Gallery, London, 1974.

537

Daniel McNaughton: His Trial and the Aftermath, by Donald J. West & Alexander Walk; Gaskell Books (Headley Bros Ltd) Ashford, Kent, 1977.

Broadmoor, by David Cohen, Psychology News Press, London, 1981.

*Notes From A Waiting Room, by Alan Reeve; Heretic Books, London, 1983.

Integration of Special Hospital Patients Into the Community, by Margaret Norris; Gower, Aldershot, Hants, 1984.

Maternal Filicides in Broadmoor: 1919-1969, by Patrick G McGrath, unpublished thesis, Broadmoor Library, [1991 but work done during 1959-83 period].

BROADMOOR PUBLICATIONS AFTER THE PERIOD OF THIS HISTORY

The Silent Twins, by Marjorie Wallace; London, Chatto & Windus, 1986; Penguin, 1987; reprinted 1993 with new chapter.

Sentenced to Hospital: Offenders in Broadmoor, by Susanne Dell & Graham Robertson; Maudsley Monographs No.32, OUP, Oxford, 1988.

Shakespeare Comes to Broadmoor, edited by Murray Cox; Jessica Kingsley, London, 1992.

*My Story, by Ron Kray with Fred Dinenage; London, Sidgwick & Jackson, 1993.

Asylum, by Patrick McGrath; Viking (Penguin Books) London, 1996.

Graham Young (1947-90); The St Albans Poisoner: His Life and Times, by Paul Bowden; in *Criminal Behaviour & Mental Health,* vol. 6, 1996, No.Suppl, pp.17-24.

The Surgeon of Crowthorne, by Simon Winchester; Viking; London, 1998.

Managing High Security Psychiatric Care, edited by Charles Kaye & Alan Franey; Jessica Kingsley, London, 1998.

OTHER PUBLICATIONS RELEVANT TO BROADMOOR DURING THE PERIOD OF THIS HISTORY
(See Bibliography for a fuller reference list)
(Arranged in chronological sequence)

The Mental Health Act, HMSO, London, 1959.

A Calendar of Murder, by T. Morris & L. Blom-Cooper; Michael Joseph, London, 1964.

Crime & Insanity in England, I: The Historical Perspective, by Nigel Walker; Edinburgh University Press, Edinburgh, 1968.

Crime & Insanity in England, II: New Solutions & New Problems, by Nigel Walker & Sarah McCabe; Edinburgh Univ. Press, Edinburgh, 1973.

Report on the Review of Procedures for the Discharge and Supervision of Psychiatric Patients Subject to Special Restrictions, (the 'Aarvold' Report); Cmnd 5191, HMSO, London, 1973.

Report of the Committee on Mentally Abnormal Offenders, (the 'Butler' Report); for the Home Office & DHSS; Cmnd 6244, HMSO, London, 1975.

A Human Condition, vol. 1: The Mental Health Act from 1959 to 1975; Observations, analysis and proposals for reform, by Larry O. Gostin; MIND, London, 1975.

A Human Condition, vol. 2: The Law Relating to Mentally Abnormal Offenders, Observations, analysis and proposals for reform, by Larry O. Gostin; MIND, London, 1977.

Secure Facilities for Psychiatric Patients - A Comprehensive Policy, a Report of The Royal College of Psychiatrists, London, 1981.

The Future of the Special Hospitals, a Report of the Royal College of Psychiatrists, London, 1983.

Mentally Abnormal Offenders, edited by Michael & Ann Craft; Baillière Tindall, Eastbourne, East Sussex, 1984.

SINCE THE END OF THIS HISTORY

The Mental Health Act, HMSO, London, 1983.

Secure Provision, A Review of Special Services for the Mentally Ill & Mentally Handicapped in England & Wales, edited by Larry Gostin; Tavistock Publications, London, 1985.

Principles & Practice of Forensic Psychiatry, by Robert Bluglass & Paul Bowden; Churchill Livingstone, Edinburgh, 1990.

Forensic Psychiatry: Clinical, Legal & Ethical Issues, edited by John Gunn & Pamela Taylor; Butterworth- Heinemann, Oxford, 1993.

The Psychology of Criminal Conduct: Theory, Research & Practice, by Ronald Blackburn; Wiley, Chichester, Sussex, 1993.

Psychology & Antisocial Behaviour, Report of the British Psychological Society, Leicester, 1993.

Special Women, the Experience of Women in the Special Hospital System, edited by Catherine Hemingway; Avebury, Aldershot, Hants, 1996.

SOME KEY PUBLICATIONS REVIEWED

Inside Broadmoor and *Asylum*

Historic Broadmoor is expanded upon by several of these books. An account of life in Broadmoor before and during the 1939-45 war is given by John Allen, a patient who escaped and stayed at large for more than two years. His account in his book *Inside Broadmoor* is very much in line with Partridge's but it adds the patient's angle and fascinating information about his experiences during his escape and as a result of his recapture.

A similar flavour is given by Dr Patrick McGrath's son, Patrick McGrath jnr, in his novel, *Asylum*. Despite writing much later and well after this history finishes, the setting of his novel is clearly Broadmoor in the immediate post-war years. How did he manage this? He grew up, of course, in the deputy superintendent's house which his parents preferred to the superintendent's house itself. This is clearly the setting for his principal characters. Patrick junior obviously drew on his memories of the childhood he spent there. He also recalls psychiatric practice as no doubt told to him by his father and overheard from the visits of prominent psychiatrists entertained by his parents in the spacious, gracious, red-brick house on the hill. More than this, he acknowledges help from Dr Brian O'Connell, an early colleague of his father's at Broadmoor, recalled at the start of this history. The picture of the several fictitious patients who figure in the book, and especially of the deterioration of his heroine, no doubt owe much to Dr O'Connell. The atmosphere evoked is redolent of Partridge's Broadmoor in the immediate post-war years.

The Surgeon of Crowthorne

Going back even further into Broadmoor history is the setting described by Simon Winchester, a journalist and writer, in his *Surgeon of Crowthorne,* which entered the best-seller lists. This might seem strange for a book about the compilation of the *Oxford Dictionary* and even stranger for a subject not having any obvious connection with Broadmoor. The 'surgeon' referred to, however, was a medical officer in the American Civil War and the encroaching insanity that brought him to England and then to Broadmoor is part of the book's fascination. Once there, however, his strange madness alternates with periods of lucidity, during which he sets to work researching and supplying the information for which the editors publicly advertised in their compilation of the first *Oxford English Dictionary.* This provides an evocative illustration of Broadmoor in Victorian times and the traumatic eruptions of schizophrenia in between the American surgeon's lucid phases. Of course, none of us remembers that era but Simon Winchester's research is impressive and his tracing of the surgeon's illness persuasively presented. One can well envisage that Broadmoor would have been as he describes it in those days.

Legal texts: about Straffen and McNaughtan; and by Nigel Walker

Two books of trials: the one of John Straffen which brought the otherwise progressive era of Dr Stanley Hopwood to an end; and the other of Daniel McNaughtan, who gave his name to the McNaughtan Rules for determining insanity in court, trace legal issues in illustrative fashion. The Straffen trial is prefaced with the account of his escape and recapture which, again, evoke the era, the locality, Broadmoor's setting and practices, and the staff organization and outlook.

The second of Professor Nigel Walker's books: "Crime & Insanity in England," this one in co-authorship with Sarah McCabe (in fact, Dr McGrath's sister), traces in painstaking detail many more of the legal procedures and niceties than could be accommodated in this history. In these several books are examined the many facets of the medico-legal element which the more legally minded reader may want.

Clinical Textbooks

The latest book from the period of the 1959 Act was that edited by the Crafts. It still contains much relevant material (and my own elaboration of special hospitals' treatment as described in this history). It has now been updated and amplified by the books of Bluglass and Bowden and of Gunn and Taylor, both encyclopaedic and including contributions from many authoritative authors. Ronald Blackburn's book, already mentioned several times in this history, spells out the psychological element and supplies analyses, not only of the historical, legal, theoretical and sociological perspectives, but also of clinical and research applications, practices and progress. Once again it supplies greater and more authoritative detail than can or should be given in a history.

Research Texts

The two reports: *The Transfer of Special Hospital Patients to NHS Hospitals,* by Susanne Dell; and *Integration of Special Hospital Patients into the Community*, by Margaret Norris; form the content of Chapter 18 and need no further mention here. However, these will lead into other work by Dell, one of which: *Sentenced to Hospital*, with Graham Robertson, is a more up-to-date report, well after the period of this history, detailing the characteristics of special hospital patients and, in particular, reporting their attitudes to their life in hospital and to their discharge prospects.

From Dell's and Robertson's thoughtful and painstaking work, patients' attitudes to their incarceration and treatment (or lack of it) are collated and analysed, the authors distinguishing the conditions and treatments of the mentally ill and the psychopathic groups as well as the attitudes of the medical staff to these. As a result they highlight the differences in the nature of the disorder in these two groups (and the mental subnormality/handicap group at the other special hospitals) and the difficulty in conceptualizing the treatment needs and the assessment of change in the psychopathic group. In this there is much agreement with the present history's account of the differences and problems, especially in explicitly acknowledging that it is effectively the antisocial behaviour of the defendant being tried in court that puts him/her into hospital classified as psychopathic, yet an assumption that this implies a pervasive 'disorder of personality' which keeps him/her there. As this, however, does not meet the traditional criterion of an illness, it frustrates the consultant psychiatrist, as 'responsible medical officer', in prescribing treatment or evaluating readiness for discharge. This continues discussion of an issue which has been a preoccupation of this history.

Of especial interest, however, in this later study which, although running well into the lifetime of the subsequent Mental Health Act of 1983 draws its data mainly from the time of the 1959 Act, is Dell's and Robertson's suggested solution. Whilst they are content to see use of the hospital order continue for the mentally ill and handicapped, they see it as irrelevant and essentially unethical for the psychopathic group who frequently continue to be held on the grounds of their disorder when the only evidence for this is the original offence; they have either completed any treatment available for this or no further treatment can be suggested.

Interestingly, their interview data suggest that it is the psychopathic group who see their stay in Broadmoor as being preferable to imprisonment, because it is more congenial, constructive, varied and offers treatment for problems they are often prepared to acknowledge. It is the mentally ill who resent a special hospital for what they see as providing the standard psychiatric treatment which they could equally well have received in a more traditional setting. Broadmoor patients are notoriously prone to see only other patients as dangerous and not themselves. They often regard their offences as untypical, 'rogue' events, indicative of special circumstances which they do not see as recurring.

Corroborating the treatment arguments in Chapter 22, Dell and Robertson describe the psychiatric staff as seeing the cause of the offence in the mentally ill group as their illness, rather than the illness more often being a trigger for underlying personality problems which themselves need attention when the illness has been resolved. Consistent with this view, they also see the cause of psychopaths' offences as their psychopathy, this time correctly, because the condition is merely a description of long-standing behavioural tendencies rather than a transient mental illness. Part of the evidence for this is the offence itself, yet either no effective treatment is on offer or, when treatment programmes have been completed, the patient continues to be held on the grounds of an enduring personality defect for which no independent evidence is forthcoming except the antisocial life-style of which the offence is an example.

Dell's and Robertson's suggested solution for this dilemma, whilst continuing the hospital order for the mentally ill and mentally subnormal (now 'mentally handicapped'), is to enable special hospitals to accept psychopaths for voluntary treatment, under civil procedures; or to sentence them in the usual manner, under criminal procedures, and then transfer them from prison to hospital. If they declined this transfer, or when treatment was complete, they would return to prison to complete their sentence.

This is an interesting proposal, although it still does not meet the problems of those who refuse or fail to respond to treatment (as psychopaths are notoriously prone to do) and who are released at the end of their sentence with a high risk of continuing to offend. The special hospital staffs often raised argument is that it is the compulsory nature of detention that 'concentrates the minds' of psychopaths on the necessity that they change. Dell and Robertson meet this by pointing out that this is hardly voluntarily accepted treatment, is unethical, and is unlikely to promote willing and effective change. This is arguable and touches again on the issues discussed earlier in this history. Their description of many psychopaths' preference for a special hospital 'sentence' as more comfortable than a prison one does, however, hold out hope for acceptance of the need for change and the prospect of return to prison might equally be said to be a coercive factor. In any case, the whole process of treatment when it is psychological rather than medical, includes a wide-ranging patient-therapist dialogue turning upon helping the patient to recognize his/her problems and accept whatever implications may emerge. Treatment is seen as a collaborative procedure.

Unfortunately, government thinking, now a decade after Dell and

Robertson made their suggestions, seems to have gone the other way and proposals have been mooted to introduce some form of institutional incapacitation of recalcitrant psychopaths, as public protection, without either conviction or hospital order, but on the strength merely of a dangerous record. There must be some sympathy for the legislators over this vexing problem, for they see the specialists who deal with these problems in disagreement over the strategies to use. It is a pity that the messages are clouded for the solutions are clear, even though they may be difficult to achieve and may not command universal agreement; at present they are obscured by the counter-messages of those who are trying to define the problem in inappropriate and irrelevant alternative terms.

Shakespeare Comes to Broadmoor

It is, therefore, heartening to come to an account which emphasizes clearly what are the appropriate and relevant messages for helping damaged personalities to mend. Perhaps the most hopeful book to have emerged since the ending of the era of the 1959 Act is the one edited by Murray Cox which describes the venture of bringing Shakespeare to the patients of Broadmoor. It confronts head on the issue of enabling the patient to get to grips with the emotionality of his or her crime, which the book sees as crucial to achieving effective treatment progress. This is, of course, plumb in line with the implications from the developments described in this history. The lack of this element is starkly revealed by both Dell's and Robertson's and Norris's findings and, I hope, by all the many initiatives described in this history. As an illustration of the continuing work of Broadmoor after 1983, Murray Cox cogently sets out the needs of patients and the process of meeting them. The powerful effect on both the patients and the Shakespearean actors is described, with numerous comments cited from both.

This history has stressed constantly the need for patients to be enabled to develop new strategies for coping with their lives, albeit entailing a period of intense effort and practice to bring this about. Psychotherapy has been described as a process enabling the patient to discover and convince him/herself of the need for change. Murray Cox's books illustrate the power of this discovery, when found through Shakespeare's dramas, and its necessity for the self-realization that precedes and enables effective change. Whilst a psychological perspective sees this as usually insufficient without developing the accompanying strategies for bringing about change, its powerful role is graphically illustrated by Murray Cox.

Behavioural therapies have been criticized as too limiting, conceptually and practically, and the term 'cognitive' has now been added. This is actually a tautology, for 'behaviour' in psychological parlance includes the entire process of perceiving, thinking, acting and storing experiences, all of which are driven by motivation, of which emotion is a major component. However, to the extent that 'behaviour' has tended to carry restricted connotations, it is understandable that 'cognitive' has been added to the term which describes this currently popular treatment method. Nevertheless, one of its forebears, social skills training, incorporated and facilitated the cultivation and understanding of emotional feelings and their portrayal through bodily signals. It has led to both assertiveness training and to anger control methods. Perhaps it did not delve deeply enough into the origins, control or meaning of these feelings but it attempted to incorporate them into the comprehension of what was significant to the process of changing behaviour. Cognitive-behavioural therapy makes explicit that re-orientation of thinking patterns and attitudes must accompany 'behavioural' change. The experienced therapist knows that emotional barriers hinder therapy and an understanding of emotional needs and problems are vital to therapeutic progress.

The introduction of Shakespeare to Broadmoor, specifically several of his tragedies, powerfully illustrated this. Through the portrayal of complex and poignant emotions by the actors, which the patient members of the audience recognized but could not always express for themselves, many patients were brought to a new realization of their problems and a fresh perspective for their solution. They were then enabled to take the next steps more readily in the ensuing treatment groups.

Murray Cox's initiative, interestingly, did not discriminate between those patients who required psychotherapy in addition to or instead of medicine. The audiences comprised about a quarter of the patient population. When allowance is made for those too confused to express a wish to attend and others whose RMO thought them unfit to attend, and then those who believed that Shakespeare was too highbrow, complicated or boring for them to enjoy, the attendance must have represented a fair cross-section of the patient population's mental disorder categories. There were clearly more than merely psychopaths attending. So a great many mentally ill patients, too, must have had their needs met through experiencing the Shakespearean approach to their predicaments. They needed more than medicine; it was not just their illness that needed treating. Their copious recorded comments indicate their awareness of the significance of the experience and their wish to see dramatherapy incorporated into the standard treatment repertoire of Broadmoor.

The small beginnings of the psychologists' social skills training (for which perhaps read: 'emotional competence training') and the psychotherapy groups of Murray Cox and the other psychotherapists, seem to have been vindicated. Reviews of the efficacy of various treatment approaches almost always seem to result in 'not proven' verdicts. 'More research is needed' is the repeated plea. In fact, of course, very few treatment methods are used in isolation, so that it will be difficult as well as restricting to try to assess the validity of any one these on its own. Professional ethics decree that the treatment module most likely to succeed is provided; withholding a crucial element would be regarded as unethical. Most patient's problems are nowadays assessed with a comprehensive but specific appraisal of their needs, not blanket prescriptions. A combination of different methods and approaches is the norm. Just as education is more than the 3-Rs, psychotherapy is more than talk and behaviour is more than cognition. If bringing Shakespeare to Broadmoor adds dramatherapy to the role-play of social skills training and adds rehearsal to the insights of psychotherapy, Shakespeare will have brought enlightenment to Broadmoor and Murray Cox will have achieved immortality.

All the emotional mayhem of Shakespeare's tragedies drew comment from numerous patients which are duly recorded in Murray Cox's book giving an account of the venture. Shakespeare not only described emotion but had his actors enact it in all its fury, despair and ecstasy. Conflicts were not merely discussed but lived through. The boundaries of fantasy and reality became blurred. Lives were lived before the audience's eyes in raw, bare reality. The emotional outpourings of love, anger, jealousy, fear, hatred: all were fully expressed by Shakespeare and enacted passionately, violently. Many patients revelled in the freedom this provided for them. They commented that their own emotions were never able to gain expression. The institutional ethic was of control. Any outburst was labelled 'an incident', a sign of patients' continuing psychiatric instability which could lengthen their stay. Control of this kind was nevertheless artificial because it failed to reflect the reality of resolving conflicts in real life. Shakespeare's coming to Broadmoor gave them a new freedom, a licence to react. Was it reflected in a new tolerance by staff? Could they see it as part of the therapeutic process and use it to resolve patients' problems? A further history is awaited. Kaye and Franey do not reach these untouched places.

One more facet of the hospital is also cogently illustrated in Murray Cox's account of bringing Shakespeare to Broadmoor, confirming my own account of the reaction of visitors to the experience of Broadmoor. Time and again the Shakespearean actors describe similarly their own reactions to meeting patients. Not only do they see them as ordinary people like themselves and not the crazed beasts the tabloid press would have us believe they are, but they discover, from portraying Shakespeare's tragedies and discussing these with the patients afterwards, how anguished and puzzled the patients' minds are and how important it is for them to work through their agony in therapy. They emphasize how irrelevant it is to see this as some kind of insult to their victims or a condoning of their crimes. It is of no help to the victims to victimize their aggressors, even though a process of expiation and rapprochement is invariably required. Patients recognize this and frequently request it. Helping the aggressor can help the victim (or the victim's family where the victim has died). Sadly, many do not recognize this: another indication of yet another unfulfilled therapeutic need.

After describing the venture of performing Shakespeare's tragedies in Broadmoor, the second half of Murray Cox's book deals with the process of psychotherapeutic drama in general, including chapters on how it is carried out and its applications in other institutional settings. These fill out the picture, for which the Shakespeare venture was the stimulus, and elevate the story from an anecdotal account to a valuable reference source on 'expressive therapies'. Some of the terminology might not be to every professional person's taste but the meaning and methods are clear and alternative expressions usually spring to mind. The potency of the therapeutic activity is also clear where the participating individuals are concerned, empowering many of them to examine themselves and their lives afresh. The processes remain to be codified and their effects verified in relation to other significant life events, such as staying free of further convictions and sustaining relationships and an independent life style. The relevance of 'expressive therapies' to patients' and offenders' needs seems to have been demonstrated by the novel initiative in bringing Shakespeare to Broadmoor.

The Patients' Own Accounts

Several books are patient's own accounts of their experiences. Allen's has already been referred to and both Thompson's and Reeve's have received comment at points during this history. Several are accounts by others of particular patients. The young poisoner, Graham Young, is one of these, whilst Ronald Kray's is assisted by a co-author. Another describes the strange history of twin girls who came to Broadmoor and communicated only between themselves, using their own private language. Historically, Daniel McNaughtan has already been mentioned but Richard Dadd only in passing. He came to Broadmoor in Victorian times, having initially been sent to Bethlem Hospital ('Bedlam') before Broadmoor was opened.

Dadd was ironically named, having murdered his father but, of course, his fame was through being already an accomplished artist of some renown. His pictures were exhibited in the Royal Academy, the principal work for which he is known being the *Fairy Feller's Master-Stroke*. However, he produced a wealth of others in his lifetime, of many different kinds, being particularly well-known for his portrayals of Victorian street characters such as the crossing-sweeper, the wooden-legged sailor and the coachman. Several of these were in the medical superintendent's office so were familiar from the many meetings held there. They were borrowed by the Tate Gallery when it mounted an exhibition of Dadd's work in 1974, in connection with which Patricia Allderidge, archivist at the Bethlem Royal Hospital, prepared the book on Dadd which is listed here. Before Dadd's tragic crime he had accompanied Sir Thomas Phillips, as his artist, on a grand tour of the Mediterranean and middle eastern countries, fulfilling the role of the present day photographer. A collection of paintings quite different from his previous work resulted. His mental wanderings into fantasy often cropped up in paintings of fairy-like and other mythical creatures but he also made many fine landscapes and figure paintings in a more traditional style.

Because much of Dadd's later work was done in Broadmoor, and although he was accorded the materials and facilities to exercise his talent, he also made use of whatever materials came to hand. Thus a number of works were done on hessian and others on internal windows, which had been whitewashed and the figure scratched upon them. A set of paintings was done on the panels fronting the stage in the central hall (now removed and preserved). It is rumoured that some works, if they have survived at all, will have found their way into the homes and families of staff and friends. One of his earlier paintings from his tour with Sir Thomas Phillips, recorded as missing in Patricia Allderidge's book, emerged from the traditional attic of a couple (of no apparent connection with Broadmoor) who brought it unsuspectingly on to the Antiques Road Show. I happened to watch that edition and remarked to my wife that it looked like a Dadd (and there was a reference to Sir Thomas Phillips on the back) but was still amazed the following week when the paintings expert reported back the results of his inquiries. It was indeed Dadd's missing *Artist's Halt in the Desert* and was valued at over £100,000. Patricia Allderidge's book contains a fine, fully annotated and illustrated record of his output.

Of the other patients' own accounts of their time in Broadmoor, I have already remarked upon the contrast between Thompson's and Reeve's which results, no doubt, from their very different personalities and backgrounds. Dell and Robertson have reported the contrasting attitudes and circumstances of the patients they interviewed. Murray Cox's book, with its plethora of patients' comments, albeit deriving from their reaction to Shakespeare but strongly reflecting their personalities and emotional strivings, comes nearer to Thompson's impressions. Whilst numerous patients resented having to be in Broadmoor and 'the gate' was an enduring aspiration, the majority did seem to resign themselves to the need to be there and, sometimes grudgingly, sometimes more enthusiastically, appreciated the treatment and help they received.

The overriding problem was the extreme length of time that most of them had to stay there, which could undoubtedly now be reduced with more modern treatments and improved knowledge of what makes for success or failure. Norris's work, summarized in Chapter 18, has particularly focused on this and provides corroboration. As remarked in Chapter 23, however, there is clearly a philosophy and outlook in the public mind, which not surprisingly extends to the lawmakers in parliament and the lawyers who apply the laws, that 'the punishment must fit the crime', as W S Gilbert wrote in *The Mikado*. The concept of missing, impaired or distorted responsibility arising from mental or personality disorder, and introduced by the Victorians whom we otherwise see as sternly unforgiving, does not seem to make any impact upon this philosophy. The scientific, medical and philosophical advances brought with the passage of time seem to have been ignored rather than assimilated. The emotional climate blowing on successive generations is more influential than knowledge and reason. The power of emotion is the element with which not only Broadmoor's patients must grapple but society itself and its political servants. Otherwise, to quote Tevye the milkman in another stage musical, *Fiddler on the Roof*: 'An eye for an eye and a tooth for a tooth - in the end everyone will be blind and toothless'.

Managing High Security Psychiatric Care by Charles Kaye and Alan Franey

And so we come to the nearest thing to a continuation of Broadmoor's history into the era of the 1983 Act - indeed the history of all the special hospitals - Kaye's and Franey's book, which has already received some mention. Charles Kaye was chief executive to the Special Hospitals Service

Authority and Alan Franey the general manager at Broadmoor, both in the period of the 1983 Mental Health Act but at the end of the 1980s, some years into its life.

The era of medical superintendents had ended. For a few years the 'hospital management teams' (HMTs) of this history had continued. They comprised a triumvirate of an RMO (consultant psychiatrist), a CNO (chief nursing officer) and the hospital secretary, an administrator. The arrival of new legislation and the retirement of long-standing office holders was the opportunity, however, for a further evolution to occur and the special hospitals followed the rest of the NHS with the appointment of general managers. Kaye's and Franey's book tells the story of the transition and how a new system was created to manage the problem hospitals which no one seemed to know what to do with. In this mode their account could not be expected to follow the pattern of Partridge. Their main concern, as managers, was how the system was now to be seen, structured and run. They tell of their struggles. It is not part of this history to try to venture into the next era, but some mention needs making of this book which, like Murray Cox's, has relevance for the clinical and psychological ideas introduced in the present history.

In contrast with Murray Cox, Kaye and Franey are concerned with the system: could it be adapted, managed and given a future or were the special hospitals to be closed? They describe their efforts to come to terms with the problem and to construe and manage it differently. Unfortunately, they came to the job at a time when the introduction of business management was thought to be the solution to service problems. Clinical personnel were thought inappropriate as hospital managers but at the same time made responsible for managing aspects of their own service, for which they had previously had expert support. They were required to do this without any compensating help for their clinical activities, which suffered as a consequence of their attentions being required elsewhere. Small wonder that they thought it a money-saving ploy. This no doubt added to the endemic problems of the special hospitals which Kaye and Franey were appointed to resolve. Improvements seem to have resulted but how fundamental and long-lasting only time will tell. Further reorganization has now followed theirs. Unfortunately, a certain ambivalence colours Kaye's and Franey's account. One feels that they could really have wished to have had the task of winding up the whole system instead of trying to rescue it. As the book unfolds, however, they seem to gain some sneaking regard for it and to be more strongly motivated to make it work.

Kaye and Franey, however, do not monopolize their book and, after a couple of sections dealing with their struggles with what they found and their further struggles in introducing change, they devote sections to the patients and the changes in clinical services. These are contributed by an appropriate range of clinical staff and are interesting and relevant. What one might have thought would be a dry subject - the buildings, or 'physical environment' as the book has it - turns out to be a fascinating exploration of the new accommodation and of the rationale of its security arrangements. There are chapters describing the patients, including the learning disability patients at the other special hospitals, by several clinical authors, and a sensitive treatment of whether and how to treat the question of enabling intimate relationships to be enjoyed under security constraints. Parts 3 and 4 are encouraging accounts of clinical advances following the era of the present history.

In this context it is disappointing, therefore, to see the sparse attention given to research and development before Kaye and Franey return, at the end, to the hospital's relationships with the outside world. They describe research as attracting 'awareness, interest and significant activity .. but .. a notable absence of co-ordination and drive'. Co-ordination may, indeed, have been less than ideal, but a start had to be made somewhere and the crude and tentative beginnings were always encouraged by Dr McGrath, as this history tells. This history also emphasizes the necessity for critical scrutiny of clinical procedures and developments, which the psychology department and SHRU always conscientiously observed.

'Drive', however, was most certainly not lacking and this history charts some of the quite remarkable research explorations into new fields of assessment, explanation, treatment and follow-up. Kaye and Franey describe 'early tender shoots of development' when they should have been describing the nurture and retraining of mature growths, with perhaps some weeding, clearing, pruning, fresh planting and fertilizing. They set out a good programme, if over-elaborate in the way of administrators, but they don't seem to have noticed the extensive foundations already provided for them. Where research is concerned they want to bulldoze the site and start again when a good garden lies hidden in the undergrowth. This is a book that is, at one and the same time, both encouraging and disappointing, stimulating and irritating.

SUMMARY AND CONCLUSIONS

An intermittent trickle of books has come out of Broadmoor in the past, flowing a little more fully as the years have gone by. Accounts by or about patients have been augmented by some researches, a history of another subject that has intriguingly also involved Broadmoor and one of its patients, and even a novel set in a fictitious but spookily convincing Broadmoor. All provide interesting extra information and colour that this history may have missed or inadequately covered; or which will have been beyond its remit; or have been written since the 1959 Act ended. By contrast, a considerable number of forensic psychiatry and psychology textbooks have included aspects deriving from or bearing upon Broadmoor, whilst there are plenty of legal tomes of relevance. Papers in the journals of all the relevant disciplines also abound. Books solely about Broadmoor, however, remain rare.

Closest to the hospital itself and its life inside, since Partridge, and since the period covered by this present history, must nevertheless be the books of Kaye and Franey, Murray Cox and Dell and Robertson. The first two of these stand in complete contrast to each other, even where they deal with clinical topics. Kaye and Franey describe the struggle to reorganize the running of the special hospitals, under the changing conditions which have followed the 1983 Mental Health Act, and against the entrenched attitudes and customs that a century-old institution always presents. Their clinical chapters, although sensitively detailed, are furthermore, mainly 'organizational' in telling of the way services were provided and what they were for.

Murray Cox, in contrast, tells of therapy as it happened: a venture providing patients with a means of expressing their needs in a compellingly effective way. He also shows how the ordinary public, in the persons of the actors who portrayed Shakespeare's tragedies inside Broadmoor, found that their audience not only understood and responded in quite startling fashion, but were also ordinary human beings, not crazed, frightening monsters.

This matches the reactions of most visitors to the hospital. There is, of course, unfortunately a limit to the visitors that can be accommodated there, otherwise many more people could experience this for themselves. Even so professional groups visit weekly and staff regularly present their work at meetings and conferences. The League of Friends, moreover, would be delighted to welcome more members.

Yet the world outside, and especially the media, continually refers to Broadmoor as a secret, shut-away place, rebuffing efforts to get to know it. I repeat what I said at the outset of this history: one can't help feeling that people have a deep felt need to believe Broadmoor is far away, mysterious and unknown. 'Out of sight, out of mind' makes them feel more comfortable.

Perhaps the last words, though, should be from Partridge himself, where we started. He wrote, not as a psychologist, psychiatrist, nurse, social worker or lawyer, but as an ordinary member of the public. He concluded that Broadmoor was 'a place for any nation to be proud of' (p.262), and that: 'if we acknowledge a duty to help the insane to recover, why not the criminally insane?' (p.263). That was 1953, before two successive Acts of modern, emancipating legislation. If his words were relevant then, they should be no less so today.

GLOSSARY OF ABBREVIATIONS

ACC	Army Catering Corps
ACMN	Assistant Chief Male Nurse
AHA	Area Health Authority
AScW	Association of Scientific Workers (succeeded by the ASTMS)
ASTMS	Association of Scientific, Technical and Managerial Staff
BASW	British Association of Social Workers
BMA	British Medical Association
BPS/BPsS	British Psychological Society
C&R	Control & Restraint
CA	Clerical Assistant
CAC	Clinical Advisory Committee
CEO	Chief Executive Officer
CJA	Criminal Justice Act(s)
CMN	Chief Male Nurse
CN	Charge Nurse
CNO	Chief Nursing Officer
CO	Clerical Officer
COHSE	Confederation of Health Service Employees
COO	Chief Occupations Officer
CPIAct	Criminal Procedures (Insanity) Act
CRO	Criminal Records Office
CSM	Company Sergeant Major
DCMN	Deputy Chief Male Nurse
DHA	District Health Authority
DHSS	Department of Health & Social Security - predecessor to the DoH

DN	Departmental Nurse - an assistant chief male nurse rank
DoE	Department of Education
DoH	Department of Health
DPP	Director of Public Prosecutions
DS	Departmental Sister - an assistant matron rank
ECT	Electroconvulsive Therapy
EEG	Electroencephalograph/Electroencephalogram
EO	Executive Officer
FW	Female Wing
GBH	Grievous Bodily Harm
GbI	Guilty but Insane (originally and later again "Not Guilty by reason of Insanity")
GCE	General Certificate of Education (O & A Levels)
GMC	General Medical Council
GP	General Practitioner
GPI	General Paralysis of the Insane
GSR	Galvanic Skin Reflex
HAS	Hospital Advisory Service
HEO	Higher Executive Officer
HMP	Her Majesty's Pleasure (also Her Majesty's Prison, but not used here)
HMSO	Her Majesty's Stationery Office
HMT	Hospital Management Team
HO	Home Office
HoD	Heads of Departments (meeting)
HORU	Home Office Research Unit
HQ	Headquarters (i.e.: at the Department of Health & Social Security)
IoA	Insane on Arraignment

IPCS	Institute of Professional Civil Servants (succeeded by the IPMS)
IPMS	Institute of Professionals, Managers & Scientists
IQ	Intelligent Quotient
ISU	Interim Secure Unit
JBCNS	Joint Board of Clinical Nursing Studies
LASS	Local Authority Social Services
LMHSA	London Mental Hospitals Sports Association
LoF	League of (Hospital) Friends
MAC	Medical Advisory Committee
MENCAP	The National Association for Mental Handicap
MHA	Mental Health Act
MHAC	Mental Health Act Commission
MHR	(The) Mental Health Register
MHRF	Mental Health Research Fund
MHRT	Mental Health Review Tribunal
MI	Mental Illness
MIND	The National Association for Mental Health
MO	Medical Officer
MoH	Ministry of Health - predecessor to the DHSS
MoW	Ministry of Works (later MPBW)
MP	Member of Parliament
MPBW	Ministry of Public Buildings & Works (later PSA)
MST(Union)	(Union for) Managers, Scientists and Technicians
NA	Nursing Assistant
NACRO	National Association for the Care & Resettlement of Offenders
NCO	Non-Commissioned Officer
NHS	National Health Service
NO	Nursing Officer
NUPE	National Union of Public Employees

OC	Office Committee (of the DoH) - previously SHOC
OO	Occupations Officer
OT	Occupational Therapy/Therapist
PA	Principal Attendant
PAC	Professional Advisory Committee
PD	Psychopathic Disorder
PhD	Doctor of Philosophy
POA	Prison Officers Association
PPG	Penile Plethysmograph
PQs	Parliamentary Questions
PSA	Public Services Agency (formerly MPBW)
PT	Physical Training
PTSD	Post Traumatic Stress Disorder
QARANC	Queen Alexandra's Royal Army Nursing Corps
QC	Queen's Counsel
RAE	Royal Aircraft Establishment
RAF	Royal Air Force
RAMC	Royal Army Medical Corps
RASC	Royal Army Service Corps
RC	Roman Catholic
RCN	Royal College of Nursing
RCPsych	Royal College of Psychiatrists
RE	Royal Engineers
REME	Royal Electrical & Mechanical Engineers
RHA	Regional Health Authority
RMN	Registered Mental Nurse
RMO	Responsible Medical Officer
RMPA	Royal Medico-Psychological Association (succeeded by the RCPsych)
RSM	Regimental Sergeant Major
RSU	Regional Secure Unit

SEC	Staff Education Centre
SEN	State Enrolled Nurse
SEO	Senior Executive Officer
SHMO	Senior Hospital Medical Officer
SHOC	Special Hospitals Office Committee
SHRU	Special Hospitals Research Unit
SN	Subnormal
SNO	Senior Nursing Officer
SOAD	Second Opinion Approved Doctor
SOO	Senior Occupations Officer
SPSS	Statistical Package for the Social Sciences
SRN	State Registered Nurse
SSN	Severely Subnormal
TB	Tuberculosis
TV	Television
UNISON	The Public Services Union
VD	Venereal Disease
VIP/VIPs	Very Important Person/People
WS	Ward Sister
WWI	Wounding With Intent (e.g.: to kill/to do GBH)
XXY/XYY	Chromosome Abnormalities
YHA	Youth Hostels Association

BIBLIOGRAPHY

This bibliography gathers together publications discussed or mentioned in the text, including those in Appendix B. However, they are here listed in standard format, i.e.: alphabetically according to principal author (except publications by official or professional bodies, which are listed according to the name of the body, and government reports or acts of Parliament under their titles). The bibliography has been extended to include an illustrative range of other publications by Broadmoor authors, or about Broadmoor work, during the time of the 1959 Mental Health Act, to give some indication of the extent of this. A fuller range is available from Elizabeth Parker's 1981 bibliography, which is included in this list.

Allderidge, P. (1974) *The Late Richard Dadd*. London: The Tate Gallery.

Allen, J.E. (1952). *Inside Broadmoor*. London: W. H. Allen.

Bancroft, J.H.J., Tennent, T.G., Loucas, K. & Cass, J. (1974) "The Control of Deviant Sexual Behaviour by Drugs: 1. Behavioural changes following oestrogens and anti-androgens." *British Journal of Psychiatry*, 125, 310-315.

Black, D.A. (1966) Psychological Methods of Assessing Psychopathy and the Psychopath. In M. Craft (ed.). *Psychopathic Disorders and Their Assessment*. Oxford: Pergamon.

Black, D.A. (1969) "Psychological Characteristics of the Abnormal Offender at an English Special Hospital." Proceedings of the 5th International Meeting of Forensic Sciences, Toronto, Canada.

Black, D.A. (1973) "A Decade of Psychological Investigation of the Male Patient Population of Broadmoor." *Special Hospitals Research Reports, No.8*. London: Special Hospitals Research Unit, DHSS.

Black, D.A. (1976) "Review of the Butler Report on Mentally Abnormal Offenders." *Bulletin of the British Psychological Society,* 29, 130-139.

Black, D.A. (1981) "Implications for Sentencing of Psychological Developments in Behavioural Assessment and Treatment." In S. Lloyd-Bostock (ed.), *Law and Psychology.* Oxford: Centre for Socio-Legal Studies, Wolfson College.

Black, D.A. (1982) "A Five-year follow up study of male patients discharged from Broadmoor Hospital." In Gunn, J. & Farrington, D.P. (eds): *Abnormal Offenders, Delinquency and the Criminal Justice System.* Chichester: Wiley.

Black, D.A. & Spinks, P. (1985) "Predicting Outcomes in Mentally Disordered and Dangerous Offenders." In D.P. Farrington, & R. Tarling, (eds.), *Prediction in Criminology.* Albany, New York: SUNY Press.

Blackburn, R. (1969) "Personality in Relation to Extreme Aggression in Psychiatric Offenders." *British Journal of Psychiatry,* 114, 821-828.

Blackburn, R. (1969a) "Personality Types among Abnormal Homicides." Proceedings of the 5th International Meeting of Forensic Sciences, Toronto, Canada, and (1971), *British Journal of Criminology,* 11, 14-31.

Blackburn, R. (1969b) "Sensation seeking, impulsivity and psychopathic personality." *Journal of Consulting & Clinical Psychology,* 33, 571-574.

Blackburn, R. (1975) "An empirical; classification of psychopathic personality." *British Journal of Psychiatry,* 127, 456-460.

Blackburn, R. (1982) "On the Relevance of the Concept of the Psychopath." In D.A. Black (ed.), *Issues in Criminological & Legal Psychology, No.2,* Leicester: The British Psychological Society.

Blackburn, R. (1986) "Patterns of personality deviation among violent offenders: replication and extension of an empirical taxonomy." *British Journal of Criminology,* 26, 254-269.

Blackburn, R. (1993) *The Psychology of Criminal Conduct: Theory, Research & Practice.* Chichester, Sussex: Wiley.

Bluglass, R., & Bowden, P. (1990). *Principles & Practice of Forensic Psychiatry*. Edinburgh: Churchill Livingstone.

Bowden, P. (1996) "Graham Young (1947-90); The St Albans Poisoner: His Life & Times." In *Criminal Behaviour & Mental Health*, 6, 1996, No. Suppl., pp.17-24.

British Psychological Society, (1973) "Memorandum of Evidence to the Butler Committee on the Law relating to the Mentally Abnormal Offender." *Bulletin of the British Psychological Society*, 26, 331-342.

British Psychological Society, (1993) *Psychology & Antisocial Behaviour*. Leicester: The British Psychological Society.

British Psychological Society, (1995) *Professional Psychology Handbook*. Leicester: The British Psychological Society.

Brittain, R.P. (1970) "The Sadistic Murderer." *Medicine, Science & the Law*, 10, 198-207.

Casey, M.D., Blank, C.E., Street, D.R.K., Segall, L.J., McDougall, J.M., McGrath, P.G. & Skinner, J.L. (1966) "YY Chromosomes and Antisocial Behaviour." *Lancet*, ii, 859-860.

Casey, M.D., Blank, C.E., Mobley, T., Kohn, P., Street, D.R.K., McDougall, J.M., Gooder, J. & Platts, J. (1971) "Patients with Chromosome Abnormality in two Special Hospitals." *Special Hospitals Research Reports No.2*. London: Special Hospitals Research Unit, DHSS.

Cleckley, H. (1964). *The Mask of Sanity*. (4th edn.) St Louis: Mosby.

Cohen, D. (1981) *Broadmoor*. London: Psychology News Press.

Cox, M. (1992) *Shakespeare Comes To Broadmoor*. London: Jessica Kingsley.

Cox, M. (1976) *Group Psychotherapy in a Secure Setting*. Proceedings of the Royal Society of Medicine, 69, 215-220.

Craft, M. (ed.), (1966) *Psychopathic Disorders and their Assessment*. Oxford: Pergamon.

Craft, M. & Craft, A. (eds) (1984) *Mentally Abnormal Offenders*. Eastbourne, East Sussex: Baillière Tindall.

Crawford, D.A. (1979) "Modification of Deviant Sexual Behaviour: the need for a comprehensive approach." *British Journal of Medical Psychology*, 52, 151-156.

Crawford, D.A. & Allen, J.V. (1979) "A Social Skills Training Programme with Sex Offenders." In: M. Cook & G. Wilson (eds.), *Love & Attraction*. Oxford: Pergamon

Crawford, D.A. (1980) "Applications of Penile Response Monitoring to the Assessment of Sexual Offenders." In D.J. West (ed.), *Sexual Offenders in the Criminal Justice System*. Cambridge: Cropwood Publications.

Crawford, D.A. (1982) "Problems for the Assessment and Treatment of Sexual Offenders in Closed Institutions and Some Solutions." In D.A. Black (ed.) *Issues in Criminological & Legal Psychology*, No.2, Leicester: The British Psychological Society.

Criminal Lunatics Act, 1800.

Dell, S. (1980) "The Transfer of Special Hospital Patients to NHS Hospitals." *Special Hospitals Research Report No.16*, London: Special Hospitals Research Unit, DHSS.

Dell, S., & Robertson, G. (1988) "Sentenced to Hospital: Offenders in Broadmoor." *Maudsley Monographs No.32*. Oxford: Oxford University Press.

Department of Health & Social Security, (1975) "Revised Report of the Working Party on Security in NHS Psychiatric Hospitals." (The 'Glancy' Report). London: HMSO.

Eysenck, H.J. (1964) *Crime & Personality*. London: Routledge & Kegan Paul.

Farrington, D.P. & Tarling, R. (eds.), (1985) *Prediction in Criminology*. Albany, New York: SUNY Press.

Fairfield, L., & Fullbrook, E.P. (1954) *The Trial of J.T. Straffen*. London, Edinburgh & Glasgow: William Hodge & Co. Ltd.

Feldman, M.P. (1977) *Criminal Behaviour: A Psychological Analysis*. Chichester, Sussex: Wiley.

Fenton, G.W., Tennent, T.G., Fenwick, P.B.C. & Rattray, N. (1972) "The EEG and Sex Chromosome Abnormalities." *British Journal of Psychiatry*, 119, 185-190.

Fenton, G.W., Tennent, T.G., Fenwick, P.B.C. & Rattray, N. (1974) "The EEG in Antisocial Behaviour; a study of posterior temporal slow activity in special hospital patients." *Psychological Medicine*, 4, 181-186.

Fenton, G.W., Fenwick, P.B.C., Ferguson, W. & Lam, C.T. (1978) "The Contingent Negative Variation in Antisocial Behaviour: a pilot study of Broadmoor patients." *British Journal of Psychiatry*, 132, 368-377.

Fransella, F. & Bannister, D., (1977) *A Manual for Repertory Grid Technique*. London, Academic Press.

Gostin, L. (1975) *A Human Condition*, vol 1: The Mental Health Act from 1959 to 1975; Observations, Analysis and Proposals for Reform. London: MIND.

Gostin, L. (1977) *A Human Condition*, vol 2: The Law Relating to Mentally Abnormal Offenders: Observations, Analysis and Proposals for Reform. London: MIND.

Gostin, L. (ed).(1985) *Secure Provision*. A Review of Special Services for the Mentally Ill & Mentally Handicapped in England & Wales. London: Tavistock Publications.

Gunn, J., & Farrington, D.P. (1982) *Abnormal Offenders, Delinquency & the Criminal Justice System*. Chichester, Sussex: Wiley.

Gunn, J., & Taylor, P. (eds) (1993) *Forensic Psychiatry: Clinical, Legal & Ethical Issues*. Oxford: Butterworth-Heinemann.

Hamilton, J.R. (1980) "The Development of Broadmoor, 1863-1980." *Bulletin of the Royal College of Psychiatrists*, Sept., 130-133.

Hamilton, J.R. & Freeman, H. (Eds.), (1982) *Dangerousness: Psychiatric Assessment & Management*. London: Gaskell.

Harbison, J.J.M., Graham, P.J., Quinn, J.T. & McAllister, H. (1973) "The Psychological Assessment of Sexual Dysfunction." In: Brengelmann & Tunner (eds.), *Behavioural Therapy*. Munich: Urban & Schwarzenberg.

Hare, R.D. (1970) *Psychopathy: Theory and Research*. New York: Wiley

Hare, R.D. & Schalling, D. (eds.), (1978) *Psychopathic Behaviour: Approaches to Research*. Chichester, Sussex: Wiley.

Hemingway, C. (ed.), (1996) *Special Women? The Experience of Women in the Special Hospital System*. Aldershot, Hants: Avebury.

Hinton, J.W, (1975) "The Development of Objective Behaviour Rating Scales for use by Nurses on Patients in Special Hospitals." *Special Hospitals Research Reports, No.13*. London: Special Hospitals Research Unit, DHSS.

Hinton, J.W. (1977) "A Psychophysiological Study of Paranoid Hostility and Defensiveness in Maximum Security Hospital Patients." *British Journal of Psychology*, 68, 371-375.

Hinton, J.W., Woodman, D.D., O'Neill, M.T. & Webster, S. (1979) "Electrodermal Indices of Public Offending and Recidivism." *Biological Psychology*, 9, 297-309.

Hinton, J.W., O'Neill, M.T., Hamilton, S. & Burke, M. (1980) "Psychophysiological Differentiation between Psychopathic and Schizophrenic Abnormal Offenders." *British Journal of Social & Clinical Psychology*, 19, 257-269.

Holden, A. (1974) *The St Albans Poisoner; The Life & Times of Graham Young*. London: Hodder & Stoughton.

Hollin, C.R. & Howells, K. (eds.) (1991) *Clinical Approaches to Sex Offenders and their Victims*. Chichester, Sussex: Wiley.

Home Office/Department of Health & Social Security (1973) "Report on the Review of Procedures for the Discharge and Supervision of Psychiatric Patients Subject to Special Restrictions." (The 'Aarvold' Report). Cmnd 5191. London: HMSO.

Home Office/Department of Health & Social Security (1975) "Report of the Committee on Mentally Abnormal Offenders." (The 'Butler' Report); Cmnd 6244, London: HMSO.

Homicide Act, 1957.

Hopwood, J.S. (1927) "Child Murder & Insanity." *J. Ment. Sc.*, 73, 300, 95-108.

Hopwood, J.S. & Snell, H.K. (1933) "Amnesia in Relation to Crime." *Journal of Mental Science*, 79, 27-41.

Howard, R.C., Fenton, G.W. & Fenwick, P.B.C. (1982) *Event-Related Brain Potential in Personality and Psychopathology: a Pavlovian approach.* Letchworth, Herts: Research Studies Press (Wiley).

Howells, K. (1978) "The Meaning of Poisoning to a Person Diagnosed as a Psychopath." *Medicine, Science & The Law,* 8, 179-184.

Howells, K. (1981) "Social Relationships in Violent Offenders." In S. Duck and R. Gilmour (eds.), *Personal Relationships (3); Personal Relationships in Disorder.* London: Academic Press.

Howells, K. (1982a) "Social Construing and Violent Behaviour in Mentally Abnormal Offenders." In J. Hinton (ed), *Dangerousness: Problems of Assessment and Prediction.* London: Allen & Unwin.

Howells, K. (1982b) "Mental Disorder and Violent Behaviour." In M.P. Feldman (ed), *Developments in the Study of Criminal Behaviour, vol.2;* Violence. London: Wiley.

Howells, K. (1982c) "Aggression: clinical approaches to treatment." In D.A. Black (ed.) *Issues in Criminological & Legal Psychology, No.2.* Leicester: The British Psychological Society.

Kaye, C. & Franey, A., (eds.) (1998) *Managing High Security Psychiatric Care.* London: Jessica Kingsley.

Kelly, G.A. (1955) *The Psychology of Personal Constructs, vols. I & II,* New York, Norton.

King's Fund. (1975) "Lost Souls: Services for mentally abnormal offenders." *Mental Handicap Papers No.7.* London: The King Edward's Hospital Fund.

Kray, R., with Dinenage, F. (1993) *My Story.* London: Sidgwick & Jackson.

Laws, D.R. (1984) "The Assessment of Diverse Sexual Behaviour in Humans: a critical review of the major methodologies." In K. Howells, (ed.) *The Psychology of Sexual Diversity.* Oxford: Blackwell.

Laws, D.R., and Marshall, W.M. (1990) "A Conditioning Theory of the Etiology and Maintenance of Deviant Sexual Preference and Behaviour." In W.L. Marshall, D.R. Laws & H.E. Barbaree (eds.), *Handbook of Sexual Assault: issues, theories and treatment of the offender*. New York: Plenum.

Lecouteur, B.N. (1966) "Arson." *Medico-Legal Journal*, 34, 112-117.

Loucas, K. & Udwin, E.L. (1974) "The Management of the Mentally Abnormal Offender." *British Journal of Hospital Medicine*, 12, 285-293.

Loucas, K. (1980) "Broadmoor's Relationship with NHS Psychiatric Hospitals." *Bulletin of the Royal College of Psychiatrists*, September, 133-135.

Lunacy Act, 1890.

McGrath, P.G. (1958) "The Treatment of the Psychotic Offender." *Howard Journal*, 10, 38-44.

McGrath, P.G. (1966a) "The Special Hospitals as they are." *Proceedings of the Royal Society of Medicine*, 59, 699-700.

McGrath, P.G. (1966b) "The English Special Hospital System." In: Craft, M. (ed.), *Psychopathic Disorders & their Assessment*. Oxford, Pergamon.

McGrath, P.G. (1967) "The Offender as an In-Patient." *Royal Society of Health Journal*, 87, 329-331.

McGrath, P.G. (1968a) "Custody & Release of Dangerous Offenders." In: A.V.S. de Rouke & R. Porter (eds.), *The Mentally Abnormal Offender: a CIBA Foundation Symposium*. London: J.& A. Churchill.

McGrath, P.G. (1968b) "The Psychopath as a Long-Stay Patient." In: D.J. West (ed.), *Psychopathic Offenders: papers presented to the Cropwood Round Table Conference*. Cambridge: Institute of Criminology.

McGrath, P.G. (1976) "Sexual Offenders." In: H. Milne & S.J. Hardy (eds.), *Psycho-Sexual Problems*. Bradford: University Press.

McGrath, P.G. (1991) "Maternal Filicides in Broadmoor: 1919-1969." Unpublished thesis, Broadmoor Hospital Library.

McGrath, P. (Jnr.) (1996) *Asylum*. London: Viking.

Megargee, E.I. (1966) "Undercontrolled & Overcontrolled Personality Types in Extreme Antisocial Aggression." *Psychological Monographs*: 80, 3, No.611.

Megargee, E.I. (1971) "The Role of Inhibition in the Assessment and Understanding of Violence." In J.E. Singer, (ed), *The Control of Aggression and Violence: cognitive and physiological factors*. New York: Academic Press.

Mental Deficiency Act, 1913.

Mental Health Act, 1959. London: HMSO.

Mental Health Act, 1983. London: HMSO.

Mental Treatment Act, 1930.

Monahan, J. (1980) *Who is the Client?* Washington, D.C.: The American Psychological Association.

Morris, T., & Blom-Cooper, L. (1964) *A Calendar of Murder*. London: Michael Joseph.

Mowat, R.R. (1966) *Morbid Jealousy & Murder; A Psychiatric Study of Morbidly Jealous Murderers at Broadmoor*. London: Tavistock Publications.

National Health Service Act, 1946.

Norris, M. (1984) *Integration of Special Hospital Patients into the Community*. Aldershot, Hants: Gower.

O'Neill, M.T. & Hinton, J.W. (1977) "Pupillographic Assessment of Sexual Interest & Sexual Arousal." *Perceptual & Motor Skills*, 44, 1278.

O'Neill, M.T. & Hinton, J.W. (1979) "Cardiac variability & Attention: the possible effects of test situational adaptation." *Biological Psychology*, 9, 151-154.

Osgood, C.E., Suci, G.J., & Tannenbaum, P.H. (1957) *The Measurement of Meaning*. Urbana, University of Illinois Press.

Parker, E. (1974) "The Victims of Mentally Disordered Female Offenders." *British Journal of Psychiatry*, 125, 51-59.

Parker, E. (1979) "The Special Hospitals Case Register: the first five years." *Special Hospitals Research Report No.5*, London: Special Hospitals Research Unit, DHSS.

Parker, E. (1981) "The Special Hospitals: a bibliography." *Special Hospitals Research Report No.17*, London: Special Hospitals Research Unit, DHSS.

Partridge, R. (1953) *Broadmoor*. London: Chatto & Windus. Reprinted in 1975 by Greenwood Press, Connecticut.

Quinn, J.T., Graham, P.J., Harbison, J.J.M. & McAllister, H. (1973) *The Measurement of Sexual Function*. New York: Appleton Century Croft.

Reeve, A. (1983) *Notes from a Waiting Room*. London: Heretic Books.

Report of the Royal Commission on the Law relating to Mental Illness and Mental Deficiency 1954-57 (The 'Percy' Report) (1957). Cmnd.169, London: HMSO.

Royal College of Psychiatrists (1981) *Secure Facilities for Psychiatric Patients; A Comprehensive Policy*. London: The Royal College of Psychiatrists.

Royal College of Psychiatrists, (1983) *The Future of the Special Hospitals*. London: The Royal College of Psychiatrists.

Second Report of the Estimates Committee: the Special Hospitals and the State Hospital. (1968) London: HMSO.

Tennent, T.G. (1972) "Has Psychiatry a Role in the Treatment of Offenders?" In: B.M. Mandelbrote & M.G. Gelder (eds.). *Psychiatric Aspects of Medical Practice*. London: Staple Press.

Tennent, T.G. (1973) "The Special Hospitals Research Unit." In: G. McLachlan (ed.) Portfolio for Health 2. *The Developing Programme of the DHSS in Health Services Research*. London: Oxford University Press.

Tennent, T.G., Bancroft, J.H.J. & Cass, J. (1974) "The Control of Deviant Sexual Behaviour by Drugs: a double-blind controlled study of benperidol, chlorpromazine and placebo." *Archives of Sexual Behaviour*, 3, 261-271. Also *Special Hospitals Research Report No.5*, (1972). London: Special Hospitals Research Unit, DHSS.

Tennent, T.G. (1974) "Psychiatric Aspects of Crime." In M. Wright (ed.). *Use of Criminology Literature*. London: Butterworths.

Tennent, T.G., Parker, E., McGrath, P.G., McDougall, J.M. & Street, D.R.K. (1976) "Female Patients in the three English Special Hospitals: a demographic survey of admissions 1961-65." *Medicine, Science & the Law*, 20, 200-207.

Tennent, T.G., Parker, E., McGrath, P.G., & Street, D.R.K. (1980) "Male Admissions to the English Special Hospitals 1961-65: a demographic survey." *British Journal of Psychiatry*, 136, 181-190.

Tidmarsh, D. (1980) "Trends in Length of Stay at Broadmoor." *Bulletin of the Royal College of Psychiatrists*, September, 135-136.

Trasler, G. (1962) *The Explanation of Criminality*. London: Routledge & Kegan Paul.

Treves Brown, C. (1973) "Assessment of Regional Differences in Rates of Referral for Special Hospitals Placement." *Special Hospitals Research Report No.7*, London: Special Hospitals Research Unit, DHSS.

Treves Brown, C. (1976) "Criteria for Admission to Special Hospitals." *Prison Medical Journal*, 16, January.

Thompson, P. (1972) *Bound for Broadmoor*. London: Hodder & Stoughton.

Thompson, P. (1974) *Back from Broadmoor*. London: Mowbrays.

Tong, J.E. & MacKay, G.W. (1959) "A statistical follow-up of mental defectives of dangerous or violent propensities." *British Journal of Delinquency*, 9, 276-284.

Vaughan, P.J. (1979) "The Key to Growth of Social Work in Broadmoor." *Health & Social Service Journal*, 89, 384-386.

Vaughan, P.J. (1980) "Letters and Visits to Long-stay Broadmoor Patients." *British Journal of Social Work*, 10, 471-481.

Verberne, T.J.P. (1972) "Blackburn's Typology of Abnormal Homicides: additional data and a critique." *British Journal of Criminology*, 12, 88-89.

Wallace, M. (1986) *The Silent Twins*. London: Chatto & Windus; and Penguin 1987, reprinted 1993, with new chapter.

Walker, N. (1968) *Crime & Insanity in England, I: The Historical Perspective*. Edinburgh: Edinburgh University Press.

Walker, N., & McCabe, S. (1973) *Crime & Insanity in England, II: New Solutions & New Problems*. Edinburgh: Edinburgh University Press.

West, D.J., & Walk, A. (1977) *Daniel McNaughton: His Trial and the Aftermath*. Ashford, Kent: Gaskell Books (Headley Bros Ltd).

Widom, C. (1976a) "Interpersonal Conflict and Co-operation in Psychopaths." *Journal of Abnormal Psychology*, 85, 330-334.

Widom, C. (1976b) "Interpersonal and Personal Construct Systems in Psychopaths." *Journal of Consulting & Clinical Psychology*, 44, 614-623.

Winchester, S. (1998) *The Surgeon of Crowthorne*. London: Viking.

Woodman, D., Hinton, J.W. & O'Neill, M.T. (1977) "Abnormality of Catecholamine Balance Relating to Social Deviance." *Perceptual & Motor Skills*, 45, 702.

Woodman, D., Hinton, J.W. & O'Neill, M.T. (1978) "Plasma Catecholamines, Stress & Aggression in Maximum Security Patients." *Biological Psychology*, 6, 147-154.

Woodman, D. (1979) "Evidence of a Permanent Imbalance in Catecholamine Secretion in Violent Social Deviants." *Journal of Psychosomatic Research*, 23, 155-157.

Young, W. (1973) *Obsessive Poisoner; The Strange Story of Graham Young*. London: Robert Hale.

INDEX

575

Index

Black, Mrs DA 279

Blackburn, Ronald 235-9, 243,
245, 262-3, 271, 287, 334-5
alcohol 431, 433
over-control 334, 431, 433
Pskylab 352
publications 471, 543
sexual abuse histories 436
under-control 335
bleeps 427-8
Block 1 (Norfolk House)
98-100, 182, 250-2
accommodation 107
break-up of unitary hospital
388
insulin ward 138
recreation 153, 156
staff 79
Block 2 (Essex House; parole
block) 98-101, 209, 249-51
accommodation 105
break-up of unitary hospital
388
clinical practice 182, 186,
191
ECT 214
mixed sex therapy 348
reappraisal 455
recreation 151, 153-6, 162,
164, 172
security 113
staff 69
Block 3 (Kent House) 98-9,
183, 212, 250, 254, 388
accommodation 105-6

occupational therapy 141
recreation 156
staff 79
Block 4 (Dorset House) 98-9,
212, 250-1, 388
accommodation 105-6
clinical practice 176, 182,
183
recreation 156
staff 69, 79
Block 5 (Gloucester House;
parole block) 98-9, 182, 249,
250
accommodation 105
break-up of unitary hospital
388
ECT 214
handicrafts 141
recreation 151, 153-5, 172
Block 6 (Monmouth/Somerset
House) 98-9, 182-3, 250-2,
461
adolescent unit 251
break-up of unitary hospital
388
handicrafts 141, 143
recreation 153, 157
staff 69, 216
Block 7 (Cornwall House) 98-9,
182, 250, 388
accommodation 105-6
demolished 292
handicrafts 141
recreation 155
blood pressure 350-1, 353-4

579

Hill, Dr Dennis 221
Hinton, Dr John 352, 354
Holland 413-14, 417
Hollerith 190, 325
Home Office 411, 496-7
  discharge 7-8, 396, 453
Home Secretary 533
  capital punishment 446
  discharge 10, 17, 20, 24, 307
  Mental Health Act (1983)
    529, 533, 534
  MHRTs 22
  restriction orders 14-15, 20,
    204, 307
home visits 204
homicide 51-2, 65, 201, 219
  after discharge 329-30
  alcohol 433
  discharge follow-up study
    327, 329, 330-1, 338
  killing in Broadmoor 311,
    417
  research 223-4, 237-8, 245
  research by Norris 375
  sex offenders 343, 347
  sexual abuse histories 435
  see also manslaughter; murder
Homicide Act (1957) 5, 10, 12,
  19, 52
homosexuality 346-7
Hong Kong 59, 208
Hooker, Newman 255
Hopwood, Dr Stanley 9, 67, 77,
  428-9, 445
  escapes 116, 413, 439

publications 542
Horticultural Society 92
Horton, Percy 79
hormone treatment 527,
  531
hospital administrator 391,
  419-20
hospital advisory service (HAS)
  382
hospital management teams
  (HMTs) 391-5, 399, 411,
  419-21
  POA 402, 419
  publications 553
hospital orders 13, 14-15, 17,
  19-20, 23
  capital punishment 226
  clinical development 199,
    200, 207
  discharge 114
  discharge follow-up study
    331, 336
  Government committees 302
  Mental Health Act (1983)
    531, 534
  publications 544-6
  reappraisal 484
  reappraisal of the law 512,
    518
  schizophrenia 29
hospital secretary 384, 391, 420,
  553
hospital shop 83, 87, 89
  patient labour 146
  recreation 154-5, 157, 166

little green men *see* Ministry of
Works
lobotomies 79, 138
local authorities 519, 533
 reappraisal 445, 459-60,
 467-8
Local Authority Social Services
 (LASS) 527, 530, 533
location of Broadmoor 1-2
Loucas, Dr Kyp 356
Lunacy Act (1890) 5
lunacy and lunatics 3-5, 11, 139
Lunacy and Mental Treatment
 Acts 11

MacCulloch, Dr Malcolm 252
Mackay, Dr GW 220, 327, 452
Maclean, Roderick 2
magistrates 307, 432, 534
 hospital orders 13, 15
 visiting 426
mail 69, 80, 118, 198, 534
main gates 86-7, 99-100, 157
 rebuilding programme 275-7,
 286, 291-2, 295
Maine, Anne 279
Maine, Dr Leife 68-9, 176, 279
Mair, Miller 230
Malta 59, 208
mania 29-31, 48
manic-depressives 29, 48, 139
manslaughter 7, 10, 51-4, 65,
 219
 discharge follow-up study
 327, 334

research 223, 237, 238
matron 70, 71-2, 75, 94, 215,
 392
 decision making 495
 occupational therapy 145
 recreation 164-5
 security 110
Matthew Trust 461
Maudsley hospital (London)
 290, 384
Max Planck Institute (Munich)
 273
maze tracing task 178-9, 229
McAlister 272
McCabe, Sarah 542
McGrath, Dr Patrick 339-40,
 341, 388, 426, 445, 464-6
 against conjugal visits 134
 buildings 97, 103
 centenary meetings 222, 225
 changing social climate 296
 clinical practice 175-6, 180,
 185-6
 clinical teams 382
 discharge 9, 205
 escapes 116-17, 119, 413-15,
 439
 HMTs 391-4
 League of Friends 277-8
 library 286, 290, 294
 maternal filicides 323
 medical centre 211-12,
 214
POA 400-3
Pskylab 351

research 244
research by Norris 373, 374,
  379-80
role of learning 479-80, 501
security 110, 111, 115
sex offenders 357, 365
staff 80
statutory procedures 209
treatment 137-40, 148-9,
  252, 321, 482-3, 491
medico-legal matters 5, 11,
  23-4, 139, 199, 516
  psychopathic disorder 39-43
  publications 542-3
  research 220, 221, 222, 241,
    247
  sex offenders 46
Megargee, Edwin 238, 334, 431,
  433
MENCAP 312, 315
mens rea 503, 510-11, 516
Mental Deficiency Acts 11
mental disorder 11-12, 17,
  25-49, 200-1, 441-2, 500-1
  buildings 103-4
  capital punishment 202
  categories 5, 11-12, 13, 19,
    25-6, 48-9, 200-1, 219
  changing social climate
    312-13
  clinical development 197-203
  clinical practice 173-4, 178,
    180-4, 186, 188-90, 194
  community 125-31
  discharge 8-9, 59, 328, 338

discussion of former offences
  429
EEG 361-2
environment 470, 472-5
escapes 117
ethics and research committees
  408
farm 103
Government committees
  299-300, 302-6
hospital orders 13, 23
library 286, 294
Mental Health Act (1983) 40,
  47, 201, 203, 524, 528, 530,
  534
Mental Health Act
  Amendment Bill 422,
  424-5
MHRTs 22
offences 50-2, 64-5
publications 548, 552
reappraisal 446, 448, 453-4,
  456, 459, 466
reappraisal of the law 505-11,
  513-14, 516, 518, 520-2
recreation 163, 171
Reeve 415, 417
research 221, 223-7, 247
research by Norris 373, 375
restriction orders 14
role of learning 475-6
state of mind 503-5
substance misuse 432, 440
transfers from hospital 202-3
transfers of prisoners 24-5

research 220, 222-3, 226,
237-8, 248, 323, 327, 334
sexual abuse histories 435
transfers of prisoners 7, 10
victims 493, 495
muscle relaxant 122
music 109, 389, 483
recreation 151, 153, 156,
158, 161-2, 168-70, 172

NACRO 315
National Association for Mental
Handicap 312
National Association for Mental
Health 312
National Health Service 7, 91,
104, 422, 441, 518, 534
changing social climate 312
clinical teams 382, 384,
387
ethics and research committees
407
Government committees 300
increasing professional
demands 339
POA 399-401, 404-5
publications 553
reappraisal 455
research 236, 366
research by Norris 372, 373,
376
seminars 427
sex offenders 343
staff 78-9
treatment 140

National Health Service Acts 6,
524
needlework 82, 166, 437
neurophysiology 42-3, 47,
359-64, 450
neuropsychiatry 361
neuropsychology 323, 359-64
neuroses and neurotic disorders
10, 35-8, 201
community 126, 130
discharge follow-up study
338
psychopathic disorder 43-4,
45, 48-9
reappraisal of the law 505,
514, 520
treatment 137-9
Neville, Dr Richard 283
newsletters 427, 440
Nolan, Tom 70
Norfolk House *see* Block 1
(Norfolk House)
normality 187, 194, 259, 490
Pskylab 356
reappraisal of the law 508,
516, 520
research 224-5
Norris, Margaret 369-78,
379-80, 391, 425, 431
publications 543, 546,
552
North, Brian 160
Northern Ireland 203
not guilty by reason of insanity
5-7, 19, 24, 54, 219

reappraisal 446, 454, 466,
473, 501
reappraisal of the law 504,
505-6, 521
Reeve 413, 414-16, 417, 440
research 42-3, 223, 234, 237,
239, 240-1, 245
research by Norris 371-5, 379
role of learning 477, 501
sex offenders 46-7
staff 83
state of mind 504
Udwin 413-17
victims 46, 493
psychophysiology 323, 350-9,
364
psychoses 9, 180-1, 191, 520
affective disorder 29-30, 48
break-up of unitary hospital
390
community 130
discharge follow-up study
331
Mental Heath Act Amendment
Bill 425
neurotic disorders 36-7
organic disorders 33, 35
reappraisal 446, 454,
474
research 223-4
schizophrenia 26, 28
sex offenders 46
treatment 137, 139, 252,
482-3
psychotherapy and

psychotherapists 85, 139-40,
148, 252-3
clinical practice 184
community 127
decision making 495
discharge follow-up study
334, 335
publications 546-50
reappraisal 449, 456
role of learning 479
sex offenders 348
treatment 139-40, 252-3,
269, 273-4, 317-19
public inquiries 403
public protection 11, 104,
524-5, 546
changing social climate 313
clinical development 198, 201
Government committees
300-1
POA 402
reappraisal of the law 506,
510, 515, 522
treatment 490, 492
publicity and public profile
340-2, 364
punched cards 190, 195, 222,
231, 243, 323, 325
pupilometry 352

qualifications 17, 78-80, 141,
210, 256, 361, 533
staff education centre 286-7,
290
questionnaires 287